D1497855

MATHEMATICS EDUCATION

Officers of the Society
1969–70

(Term of office expires March 1 of the year indicated.)

N. L. GAGE
(1972)
Stanford University, Stanford, California

ROBERT J. HAVIGHURST
(1971)
University of Chicago, Chicago, Illinois

W. C. KVARACEUS
(1970)
Clark University, Worcester, Massachusetts

HERMAN G. RICHEY
(Ex-officio)
University of Chicago, Chicago, Illinois

HAROLD G. SHANE
(1972)
Indiana University, Bloomington, Indiana

RUTH M. STRANG
(1971)
Wantagh, Long Island, New York

RALPH W. TYLER
(1970)
Director Emeritus, Center for Advanced Study in the Behavioral Sciences
Stanford, California

Secretary-Treasurer

HERMAN G. RICHEY
5835 Kimbark Avenue, Chicago, Illinois 60637

MATHEMATICS EDUCATION

The Sixty-ninth Yearbook of the National Society for the Study of Education

PART I

By

THE YEARBOOK COMMITTEE
and
ASSOCIATED CONTRIBUTORS

Edited by

EDWARD G. BEGLE

Editor for the Society

HERMAN G. RICHEY

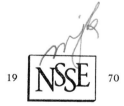

19 NSSE 70

Distributed by THE UNIVERSITY OF CHICAGO PRESS • CHICAGO, ILLINOIS

The responsibilities of the Board of Directors of the National Society for the Study of Education in the case of yearbooks prepared by the Society's committees are (1) to select the subjects to be investigated, (2) to appoint committees calculated in their personnel to insure consideration of all significant points of view, (3) to provide appropriate subsidies for necessary expenses, (4) to publish and distribute the committees' reports, and (5) to arrange for their discussion at the annual meeting.

The responsibility of the Society's editor is to prepare the submitted manuscripts for publication in accordance with the principles and regulations approved by the Board of Directors.

Neither the Board of Directors, nor the Society's editor, nor the Society is responsible for the conclusions reached or the opinions expressed by the Society's yearbook committees.

Published 1970 by

THE NATIONAL SOCIETY FOR THE STUDY OF EDUCATION
5835 Kimbark Avenue, Chicago, Illinois 60637

First Printing, 10,000 Copies

Printed in the United States of America

The Society's Committee on Mathematics Education

EDWARD G. BEGLE
(*Chairman*)

Director, School Mathematics Study Group
Stanford University
Stanford, California

WILLIAM A. BROWNELL
Professor Emeritus
University of California
Berkeley, California

J. F. WEAVER
Professor of Mathematics Education
University of Wisconsin
Madison, Wisconsin

STEPHEN S. WILLOUGHBY
Professor of Mathematics Education and Mathematics
and Chairman, Mathematics Education Department
New York University
New York, New York

Associated Contributors

TRUMAN BOTTS
Executive Director, Conference Board of the Mathematical Sciences
Washington, D.C.

R. CREIGHTON BUCK
Professor of Mathematics
University of Wisconsin
Madison, Wisconsin

RICHARD A. DEAN
Professor of Mathematics
California Institute of Technology
Pasadena, California

M. VERE DEVAULT
Professor of Curriculum and Instruction
University of Wisconsin
Madison, Wisconsin

v

ROY DUBISCH
Professor of Mathematics
University of Washington
Seattle, Washington

JOHN L. KELLEY
Professor of Mathematics
University of California
Berkeley, California

MILDRED KEIFFER
Administrative Supervisor of Secondary School Mathematics
Cincinnati Public Schools
Cincinnati, Ohio

THOMAS E. KRIEWALL
Research Associate
Institute for Educational Research
Downers Grove, Illinois

H. STEWART MOREDOCK
Professor of Mathematics
Sacramento State College
Sacramento, California

HENRY O. POLLAK
Director of Mathematics Research
Bell Telephone Laboratories
Murray Hill, New Jersey

LEE S. SHULMAN
Professor of Educational Psychology and Medical Education
Michigan State University
East Lansing, Michigan

R. L. WILDER
Professor Emeritus
University of Michigan
Ann Arbor, Michigan

JAMES W. WILSON
Associate Professor and Head, Department of Mathematics Education
University of Georgia
Athens, Georgia

Preface

In 1966, the Board of Directors of the National Society, sensing that the shock wave of the radical changes in precollege mathematics of the past decade or so was subsiding, concluded that it would be appropriate to prepare a clear account of the changes that had occurred and to examine the implications of those changes for mathematics teaching in the near future.

The Board reexamined all suggestions for yearbooks on mathematics education that had been submitted during the immediately preceding years and obtained the advice of specialists and teachers regarding the needs that a yearbook on mathematics education should meet. After having done so, the Board asked Dr. Edward G. Begle, Director of the School Mathematics Study Group (Stanford), to prepare, with the assistance of a committee to be appointed, a proposal for a volume which would explain the educational and psychological problems in the selection, organization, and presentation of mathematics materials at all levels from the kindergarten through the high school. After studying the proposal developed by Dr. Begle, Stephen S. Willoughby, J. F. Weaver, and William A. Brownell, the Board authorized the publication of the proposed yearbook, appointed Dr. Begle Chairman of the Yearbook Committee, and approved the membership of the Committee.

Dr. Begle, the members of the Committee, and other outstanding scholars in the field who contributed to the yearbook have produced a magnificent volume—one that represents a landmark in the history of mathematics education. It is broader in scope than the Society's influential earlier yearbooks on arithmetic, placing the new mathematics at all levels in the perspective of the school. The volume will be of help to everyone who wishes to learn what the new mathematics is about. It will be of great use to those who teach mathematics at any level from the kindergarten to the college. It will fill a very positive need in programs of teacher education and in the training of curriculum specialists. The influence of the yearbook will be felt throughout the nation for many years to come. The Society is proud to present the yearbook.

HERMAN G. RICHEY
Editor for the Society

Table of Contents

ects. Evaluations of Mathematics Programs. National Longitudinal Study of Mathematical Abilities. Design of NLSMA. Mathematics Tests in NLSMA. Textbook Comparison Analyses in NLSMA. An Illustrative Analysis from NLSMA. General Observations on the NLSMA Results. Concluding Remarks. NLSMA Reports.

SECTION IV

School Organization for Mathematics Instruction

SECTION V

A Brief Look Ahead

Introduction

Not quite two decades have elapsed since the appearance of the last
NSSE yearbook on mathematics education. During that period a
revolution in school mathematics has taken place. This yearbook represents an attempt to make clear both the nature and the extent of
this revolution and also to point out some of its implications important to classroom teachers, school administrators, and curriculum
workers.

This revolution in school mathematics was, in a sense, a byproduct
of a revolution in mathematics itself. Chapter i is devoted to a historical account of changes that have taken place in mathematics and
points out how these contributed to the origin of the revolution in
school mathematics.

During the past two decades new concepts have been developed in
psychology, particularly in learning theory, which are very relevant
to the approaches now taken to mathematics in the schools. A discussion of these concepts and their role in mathematics education is contained in chapter ii.

New school mathematics programs differ very little from old ones
as far as subject matter is concerned. Only a few old topics have been
de-emphasized and only a few new topics have been added. The chief
difference between the old and the new programs is the point of view
towards mathematics. No longer is computational skill the be-all and
end-all of mathematics. Now there is an equal emphasis on an understanding of the basic concepts of mathematics and of their interrela-
tionships, i.e., the structure of mathematics. However, it is extremely
difficult to develop the full meaning of the preceding sentence without a detailed consideration of new school mathematics programs
themselves. Consequently, the next three chapters are devoted to detailed presentations, from the modern point of view, of the three
major strands of mathematics taught in the precollege programs.

Arithmetic and algebra have always constituted the most impor-

I

tant strand of the school mathematics program, and the importance of this strand has not decreased. The exposition in chapter iii is intended to convey the flavor of modern mathematics and to show how the basic concepts and the structure of this strand can be developed, starting in the earliest school years.

A striking difference between the traditional and the modern mathematics program is in the treatment of geometry. In the traditional program, a senior high school level, formal, axiomatic treatment of geometry was preceded by only a small amount of work with elementary mensuration problems. In modern programs, informal and intuitive geometric concepts appear throughout the elementary school program and develop a much sounder intuitive foundation for the more formal work of the secondary school. Chapter iv is devoted to an exposition of these geometric concepts and concludes with a discussion of various approaches to formal geometry now being considered for the secondary school.

Another major strand of mathematics is that of functions. In the traditional program, functions did not appear explicitly until late in the secondary school program. Actually, however, functions are implicit from the beginning of the primary school study of arithmetic and, as shown in chapter v, the concept of function plays a unifying role throughout the entire curriculum.

These new developments in the content and objectives of the school mathematics program have been accompanied by new concepts about the teaching of mathematics. One does not teach for an understanding of basic mathematical concepts the same way one teaches for the development of purely mechanical mathematical skills. Many other important pedagogical issues have also been the subject of discussion in recent years and these are carefully reviewed in chapter vi. In the same way, the training needed by prospective mathematics teachers or the retraining needed by experienced teachers, in order to satisfactorily handle a modern program, is more complex than the training needed in the past. Chapter vii is devoted to a review of modern teacher training programs.

The multivariate nature of the objectives of mathematics education in a modern program has made evaluation on the one hand considerably more important and on the other hand considerably more difficult. Chapter ix contains a discussion of evaluation problems from the point of view of the classroom teacher, and chapter x a discussion of the kinds of evaluation of mathematics programs that are the concern of the school administrator.

Individual differences among students and the desire to adapt instruction in such a way as to take into account these differences have not been neglected in recent years. A review of recent developments in this area is found in chapter xi, together with some suggestions for potentially fruitful further investigation.

Among school administrators, the ones who have probably been most affected by the revolution in school mathematics have been the mathematics supervisors, at both the local and the state levels. Chapter xii contains a discussion of problems now facing these supervisors, and other school administrators, in their efforts to adapt new mathematics programs to their own local conditions.

The initial chapters of the yearbook were devoted to the nature and extent of the revolution in the school mathematics program that has taken place over the past decade. As was pointed out in the first chapter, the nature of the revolution was dictated by changes within mathematics itself. However, there are other forces that act on the school mathematics program and lead to changes in it. In this country every student is required to take mathematics, of some form, through the first nine years of school. This requirement exists because, presumably, it is generally agreed that mathematics is useful to everyone and that everyone will have to use a certain amount of mathematics in everyday life after leaving school.

What has not generally been realized is the tremendous extension in the range of the applications of mathematics which started during World War II and has continued at an ever increasing rate since then. In the classical areas of application of mathematics, such as science, engineering, the accounting and actuarial sciences, etc., mathematics still plays a very heavy role and in fact many new kinds of mathematics are finding applications in these areas. Outside these classical areas, mathematics is finding increasing use in the biological sciences and medicine, in the social sciences, in government, and in business and industry.

The applications of mathematics are therefore of concern to everyone involved in mathematics education. Unfortunately, few classroom teachers, few mathematicians, and even fewer of the general public have a clear understanding of the process of applying mathematics to real problems. Chapter viii is therefore devoted to a careful discussion of this process and of the task of conveying to students an understanding of the nature of applications.

The uses to which our society puts mathematics have always influenced the mathematics curriculum in the schools, and changes in these uses have usually been followed by changes in the curriculum. What is different today is that our society is changing more rapidly than in the past. Consequently, changes in the content of the curriculum come about more rapidly. (For example, in 1970 two major mathematical topics, statistics and computer mathematics, are being brought into the general mathematics curriculum. A decade ago these topics were reserved for study by a few specialized students at the undergraduate or graduate level, mostly the latter.) Chapter xiii represents an attempt to look a short way into the future and to predict what the effects will be on the precollege mathematics program of changes now going on both in our society and in mathematics itself.

SECTION I

HISTORICAL BACKGROUND AND PSYCHOLOGICAL BASES

CHAPTER I

Historical Background of Innovations in Mathematics Curricula

R. L. WILDER

The Phenomenon of Change

No phenomenon is so constantly before our eyes, and yet so little perceived, as that of *change*. Perhaps it would be more accurate to say that our awareness of natural phenomena is in no way more subject to such extremes as in the case of change. For in certain of its aspects, such as weather changes, growth of children, and variation in the seasons (in temperate zones), change is not only perceived but is a perennial topic of conversation. Yet over long periods, changes in these phenomena are largely unnoticed, inasmuch as they follow regular patterns or cycles. We have become accustomed to the constant cycling of the seasons—summer, autumn, winter, spring, and back to summer again—and, similarly, to the growth of children which follows patterns subject to little variation.

What we do not realize (or, if we do, tend to forget) is that all phenomena are subject to long-term changes that seem not to affect our brief individual lives and hence go unperceived. It is much as with the curvature of the earth; we know it exists, but from the point of view of the individual observer, it is something of which he need take no account in the ordinary affairs of life. Thus, in the case of the weather, we know that the incidences and recessions of great ice ages have effected profound changes in the weather patterns of Canada and the northern United States. And from a long-range evolutionary point of view, the patterns of child growth to which we have become accustomed are but the latest and perhaps final stage of a long series of biological and behavioral changes.

Change is universal. But it is short-range change, such as that from day to night, that we have to take into account in our daily lives.

The long-range evolutionary changes we rarely perceive and hence tend to ignore in our adjustments to reality. Some of these, chiefly in the cultural realm, we resist, under the impression that we can control them. This is especially the case with certain social, political, and religious aspects of culture, in which change is likely to produce disruption of our ways of life or thinking. If our political environment is satisfactory, we resist any change in it, particularly if the change is of such a fundamental nature as to threaten our means of livelihood. And in an area such as religion, where the emotions are more deeply involved, radical change is stoutly resisted.

It may seem strange that change is resisted even in the scientific area of culture, a sphere in which change is something that we have come to expect. Even a well-informed person in his twenties is already aware of this type of change, which he can see in transportation changes, the development of space travel, and the constant flow of new gadgets. What he may not appreciate is that these are applied or technological aspects of science, which are generally but the reflections of evolutionary changes that are taking place in the basic parts of science. The latter changes, being more abstract and usually comprehended only by their practitioners, do not ordinarily come to the attention of the non-scientist. There are exceptions, of course, as in the cases of genetics, medicine, and even parts of modern physics, certain aspects of which are both susceptible of popular exposition and dramatic in nature.

Change in the more abstract parts of basic science does not, however, come to popular notice as a rule.[1] It is not surprising, then, that in the most fundamental and abstract of all basic sciences, viz., mathematics, change should not be known or comprehended by the non-mathematician. The popular notion of mathematics as a science of computation is a misconception based on outdated curricula emphasizing drill methods, and the "mathematical prodigy" who can perform feats of mental arithmetic often turns out to be quite stupid

1. An unfortunate effect of this fact is that governmental committees, engaged in the dispensing of funds for the support of science, have been (understandably) reluctant to provide adequately for basic science. Consequently, scientists have been compelled to devote precious time to lengthy and necessarily hazy explanations of the importance of basic science in order to ensure that the abstractions from which all technological changes and improvements flow do not cease from lack of support.

when faced with modern mathematical concepts. Moreover, this state of affairs is aggravated by the fact that those technological changes which are the direct result of basic mathematical developments are not recognized as such. A common case is that of computer technology. Possibly the occasional "man in the street" assumes that the revolutionary changes due to computer technology (of which he is becoming acutely aware) are somehow connected with basic mathematics. But if so, he seldom knows that change, as represented in the development of mathematical logic and automata theory during the past half-century, has anything to do with the matter; he is not even aware of the existence of such fields. Indeed, he usually believes that no change has ever occurred in basic mathematics, and that computer technology is just another application of the unchanging "truths" of mathematics as represented, for him, by such formulas as "$2 + 3 = 5$." Presumably the well-educated layman is at least vaguely aware that such mathematical facts must have been "discovered" by man at some time during his evolution from the primitive state; the common use of such terms as "Hindu-Arabic numerals," implying some connection between the numerals and the Hindu and Arabic cultures, must suggest this to him.

The situation has not been remedied by the fact that, until very recent years, the mathematics taught in the elementary and secondary schools had not substantially changed for over a century. Of course there have been minor changes—some, pedagogical in nature, and some, substantive. For example, during the 1920's more material concerning commercially useful types of arithmetic and algebra was introduced. But such changes involved only applications and were not indicative of any change in basic mathematics. Nevertheless, fundamental changes were occurring in basic mathematics, both in content and in method, and in order to understand the influence of these on the present school curriculum, and the reasons therefor, it is necessary to understand both their character and their relationship to the other sciences. Toward providing such an understanding, a brief sketch of the ways in which mathematics first became a recognized discipline, followed by a description of the types of revolutionary changes that have occurred in basic mathematics during the past century and a half—particularly during the past half-century— is presented in the section which follows.

Development of Mathematics as a Discipline

BEGINNINGS OF MATHEMATICS

Both mathematicians and historians are familiar with the fact that the evolution of *counting* was an extremely slow process. This has been ascertained by piecing together remains of ancient cultures turned up by archeologists and by observing the counting habits of those primitive societies that still existed during the last century.[2] The evolution of counting was a social process—the anthropologist would say a cultural process—and not the invention of a single individual. As in other aspects of his life, primitive man got along with as little effort as he could in the employment of numerals; and most primitive societies found the distinction between "one," "two," and "many" quite sufficient for their needs. Whenever higher numerals were needed, some kind of tallies (such as notches in a stick, knots in a string, or pebbles in piles) were used. Actual *need* seemed to govern the process; just what needs forced the development of higher numerals, however, can only be conjectured and seemingly varied from one society to another. A society had to be considerably advanced both in its political and in its religious structures before higher numerals evolved. In some cases this evolution took the form of descriptive numerals which varied from one category of objects to another. Vestiges of this still appear in the Japanese numerals *1* to *10*. For long thin objects such as a pencil, one form of the numeral is used; for flat objects, another form; and so on. Evolution of the abstract notions of *two-ness, three-ness*, etc., irrespective of objects to which the numerals may be attached, was apparently a long process. The modern, educated Japanese is just as much aware of the property of three-ness as his contemporaries in other societies, but the ancient forms persist as a matter of common usage and tradition.

Just what does "three-ness" consist of? Certainly it is not just the symbol *3*, or *III*, or *iii*, or any of the other forms used to denote it. On reflection, one will probably conclude that "three-ness" constitutes an abstract *structure*—the most elementary type of structure one can conceive of, perhaps—which applies only to those collections that contain exactly three elements. This sounds circular, to be sure,

2. Some still exist, but usually have been "contaminated" by contacts with advanced societies.

but "three-ness" is a *noun*, whereas in the term "three elements," the "three" is an adjective; and if forced to define the latter, we can point to any triple of objects and use a matching process. Of course we do not usually say of a given collection of three objects, "This collection has the property of three-ness"; we use the adjective form and say, "This collection has three elements." But the two statements mean the same thing, although the latter obscures the fact that it is really a structural property, that of three-ness, that is being applied to the collection.

Geometry went through a similar development, culminating in the abstract structures created by the Greeks who recognized, in all the clutter of ancient formulas for measuring special objects, a uniformity which is preserved for us in the classical work of Euclid. One of the most fundamental of their achievements was the Eudoxian theory of proportion which we now recognize as embodying a description of the structure of the real line (in terms of magnitudes instead of number) and which was not matched in modern numerical terms until less than a century ago.

Of course the foregoing remarks can be labeled "hindsight"; we have the advantage of knowing what happened in those ancient times and are able to interpret it within the framework of our ways of thought. But the significance of great events is rarely realized during their occurrence, and it is the duty of the historian to point it out so that succeeding generations may be better able to interpret developments of a similar nature within their own times. This is the reason why we are now recalling and interpreting these past mathematical events; they will enable us to understand current trends.

TREND TOWARD THE STRUCTURAL NATURE OF
MATHEMATICAL CONCEPTS

The closer we come to our own era in mathematical history, the clearer becomes the trend toward the structural nature of mathematical concepts. First we must note, however, the groundwork laid in algebra, analysis, and new types of geometries during the period from the sixteenth to the eighteenth century A.D. This was a new phenomenon distinct from (albeit aided and abetted by) the ancient achievements in arithmetic and geometry. Neither algebra nor analysis (the mathematical theory of operations with limits and, generally, infinite processes) developed noticeably in ancient times. We can detect elements of both in the Babylonian-Greek-Hindu-Arabic cultures (hindsight), but their principal development was modern. We are indebted particularly to the Arabic civilization for preserving, developing, and passing on to European cultures the elements of algebra and arithmetic which stimulated the Italian flair for the solution of algebraic equations. There is a direct line from this work to the researches of Abel and Galois, which culminated in the earliest major achievement of modern times in the recognition of structure, viz., the theory of groups. Since this was a typical example of the conscious recognition of a structural type occurring in numerous particular instances, we shall give a brief description of it.

Methods for solving second-degree equations (i.e., quadratic equations of type $ax^2 + bx + c = 0$) were known to the Babylonians and probably exerted some influence on the later incorporation of the numerical and the geometric into the one science, mathematics, since most of the methods of solution were geometrical in nature. The formula

$$\frac{-b \pm \sqrt{b^2 - 4ac}}{2a}$$

for the two roots was implicit in some of this early work, although not explicitly formulated. Negative and complex (for the case $b^2 - 4ac < 0$) roots were not accepted as "real"; and this was still the case when the Italian mathematicians of the sixteenth century found formulas[3] for solutions of the cubic and quartic equations of the form $ax^3 + bx^2 + cx + d = 0$ and $ax^4 + bx^3 + cx^2 + dx + e = 0$ respectively. Strangely, the solution of the latter depended upon operations with complex numbers of the form $a + b\sqrt{-1}$, even though these were regarded only as "fictitious"; but so long as "real" roots were produced by the process, use of the complex numbers during the process was accepted.[4]

Now the solutions of the quadratic, cubic, and quartic equations all involve only the five operations of addition, subtraction, multi-

---

3. For details and the actual identities of the discoverers of these solutions, see Carl B. Boyer, *A History of Mathematics* (New York: John Wiley & Sons, 1968), pp. 310–17.

4. As observed by Struik, ultimate acceptance of the complex numbers within orthodox mathematics was more influenced by the work on cubic equations than on quadratics. See Dirk Jan Struik, *A Concise History of Mathematics* (2 vols.; New York: Dover Publications, 1948), I, 114.

plication, division, and taking roots (radicals)—what may be termed algebraic operations. It was natural, therefore, that the same type of solution would be sought for the fifth-degree equation, the quintic. But so long as the attack on the problem took the form of searching for special algorithms, i.e., formulas embodying only algebraic operations, it was doomed to failure. An entirely new approach was needed.

In 1770, the French mathematician Lagrange took such a new approach by asking the question, "Why do the methods which are successful in solving equations of degree at most 4, all fail when the degree is greater than 4?" Although Lagrange was not able to answer this question, it was apparently his work that induced both the Italian physician Ruffini and, a few years later, the Norwegian mathematician Niels Abel to come to grips with the question, "Can there be given any algorithm, using only algebraic operations, for the solution of the quintic?" Although neither of these gentlemen gave a proof that would be considered rigorous by modern standards, they did arrive as proofs satisfactory enough to be convincing that the answer was negative. And soon after, the young French mathematician Evariste Galois went further and asked, "Can there be given criteria for establishing the solvability, by algebraic methods, of equations of degree higher than 4?" For not all quintics are unsolvable by algebraic methods, as trivial examples show; but no general formula exists, using algebraic methods alone, that is applicable to all cases.

The concept of group.—If we pause to consider the great generality of questions such as these, as opposed to the finding of a solution for a particular given equation having numerical coefficients, we will not be surprised (if we do not already know) that the answers required a searching inquiry into the structure of the so-called group of an equation. Although Galois apparently originated the name "group" for the structure referred to, he did not originate the concept of group; nor, indeed, did he (or anyone else until nearly a century later) give a precisely formulated definition of the concept. Like most profound ideas, it evolved only gradually out of recognition of its occurrences and its importance in various special cases—as in Galois' use of it, for instance. However, only from the common knowledge of the arithmetic of the integers (positive, negative, and zero) and their addition, could the concept of group have been invented. Consider the following statements:

Statement 1. Addition of integers gives an integer, and the order in which they are added does not change the result (in the sense that if *a*, *b*, and *c* are integers, adding *a* to *b* and then the result to *c*, gives the same as adding *a* to the sum of *b* and *c*); and there is an integer *zero*, addition of which to any integer gives the same integer, and such that if *x* is an integer, there is an integer − *x* which when added to *x* gives zero.

Now let us paraphrase this statement by substituting the word "element" for "integer" and "combination" for "addition":

Statement 2. Combination of elements gives an element, and the order in which they are combined does not change the result; and there is an element *e*, combination of which with any element gives the element, and such that if *x* is an element, there is an element − *x* which when combined with *x* gives *e*.

One unfamiliar with this would probably react by asking, "What has been accomplished by such a paraphrase? One has only substituted meaningless or indefinite terms for meaningful terms!" But this is precisely the point. It is quite correct to say that *Statement 2*, in view of the meaningless terms, is itself meaningless; but it is the wide variety of meanings, or interpretations, that we can give to the terms "element" and "combination" that make the meaningless paraphrase important. It is this latter fact (together with the fact that the properties implied by the so-called "meaningless paraphrase" turn out to form a substantive and useful abstract theory which can be applied to every meaningful interpretation of the paraphrase) which renders it important. Specifically, if one can find, in mathematics or anywhere else (such as in physics), a collection of things which we may call elements and a means of combining them which will satisfy *Statement 2*, then one has found an example of a group; and the combination used is called the *operation* of the group. Thus in *Statement 1* we have an example of a group in which the operation is ordinary addition of integers.

As we have observed, the concept of a group could have been formulated solely out of the arithmetic of integers, in fact out of their additive properties alone. But it is safe to say that nobody, not even the most perceptive mathematician, would ever have discovered it if the same type of structure had not been turning up almost everywhere in mathematics, even (and especially) in geometry (as in groups of rotations), and gradually forcing itself upon the attention of the mathematical world. In particular, the group formed by combining permutations of the coefficients of an equation had impressed Galois, and it was the solvability[5] of this so-called group of the equation that turned out to be the criterion for the existence of a solution of the equation by algebraic methods.

A formal development of group theory today usually employs the axiomatic method, i.e., axioms are stated incorporating the four parts of *Statement 2*, and then the properties of groups are proved in theorem form from these axioms much as Euclid did for his geometry. Every professional mathematician is expected to know the most important of these properties, although the theory of groups, unlike Euclidean geometry (which is a relatively closed field), is a very active field of research today. Group structures, embodying interpretations of the group axioms (or, equivalently, of *Statement 2* above), are found in all fields of mathematics, and the theorems derived from the group axioms must hold true in all such interpretations. The economy involved in the recognition of a group structure in a particular situation is obvious; the properties needed for the particular situation have usually already been proved in the abstract theory and are available for each special case. In modern physics, especially quantum physics, important applications of group theory have been found—neither the first nor the only time that a theory developed for purely mathematical purposes was found to furnish the appropriate structure in a physical or social science.[6]

But it is not just this fact which justifies establishing the properties of an abstract group once and for all; it is rather the perspective and power usually achieved by the recognition of a group structure in a given situation. Galois could hardly have solved the question of the solvability of a general algebraic equation by using the older methods

---

5. To define what is meant by the solvability of a group would take us too far afield. The definition and reference to Galois' work may be found in Eric T. Bell, *The Development of Mathematics* (2d ed.; New York: McGraw-Hill Book Co., 1945), pp. 231–36.

6. Eugene P. Wigner, "The Unreasonable Effectiveness of Mathematics in the Natural Sciences," *Some Uses of Mathematics*, ed. Max S. Bell (School Mathematics Study Group, *Studies in Mathematics*, Vol. XVI), pp. 31–44. This Richard Courant Lecture in Mathematical Sciences is reprinted from *Communications on Pure and Applied Mathematics*, Vol. XIII (New York: John Wiley & Sons, 1960).

which preceded his work. And as we shall see, it is really this kind of structural approach that has given modern mathematics its power and its ability to consolidate and simplify the diverse mathematical theories that have evolved during the past three centuries.

New types of abstract structure.—During the nineteenth century, the study of new number systems (real numbers, complex numbers, quaternions, matrices, etc.) led to the formulation of new types of abstract structures such as rings, ideals, modules, and so on. These usually involve two operations instead of one, with one of the operations forming a group. Such structures were fundamental in the study of the various types of algebras which have found important applications in mathematics and physics.

In the case of geometry, which during the Hellenistic era was basically all of the Euclidean type, the nineteenth century saw the creation of new types (inverse, projective, descriptive, etc.) including the beginnings of topology. Freedom to investigate hitherto undreamed-of geometric structures was enhanced by the creation of non-Euclidean geometries and the *Erlanger Programm* of Felix Klein, in which it was pointed out that each of the known geometries could be characterized by its group of transformations. From the latter point of view, plane (Euclidean) geometry is the study of those properties (length, area, angles, etc.) of plane figures that remain unchanged by the group of "rigid" transformations of the plane, i.e., by translations and rotations. Klein's formulation is another example of the perspective provided by the theory of groups.

The beginnings of topology were geometric—more precisely, a series of seemingly unrelated studies concerning knots (Listing, Tait), graphs modeled after electric circuits (Kirchhoff) and chemical bonds (Cayley), and surfaces (Riemann, Betti, Poincaré). Early in the present century, the concept of a topological space was introduced (Fréchet, Riesz, Hausdorff) and later became a unifying structure for all of topology.[7] In slightly more general form than conceived by its original proponents, it serves as a starting point for the various types of structures, called spaces, that are employed in topological research and the applications of topology. Depending upon its special characteristics, every collection whatsoever can be considered as a topological space, and consequently the notion is of

7. See the works referred to in footnotes 3, 4, and 5.

much more general application than that of an abstract group. Every professional mathematician is expected to be familiar with the basic properties of topological spaces, since so many theorems are most easily proved when the collections involved are regarded as topological spaces in a suitable manner.

An easily understood and brief exemplification of this can be presented through the notion of metric space, a very common type of topological space. Consider the ordinary plane of plane geometry. Basic to length, area, and all other measurements is the distance between two points: if p and q are points of the Euclidean plane, then the distance between p and q is a unique, non-negative real number which we may denote by the symbol $d(p, q)$. If p and q are the same point, $d(p, q)$ is zero, but unless this is the case, it is positive. In plane geometry we prove the so-called triangle law as a theorem. It may be stated as follows: If p, q and r are points, then $d(p, q) \leqq d(p, r) + d(q, r)$. Now if S is any collection whatsoever, and we call its elements "points" and set up a distance $d(p, q)$ for every pair of points p and q in such a way that the triangle law is satisfied, then S is thereby converted into a metric space. A trivial way of doing this is to make $d(p, q)$ always equal to 1 (unless p and q are the same point, in which case $d(p, q)$ is put equal to zero of course). However, we usually try to choose $d(p, q)$ in such a way that it suits the special properties of the collection; for example, in the plane as p and q get closer together, $d(p, q)$ becomes smaller.

Anyone who has had a beginning course in calculus—or at least enough to know what is meant by a continuous real function $f(x)$ and its derivative $f'(x)$—should understand the following example: Consider the collection (C) of all continuous real functions defined over the interval $[0, 1]$. Now call each element of C a point—i.e., by "point" we mean some function $f(x)$ of the collection C—and for any two points p and q define $d(p, q)$ as follows: p and q are functions $f_1(x)$ and $f_2(x)$, respectively; let $d(p, q)$ be the maximum value of $|f_1(x) - f_2(x)|$ for all x in $[0, 1]$. With this definition it is easy to show that C becomes a metric space, and this means that we may use all the properties and theorems concerning metric spaces that are applicable. One very interesting theorem that can be proved relates to the existence of functions having no derivatives anywhere.

Until Bolzano and Weierstrass showed, a little over a century ago, that such functions existed, most mathematicians felt intuitively that every function in C must have derivatives at "most" points; that is, although a function might fail to have a derivative at some singular point here and there, at most points its derivative—geometrically, a tangent to its graph—must exist. The examples given by Bolzano and Weierstrass were very surprising and unexpected, but since then many examples have been given of such "pathological" functions. Today, using the concept of C as a metric space, it is easily proved that "points" of C which correspond to functions having no derivatives are scattered all through C. Indeed, if one introduces the idea of a "sphere" in C (exactly as defined in plane geometry), then arbitrarily close to each point of C, one can find entire spheres all of whose interior points represent functions having no derivatives. Thus, by introducing the topology in C, one gets a much broader perspective concerning the existence of these pathological functions, not to mention an easier and more elegant proof than is obtainable by the classical methods of calculus.

The idea of dimension.—Another idea that was never satisfactorily cleared up until the first quarter of the present century was that of *dimension*. For a long time mathematicians had sought satisfactory definitions of the notion, but without success. Although the concept now can be given a precise meaning in many different ways, and for any kind of topological space, all the meanings agree in the case of Euclidean spaces and can be explained as follows: Let empty space—i.e., space containing no points at all—have dimension -1, by definition. Then given a Euclidean space E, and point p of E, let n be the smallest integer such that p is the center of arbitrarily small spheres of E whose boundaries have dimension $n-1$; then n is the dimension of E at p—and, for the Euclidean case, that of E. This defines dimension for all cases by mathematical induction. In particular, the line has dimension one, the plane dimension two, and so on. For more general metric spaces, other kinds of neighborhoods of a point than just spheres must be permitted—but the idea is the same.

Characteristic Features of Modern Mathematics

Further examples of interesting mathematical structures and their applications could be given, but the aim of this chapter is only to give some inkling of what have become recognized as the most characteristic features of modern mathematics. During the past half-century, new types of structures have been created which not only have furnished means for the solution of long-outstanding, unsolved problems but also have provided an instrument without which the student would hardly be able to comprehend the vast accumulation of new mathematics which is being discovered (or invented). Consider the following diagram:

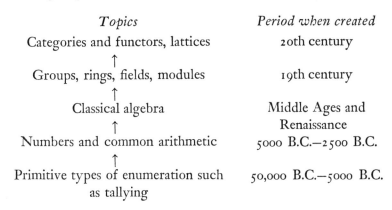

FIG. 1.—Accelerating rate of evolution of levels of abstraction

The five levels in Figure 1 correspond to levels of abstraction, the arrows indicating direction of higher abstraction. The dates at the right are rough approximations, intended only to emphasize the gradual but accelerating rate of evolution of the levels. Starting at the bottom line, the various forms of primitive enumeration ultimately led to the introduction of the abstract concept of number, along with the operations of arithmetic which made unnecessary the use of tallying or the abacus. With the evolution of the classical algebra, using symbols which could denote any one of a collection of numbers without specifying particular ones, a still higher level of abstraction was reached.

Then, as described above, the structures of the fourth level provided means for treating problems concerning any of a whole collection of third-level structures. (In the diagram, only algebraic structures have been indicated on the fourth level; in a complete diagram, topological structures would appear on this level—as well as other types which have not been mentioned). The highest (i.e., fifth) level is of more recent origin and was designed especially for the handling of collections of fourth-level structures and their relations to one another. It would take too long to treat this level in detail. A "category," as the term is used here, is a collection whose elements consist of fourth-level structures and their mappings; for instance, it might consist of groups along with a set of mappings (homomorphisms) from one group into another. "Functors" are mappings of categories into one another. All mappings involved in these structures are required to satisfy certain conditions (axioms).

It must be emphasized that the particular items mentioned on each level of the above diagram are not exhaustive; as we have already mentioned, topological structures would appear on the fourth level of a more complete diagram (as would various types of geometries on lower levels). We have also not mentioned at all some of the most interesting structures in modern mathematics, to be found in a field which is only a few decades old, viz., mathematical logic. Although its beginnings can be traced back more than a century (see especially the work of the English mathematician George Boole), it is chiefly a product of the present century. Originally used as a tool for substantiating certain philosophical viewpoints (e.g., "Mathematics consists of logical tautologies") and to provide a "rigorous" foundation for arithmetic (which later turned out to be not so rigorous after all), mathematical logic has provided a means whereby fundamental questions, long unyielding to older methods, have been answered. And to the surprise of most of those who forty years ago considered it as the most cryptic and esoteric of mathematical fields, it has provided structures that are basic in both mathematics and applications of mathematics to modern technology. This kind of development is no longer astonishing to those acquainted with the evolution of modern mathematics; indeed, a mathematics of the classical type, which busied itself mainly with complicated computational problems, would be totally inadequate to the needs of modern science and technology.

Moreover, teachers in the university graduate schools, faced with the problem of investing students with increasing amounts of new mathematical methods (the results of continuing research), were forced to explore ways of utilizing the newly created structures for simplifying and consolidating diverse older mathematical theories. They were pleasantly surprised to find that the newly developed structures afforded a valuable educational device, while at the same time accomplishing the objective of simplification and consolidation. As might be expected, this activity was accompanied by a breaking-down of traditional barriers between fields—a characteristic feature of modern mathematics which is being reflected to some extent in the undergraduate colleges and secondary schools.

Reshaping the Mathematics Curriculum

It was not long before explorations were initiated for taking advantage of some of the new methods in the undergraduate curriculum, not only to make simpler and more efficient the assimilation of ideas on that level of instruction, but to prepare for what was to come on the graduate level. As might be anticipated, some resistance was encountered from undergraduate teachers as well as teachers in allied fields who had not kept up with the way in which new mathematical concepts were being utilized. But these matters have a way of working themselves out as the advantages accruing from the new approaches become manifest. And once started, it was inevitable that the changes being made would influence the secondary- and, ultimately, the primary-school curriculum. The impetus to change was accelerated in this country by the news of "Sputnik," whose ascent stimulated criticism of the scientific aspects of education and demands for accelerated programs.

This is a good place to recall that the algebra and the plane and solid geometry, which for many years have been part of the secondary-school curriculum in this country, were part of the *college* curriculum only a little over a century ago. Moreover, only at such an outstanding college as Princeton was calculus taught. Indeed, nothing more advanced than differential and integral calculus was offered in any of the colleges; and in those institutions where it was part of the curriculum, it was considered of Junior- or Senior-year caliber! Not until Johns Hopkins started graduate work in 1876 was there any mathematics taught beyond the calculus. Today, calculus is often available in the high school.

Over the long term, then, changes in mathematics and mathematics curricula have been taking place; and as mathematics itself grows—and it is growing more rapidly now than ever before both in its basic and applied aspects—we can expect that more topics which are considered university subjects in the recent past,[8] will be provided at the high school level. Paralleling this, more of the high school curriculum must be (and is being) moved into the primary grades. To accomplish this transfer, more emphasis will have to be placed on mathematics as a study of structures. This does not mean that what would correspond to the three lowest levels in Figure 1 can be neglected. Accounts will still have to be figured and areas measured; and the significance of (and the benefit to be derived from) the concepts of levels four and five cannot be appreciated without an acquaintance with the lower levels. However, whenever an acquaintance with structures of the fourth level will lead to better comprehension or make easier the assimilation of materials on the lower levels, they should be introduced. After all, except for those areas in traditional engineering and science in which special mathematical skills are still required, the chief requirement for the mathematically trained individual who goes into the ramified branches of modern industry and government is that he be trained in mathematical *ways of thought*. Probably the major task of the framers of modern curricula is to keep this latter requirement always in mind while still heeding the necessity for supplying those technical skills without which the purpose of the new structures cannot be made clear.

Like the rest of history, the history of mathematics is a record of progress through change. And as mathematics grows, curricular changes on all levels of the schools, from the primary to the graduate schools, are inevitable. It is unfortunate that the primary and secondary curricula remained fixed in basic content for so many years, and that current changes have had to be made so abruptly. However, once the changes now underway have settled into a satisfactory pattern, it is probable that no further changes of a radical nature will need to be made for some time; at least, this is what the history of curricular change seems to portend.

8. Probability and statistics are examples.

CHAPTER II

Psychology and Mathematics Education

LEE S. SHULMAN

Psychology and mathematics education are neither strange nor merely transient bedfellows. Their affair has a long and occasionally torrid past, during which mathematics instruction has been quite sensitive to shifts in psychological theories. However, much like the advice given to new mothers in successive editions of Doctor Spock, the psychological "word" has frequently changed each decade. For this reason, earlier yearbook chapters paralleling this one, by Knight,[1] Wheeler,[2] McConnell[3] and Buswell,[4] can almost be read as a history of controversies, cease-fires, and temporary truces among educational learning theorists over the last forty years. It would surely be an error to suggest that innovations in mathematics education have been caused wholly by developments in psychology. On many occasions the two disciplines may have responded commonly to a more general change in the *Zeitgeist* of education and the sciences. Most often, mathematics educators have shown themselves especially adept at taking hold of conveniently available psychological theories to buttress previously held instructional proclivities.

1. F. B. Knight, "Some Considerations of Method," *Report of the Society's Committee on Arithmetic* (Twenty-ninth Yearbook of the National Society for the Study of Education [Chicago: University of Chicago Press, 1930]), pp. 145–267.

2. R. H. Wheeler, "The New Psychology of Learning," *The Teaching of Arithmetic* (Tenth Yearbook of the National Council of Teachers of Mathematics [New York: Teachers College, Columbia University, 1935]).

3. T. R. McConnell, "Recent Trends in Learning Theory: Their Application to the Psychology of Arithmetic," *Arithmetic in General Education* (Sixteenth Yearbook of the National Council of Teachers of Mathematics [New York: Teachers College, Columbia University, 1941]), pp. 268–89.

4. Guy T. Buswell, "The Psychology of Learning in Relation to the Teaching of Arithmetic," *The Teaching of Arithmetic* (Fiftieth Yearbook of the National Society for the Study of Education, Part II [Chicago: University of Chicago Press, 1951]), pp. 143–54.

The curriculum revolution which laymen and professionals alike have called the "new math" has been supported by a "new psychology." What are the characteristics of this ostensibly new approach to the psychological analysis of the educational process? Just as the mathematician recognizes that, in point of age, there is nothing particularly new about the new mathematics, the psychologist must observe that many aspects of the "new psychology" are practically candidates for "intellectual medicare."

Scott[5] has attempted to state the basic principles of this new psychology in the following series of ten statements.

1. The structure of mathematics should be stressed at all levels. Topics and relationships of endurance should be given concentrated attention.
2. Children are capable of learning more abstract and more complex concepts when the relationship between concepts is stressed.
3. Existing elementary arithmetic programs may be severely condensed because children are capable of learning concepts at much earlier ages than formerly thought.
4. Any concept may be taught a child of any age in some intellectually honest manner, if one is able to find the proper language for expressing the concept.
5. The inductive approach or the discovery method is logically productive and should enhance learning and retention.
6. The major objective of a program is the development of independent and creative thinking processes.
7. Human learning seems to pass through the stages of preoperations, concrete operations, and formal operations.
8. Growth of understanding is dependent upon concept exploration through challenging apparatus and concrete materials and cannot be restricted to mere symbolic manipulations.
9. Teaching mathematical skills is regarded as a tidying-up of concepts developed through discovery rather than as a step-by-step process for memorization.
10. Practical application of isolated concepts or systems of concepts, particularly those applications drawn from the natural sciences, are valuable to reinforcement and retention.[6]

It must be recognized that the theoretical and empirical foundations for many of these assertions reach back to the truly excellent work of an earlier generation of investigators in the psychology of

5. Lloyd Scott, *Trends in Elementary School Mathematics* (Chicago, Illinois: Rand McNally & Co., 1966), pp. 15–16.

6. *Ibid.*, pp. 15–16.

mathematics learning. Such outstanding contributors as Brownell[7] anticipated many current developments both in the studies they conducted and in the pedagogical techniques they advocated.

The extent to which Scott's ten principles accurately reflect the general psychological foundation of many of the new approaches to mathematics instruction bespeaks the pervasive influence of a small book, *The Process of Education*,[8] and its author, Jerome S. Bruner. No single work embodied the letter and spirit of that psychology which undergirds the new curricula as did Bruner's short distillation of the deliberations of a conference of scientists and educators. Each of Scott's ten points can be found highlighted in the barely one hundred pages of that volume. Although we have come to associate with Bruner such ideas as *discovery, structure, early readiness,* and *intuitive thinking,* his writings did not initially stimulate those early renovative efforts in mathematics education. Yet, at the end of the 1950's, he managed to capture their spirit, provide them with a framework of cognitive theory, and stimulate the development of their later forms and eventual successors.

The phrase around which much of the new psychology of learning developed was "learning by discovery." It was far from a new idea.[9] Bruner's version of learning by discovery involved a theoretical mélange of Piaget and Plato—an environmentally dynamic version of contemporary developmental theory in conjunction with a twentieth-century form of classical rationalism.

Our discussion of the psychological issues surrounding the teaching of mathematics will begin as do so many of the new curricula—concretely. We shall begin our examination of these issues by citing

7. The psychology of school subjects has long been an area of active research. No other school subject has even approached the level and frequency of studies conducted in the area of arithmetic. See especially William A. Brownell, *Learning as Reorganization: An Experimental Study in Third Grade Arithmetic.* (Durham, N.C.: Duke University Press, 1939); William A. Brownell and Gordon Hendrickson, "How Children Learn Information, Concepts, and Generalizations," *Learning and Instruction* (Forty-ninth Yearbook of the National Society for the Study of Education, Part I [Chicago: University of Chicago Press, 1950]), pp. 92–128. Excellent reviews of this body of research can be found in McConnell, *op. cit.,* and Buswell, *op. cit.*

8. Jerome S. Bruner, *The Process of Education* (Cambridge, Mass.: Harvard University Press, 1960).

9. Cf. M. C. Wittrock, "The Learning by Discovery Hypothesis," in Lee S. Shulman and Evan R. Keislar (eds.), *Learning by Discovery: A Critical Appraisal* (Chicago: Rand McNally & Co., 1966), pp. 33–75.

in some detail an example of what Bruner considers learning by discovery. We will then analyze that example in order to relate it to the principles stated by Scott as well as to derive any further insights or clarifications. After characterizing what is meant by discovery learning, we will examine two additional theories which will serve as useful counterpoints to the discovery approach.

We will then attempt to disentangle the many complexities of this instructional question from the vantage point of the educational psychologist. We will use that analysis as a jumping-off point for a systematic analysis of a number of critical contemporary issues in the psychology of education.

This chapter will *not* attempt a comprehensive review of literature in the psychology of mathematics learning. It will instead examine some of the current theoretical issues in psychology that have relevance to education in mathematics, citing empirical literature only for illustrative purposes.

An Example of Discovery Learning

In a number of his papers, Bruner uses an instructional example from mathematics that derives from his collaboration with the mathematics educator, Z. P. Dienes.[10]

The class is composed of eight-year-old children who are to learn some mathematics. As one of the instructional units, children are first introduced to three kinds of flat pieces of wood or "flats." The first one, they are told, is to be called either the "unknown square" or "x square." The second flat, which is rectangular, is called "$1\ x$" or just x, since it is x long on one side and 1 long on the other. The third flat is a small square which is 1 by 1, and is called 1.

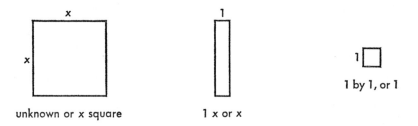

unknown or x square   1 x or x   1 by 1, or 1

10. Jerome S. Bruner, *Toward a Theory of Instruction* (Cambridge, Mass.: Belknap Press, 1966), pp. 59–68.

After allowing the children many opportunities simply to play with these materials, to do things with them, and to get a feel for them, he presents them with a problem. The problem is "Can you make larger squares than this **x** square by using as many of these flats as you want?" This is not a difficult task for most children and they readily make another square such as the one illustrated below.

Bruner then asks them if they can describe what they have done. They might reply, "We have one $x^\square$, with two x's and a 1." He then asks them to keep a record of what they have done. He may even suggest a notational system to use. The symbol $x^\square$ can represent the square x, and a $+$ for "and." Thus, the pieces used can be described as $x^\square + 2x + 1$.

Another way to describe their new square, he points out, is simply to describe each side. With an x and a 1 on each side, the side can be described as $x + 1$ and the square as $(x + 1)(x + 1)$ after some work with parentheses. Since these are two basic ways of describing the same square, they can be written in this way: $x^\square + 2x + 1 = (x + 1)(x + 1)$. This description, of course, far oversimplifies the procedures used.

The children continue making squares and generating the notation for them (see page 28).

Bruner hypothesizes that at some point they will begin to discern a pattern. While the x's are progressing at the rate of 2, 4, 6, 8, the ones are going 1, 4, 9, 16; on the right side of the equation, the pattern is 1, 2, 3, 4. Provocative or leading questions are often used Socratically to elicit this discovery. Even if they are initially unable to break the code, Bruner maintains, they will sense that there is a pattern and try to discover it. Bruner then illustrates how the pupils transfer what they have learned to working with a balance beam. The youngsters are ostensibly learning not only something about quadratic equations but, more important, something about the discovery of mathematical regularities.

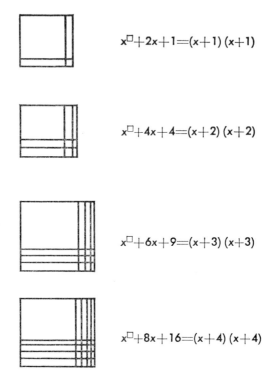

$x^{\square}+2x+1=(x+1)(x+1)$

$x^{\square}+4x+4=(x+2)(x+2)$

$x^{\square}+6x+9=(x+3)(x+3)$

$x^{\square}+8x+16=(x+4)(x+4)$

The general learning process described by Bruner occurs in the following manner. First, the child finds in his manipulation of the materials regularities that correspond with intuitive regularities he has already come to understand. Notice that what the child does for Bruner is to find some sort of match between what he is doing in the outside world and some models or templates that he has already grasped intellectually. For Bruner, it is rarely something *outside* the learner that is discovered. Instead, the discovery involves an internal reorganization of previously known ideas in order to establish a better fit between those ideas and the regularities of an encounter to which the learner has had to accommodate.

This is precisely the philosophy of education we associate with Socrates. Remember the lovely dialogue of the *Meno* by Plato, in which the young slave boy is brought to an understanding of what is involved in doubling the area of a square. Socrates maintains throughout this dialogue that he is not teaching the boy anything new; he is simply helping the boy reorganize and bring to the fore what he has always known.

Bruner almost always begins with a focus on the production and manipulation of materials. He describes the child as moving through three levels of representation as he learns.[11] The first level is the *enactive level,* where the child manipulates materials directly. He then progresses to the *ikonic level,* where he deals with mental images of objects but does not manipulate them directly. Finally he moves to the *symbolic level,* where he is strictly manipulating symbols and no longer mental images of objects. This sequence is based on Bruner's interpretation of the developmental theory of Jean Piaget. The combination of these concepts of manipulation of actual materials as part of a developmental model and the Socratic notion of learning as internal reorganization into a learning-by-discovery approach is the unique contribution of Bruner.

The Process of Education was written in 1959, after most mathematics innovations that use discovery as a core had already begun. It is an error to say that Bruner initiated the learning-by-discovery approach. It is far more accurate to say that, more than any one man, he managed to capture its spirit, provide it with a theoretical foundation, and disseminate it. Bruner is not the discoverer of discovery; he is its prophet.

Counterpoints to Discovery

As Hegel recognized nearly two centuries ago, there is a dialectical quality to history. Every successfully advanced thesis seems to generate its own antithesis. In the present instance, the success of the discovery position (as expounded by Bruner and as reflected in a multitude of curricular innovations in mathematics, the sciences, and the social studies) inevitably resulted in the calling forth of antagonistic positions. These positions were by no means created solely to oppose learning by discovery. Since the days of William James, psychology has always harbored opposing camps on the battleground of learning theory.[12] The respective banners might read

11. Jerome S. Bruner, Rose R. Olver, and Patricia M. Greenfield, *et al.,* *Studies in Cognitive Growth* (New York: John Wiley & Sons, 1966), pp. 12 ff.

12. Cf. E. G. Boring, "Human Nature and Sensation: William James and the Psychology of the Present," in Robert I. Watson and Donald T. Campbell (eds.), *History, Psychology and Science* (New York: John Wiley & Sons, 1963), pp. 92–108.

"behaviorists and mentalists," "connectionists and gestalt psychologists," "neobehaviorists and cognitive psychologists"—the fundamental epistemological stances which stand opposed to each other have
been only moderately changed from the early confrontation of
Hume and Kant or, for that matter, from that of Plato and Aristotle. We shall examine these epistemological assumptions in detail
at a later point in this chapter.

Although it is often B. F. Skinner who is identified as Bruner's
primary antagonist, for purposes of the present chapter the work of
two other learning theorists, Robert M. Gagné and David Ausubel,
each of whom has taken a position in marked opposition to Bruner,
will be examined. Each of these men is an advocate of approaches to
instruction that may be interpreted as the antithesis of discovery.
Such an approach may be called "guided learning," "expository
learning," or "reception learning." Each has written at least one
major volume elucidating his position.[13] They are by no means
wholly in agreement with each other on all matters. Both, however,
represent a theoretical position which raises serious questions concerning the fruitfulness of encouraging students to discover answers
for themselves as a major vehicle for general instruction. We shall
first examine the work of Gagné.

Instructional Example: Guided Learning

Gagné begins with a task analysis of the instructional objectives.
He always asks the question, "What is it you want the learner to be
able to do?" This *capability*, he insists, must be stated *specifically* and
behaviorally.

By "capability," he means the ability to perform certain specific
functions under specified conditions. A capability could be the ability to solve a number series. It might be the ability to solve some
problems in non-metric geometry.

This capability can be conceived of as a terminal behavior and
placed at the top of what will eventually be a complex pyramid.
After analyzing the task, Gagné asks, "What would you need to
know in order to do that?" Let us say that one could not complete

13. Robert M. Gagné, *The Conditions of Learning* (New York: Holt, Rinehart & Winston, 1965); David P. Ausubel, *Educational Psychology: A Cognitive
View* (New York: Holt, Rinehart & Winston, 1968).

the task unless he could first perform prerequisite tasks *a* and *b*. So a pyramid begins.

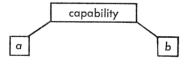

But in order to perform task *a*, one must be able to perform tasks *c* and *d* and for task *b*, one must know *e*, *f*, and *g*.

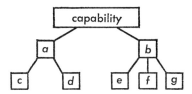

So one builds a very complex pyramid of prerequisites to prerequisites to the objective which is the desired capability.

Gagné has developed a model for discussing the different levels of such a hierarchy. If the final capability desired is a *problem-solving* capability, the learner first must know certain *principles*. But to understand those principles, he must know specific *concepts*. But prerequisite to these are particular *simple associations* or *facts* discriminated from each other in a distinctive manner. He continues the analysis until he ends up with the fundamental building blocks of learning—classically or operantly conditioned responses.

Gagné, upon completing the whole map of prerequisites, administers pretests to determine which have already been mastered. The pattern of responses to these diagnostic tests identifies precisely what must be taught. This model is particularly conducive to subsequent programing of material and programed instruction. When prerequisites are established, a very tight teaching program or package can develop. Figure 1 illustrates such a task hierarchy for the terminal objectives identified by the boxes labeled Task 1 and Task 2.[14]

The work of Ausubel also stands in dramatic counterpoint to the body of theory and research which advocates discovery over exposition in teaching. Ausubel has long argued against the "mystique" of

14. Robert M. Gagné, "Contributions of Learning to Human Development," *Psychological Review*, LXXV (May, 1968), 177–91.

discovery. He argues that much of the apparent superiority of discovery approaches in empirical studies derives from the use of a straw man, *rote learning*, as the basis for comparison. The opposite of discovery learning need not be rote learning, insists Ausubel. It ought to be *meaningful verbal learning*.

Ausubel, like Gagné, emphasizes the great importance of systematically guided exposition in the process of education. The key is the careful sequencing of instructional experiences so that any unit taught is clearly related to those that precede it. It is this continuity

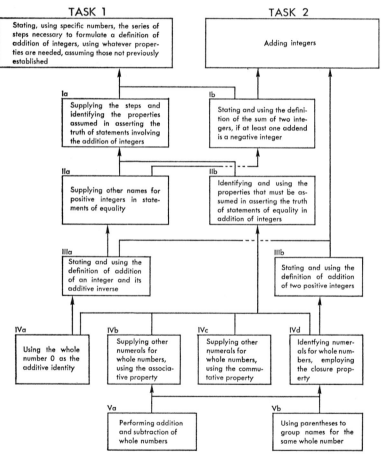

Fig. 1.—A task hierarchy for objectives of assigned tasks. (From Robert M. Gagné, "Learning Hierarchies," *Educational Psychologist*, VI [November, 1968], 1.)

between the learner's existing cognitive structure and the new material to be learned that makes the new material meaningful. There is certainly no basis for asserting that anything learned through reception has been learned rotely.

Ausubel discusses this problem of the confounding of discovery and meaningfulness in the following manner.

> In reception learning (rote or meaningful) the entire content of what is to be learned is presented to the learner in final form. The learning task does not involve any independent discovery on his part. He is required only to internalize or incorporate the material ... that is presented to him so that it is available or reproducible at some future date. In the case of meaningful reception learning, the potentially meaningful task or material is comprehended or made meaningful in the process of internalization. In the case of rote reception learning, the learning task either is not potentially meaningful or is not made meaningful in the process of internalization.
>
> The essential feature of discovery learning ... is that the principal content of what is to be learned is not given but must be discovered by the learner *before* he can incorporate it meaningfully into his cognitive structure. The distinctive and *prior* learning task, in other words, is to discover something. ... The first phase of discovery learning involves a process quite different from that of reception learning. The learner must rearrange information, integrate it with existing cognitive structure, and reorganize or transform the integrated combination in such a way as to generate a desired end-product or discover a missing means-end relationship. *After* discovery learning itself is completed, the discovered content is made meaningful in much the same way that presented content is made meaningful in reception learning.
>
> It is evident, therefore, that reception and discovery learning are two quite different kinds of processes, and ... that most classroom instruction is organized along the lines of reception learning. In the next section it will be pointed out that verbal reception learning is not necessarily rote in character, that much ideational material (concepts, generalizations) can be internalized and retained meaningfully without prior problem-solving experience, and that at no stage of development does the learner have to discover principles independently in order to be able to understand and use them meaningfully.[15]

In contrast to Bruner, Ausubel sees no reason why problem-solving activity must precede the internalization of new facts, concepts, or principles. If the material can be meaningfully organized by the

15. Ausubel, *op. cit.*, p. 22.

instructor, the need for student discovery is removed and the process of learning rendered far more efficient.

Although often approached simplistically, the learning-by-discovery controversy is in fact a vast psychoeducational collage—a heterogeneous mixture of many issues bound together indiscriminately. In the following pages, we shall attempt to disentangle the separate issues and discuss them individually. We will then return to instructional problems and attempt to assess these in the light of our discussion.

Any discussion of a psychology of instruction must deal with the three basic components of that process: (*a*) the entering characteristics of the students, (*b*) the teaching-learning activities and processes, and (*c*) the instructional objectives. We shall discuss each of these in turn, beginning with the ends of education—the objectives of instruction.

Objectives

What are the ends of education? What objectives should we seek? Although such questions may appear, at first blush, better suited to a discussion of philosophy than of psychology, they in fact form the very crux of the issues being examined.

For Bruner, the emphasis is upon the kinds of *processes* learned by the student, in contrast to the specific subject-matter *products* he may acquire. One paragraph from *Toward a Theory of Instruction*[16] communicates the essence of educational objectives for Bruner. After discussing the mathematics example previously mentioned, he concludes:

> Finally a theory of instruction seeks to take account of the fact that a curriculum reflects not only the nature of knowledge itself [the specific capabilities] but also the nature of the knower and of the knowledge-getting process. It is the enterprise *par excellence* where the line between the subject matter and the method grows necessarily indistinct. A body of knowledge, enshrined in a university faculty and embodied in a series of authoritative volumes, is the *result* of much prior intellectual activity. To instruct someone in these disciplines is not a matter of getting him to commit results to mind. Rather, it is to teach him to participate in the process that makes possible the establishment of knowledge. We teach a subject not to produce little living libraries on that subject, but rather

16. Bruner, *Toward A Theory of Instruction, op. cit.*

to get a student to think mathematically for himself, to consider matters as a historian does, *to take part in the process of knowledge-getting. Knowing is a process, not a product.* (italics mine)[17]

Gagné has come out in substantial agreement with Bruner on the priority of processes over products as the objectives of instruction. His emphasis, however, is not on teaching general strategies or heuristics of discovery; he is much more concerned with the teaching of the rules or intellectual skills that are relevant to particular instructional domains. The following paragraph could well be read as a clear, if gentle, demurrer to Bruner's approach to the issue of objectives.

Obviously, strategies are important for problem-solving, regardless of the content of the problem. The suggestion from some writings is that they are of overriding importance as a goal of education. After all, should not formal instruction in the school have the aim of teaching the student "how to think"? If strategies were deliberately taught, would not this produce people who could then bring to bear superior problem-solving capabilities to any new situation? Although no one would disagree with the aims expressed, it is exceedingly doubtful that they can be brought about solely by teaching students "strategies" or "styles" of thinking. Even if these can be taught (and it is likely that they can), they do not provide the individual with the basic firmament of thought, which is a set of externally-oriented intellectual skills. Strategies, after all, are rules which govern the individual's *approach* to listening, reading, storing information, retrieving information, or solving problems. If it is a mathematical problem the individual is engaged in solving, he may have acquired a strategy of applying relevant subordinate rules in a certain order—but he must also have available the mathematical rules themselves. If it is a problem in genetic inheritance, he may have learned a way of guessing at probabilities before actually working them out—but he must also bring to bear the substantive rules pertaining to dominant and recessive characteristics. Knowing strategies, then, is not all that is required for thinking; it is not even a substantial part of what is needed. *To be an effective problemsolver, the individual must somehow have acquired masses of organized intellectual skills.* (italics mine)[18]

For Gagné, the objectives of instruction are intellectual skills or capabilities that can be specified in operational terms, can be taskanalyzed, and then can be taught. Gagné would subscribe to the posi-

17. *Ibid.*, p. 72.

18. Gagné, *Conditions of Learning*, 2d ed. This second edition of Gagné's book is in preparation and contains several major departures from the first edition. This passage is quoted from the manuscript.

tion that psychology has been successful in suggesting ways of teaching only when objectives have been made operationally clear. When objectives are not clearly stated, the psychologist can be of little assistance. Objectives clearly stated in behavioral terms are the cornerstones of Gagné's position.[19]

Ausubel strongly rejects the notion that any kind of process, be it strategy or skill, should hold priority among the objectives of education. He remains a militant advocate of the importance of mastering well-organized bodies of subject-matter knowledge as the most important goal of education.

... As far as the formal education of the individual is concerned, the educational agency largely transmits ready-made concepts, classifications, and propositions. In any case, discovery methods of teaching hardly constitute an efficient *primary* means of transmitting the *content* of an academic discipline.

It may be argued with much justification, of course, that the school is also concerned with developing the student's ability to use acquired knowledge in solving particular problems, that is, with his ability to think systematically, independently, and critically in various fields of inquiry. *But this function of the school, although constituting a legitimate objective of education in its own right, is less central than its related transmission-of-knowledge function* [italics mine] in terms of the amount of time that can be reasonably allotted to it, in terms of the objectives of education in a democratic society, and in terms of what can be reasonably expected from most students . . .[20]

We may thus observe that, while Gagné and Ausubel tend to agree that exposition is a more generally useful form of instruction than discovery, they disagree regarding the appropriate objectives of instruction. More generally, we may see that a theorist's preferred mode of instruction can be, and often is, independent of the objectives he holds most important. Decisions about objectives reflect more than the psychologist's preferred theory of learning. They also reflect his judgments concerning the nature of knowledge and the social utility of the different kinds of intellectual accomplishment.

Differences among competing theorists with respect to the objectives of education contribute to the difficulty of assessing the relative potencies of the theories they espouse. One can argue endlessly over the relative merits of a jeep and a Cadillac because the purposes to

19. See the 1965 edition, footnote 13.   20. Ausubel, *op. cit.*, p. 23.

which each is put are generally so disparate; the criteria of success are thus different. One can also dispute over the respective qualities of the White Sox and the Bears, but no meaningful resolution is likely to emerge. Thus, though most learning theorists espouse the acquisition of knowledge as the major objective of education, their respective definitions of *knowledge* and *knowing* are often so incongruent that they scarcely overlap.

The psychological and philosophical bases for these differences will be discussed later in this chapter. For the moment, we may note that when conflicting approaches seek such contrasting objectives, the conduct of comparative educational experiments becomes extremely difficult. How can one investigate the conflicting claims of two points of view when each aims at distinctly different goals?

One solution that deserves attention is that of planning educational experiments with multiple criterion measures.[21] For example, evaluate the extent to which both processes and product objectives are reached through employment of a particular approach. One might further assess such additionally important outcomes as attitudes, motivation, and self-esteem. In this way we can generate a sufficiently broad range of criteria to compare meaningfully across instructional approaches which begin with radically disparate assumptions.

We may, at this point, pause to reflect on the analyses we have completed. Ausubel has made the important observation that the rote-meaningful and reception-discovery continua are not coextensive. They are logically independent.

For Ausubel, something has been learned meaningfully:

. . . if the learning task can be related in nonarbitrary, substantive (nonverbatim) fashion to what the learner already knows, and if the learner adopts a corresponding learning set to do so. Rote learning, on the other hand, occurs if the learning task consists of purely arbitrary associations; . . . if the learner lacks the relevant prior knowledge necessary for making the learning task potentially meaningful; and also, . . . if the learner adopts a set merely to internalize it in an arbitrary, verbatim fashion (that is, as an arbitrary series of words).[22]

21. Cf. Lee J. Cronbach, "The Logic of Experiments on Discovery" in Shulman and Keislar (eds.), *op. cit.*, pp. 88–90.

22. Ausubel, *op. cit.*, p. 24.

Thus, the reception-discovery dimension reflects what the learner is doing in the course of instruction—the cognitive processes in which he is engaged as he learns. The rote-meaningful dimension represents the degree to which what is learned articulates with the learner's prior knowledge and cognitive structure, with no reference to how he learns it.

Table 1 reflects the orthogonality of these two dimensions and provides examples of the kinds of activities that can be classified in each of the four cells.

TABLE 1

	ROTE	MEANINGFUL
RECEPTION	Memorize multiplication tables	Learn to solve problems of adding number series
DISCOVERY	Use trial-and-error procedures to calculate square roots	Work from a set of specific examples to induce a mathematical rule.

TABLE 2

	ROTE	MEANINGFUL
PRODUCT	$2 + 2 = 4$	Multiplication tables
PROCESS	"Invert and multiply"	Application of heuristics in estimation problems

NOTE: Any of these examples could shift between the rote and meaningful categories as a function of how, when, and why they are taught.

Hence, all that is discovered is not meaningful; all that is received is not rote.

Our discussion of objectives has introduced yet another dimension into our analysis—the product-process distinction. In Table 2 we can observe that another typical plaint, that products are learned by rote while processes are mastered meaningfully, is also a *non sequitur*.

Learning to parrot the words "two plus two equal four" would be an example of the student learning a rote product. The student who, when confronted with a problem of dividing one fraction by another, knows that he must "invert and multiply" but has not the faintest idea why, has mastered a process rotely. The student who has mastered his multiplication tables and understands the conceptual relationships among the various orders of multiplication has mastered a product or set of products meaningfully. Finally, the student who has learned to apply a heuristic or set of heuristics when confronted with the problem of estimating a particular solution in an arithmetic problem and who understands why the heuristic works has come to master a process meaningfully.

By the end of the 1960's, it appears that the rote-meaningful argument has been mercifully put to rest. In contrast to the 1920's and 1930's, general advocates of drill without understanding either have retired or are in hiding. This is not to imply that rote learning has ceased to occur in our classrooms. Far from it. It now occurs, however, through inadvertence rather than through careful planning.

We have now observed that a number of dimensions that are usually confounded in discussions of discovery learning can and must be distinguished. These include matters of student learning (reception-discovery), educational objectives (product-process), and instructional articulation with past learning (rote-meaningful). There are yet other aspects of the psychology of instruction that have become inextricably bound up in the polemics over discovery. We shall now turn to one of the most critical of these, the concept of readiness for learning.

Entering Characteristics

What does the student bring with him to the instructional situation? In what manner do the characteristics of the students at the inception of instruction affect the subsequent teaching-learning process? We shall examine this topic under two traditional educational headings: (a) readiness for learning, and (b) aptitude for learning.

READINESS

One indication of the rapidity of change in the psychological theories underlying mathematics instruction is reflected in the role assigned to Piaget.[23] Twenty years ago the work of this eminent

23. Jean Piaget has produced an enormous body of work. See especially Jean Piaget, *The Child's Conception of Number* (New York: Humanities Press,

Swiss psychologist received not a single mention in the yearbook on mathematics education.[24] Today it is literally impossible to discuss the psychology of instruction in mathematics without placing his contributions at center stage. His influence is not limited to the psychology of instruction. Many psychologists are seriously suggesting that his stature will eventually equal that of Freud as a pioneering giant in the behavioral sciences.

Piaget is a man of multiple talents and widespread contributions. He is an epistemologist, logician, biologist, and developmental psychologist. It is only in the latter capacity that we will consider his work in the present chapter. We will examine the implications of Piaget's view of cognitive development as it relates to readiness to learn.

Piaget first became fascinated with problems of cognitive growth while translating and standardizing into French a series of English intelligence tests. He was struck by the observation that the character of the *errors* made by children held as much interest as the nature of their correct answers. In fact, there were systematic internal consistencies in the kinds of errors made by children of different ages. It was as if they were operating with their own forms of logic which, though unlike adult logical forms, were regular and amenable to formal analysis. These observations of the character of children's errors stimulated a half-century of research into the problems of cognitive development.

We shall not in this chapter reiterate the Piagetian stages of cognitive development. This task has been ably performed in many other volumes.[25] Instead, we shall focus on the characteristics of Piaget's

1952); Jean Piaget, *Logic and Psychology* (New York: Basic Books, 1957); Barbel Inhelder and Jean Piaget, *The Growth of Logical Thinking from Childhood to Adolescence* (New York: Basic Books, 1958). The best overviews of Piaget's work are through his interpreters. See note 25.

24. *The Teaching of Arithmetic*, ed. Guy T. Buswell (Fiftieth Yearbook of the National Society for the Study of Education, Part I [Chicago: University of Chicago Press, 1951]).

25. See especially John Flavell, *The Developmental Psychology of Jean Piaget* (Princeton, N.J.: Van Nostrand Co.), 1963; J. McV. Hunt, *Intelligence and Experience* (New York: Ronald Press, 1961); Hans G. Furth, *Piaget and Knowledge* (Englewood Cliffs, N.J.: Prentice-Hall, 1969); Irving E. Sigel and Frank H. Hooper (eds.), *Logical Thinking in Children* (New York: Holt, Rinehart & Winston, 1968).

view of the growth of intelligence as they may relate to the process of instruction.

Piaget views the development of intelligence as part of the more general process of biological development. Gallagher[26] has suggested five major themes running through Piaget's work.

1. Continuous and progressive changes take place in the structures of behavior and thought in the developing child.
2. Successive structures make their appearance in a fixed order.
3. The nature of accommodation (adaptive change to outer circumstances) suggests that the rate of development is, to a considerable degree, a function of the child's encounters with his environment.
4. Thought processes are conceived to originate through a process of internalizing actions. Intelligence increases as thought processes are loosened from their basis in perception and action and thereby become reversible, transitive, associative, and so on.
5. A close relationship exists between thought processes and properties of formal logic.[27]

For Piaget the child is a developing organism passing through biologically determined cognitive stages. These stages are more or less age-related, although wide variations in cultures or environments will yield differences in individual rates of development. One might view the process of cognitive growth as a drama. The script or scenario describing the drama's plot and characters is given by the biological component. The role of the director—that of determining the onset and pace of the episodes—is a function of the environment.

Although development is a continuous process of structural change, it is still possible to characterize certain growth periods by the formal logical structures most useful for describing the child's cognitive functioning during that time span. These growth periods, when a temporary stability of cognitive functioning is achieved, define for Piaget the major stages of intellectual growth.

There is one other principle which is extremely important for an understanding of Piaget's system and its impact on education. This is the princicple of *autoregulation* or *equilibration*. Piaget sees the development of intelligence as a sequence of successive disequilibria followed by adaptations leading to new states of equilibrium. The

26. James J. Gallagher, "Productive Thinking," in Martin L. Hoffman and Lois W. Hoffman (eds.), *Review of Child Development Research* (2 vols.; New York: Russell Sage Foundation, 1964), I, 349–81.

27. *Ibid.*, p. 355. This listing is itself taken from Hunt, *op. cit.*

imbalance can occur because of an ontogenetic change occurring naturally as the organism matures. It can also occur in reaction to an input from the environment. Since disequilibrium is uncomfortable, the child must accommodate to new situations through active modification of his present cognitive structure.

Piaget observes that only in man can intelligence develop to the point where the domain of ideas and symbols can serve as the "environmental" source of disequilibrium. That is, we can construct intellectual universes, for example, transintuitive spaces, which can stimulate our own cognitive growth as surely as the confrontation by a baby with the problem of reaching his pacifier can lead to new insights or equilibria on his part.

Piaget has written little specifically directed at problems of education. He has repeatedly disavowed any expertise in the pedagogical domain. Yet, either directly or through such interpreters as Bruner, his influence has been strongly felt.

Piaget's emphasis upon action as a prerequisite to the internalization of cognitive operations has stimulated the focus upon direct manipulation of mathematically relevant materials in the early grades. His description of cognitive development occurring through autoregulation has reinforced tendencies to emphasize pupil-initiated, problem-solving activities as a major vehicle of mathematics instruction. His characterization of the number-related concepts understood by children of different ages (e.g., one-to-one correspondence, reversibility, conservation, and the like) has influenced our grasp of what children at different stages can be expected to learn meaningfully.

The latter point reflects Piaget's influence on some current conceptions of readiness. To determine whether a child is ready to learn a particular concept or principle, one analyzes the structure of that to be taught and compares it with what is already known about the cognitive structure of the child of that age. If the two structures are consonant, the new concept or principle can be taught; if they are dissonant, it cannot. One must then, if the dissonance is substantial, wait for further maturation to take place. If the degree of dissonance is minimal, there is nothing in Piaget's general theory to preclude the introduction of training procedures to achieve the desired state of readiness. However, Piaget seems to prefer the "waiting" to the "training" strategy under such conditions. Though his theory admits of both external and internal sources of developmental change, he seems to favor the internal ontogenetic mechanisms.

The chapter in *The Process of Education* entitled "Readiness for Learning" was ostensibly based on the work of Piaget. The largest single segment of that chapter was written by Piaget's chief collaborator, Barbel Inhelder. Imagine then the shock of that chapter's opening assertion: "We begin with the hypothesis that any subject can be taught effectively in some intellectually honest form to any child at any stage of development."[28] Considering the earlier description of Piaget's position, it seems hardly consistent.

Many are puzzled by this stand, including Piaget. In a paper delivered in the United States, he admitted that he (in the light of his own experiments) did not understand how Bruner could make such a statement. If Bruner meant the statement literally (i.e., *any* child can learn *any*thing), then it just is not true! There are always things a child cannot learn, especially not in an intellectually honest way. If he meant it homiletically (i.e., we can take almost anything and somehow resay it, reconstruct it, restructure it so that it now has a parallel at the child's level of cognitive functioning), then it may be a truism.

What Bruner is saying, however (and it is neither trivial nor absurd), is that our older conceptions of readiness have tended to apply Piagetian theory in the same way as some have for generations applied Rousseau's. There has been the belief that neither the nature of the child nor that of the subject matter can tolerate systematic tampering. We take the subject matter as our starting point, carefully observe as the child develops, and feed in the content as "readiness" is reached.

Bruner is suggesting that we must modify our conception of readiness so as to include not only the child, but the subject matter as well. Subject matter, too, can be passed through stages of readiness. We view the child as evolving through stages in which his preferred modes of representation are (serially) enactive, ikonic, and symbolic. Similarly, the basic principles or structures of a discipline can be represented manipulatively, as visual representations or as formal symbolic expressions.

28. Bruner, *Process of Education, op. cit.*

We may look to the example of discovery presented earlier in this chapter to illustrate the principles of alternative modes of representation. When the pupil is working solely with the flat pieces of wood, he is contending with problems presented in the enactive mode. When we help the child conceive of the problem in terms of manipulating the placement of any number of "flats," we have shifted to an ikonic mode, wherein visual images of objects are manipulated. When the learner can finally begin to manipulate the abstract symbols by themselves, thinking of x^2, $2x$, and 1 without invoking their imaginal or concrete manifestations, he has managed to deal with the problem at a symbolic level. The problem itself has remained the same. Only the modality in which it is being represented has been changed. Bruner would assert that similar transformations through modes of representation could be achieved for any fundamental concept or principle in mathematics.

How is it that Bruner, though beginning from a Piagetian starting point, reaches such a contrasting conclusion? It appears that they do not use the same criteria for determining whether a stage has been reached. Piaget employs far more stringent criteria for establishing whether a child has achieved, for example, the stage of concrete operations, including the expectation that the child should be able to provide a coherent verbal rationale for his assertions about phenomena. Bruner, viewing cognitive growth in terms of progressive changes in modes of representation, is prepared to accept non-verbal, behavioral evidence for the onset of a given stage. Thus, a child may appear "ready" to Bruner substantially earlier than he will to Piaget.

Bruner's position also appears to rest on an assertion about the nature of knowledge itself. The spiral curriculum, wherein the structures of disciplines are represented *seriatim* enactively, ikonically, and symbolically, may represent Bruner's conception of how any idea becomes known. The assertion is double-barreled. First, it is asserted that the fundamental principles or structures of disciplines are essentially simple; second and consequently, these simple structures can be taught and learned in an intellectually honest form through any mode of representation.

This conception of the simplicity of fundamental principles is neither unique to Bruner nor attributable only to Plato. The Nobel laureate Szent-Györgyi has written:

Science tends to generalize, and generalization means simplification. My own science, biology, is today not only very much richer than it was in my student days, but is simpler, too. Then it was horribly complex, being fragmented into a great number of isolated principles. Today these are all fused into one single complex, with the atomic model in its center. Cosmology, quantum mechanics, DNA and genetics, are all, more or less, parts of one and the same story—a most wondrous simplification. And generalizations are also more satisfying to the mind than details. We, in our teaching, should place more emphasis on generalizations than on details.[29]

We may thus observe and understand how, through the interpretation of Bruner, Piaget's essentially conservative position regarding readiness becomes a major impetus for the trend toward earlier introduction of subject matter to elementary school children.

Piaget himself remains quite dubious over the attempts to accelerate cognitive development that are reflected in many modern mathematics and science curricula. On a recent trip to the United States, Piaget commented:

. . . we know that it takes nine to twelve months before babies develop the notion that an object is still there even when a screen is placed in front of it. Now kittens go through the same stages as children, all the same substages, but they do it in three months—so they're six months ahead of babies. Is this an advantage or isn't it? We can certainly see our answer in one sense. The kitten is not going to go much further. The child has taken longer, but he is capable of going further, so it seems to be that the nine months probably were not for nothing.

It's probably possible to accelerate, but maximal acceleration is not desirable. There seems to be an optimal time. What this optimal time is will surely depend upon each individual and on the subject matter. We still need a great deal of research to know what the optimal time would be.[30]

The question that has not been answered, and which Piaget whimsically calls the "American question," is the empirical experimental question—to what extent is it possible through instruction to accelerate what Piaget maintains is the invariant clockwork of the order?

29. Albert Szent-Gyorgyi, "Teaching and the Expanding Knowledge," *Science*, CXLVI (December 4, 1964), 1278–79.

30. Quoted in Frank G. Jennings, "Jean Piaget: Notes on Learning," *Saturday Review* (May 20, 1967), 82.

Studies conducted by Smedslund,[31] Sigel,[32] Mermelstein[33] and others are attempting to identify the degree to which these processes can be accelerated. At this point the results remain equivocal. Successful acceleration is usually not achieved. When it is achieved, the success is relatively modest. However, we are far from having exhausted the full range of creative approaches to the problem. Much more work is needed. Even if successful, is there a long-term danger in such acceleration, as Piaget suggests? Or is early introduction to the basic principles of disciplines the key to educating a generation of citizens who, rather than patronizingly tolerating the sciences and mathematics, truly understand and appreciate them? (This is not to mention its value to those who will devote their lives to such pursuits.) These are questions to which future inquiries need be directed, for at the moment we have access only to opinions and personal prejudices.

For those theorists who advocate the systematic guidance of learning, the problem of readiness is free of ontogenetic and epistemological encumbrances. Gagné maintains that readiness is essentially a function of the presence or absence of prerequisite learning. When the child is capable of tasks d and e, he is by definition ready to learn b.

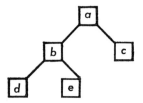

Until then, he is not ready. Gagné is not concerned with genetically developmental considerations except of the most gross variety. If the child at age five does not have the concept of the conservation of liquid volume, it is not because a natural mental unfolding has failed to take place; he has not had the necessary prior experiences. Ensure

31. Four of Jan Smedslund's studies are reprinted in Sigel and Hooper, *op. cit.*, pp. 265–94.

32. Irving E. Sigel, Anna Marie Roeper and Frank H. Hooper, "A Training Procedure for Acquisition of Piaget's Conservation of Quantity: A Pilot Study and Its Replication," in Sigel and Hooper, *op. cit.* pp. 295–307. The entire Sigel and Hooper volume is extremely relevant to mathematics education research.

33. Egon Mermelstein and others, *The Effects of Various Training Techniques on the Acquisition of the Concept on Conservation of Substance.* (U.S. Office of Education Project No. 6-8300, Hofstra University, February, 1967).

that he has acquired the prerequisite capabilities and he will be able to conserve.[34]

The key for understanding readiness is *prerequisite* knowledge or capabilities. Ausubel, who is in fundamental agreement with Gagné on this issue, has stated the point eloquently in the following aphorism.

If I had to reduce all of educational psychology to one principle, I would say this: The most important single factor influencing learning is what the learner already knows. Ascertain this and teach him accordingly.[35]

Ausubel felt that this point was so central to his general theoretical position as an educational psychologist that he placed it in the frontispiece of his textbook on educational psychology.

Problems of readiness, early learning, and acceleration are, thus, far less complex for the proponents of expository teaching than for their discovery-oriented counterparts. It is a matter of identifying prerequisite knowledge or capabilities and teaching these. Ironically, one might contend that Bruner's "shocking" proposition regarding readiness is as consistent (if not much more so) with the theories of Gagné and Ausubel as with that of Piaget. Surely, they (Gagné and Ausubel) might find the assertion less shocking to their conceptions of intellectual development. Their doubts, and they are major ones, would grow out of the unlikely probability of providing sufficient prerequisite understanding in a given time period to prepare "any child" to learn "any subject."

The psychological stance of those advocating guided expository learning has had interesting and potentially revolutionary consequences for our perspective on a concept that falls somewhat beyond the pale of considerations of discovery learning. This is the question of *aptitude for learning*. Working within the guided-learning tradition, theorists such as Carroll[36] and Bloom[37] have challenged educators to recast their ancient conceptions of mental ability. The next section is devoted to that challenge.

34. Gagné, "Contributions of Learning to Human Development," *op. cit.*

35. Ausubel, *op. cit.*, frontispiece.

36. John Carroll, "A Model of School Learning," *Teachers College Record*, LXIV (1963), 723–33.

37. Benjamin S. Bloom, "Learning for Mastery," in *Evaluation Comment* (Bulletin of the U.C.L.A. Center for the Study of Evaluation of Instructional Programs), May, 1968.

APTITUDE

When we discuss the entering characteristics of students, we are generally referring either to their readiness or to their aptitudes. Typically these two topics have been handled separately. Discussions of aptitude have usually centered about such issues as: What are the respective contributions of nature and nurture to individual intelligence? Is intelligence general or subject-specific? How stable or unchanging is aptitude?

Problems of planning for particular instructional units or curricula have usually treated student aptitude as a given. A student's aptitude was perceived as setting a theoretical limit on the level of complexity or abstraction he could be expected to attain in his attempts to master a given capability or substantive domain. It has always seemed a quite reasonable proposition, and few educators have bothered to question it.

Not so Carroll and, more recently, Bloom. Carroll[38] has challenged us with the view that *aptitude is the amount of time required by the learner to attain mastery of a learning task.* As Bloom has observed:

Implicit in this formulation is the assumption that, given enough time, all students can conceivably attain mastery of a learning task. If Carroll is right, then learning mastery is theoretically available to all, if we can find the means for helping each student. It is this writer's belief that this formulation of Carroll's has the most fundamental implications for education.[39]

Carroll's formulation bridges the gap between aptitude and readiness. If aptitude is seen as a measure of the *rate* at which a given student can master an instructional objective, clearly the prerequisite capabilities he brings to the learning task achieve major importance. Gagné[40] has demonstrated that once a carefully sequenced learning unit has begun, it is not the student's general aptitude that predicts best how well he will achieve any particular step. It is the extent to which he has attained the prerequisites to that step that predicts best. Thus, his readiness and aptitude come to coincide. Aptitude becomes a matter of *how long* it takes to achieve readiness, rather than *whether* a student is or can ever become ready.

38. Carroll, *op. cit.*   39. Bloom, *op. cit.*, p. 3.

40. Robert M. Gagné, "The Acquisition of Knowledge," *Psychological Review,* LXIX (1962), 355–65.

Our traditional conceptions of readiness happen to fit nicely with the institutionalized tempo of our school systems. In education we characteristically treat *time* as a constant while allowing *achievement* to act as a variable. That is, we provide a predetermined span of time for the mastery of a given body of subject matter and then measure the varying degrees of learning mastery attained by the students at the end of that time. We not only expect variability in achievement; we welcome it, for it serves as the basis for our grading systems. We then attribute the variability (wherein, as Bloom observed, hardly one-third of our students ever truly attain the objectives of instruction under the best of conditions) to those mystically immutable student characteristics—aptitude and motivation.

Let us use the analogy of a track meet.[41] Imagine the mile run if it began with the firing of a gun and ended at the end of four minutes when another gun went off and everyone had to stop wherever they were. It would be even more startling if about five minutes later another gun went off for the next race and everyone began that race from the same point at which they had ended the previous one.

By repeating such a process, we would guarantee the development of cumulative deficits for some runners as they fell progressively further behind after each successive race. As long as time were held constant and no source of external assistance or remediation were provided, such a consequence would be inevitable. We would find such a practice ludicrous in track, yet we run our educational programs in precisely this manner. Our purposes in education are to see to it that a certain minimal level of competence is achieved by each learner. To do so, we should logically set *levels of achievement* as constants and let *time* act as a variable.

Such a study has already been carried out in mathematics education. Herriot[42] reports that "slow-learning" students achieve as well in SMSG math as average students when they are allowed substantially more time than is usually allotted to the mathematics curriculum. In this case, they spent two years studying material originally designed for a one-year program. We are not arguing here whether

41. I am grateful to Professor Joe L. Byers for suggesting this analogy, as well as for much advice and helpful criticism concerning this chapter.

42. Sarah T. Herriot, "The Slow Learner Project: The Secondary School 'Slow Learner' in Mathematics," *SMSG Reports*, No. 5 (Stanford University, 1967).

certain topics in mathematics are really worth such extra time ex-
penditures. It is merely our purpose to demonstrate that one's aptitude does not determine the amount that can be learned, but merely
the amount of time necessary for that learning.

Such a modification in our view of aptitude for learning would
have multiple consequences. It would quickly broaden the range of
instruments used to measure aptitude, probably leading to the use of
many more differential aptitude measures in place of general aptitude
tests. In addition, tests of prerequisite knowledge would also be used.
We would find ourselves blending testing and teaching into a more
integrated general process of instruction. Student-entering characteristics would be used diagnostically, rather than prophetically—that is,
to plan for differentiated programs of instruction, rather than to
anticipate "inevitable" instructional disasters. It is such an approach
to the question of aptitude that has developed from the analyses of
learning exemplified by the work of Gagné and carried forward by
Carroll, Bloom, and others.

Having examined the objectives of instruction and the entering
characteristics of students, we turn in the next section to the tactics
of instruction and the problem of transfer of training.

Tactics and Sequence of Instruction

The theoretical issues we have been examining are educationally
relevant because they are related to what people actually do in
classrooms. Those who march under the learning-by-discovery ban-
ner behave quite differently as instructors from those whose pulses
quicken at the thought of guided learning. Though we have already
described some instructional examples and briefly characterized
them, it would now seem appropriate to treat in greater detail certain
of these specific pedagogical contrasts. For purposes of clarity, the
major distinction will be between the guided-learning approach of
Gagné and the discovery-learning strategy of Bruner.

The task analysis of subordinate capabilities that are prerequisite
to attainment of a given objective generates, for Gagné, a hierarchical structure of learning. Gagné[43] is quick to point out that this resultant structure by no means describes a universally necessary single

43. Robert M. Gagné, "Learning Hierarchies," *Educational Psychologist,* VI
(November, 1968).

pathway to the terminal objective. Specific individuals may vary from the derived learning hierarchy in the absence of specified stages, the interpolation of other stages not specified in the particular hierarchy, or in the reordering of the sequence. However, the structure and sequence suggested by the analysis of subordinate capabilities will generally describe a teaching program that will effectively accomplish the desired objective. That is, although it is possible to achieve the terminal capability via alternate routes, the pathway identified in the learning hierarchy will be preferable in general.

The model of teaching most closely following Gagné's expository or guided approach would be some form of programed instruction. Here the specific steps undertaken by the learner are carefully specified and sequenced. The medium may be a machine, a book, or a programed teacher closely following a predetermined instructional sequence. The achievement of each prerequisite step is firmly established before instruction on its successor is begun. Hence, learning is highly guided, errors are minimized, and meaningfulness—in the sense of articulation of new material with what the learner already knows or can do—is thereby assured.

In contrast, Bruner would emphasize much less system or order in his approach, although he would not, in principle, preclude such structure. He prefers to have the learner begin with manipulation of materials or tasks that present problems. These problems may take the form of (*a*) goals to be achieved in the absence of readily discernible means for reaching those goals, (*b*) contradictions between sources of information of apparently equal credibility, or (*c*) the quest for structure or symmetry in situations where such order is not readily apparent.

For Bruner the first step of discovery is a sensed incongruity or contrast.[44] He is always attempting to build potential or emergent incongruities into the materials of instruction. An example of such teaching is the use of "torpedoing" by Davis[45] in the Madison Project. Davis will teach something to a child (or have the child derive a rule inductively for himself) until the learner is confident of his mastery of the principle and its application. He then provides the

44. Jerome S. Bruner, "Some Elements of Discovery," in Shulman and Keislar (eds.), *op. cit.*, pp. 101–13.

45. Robert B. Davis, "Discovery in the Teaching of Mathematics," in Shulman and Keislar (eds.), *op. cit.*, pp. 118–19.

child with a "whopper" of a counterexample. Such contradictions are used to engage the child, because of the resulting intellectual discomfort, in an attempt to resolve this disequilibrium by making some new discovery in the form of a reorganization of his understanding— what the Gestalt psychologists would have called "cognitive restructuring."

This discovery may require forming a new distinction, thus creating a new category of experience which will account for the now-recognized complexity of the situation. Or the discovery may involve a higher-order synthesis, whereby the two apparently discrepant events—the previous understanding and the unexpected counterexample—are now seen jointly accounted for through some more abstract rule. As indicated earlier, the essence of the discovery for Bruner is something which takes place inside the learner, through the eduction of new relations and the creation of new structures.

The use of a technique like "torpedoing" reflects the dual roots of Bruner's approach both in the Piagetian model of cognitive development and in the Socratic model of teaching. Piaget maintains that the growth of intelligence follows the path of successive disequilibria and equilibria. The child, confronted by a new situation which is not directly assimilable, gets out of balance and must accommodate to achieve a new balance by modifying his existent cognitive structure. This modification will usually take one or both of the forms described earlier: increased differentiation of cognitive structure and/or enhanced generalizability and integration of structure.

The Socratic method is simply a pedagogical approach in which it is not nature which supplies the source of contrast or contradiction, but a community gadfly—the teacher. Through dialogue, Socrates manages to help his friends make their principles explicit. Through further questioning, he leads them to recognize that they inevitably practice or value certain other behaviors which, in principle, must contradict their earlier stated belief. Clearly something has got to give. Usually the principle as stated must be modified, and a higher, more abstract, yet better differentiated understanding must take its place.

It can also be argued that the dialectical quality of Socratic learning sequences simulates most accurately the manner in which new knowledge is actually discovered in a scientific community. Such a model for the creation of new theoretical paradigms would be quite consistent with Kuhn's characterization of the dynamics of theoretical changes in science.[46]

Even Davis' term "torpedoing" refers to the Socratic approach from which it derives. Meno refers to Socrates as a "torpedo fish, who torpifies those who come near him and touch him," thus shocking them into recognition of their own ignorance and self-contradiction.

We may thus characterize the difference between the instructional approaches of expository and discovery teaching in the following manner: For Gagné, instruction is a smoothly guided tour up a carefully constructed hierarchy of learning tasks; for Bruner, instruction is a roller-coaster ride of successive disequilibria and equilibria terminating in the attainment or discovery of a desired cognitive state.

The implications for the sequence of the curriculum growing from these two positions are quite different. For Gagné, the highest level of learning is problem-solving; lower levels involve facts, concepts, principles, and so on. Clearly, for Gagné, the appropriate sequence in learning is, in terms of the diagram below, from the bottom up. One begins with simple prerequisites and works up, pyramid fashion, to the complex capability sought.

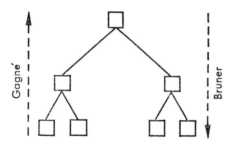

For Bruner the same diagram may be appropriate, but the direction of the arrow would be changed. He has the learner begin with *problem-solving*. Once confronted with a problem, whether embedded in the materials of instruction or directly presented by the teacher, the learner will be led to move back through the hierarchy to form the needed associations, attain the necessary concepts, and, finally, derive the appropriate rules for solving the problem.

46. Thomas F. Kuhn, *The Structure of Scientific Revolutions* (Chicago: University of Chicago Press, 1962).

This strategy appears to have two rationales. First, it is thought to be, in contrast to the guided-learning sequence, a more motivating approach to learning. That is, children may be more motivated when confronted with an enticing problem they cannot solve than they are when given some specific objectives to master on the promise that, if they learn them well, at some indeterminate future point they may be able to solve an exciting problem.

The second rationale for this strategy is based on the ostensibly greater transferability of knowledge discovered in a problem-solving context over that learned in a didactic mode. We may note that two separable issues are confounded in this question: (*a*) the organization of the material to be learned—by problem or by logical learning structure—and (*b*) the optimal sequence of the learning process—inductively from problems to rules or deductively from rules to problems. Suffice it to observe that the fundamental argument here is over which of these approaches will optimize transfer of training most effectively. As usual, current statements of the problem manage to confound more aspects of the issue than they usefully clarify.

Ausubel's concept of instructional sequence once again reflects certain positions of both the other theorists. Like Gagné, he advocates a carefully guided, expository sequencing. However, like Bruner, he would advocate initiating the sequence at a higher point on the hierarchy. This is Ausubel's principle of the *advance organizer*.[47]

Ausubel begins the instructional sequence with a set of organizing statements at a level of abstraction *higher* than what must be learned subsequently. He uses it to establish an "ideational scaffolding" which both links what is to be learned with what the learner already knows and creates an organization or structure within which the new learning will be embedded. These organizers are expositorily taught to the learners as the first step in a unit of instruction. They are not to be discovered, as would be the initial stage of a Bruner program of instruction.

All these positions have but one major objective—that of optimizing subsequent retention and transfer of learning. It is to a consideration of transfer that we now turn.

47. Ausubel, *op. cit.*, pp. 148–49.

Transfer of Training

Transfer of training is the most important single concept in any educationally relevant theory of learning. Without transfer, our students could be expected only to practice what we teach. The span of their learning could never exceed the range of situations or problems actually encountered in the course of instruction. The phenomenon of transfer makes it possible to collect many educational dividends from a relatively modest initial learning investment. In Bruner's apt phrase, it allows us "to go beyond the information given."[48]

There are none who would deny the reality of transfer. The disagreements revolve around such questions as the breadth of transfer —whether the concept applies only to acquisition of specific products and narrow processes or can account equally well for the generalizable learning of broad principles, general strategies of inquiry, motivations to learn in certain domains, and attitudes about learning and about oneself as a learner. The contrasts of the preceding section on tactics of instruction reflect yet another dimension of the transfer question, i.e., identification of the optimal instructional conditions for the facilitation of transfer.

It may be useful here to invoke a distinction suggested by Gagné between *lateral* and *vertical* transfer. *Lateral transfer* refers to the manner in which the learning of a capability in one domain can facilitate the mastery of some parallel capability in another domain. These parallel capabilities would be at the same levels of their respective learning hierarchies. *Vertical transfer* refers to the manner in which the learning of a subordinate capability serves to facilitate the mastery of some subsequent learning at a higher level of the same hierarchy.

An example of lateral transfer would be learning certain elements of logical inference in the proof of geometric theorems subsequent to initially learning similar logical principles while deriving and proving theorems relating to numbers and arithmetic operations. We would expect that there would be positive lateral transfer across the two parallel kinds of problems.

We would expect to observe vertical transfer in the manner in

48. Jerome S. Bruner, "Going Beyond the Information Given," in Jerome S. Bruner *et al.*, *Contemporary Approaches to Cognition* (Cambridge, Mass.: Harvard University Press, 1957), pp. 41-70.

which previous mastery of multiplication would transfer to subsequent learning of the more complex task of long division.

As we examine the topic of transfer, we will ask (*a*) what is transferred, (*b*) how broadly does the transfer occur, and (*c*) what are the optimal instructional conditions for transfer? Finally, some recent research on transfer in mathematics learning will be reviewed and evaluated.

The major theorists differ in their respective emphases upon *what* is transferred in learning. Bruner stresses the lateral transfer of broad principles and strategies from one domain or topic to another. Bruner believes that we can have massive transfer from one learning situation to another. He recognizes that some may find his position reminiscent of *faculty psychology*—the theory that a person can study geometry and become a better logical thinker, or study Latin and come to know more English vocabulary. This theory and its concept of broad massive transfer was thought to have been put permanently to rest by William James and Edward Lee Thorndike at the turn of this century.

Bruner adheres to an analogous concept of transfer. His theory is not faculty psychology in the sense that the mind is perceived as a muscle made stronger through exercise. Broad transfer of training occurs when one can identify in the structures of subject matters basic, fundamentally simple concepts—principles or strategies which, if learned well, can be transferred both to other topics within that discipline and to other disciplines as well. He gives examples such as the concept of conservation or balance. Is it not possible to teach balance of trade in economics so that, when ecological balance is considered, pupils see the parallel? This could then be extended to balance of power in political science, or to balancing equations. Of equal, if not greater, importance for Bruner is the broad transferability of the knowledge-getting processes—strategies, heuristics, investigatory methods, and the like. In his view, learning by discovery leads to the ability *to* discover, that is, to the development of broad inquiry competencies in students.

Bruner does not ignore vertical transfer in his theorizing. His conception of learning moving from enactive through ikonic and symbolic modes of representation is a theory of vertical transfer. Bruner would use such learning sequences wherein learners make the necessary discoveries themselves for the teaching of the most broadly transferable principles and processes.

Gagné considers himself a conservative on matters of transfer. He states that "transfer occurs because of the occurrence of specific identical (or highly similar) elements within developmental sequences."[49] To the extent that an element which has been learned (be it association, concept, or principle) can be directly employed in a new situation, transfer will occur. If the new context requires a behavior substantially different from the specific capability mastered earlier, there will be no transfer. He thus clearly identifies himself with the "identical elements" position of Thorndike, a point of view in clear contrast to Bruner.

Gagné is concerned primarily with the conditions for *vertical* transfer. His theory of learning hierarchies is clearly a theory of positive vertical transfer. Though not denying the possibility of lateral transfer—he goes so far as to describe the theoretical conditions for such transfer, such as practicing the capability to be transferred in as wide a variety of contexts as is feasible—his massive body of theoretical and empirical work is directed at the vertical transfer problem.

Gagné distinguishes between the learning of "verbalizable knowledges" and "intellectual skills or strategies,"[50] which are parallel to what we earlier referred to as products and processes. He asserts that his hierarchical model of learning is only appropriate to the acquisition of intellectual skills. Furthermore, like Bruner, he finds the acquisition of such processes far more important for learners than the acquisition of verbalizable knowledge.

Ausubel asserts that *what* is transferred is subject matter knowledge. This places him in clear contrast to the positions of Bruner and Gagné. With respect to the breadth of transfer, he maintains an intermediate position between Bruner and Gagné—less conservative than Gagné's insistence on identical elements, yet more moderate than Bruner's claims of the most far-reaching process transfer. He compares his position to that of Judd, who spoke of transfer by generalization. Finally, like Gagné, he prescribes guided learning as

49. Gagné, "Contributions of Learning to Human Development," *op. cit.* p. 186.

50. Gagné, "Learning Hierarchies," *op. cit.*

providing the optimal conditions for transfer but differs with Gagné on the optimal sequence. While Gagné recommends an instructional sequence in which learning proceeds from less abstract to more abstract materials, Ausubel advocates *progressive differentiation,* where material is initially presented in the more abstract form of an *advance organizer.* This is then followed by the less abstract material to be mastered.

In summary, Bruner argues that the kinds of approaches to which the rubric *discovery* has been applied establish the optimal conditions for transfer, and that the most important things to be transferred are the broadest kinds of processes and principles. Gagné and Ausubel both argue for the general superiority of the guided or expository approaches to learning in optimizing transfer, though they would differ both in the specific type of expository sequence advocated and in the form of knowledge—product or process—which is transferred.

What does the evidence from empirical studies of this issue seem to demonstrate? The findings are not all that consistent. Most often guided or expository sequences seem to be superior methods for the *acquisition* of immediate learning. With regard to long-term *retention,* the results seem equivocal, with neither approach consistently better. Discovery-learning approaches appear to be superior when the criterion of *transfer* of principles to new situations is employed. Notably absent are long-term studies which deal with the question of whether general techniques, strategies, heuristics of discovery can be learned—by discovery or in any other manner—which will transfer across grossly different kinds of tasks. Also absent are studies which assess whether long-term use of particular instructional approaches results in fairly stable attitudinal or motivational changes. The latter achievement is frequently claimed by advocates of "the discovery method."

Craig[51] has reviewed the results of a number of studies of transfer in discovery learning by Gagné and Brown,[52] Guthrie,[53] Roughead

51. Robert C. Craig, "Recent Research on Discovery," *Educational Leadership,* XXVI (February, 1969), 501–8.

52. Robert M. Gagné and Larry T. Brown. "Some Factors in the Programming of Conceptual Learning," *Journal of Experimental Psychology,* LXII (1962), 12–18.

53. John T. Guthrie, "Expository Instruction Versus a Discovery Method," *Journal of Educational Psychology,* LXIII (1967), 45–59.

and Scandura,[54] and Worthen.[55] He concludes that "the discovery treatment has been inadequately tested; but, when differences among treatment groups in later ability to infer and use new principles have been found, they favor discovery techniques over the giving of guidance."[56]

Although Worthen's study contains certain inconsistencies that raise some serious questions concerning its generalizability,[57] his investigation possesses a number of characteristics which could well serve as a model for future research in this area. He conducts the research in the classroom rather than in the laboratory, thus reducing the inevitable credibility gap encountered whenever generalizing from the psychologist's hothouse to the educator's garden. The duration of the experimental treatments is six weeks instead of the all-too-frequent sixty minutes. An attempt is made to specify carefully the particular experimental variables manipulated—in this case, example-rule and rule-example sequences. Tests of retention cover a reasonably long term, in contrast to the ludicrous habit among experimental psychologists of referring to a posttest twenty-four hours after initial learning as the measure of "long-term retention." Finally, attitude measures as well as intellectual measures are employed as criterion variables.

The superiority of transfer for the discovery treatment in the cited studies is impressive, but no swift generalizations can be made. For example, in the Worthen research, the discovery treatment had only one characteristic of discovery approaches, the withholding of rules until presentation of examples had been completed. There is every indication that the discovery treatment was highly guided. The students were by no means engaging in long periods of relatively undirected "messing around" with materials or problems as in some of Bruner's favorite examples. Furthermore, there is no indication that the expository treatment in any way reflected an attempt to apply

54. W. G. Roughead and Joseph M. Scandura, " 'What is Learned' in Mathematical Discovery," *Journal of Educational Psychology,* LIX (1968), 283–89.

55. Blaine R. Worthen, "Discovery and Expository Task Presentation in Elementary Mathematics," *Journal of Educational Psychology Monograph Supplement,* Part II, LIX (February, 1968).

56. Craig, *op. cit.,* p. 503. Craig also points out that when the criterion has been application of the specific rules taught, expository forms of presentation are superior.

57. Vernon Hall and Harold Cook, "Discovery vs. Expository 'Instruction': A Comment" (Unpublished Manuscript, Syracuse University, 1968).

systematically the tenets of either Gagné's or Ausubel's models. Hence, though in some ways exemplary in its research design, the Worthen investigation or any of the others cannot be said to have resolved the theoretical issue. No single study is capable of doing so. Only a carefully planned *program* of research is likely to clarify this issue in some ultimate sense.

Epistemology

When theorists differ so systematically over principles of learning and teaching, it is not surprising to find that their differences are rooted deeply in far more fundamental issues. Although the field of psychology ostensibly achieved emancipation from philosophy some eighty years ago, contemporary psychologists continue to fight the same battles that bloodied their philosophical forebears. Thus, the clamor over the relative merits of expository and discovery teaching is much more than a mere disagreement concerning pedagogical policy. It can best be understood in terms of certain basic controversies relating to the manner in which *anything* becomes known. These issues of the nature of knowledge and the knowing process are the domain of epistemology.

The Gagné position grows directly out of the epistemology that began with Aristotle, bore fruit with the British associationists (Hume, Berkeley, Locke), and took root in psychology with the American associationists (Thorndike, Watson, Hull, Skinner, and Osgood). The essence of this epistemology is simple. The child begins as a blank slate, a *tabula rasa*. Human development can be described as the cumulative effects of experience; what is learned is strictly a function of the imprint that experience makes upon this blank slate. Therefore, learning can be thought of additively and connectively; what is learned is something that is added and connected to what was learned before.

Bruner's thinking traces back to Plato, through Hegel and Dewey. Psychologically, it is influenced by the Gestalt psychologists in the thirties, and, most recently, by Piaget. If we can call the Gagné tradition one of neobehaviorism, the position of Bruner is a particularly Platonic branch of cognitive psychology, or genetic-cognitive psychology. In general, there is a bit of Plato in any man who advocates teaching by discovery because of the way in which the approach attempts to elicit from the learner things that he has always known, but in a reconstructed structural form. There is an emphasis upon structure, upon meaning, upon relationships, upon organization, which is reminiscent of Gestalt psychology. If we drew a diagram of what is to be learned, Gagné would be more interested in what is inside the boxes and Bruner, in the arrows between the boxes. For Gagné the fundamental question is, "What is to be learned?" For Bruner, it is, "How do you get there and to similar places?" These are quite consonant with their contrasting epistemologies. The nature of knowledge is different for Bruner and for Gagné. In contrast to Gagné's additive and cumulative notion, Bruner would maintain that the whole is greater than the sum of its parts and that the process cannot be taught didactically but must be undergone *in toto*.

To understand the Bruner position on learning by discovery, one must surely understand the pervasiveness of his Platonic idealism—a characteristic that sets Bruner apart from almost all other cognitive psychologists. We observed earlier that Bruner views the most fundamental and abstract ideas as inherently simple. Ultimate knowledge of these ideas consists of freeing oneself from the encumbering effects of their enactive and imaginal aspects and dealing with them in their purely symbolic, most efficiently transferable form. Most individuals have the "basic stuff" of which these ideas are made, but must confront suitable problems or contrasts in order to clarify and restructure them. Hence, some variation of Socratic teaching suggests itself.

For the empiricist, such as Gagné, the ultimate source of all knowledge is *experience*. Hence, one learns best through having experience organized optimally and presented expository. For the rationalist, such as Bruner, it is not experience but *reason* which is the ultimate source of understanding. Therefore, that mode of instruction is best which aids the learner to reflect on his own thinking and to reorganize his own understanding to grasp the world of experience more effectively.

A distinction originally made by Aristotle may be usefully invoked at this point. Aristotle distinguished between two different structures of knowledge: *ordo essendi*, the order of being, and *ordo cognoscenti*, the order of knowing. There is an important difference between the way things *are* and the manner in which they *become known*. Aristotle's implication is that we must distinguish between the structure of some knowledge in its fully developed form as grasped by the mature intellect and the structure of that same idea as it is presented for most effective and expeditious acquisition. Both Bruner and Gagné use the term *structure* in their writings; Bruner speaks of the centrality of the "structure of the subject matter," while Gagné calls his hierarchies "learning structures."

In referring to the structure of the subject matter, Bruner collapses the distinction between the structure of being and the structure of knowing. The activities of the child and those of the mature scholar are to be quite parallel for Bruner, and will differ mainly in the mode of representation used to cope with the fundamental ideas or structures. In contrast, Gagné clearly distinguishes between the two kinds of structures. The order of knowing is reflected in the optimal sequence of a learning hierarchy. The order of being is a more abstract set of relationships that can only be comprehended when learning is complete.

The epistemological roots of Ausubel's position do not flow as directly from the traditions of rationalism and empiricism as do those of Bruner and Gagné, respectively. He assumes a somewhat more eclectic epistemological stance which reflects some elements of both approaches.

There is another aspect of an educator's theory of knowledge which is relevant to our discussions, and which has been mentioned somewhat obliquely earlier in this chapter. This is the question of which kind of knowledge is of most value or worth. Bruner and Gagné are both of the persuasion that *processes* of knowledge-getting and knowledge-using are the most valuable forms of knowledge and are, therefore, the most important objectives of education. Ausubel asserts that it is the organized bodies of subject matter understanding themselves, the *products* of knowledge, which are most important as educational objectives.

We may thus see that the implicit theories of knowledge or epistemologies underlying the positions we have been discussing go a long way toward accounting for many specific characteristics of the positions themselves.

Prerequisites for a Psychology of Mathematics Education

Where is the practitioner to turn when confronted by such a confusing array of positions, theories, and prescriptions? How can he sort out the strengths, weaknesses, and implications of these positions in order to assist in his own curriculum-planning and instructional decision-making?

In this concluding section, we shall present a model for examining those variables which must be considered in formulating any propositions about the best forms of instruction. We shall then discuss the characteristics of those positions examined in the preceding sections and evaluate their claims and implications.

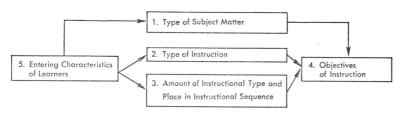

Examples of each kind of variable

1. Mathematics, foreign languages, social studies (subject matter defined in task terms)
2. Expository-discovery (degree of guidance); inductive-deductive
3. Number of minutes or hours of instruction; position in sequence of instructional types
4. Products; processes; attitudes; self-perception
5. Prior knowledge; aptitude; cognitive style; values

Fig. 2.—Theoretical generalization about the nature of instruction

In a paper concerning "the logic of experiments on discovery," Cronbach[58] suggests that any theoretical generalization about the nature of instruction must necessarily take the form of the following five-fold interaction:

> With subject matter of this nature,
> inductive experience of this type,
> in this amount,
> produces this pattern of responses,
> in pupils at this level of development.[59]

Figure 2 presents our paraphrase and generalization of Cronbach's admonition, along with examples of each of the five kinds of variables.

This chapter began with the perennial pedagogical question: Which mode of instruction is best—discovery or exposition? We may now observe that any such question involves a number of issues

58. Cronbach, *op. cit.*, pp. 76–92.   59. *Ibid.*, p. 77.

which must be considered jointly. Previous sections have already established that both the preferred objectives of instruction and the entering characteristics of learners will affect one's choice of instructional mode. Moreover, the particular subject matter to be learned will also influence the selection of approach. A teaching method deemed suitable for instruction in mathematical reasoning may be wholly inappropriate for the teaching of Latin noun declensions. Furthermore, the type of instruction itself cannot be judged *in vacuo*. As Cronbach observes, ". . . A particular educational tactic is part of an instrumental system; a proper educational design calls upon that tactic at a certain point in the sequence, for a certain period of time, following and preceding certain other tactics. No conclusion can be drawn about the tactic considered by itself."[60]

ENTERING CHARACTERISTICS

A whole host of student-entering characteristics can be considered in any discussion of instruction. Although many theorists, most notably Cronbach,[61] have argued persuasively for the importance of individual differences in learning, the research literature in this area is remarkably underrepresented with studies demonstrating the differential effectiveness of contrasting instructional tactics for different types of individuals. Nevertheless, there may be a number of such kinds of characteristics worth considering in our discussions.

The student's *knowledge* of the area in which instruction must proceed will be an important factor. Successful inductive or Socratic teaching is clearly contingent upon some previously attained knowledge base. This would suggest that certain minimal prerequisites of understanding may be necessary before effective instruction leading to cognitive reorganization can be successful.

The learner's *developmental level* may also be significant. Ausubel[62] describes discovery learning as much more characteristic of the intellectual activities of the preadolescent child than of the more mature individual. He maintains that the trial-and-error concrete coping of discovery learning is useful in first establishing those conceptual foundations necessary for future understanding. However, once this

60. *Ibid.*, p. 77.
61. Lee J. Cronbach, "How Can Instruction Be Adapted to Individual Differences?" in Robert M. Gagné (ed.), *Learning and Individual Differences* (Columbus, Ohio: Charles E. Merrill Books, 1967), pp. 23–39.
62. Ausubel, *op. cit.*, pp. 23–24.

initial underpinning has been established through discovery learning, most subsequent instruction can proceed both more effectively and more efficiently through meaningful expository learning. Hence, Ausubel would view the child's level of cognitive development, however attained, as a major criterion in selecting among instructional tactics.

An additional variable to consider, if only we knew more about it, would be the learner's *cognitive style*. Here again we confront a type of variable that combines intuitive feast with empirical famine. The convincing data on learning-relevant individual differences in cognitive style are rare indeed. One promising stylistic variable is Kagan's *conceptual tempo*[63] dimension. Others include *achievement motivation*,[64] *extraversion-introversion*,[65] *creativity*,[66] and *anxiety*.[67] Though it is intuitively obvious that such aspects of entering characteristics *ought* to interact significantly with mode of instruction, there is as yet no convincing empirical evidence that supports our intuitions. To assert that such is likely to be the case, as the writer would, is to utter a wish rather than a demonstrated reality.

TYPE AND AMOUNT OF INSTRUCTION

The discovery issue has revolved almost totally around the question of instruction. However, it has been demonstrated repeatedly that the very term *discovery* is itself instructionally ambiguous. We earlier attempted to clarify the multiple meanings of discovery when used to describe an intervening process within the learner, distinguishing reception learning from discovery learning, and rote learning from meaningful learning. We shall now attempt to do the same for discovery as a description of a method of teaching.

63. Jerome Kagan, "Impulsive and Reflective Children: The Significance of Conceptual Tempo," in John D. Krumboltz (ed.), *Learning and the Educational Process* (Chicago: Rand McNally & Co., 1965), pp. 133–61.

64. John W. Atkinson, "The Mainsprings of Achievement-Oriented Activity," in Krumboltz, *op. cit.*

65. Hans J. Eysenck, *The Structure of Human Personality* (2d ed.; New York: John Wiley & Sons, 1960).

66. Michael A. Wallach and Nathan Kogan, *Modes of Thinking in Young Children*. (New York: Holt, Rinehart & Winston, 1965). See also, Lee J. Cronbach, "Intelligence, Creativity, A Parsimonious Reinterpretation of the Wallach-Kogan Data," *American Educational Research Journal*, V (November, 1968), 491–512.

67. Wallach and Kogan, *op. cit.*

Once again, at least two somewhat independent dimensions must be distinguished. The first is the *degree of guidance*. In the act of teaching anything, a teacher may exercise nearly total guidance over the learner's behavior or practically none. In the former case, we generally speak of expository or didactic teaching. In the latter instance, we would be likely to call the teaching method discovery. However, these two characterizations merely highlight the extreme ends of a continuum. Much instruction occupies intermediate points between them.

Wittrock[68] has suggested that we characterize the degree of guidance in terms of whether the rule and the solution to the problem being taught are given. Table 3 depicts the four possibilities.

TABLE 3

RULE	SOLUTION	TYPE OF GUIDANCE
Given	Given	Exposition
Given	Not Given	Guided Discovery (deductive)
Not Given	Given	Guided Discovery (inductive)
Not Given	Not Given	"Pure" Discovery

When both the rule and solution are given, the teaching method is thoroughly expository. When neither rule nor solution is given, we are engaging in "pure" discovery teaching. When one of the two is given, we are in an intermediate instructional situation that may best be characterized as *guided discovery*. However, it is usually the case that situations where the rule is given get labeled "exposition," irrespective of the tactics regarding the solution. Furthermore, situations where the rule must be generated to fit the given examples are almost inevitably dubbed with the title "discovery."

The reason for this apparent anomaly is that a second dimension, somewhat independent of degree of guidance, is also used to discuss teaching. This dimension is *sequence of instruction*. Inductive sequences, in which learners must invent the rule underlying a series of examples, are considered expository sequences. As can be seen in Table 4, the two dimensions can be considered separately. Thus, for example, in the Worthen[69] study cited earlier, what distinguishes ex-

68. M. C. Wittrock, "Verbal Stimuli in Concept Formation: Learning by Discovery," *Journal of Educational Psychology*, LIV (1963), 183–90.

69. Worthen, *op. cit.* See note 55.

pository from discovery treatments is strictly instructional sequence, since both forms of instruction occupy roughly the same position on the degree of guidance dimension.

A further wrinkle may be introduced when one observes that the breakdown provided in Table 3, wherein either or both rule and solution are given, assumes that a *problem* is already formulated for the learner. Clearly, one can conceive of many situations that are considerably less guided by an order of magnitude, because not even the formulated problem is given. Rather, the learner is simply placed in a potentially problematic instructional situation. Shulman[70] has referred to this latter type of situation as requiring the process of

TABLE 4

	GUIDED	UNGUIDED
INDUCTIVE	Discovery Treatment (Worthen)	Bruner Mathematics Example
DEDUCTIVE	Expository Treatment (Worthen)	Hypothetical Example: Provide learner with rule, must discover relevant examples

inquiry, in contrast to situations where the formulated problem is given, which require *problem-solving*. Since much of significant human endeavor involves situations in which the critical problems must first be sensed and formulated before they can be solved, the relevance of inquiry as a process to be taught and investigated should be clear. A similar model, involving the interplay of problem, rule, and solution, is discussed in an earlier yearbook by Getzels.[71]

Although we are far from exhausting the possible dimensions along which instructional types can be classified, only one more will be discussed. It, too, is partially independent of the dimensions discussed above. This is the *didactic-Socratic* dimension. Didactic instruction is most similar to maximally guided, deductive teaching. Socratic in-

70. Lee S. Shulman, "Seeking Styles and Individual Differences in Patterns of Inquiry," *School Review*, LXXIII (1965), pp. 258–66. See also Lee S. Shulman, Michael J. Loupe and Richard M. Piper, *Studies of the Inquiry Process* (Cooperative Research Project No. 5-0597, Michigan State University, 1968).

71. Jacob W. Getzels, "Creative Thinking, Problem-Solving, and Instruction," in Ernest R. Hilgard (ed.), *Theories of Learning and Instruction* (Sixty-third Yearbook of the National Society for the Study of Education, Part I [Chicago: University of Chicago Press, 1964]), pp. 240–67.

struction refers to teaching in which the dialectic of the "torpedo-ing" process, as discussed earlier, is paramount. Socratic teaching may range along a large portion of the continuum of guidance, including situations so highly guided that the learner merely answers "yes" or "no" to the teacher's questions.

An interesting corollary to Socratic teaching is the inverse of that process, as reflected in Suchman's[72] inquiry-training approach. In this approach, the learner is visually confronted by an apparently anomalous physical event, and must remove the anomaly by directing questions to the teacher, who answers "yes" or "no." Hence, once the initiating problem has been presented, guidance by the teacher is essentially absent.

Cronbach[73] cites briefly a number of other dimensions along which instruction can be classified—e.g., hints given or not given, individual versus group instruction, and verbalized or unverbalized rules. We will not be able to deal with such examples in the present chapter, but the possibility of generating many more examples should be recognized.

It should now be clear why the simple descriptor *discovery* can in no way characterize adequately a type of instruction. The term may be associated with any number or combination of approaches. The range of tactics excluded by the term is even more vast. One obvious prerequisite to further progress in this area is the replacement of such general terms as *discovery* and *exposition* with far more precise descriptors, except in the most informal discourses on education. The growing body of research being produced by Scandura[74] and his co-workers is exemplary of the fruitfulness of orienting research in mathematical learning toward the experimental study of psychologically meaningful variables rather than ambiguously labeled techniques.

SUBJECT MATTER

The characteristics of the subject matter to be taught are a major determinant of the suitability of inductive and/or minimally guided

72. J. Richard Suchman, "Inquiry Training: Building Skills for Autonomous Discovery," *Merrill-Palmer Quarterly of Behavior Development*, VII (1961), 147–69.

73. Cronbach, "The Logic of Experiments On Discovery," *op. cit.*, pp. 85–86.

74. Joseph M. Scandura, "An Analysis of Exposition and Discovery Modes of Problem Solving Instruction," *Journal of Experimental Education*, XXXIII (1964), 149–59. See also Roughead & Scandura, *op. cit.*

forms of instruction. Cronbach[75] has suggested that methods in which learners are called upon to discover rules and solutions are likely to be most fruitful with tasks in which the system or discipline of which they are a part is logical or rational. One may here contrast the task of finding the sum of a number series with that of finding which nouns take *le* and which *la*. The solution to the first problem is rational and is thus amenable to an inductive approach. The latter task is apparently arbitrary, hence would make less sense as the subject of inductive instruction.

If the logic or rationality of a subject matter is of prime importance in assessing its teachability via inductive methods, the signal popularity of such "discovery" tactics in mathematics instruction may be more easily understood. If it can also be asserted that mathematics is the discipline which has the most easily discernible structure, then the powerful impact of Bruner's theorizing becomes easier to explain. Which among the disciplines could be better fitted than mathematics to a neo-Platonic epistemology wherein true understanding is reached when ideas can be represented as formal symbols, free from the shackles of actions and images? Such concepts as number, point, and line are parts of a discipline far more "discoverable" in Bruner's terms than one whose concepts might be epoch, *Zeitgeist*, and king. In recognizing the relationship between subject matter and teaching mode, we may also be seeing the reason for the long romance of mathematics education and Brunerian discovery.

EDUCATIONAL OUTCOMES

Even within a single discipline, the objectives of instruction may vary. We earlier examined an important distinction between products and processes as objectives of instruction. Both these terms refer to clearly specifiable cognitive or intellectual consequences of education. There are other outcomes as well, which include broad cognitive strategies and expectancies, motives, values, and self-perceptions. For example, in addition to mastery of a particular set of principles and/or capabilities, we could seek as objectives of instruction: (*a*) the desire to learn more mathematics, (*b*) the judgment of mathematical knowledge as worthwhile, and (*c*) self-confidence in oneself as a mathematical reasoner and problem-solver. Under what instructional conditions can such objectives be achieved? Advocates of dis-

75. Cronbach, "The Logic of Experiments on Discovery," *op. cit.*, p. 79.

covery approaches claim such benefits for their methods. We currently have no evidence either to confirm or to disconfirm these claims. Furthermore, the necessary evidence is likely to be forthcoming only if we begin to perform more of the systematic long-term studies such as the SMSG longitudinal research of Begle.[76]

If the writer had to identify a single dimension most critical as a determinant of the choice of an instructional strategy, it would be the objectives sought. Since an entire earlier section of this paper was devoted to that topic, we will not belabor the point here.

Summing Up

Dewey observed that a problem well put is half solved.[77] Those who might have anticipated that this chapter would report a great number of psychologically rooted solutions to the problems of mathematics instruction must remain disappointed. Though psychology can provide numerous answers, they fall short of the myriad questions mathematics educators can raise. The major contribution that psychology can presently make, the examination of which was the major objective of this chapter, is to ensure that the questions formulated are "well put." The primary prerequisite of any developing theory of mathematics education is the most fruitful formulation of its questions.

We must see that decisions concerning such theories cannot rest upon comparisons of positions, in principle. One must also invoke an understanding of the structure of knowledge and inquiry within the particular subject matter discipline whose mastery is sought. For example, if one perceives "mathematics" as basically a body of strategies, heuristics, or methods of inquiry, then clearly an approach to instruction calculated to optimize process learning is most advisable. If mathematics is seen as a compendium of subject matter understandings (e.g., arithmetic facts, computational algorithims, specific postulates or theorems), an approach which optimizes subject matter mastery would be preferred.

It is when one's conception of the structure and contents of an entire discipline is put in such starkly contrastive terms that the

76. Edward Begle, chapter x of this volume.

77. John Dewey, *Logic: The Theory of Inquiry* (New York: Henry Holt & Co., 1938), p. 108.

absurdity of a parallel forced choice between learning theories becomes evident. The mathematician will surely respond that mathematics is both an organized body of knowledge *and* a set of methods for critiquing and extending that knowledge. Both aspects are equally important to the mathematician, though the problem at hand may dictate that one or another aspect hold transient attention. Similarly, the individual careers of mathematicians may focus primarily upon a single aspect for scholarly purposes.

The mathematics curriculum designer cannot, therefore, select a particular psychologically based strategy of instruction because it is, in principle, most consonant with the nature of man, the knowing process, or the essential nature of mathematics. He must first identify (*a*) the precise characteristics of the subject matter to be mastered as objectives, and (*b*) *the* distinctive qualities of the learners who will be engaged; only then can an intelligent choice of teaching strategy be made. As learning continues, both the learner's characteristics and the objectives sought are likely to change. We need to think of instruction in terms of the selection of teaching modules chosen to fit optimally with specific objectives and student characteristics. Our problem then ceases to be "which method?" and becomes one of identifying the most effective sequences and combinations of methods for achievement of a wide range of instructional goals.

The solutions to such problems are likely to grow neither out of intuition nor out of common sense. These are empirical questions demanding empirical answers. Once well put in terms of psychologically meaningful variables rather than in terms of stirring slogans, these issues are amenable to systematic scientific investigation.[78] It is hoped that the present chapter and the volume in which it is contained will assist in the effective formulation of these questions. If so, our problems in mathematics education may soon be half solved.

78. Readers interested in the large body of empirical research in the psychology of mathematics instruction, both past and present, have a number of sources from which to choose. These include periodic issues of the *Review of Educational Research* dealing with mathematics education; the *Arithmetic Teacher* and *Mathematics Teacher*, journals; and occasional papers in the *Journal of Educational Psychology, American Educational Research Journal, Journal of Research in Science Teaching*, and *Child Development*, among many others. Reviews of earlier research can be found in past issues of this yearbook (Notes 1 and 4) as well as periodic issues of the Yearbook of the National Council of Teachers of Mathematics.

CURRICULUM CONTENT AND PEDAGOGY

CHAPTER III

Number Systems

JOHN L. KELLEY AND RICHARD A. DEAN

Part I

NUMBER SYSTEMS OF ARITHMETIC

JOHN L. KELLEY

This is a brief description of the development of the number system. This presentation requires very little mathematical background; it is an attempt to provide, for nonspecialists, an overall view of the successive enlargements of the concept of number which take place in the early school years. The approach we use is very near that of the best currently available commercial textbooks. These comprise the so-called second generation new math programs. But we do not discuss current and projected experimental curricula.

A single further note of explanation may be appropriate. We give in the following pages a number of descriptions of various sorts of numbers and operations with numbers. A mathematician might say these descriptions are models (some, physical; and some, mathematical) for the underlying abstract mathematical structure. A scientist, with equal justification, might consider many of the properties of numbers to be physically verifiable facts and the logical structure of the number system to be a mathematical model of a physical situation. Mathematician and scientist will agree that numbers are remarkably useful objects for dealing with a variety of physical situations.

WHY NUMBERS?

We all know that mathematics begins in kindergarten and first grade with the study of numbers. But before we begin this study, we want to think briefly about what numbers are good for, and, in fact, what

75

numbers are. Probably the best way to get at this question is to think about how numbers are used in the classroom and in daily life. The following sorts of questions come to mind. Are there more boys or more girls in the classroom? Are there enough desks for all of the students? Is there a crayon box for each desk? Are there as many books on the bookshelf this afternoon as there were this morning?

All of these questions are usually answered by counting, but all of them may be answered without counting. We can march the boys and girls out of the room in couples and observe whether there are boys or girls left over, to answer the first question. If we seat the children, as many as possible, we can observe whether we have desks left over or children left over, and so answer the second question. If we simply pass out crayon boxes as long as possible, we find out whether there is a crayon box for each desk. The last question (Are there as many books this afternoon as there were this morning?) can be managed by keeping a tally of each book as it is removed or returned. This last example is much the same thing as a very old problem involving the pairing of sheep and pebbles: shepherds, long before numbers were named, were able to discover whether sheep had strayed from a flock during the day by using a stack of pebbles to keep tally.

All of these problems involve a single process: we have two bunches of things and we pair off the things in one bunch with the things in the other. Thus we pair boy with girl, child with desk, crayon box with desk, or book with tally mark. This pairing process decides for us whether there are just exactly as many things in one bunch as in the other or whether there are more in one bunch than in the other. *Counting the number of things in a bunch is an abstract process which saves us the bother of doing the actual physical pairing off.* Counting gives us the information the pairing would have given.

Summing up: numbers and counting are mathematical inventions devised for the purpose of comparing bunches of things.[1]

SETS

Of course, talking about bunches of things is too undignified to pass as mathematics, so mathematicians talk about sets. A *set* is a bunch of things, and the things that belong to the bunch are called *members* of the set, or *elements* of the set. The particular arrangement of the members of

---

1. It is worth noticing that we frequently do the counting by pairing off the members of the set with a set of numbers.

a set is of no importance. If a sixth-grade class reconstitutes itself after school as the little people's marching and chowder society, then "the sixth-grade class" and the "little people's marching and chowder society" are just two different names for the same set. Two sets are the same (or are equal, or are identical) if and only if each member of the first set also belongs to the second set and each member of the second set belongs to the first. Thus the sixth-grade class equals the little people's marching and chowder society because each member of the class belongs to the society and each member of the society is a member of the class. This agreement as to the meaning of "set" can be stated formally as:

AXIOM ON SETS: If A *and* B *are sets, then* A = B *if and only if each member of* A *is a member of* B *and each member of* B *is a member of* A.

We want to emphasize again: here, and throughout this presentation, "$A = B$" means that A and B are the same thing, that A is identical with B, and that "A" and "B" are just different names for the same thing.

We sometimes designate sets by listing the members of the set within braces. Thus {Mary,John,Joe} is the set whose members are Mary, John, and Joe. This is precisely the same set as {John,Mary,Joe} because these two sets have the same members and the order of the listing is irrelevant. The set {2,3,4} is a set whose members are the numbers 2, 3, and 4. All of the following sets {2,3,4}, {3,2,3,2,4} and {4,4,4,3,2} are equal because they have the same members (an object cannot belong to a set twice). A set which has just one member is sometimes called a *singleton* (the terminology comes from the game of bridge) and a set which has no member at all is an *empty set*, or a *void set*. There is just one empty set because, in view of the axiom on sets, the only way for two sets to be unequal is for one of them to have a member which the other does not, and no empty set has any member. Consequently the set of men who are thirty feet tall, the set of 500-pound hummingbirds, and the set of flying ostriches are all identical. There is a ready-made name, { }, for this set.

We have just given several different descriptions for the empty set. In general, a set may have many different descriptions, and it is often a difficult and basic problem to find out whether two different descriptions give the same set. Here is an example. Consider the set of all people who have caught yellow fever. Consider the set of all people who have caught yellow fever as a consequence of a mosquito bite. The question of whether these sets are identical is the same as the question of whether yellow fever is transmitted in any way other than by mosquitoes.

Mathematicians have a passion for abbreviation which matches their passion for giving long, strange, technical meanings to everyday words. The symbol " $\in$ " is read "is a member of," and the symbol " $\notin$ " is read "is not a member of." Thus Mary $\in$ {Mary, Jane} and John $\notin$ {Mary, Jane}. The axiom on sets can be rewritten: $A = B$ if and only if for each object x, it is true that $x \in A$ when and only when $x \in B$.

There is another mathematical abbreviation which is frequently used. We read " $\{x: \ldots.\}$ " as "the set of all objects x such that . . .". Thus $\{x: x$ is a flying ostrich$\}$ is the set of all objects which are flying ostriches, or just the set of flying ostriches. Roughly speaking, an object belongs to $\{x: \ldots.$ something about $x \ldots\}$ if and only if . . . . something about the object . . . . is correct. Here are some more examples of the usage: if A is a set, then $\{x: x \in A\}$ is just the set A; $\{x: x \in A$ and $x \notin A\} = \{\ \}$; and $\{x: x \in A\}$ is identical with $\{y: y \in A\}$.

COUNTING NUMBERS

We return to the notion of pairing off members of one set with members of another which underlies the idea of number. We want to say (eventually) that two sets have the same number of members provided the members of the first set can be paired off with the members of the second set so that both sets are used up. There is no difficulty in describing the notion of pairing off members. For example, we may think of pairing off the members of $\{1,2,7\}$ with those of $\{7,3,6\}$ by making the correspondence: $1 \leftrightarrow 7$, $2 \leftrightarrow 3$ and $7 \leftrightarrow 6$. Of course we might equally well pair off 1 with 3, 2 with 6, and 7 with 7. A systematic way of indicating the way the members of the two sets are paired off is just to list the pairs of corresponding members so that, for example, the members of $\{1,2,7\}$ are paired off with those of $\{7,3,6\}$ by the following list: (1,7), (2,3), (7,6). Going a little further, we might think of a one-to-one correspondence between the sets $\{1,2,7\}$ and $\{7,3,6\}$ as the set of ordered pairs $\{(1,7),(2,3),(7,6)\}$. Thus a one-to-one correspondence between two sets is a set of ordered pairs, each pair consisting of a member of the first and a member of the second, such that each member of the first set is the first coordinate of just one of the pairs and each member of the second set is the second coordinate of just one pair. We will describe such a correspondence by listing the ordered pairs,

or by indicating with arrows the corresponding members of the two
sets, or just by describing the correspondence in words.

There is one matter here which may be of concern. Suppose we pair
off the members of one (finite) set with those of another and the process
comes out even so that we have a one-to-one correspondence between
the two sets. Suppose we now separate the pairs and reconstitute the
two sets, and then start pairing off members in a different way? Will
the process come out even so that we again have a one-to-one correspondence? It seems obvious to us that it will. It may not be obvious to
a very young child. There is a conservation principle needed, and it may
be that a child will need to experiment with bunches of things until this
seems clear to him.[2]

One set *matches* another, and the two sets are *equivalent* if and only if
it is possible to find a one-to-one correspondence between them. Here
are some examples. The set $\{2,1,4,5\}$ matches the set $\{$Caesar,Brutus,
Caius,Anthony$\}$, as the one-to-one correspondence $\{(2,$Caesar$),(1,$Bru-
tus$),(4,$Caius$),(5,$Anthony$)\}$ shows. The correspondence, *Adam* ↔ *Eve*,
Romeo ↔ *Juliet*, *Abelard* ↔ *Heloise* shows that $\{$Adam,Romeo,Abelard$\}$
matches $\{$Eve,Juliet,Heloise$\}$. Matching sets need not be equal because
sets are equal only if they have the same members. It is true that equal sets
are matching so, for example, $\{1,2,4\}$ matches $\{1,2,4\}$, and the correspondence $1 ↔ 1$, $2 ↔ 2$, $4 ↔ 4$ shows this fact.

There is another important fact about matching sets. If a set A matches
a set B and the set B matches a set C, then A matches C. This is true for
the following reason. Think of each member of A being paired to a member of B and each member of B being paired to a member of C. Then
we can pair a member of A with a member of C by looking at the member of B it is paired with and then choosing the member of C which is
paired with that member of B. Figure 1 pictures a special case of this
procedure.

The notion of matching sets can be pictured in the following way.
Think of all possible sets of things, each set in its sanitary cellophane
bag. Just one of the bags is empty. Now picture a red ribbon joining each
bag containing a set to every other bag which contains a matching set.
If each of two bags is connected to another bag, then the two are con-

---

2. If lack of understanding of this conservation principle causes difficulty, then it
is probably a difficulty that must be overcome by the child's playing with things, not
by being told about it. Piaget holds that various conservation principles are acquired
by children at certain rather definite ages.

nected to each other. Why? The ribbons then separate the collection of all bags into bunches such that each bag in one bunch is connected to every other bag in the bunch and to no bag in any other bunch. (Mathematicians call these bunches *equivalence classes*.)

We can describe what a number is in terms of these bunches. Each bunch of bags is to be associated with a number; we agree that the number of members of each set is the number associated with the bunch of

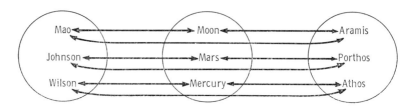

Fig. 1

The bunch 0

Part of the bunch 2

Fig. 2

bags connected to the bag the set is in. We will name all of the various bunches of bags in a systematic way later, but here is a picture (Figure 2) of part of some bunches. The sets in the different bags in the bunch labeled "2" have just one property in common, and it is this property that we could call "twoness."

There is an objection which could be raised to this description of number. We have agreed that a number is to be associated with each of the bunches of bags of objects, and that the number so associated is the property common to the sets belonging to each bunch. But we have not really said what a number *is*—in fact, we've bagged the question. One way out of the dilemma is this. We could agree that the bunches of sets (the equivalence classes) *are* numbers. That is, a number is just one of these bunches of bags of sets.

Let us summarize. The collection of all sets is split up into bunches by putting sets into the same bunch if they are matching. With each bunch we associate a counting number or, in other words, each bunch is a counting number. The number of members in a set is the counting number associated with the bunch of sets which match it. In other words, the number of members in a set is the bunch of all sets which are equivalent to it. Here is the important property of counting numbers: *Two sets have the same number of members if and only if they are matching sets.* This is sometimes stated in symbols in the following way: For each set A, let $N(A)$ be the number of members in A. Then, if A and B are sets, $N(A) = N(B)$ if and only if the set A is equivalent to the set B. The process of assigning the number $N(A)$ to each set A can be called *counting*.

COMPARISON OF SETS

We may always decide whether two sets have the same number of members by pairing the members of one set with those of the other and continuing until we have run out of members of one of the sets. If this process "comes out even" so that both sets are used up at the same time, then the two sets have the same number of members. But if the process does not come out even, then there are two different things that can occur: (*a*) we may run out of members of the first set but not of the second, or (*b*) we may run out of members of the second set but have members of the first left over. Thus, comparing sets by pairing off members can give three different results. For example, a shepherd upon returning with his flock to the fold at night and matching sheep against tally stones may find any one of the following has happened: (*a*) he may have lost some sheep, (*b*) he may have just as many sheep as he had in the morning, or (*c*) he may have acquired stray sheep and have more sheep than he had in the morning. The three possible outcomes of this sort of physical experiment are reflected in the three possible things which can occur if two counting numbers are compared. We want to describe these possible outcomes in some detail.

We begin with an example. Let us compare the sets {Rome,Carthage} and {Caesar,Hannibal,Pericles}. If we make the pairings, Rome ↔ Caesar and Carthage ↔ Hannibal, then we run out of members of the first set. Thus {Rome,Carthage} matches {Caesar,Hannibal}, and the latter set is only part of {Caesar,Hannibal,Pericles}. There is a standard terminology which is used in this situation.

A set A is a *subset* of a set B if every member of A is a member of B. We sometimes write "$A \subset B$" as an abbreviation of the statement "A is a subset of B." Thus {Caesar,Hannibal} $\subset$ {Caesar,Hannibal, Pericles}. As a further example, let us list all of the subsets of {1,2,3}. Here are some of them: {1,2}, {1,3}, {2,3}, {1}, {2}, {3}. There are, however, two subsets which are not in this list. First ,{ } $\subset$ {1,4,3}, because if it were not true that the empty set is a subset of {1,2,3}, then there would be a member of { } which did not belong to {1,2,3} and { } has no members. Next, {1,2,3} $\subset$ {1,2,3} because every member of {1,2,3} is a member of {1,2,3}. In fact, if A is any set, then { } $\subset A$ and A $\subset$ A. This last fact, that $A \subset A$, is rather unfortunate. It means that we *cannot* assert that A has fewer members than B if A matches a subset of B, because A in fact matches a subset of itself (namely A) and we do not want to say that A has fewer members than A! We indicate our disapproval of this situation by agreeing that a set A is a *proper* subset of a set B if each member of A is a member of B and there is at least one member of B which does not belong to A. Thus {Caesar,Hannibal} is a proper subset of {Caesar,Hannibal,Pericles}.

We could now make some definitions: one set has *fewer* members than another, and the latter has *more* members than the former, if and only if the first set matches a proper subset of the second. From the correspondence

$$\text{Rome} \longleftrightarrow \text{Caesar}$$
$$\text{Carthage} \longleftrightarrow \text{Hannibal}$$
$$\text{Pericles}$$

we conclude that {Rome, Carthage} has fewer members than {Caesar, Hannibal,Pericles} and that {Caesar,Hannibal,Pericles} has more members than {Rome,Carthage}.

It seems quite evident that if we compare two sets by pairing off members, precisely one of the following three things occurs: (*a*) the first set has fewer members than the second, (*b*) the first set matches the second, or (*c*) the second set has fewer members than the first. We can state this fact in the following form:

AXIOM (TRICHOTOMY) If A *and* B *are sets, then precisely one of the following occurs:* A *matches a proper subset of* B, A *matches* B, *or* B *matches a proper subset of* A.

Let us look at a mathematical example. Suppose A is the set of all counting numbers, so that the members of A are 0, 1, 2, and so on. Consider the following one-to-one correspondence.

It is clear that the set A of all counting numbers matches the set of all counting numbers which are different from zero. Consequently A matches a proper subset of itself, so A has fewer members than A. But A matches A, and this directly contradicts the axiom of trichotomy.

The point of the preceding discussion is this: The set $\{0,1,2,3, \ldots\}$ is not the sort of set that we want to talk about. It does not have a finite number of members and, in order to have the axiom of trichotomy correct, we must require that the sets under consideration be finite. It turns out mathematically that a set is finite if and only if it is not equivalent to a proper subset of itself, but we need not concern ourselves with the details of this mathematics. Intuitively, we can just think of sets of physical objects. For these, we can consider the axiom of trichotomy to be an experimentally verifiable truth.

There is one property of "fewer than" that we will need presently. If a set A has fewer members than a set B and B has fewer members than C, then A has fewer members than C. Here is a picture (Figure 3) that illustrates why this is so—that is, why it is true that:

Transitivity Property: If A *matches a proper subset of* B *and* B *matches a proper subset of* C, *then* A *matches a proper subset of* C.

(There is a one-to-one correspondence between A and a proper subset of C.)

Here is another picture (Figure 4) which illustrates the reason for the following fact.

Invariance Property: Suppose that A *matches a proper subset of* B, *and suppose* A* *matches* A *and* B* *matches* B; *then* A* *has fewer members than* B*.

(There is a one-to-one correspondence between A^* and a proper subset of B^*.)

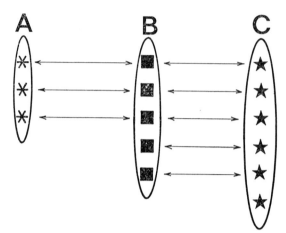

FIG. 3

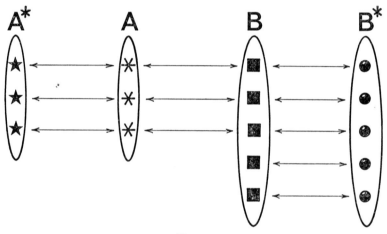

FIG. 4

COMPARSION OF NUMBERS

We now use the notion of "fewer than" for sets to define an order for counting numbers. A counting number m is *less than* a counting number n, and we write $m < n$, provided that a set which contains m members matches a proper subset of a set which consists of n members. Thus $5 < 7$, not because "5" occurs before "7" in the nursery rhyme "One, two, buckle my shoe, etc.," but because a set containing 5 members matches a proper subset of a set containing 7 members.

There is one question which might well be asked about this definition of "less than." Suppose one is asked to compare two numbers, *m* and *n*, and he chooses a set *A* with *m* members and a set *B* with *n* members and finds that *A* matches a proper subset of *B* and consequently $A < B$. Suppose another person chooses a different set A^* which has *m* members, and a different set B^* which has *n* members. Is he going to discover that A^* matches a proper subset of B^*, and so also conclude that $m < n$? Or is it possible that he will come to the opposite decision? If we appeal to the *Invariance Property* stated in the preceding section, we can conclude that he *will* find that A^* matches a proper subset of B^*, and so also conclude that $m < n$. That is, it makes no difference which set with *m* members is compared with what set of *n* members in deciding on which of the two numbers is less than the other.

There are just two important properties of inequality which we want to describe. Each is a direct consequence of properties of comparison of sets. Suppose that *m* and *n* are counting numbers and that we choose a set *A* with *m* members and a set *B* with *n* members. According to the Trichotomy Axiom for Comparison of Sets, just one of three things happens: *A* matches a proper subset of *B*, or *A* matches *B*, or *B* matches a proper subset of *A*. Because of the definition of inequality, we then conclude that in the first case $m < n$, in the second case $m = n$, and in the third case $n < m$. Consequently we have the following property of inequality:

TRICHOTOMY AXIOM FOR COUNTING NUMBERS: If m *and* n *are counting numbers, then just one of the following three statements is true:* m $<$ n, *or* m $=$ n, *or* n $<$ m.

The other property of inequality that we want to notice is the following: Suppose that *m*, *n* and *p* are counting numbers and that $m < n$ and $n < p$. This means that if *A* is a set with *m* members, *B* is a set with *n* members, and *C* is a set with *p* members, then *A* matches a proper subset of *B* and *B* matches a proper subset of *C*. But in this case, according to the *Transitivity Property* of the preceding section, *A* matches a proper subset of *C*. Consequently the number *m* of members of *A* is less than the number *p* of members of *C*. That is: *Transitivity of Inequality: If* m, n *and* p *are counting numbers such that* m $<$ n *and* n $<$ p, *then* m $<$ p.

(Here is a little puzzle to check one's understanding of the consequences of the two properties. Suppose *a*, *b*, *c*, and *d* are numbers, that *a* is less than c, and that although it is not true that d is less than b, it is true that c is less than b. Decide whether a is less than d, and how many members there are in the set $\{a,b,c,d\}$. The answers: yes; three or four.)

Intuitively, we may think of the notion of inequality as a way of arranging the numbers in an order—a way of lining them up. If we put smaller numbers to the left of larger numbers in this lining-up process, then the lineup of numbers begins with zero on the extreme left and continues with one, two, three, and so on.[3] We picture the numbers as lying on a *number line*, an initial chunk of which is shown in Figure 5. In terms of this number line, "less than" is the same thing as "to the left of," and "greater than" is the same as "to the right of."

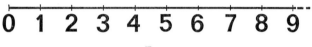

FIG. 5

Finally, we agree that if m and n are counting numbers, then $m < n$ if and only if n is greater than m. A way of remembering the meaning of the symbols "$<$" and "$>$" is to think of the symbols as arrow heads which in each case point to the smaller number. We shall also use $m \geqq n$ and $n \leqq m$ to mean, respectively, $m > n$ or $m = n$, and $n < m$ or $n = m$.

NAMING OF NUMBERS

In order to use the concept of number effectively, we have to have names for particular numbers. Numbers, like people, may have many names. Here, for example, is a list of some of the names you already know for a single number: five, 5, V, $4 + 1$, $7 - 2$, cinq. We want to assign a standard name—more precisely, the Hindu-Arabic name—for each counting number.[4]

Here is the way the system begins. (Recall that if A is a set, then $N(A)$ is the number of members of A.)

$$0 = N(\{\ \}), \quad 1 = N(\{\text{Archimedes}\}), \quad 2 = N(\{\text{Plato,Aristotle}\})$$
$$3 = N(\{\text{Arthur,Lancelot,Guinevere}\}),$$
$$4 = N(\{\text{Lyndon,Lady Bird,Luci,Linda}\})$$

3. Eventually we will have numbers corresponding to every point on the line.

4. This system of naming numbers was invented in India, then adopted by Arab traders who brought it to the backward countries of Europe.

So far there is nothing particularly special about the notation; this sort of naming of numbers happens in every notational system. It is also clear that this simpleminded sort of naming isn't practical for naming very many numbers, and the task of assigning names to all counting numbers seems formidable. It is not even clear that all of the counting numbers *can* be named effectively, since there are infinitely many of them. An idea is needed. We explain the idea in terms of a special numeration system, which could be called Hindu-Arabic-with-one-hand-behind-the-back or numeration base five, where five is defined to be the number of members of a basketball team. Operationally, it works like this. Given a set, we split it up into groups of five, as many as possible, so that the remaining set has 0, 1, 2, 3 or 4 members. For example (see Figure 6):

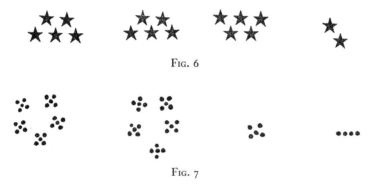

Fig. 6

Fig. 7

The set shown consists of 3 fives and 2 left over and the number of members is 3 fives and 2, or 32_{five} (the "five" shows that the grouping is by fives).

This procedure is all that is needed to give base five names to numbers up to 44_{five} (that is, up to 24_{ten}), but a new wrinkle is needed for the number of members in this set (see Figure 7). The trick is this. We first split a set into fives, with at most 4 left over. We then split the groups of five into fives, getting bunches of five fives. Thus the set shown in Figure 7 consists of 2 fives of fives, 1 five, and 4, and the number of members is 214_{five}. And that is the system. We count by ones, fives, five of fives, fives of fives of fives, and so on. Thus 3143_{five} is 3(fives of fives of fives) and 1(five of fives) and 4(fives) and 3. In terms of addition and multiplication, which we are presently going to define, $3143_{\text{five}} = 3 \times (5 \times 5 \times 5) + 1 \times (5 \times 5) + 4 \times 5 + 3$, and after we have defined exponentiation we can write $3143_{\text{five}} = 3 \times 5^3 + 1 \times 5^2 + 4 \times 5 + 3$.

Summing up, this method permits us to assign a "base five" name, consisting of a string of digits chosen from the list 0, 1, 2, 3, 4, to each number. Notice that we need no digit for five because five is just 1 five and 0 ones and consequently is 10_{five}.

Let us return to the Hindu-Arabic system. Very little need be said. We can just do the same thing with both hands. We need no digit for ten in this system, just as we needed no digit for five in the base five system. The result is that we assign to each number a unique numeral (a numeral[5] is a name for a number) which consists of a string of digits chosen from the list 0, 1, . . . , 9. We call this standard name for a number the *decimal name*.

There are several general observations about our naming system which should be made. First, it is, conceptually, an operational procedure. By counting to ten, repeatedly, we can assign to each set of objects the string of digits which is the decimal name of the number of objects. Counting beyond ten is not necessary.[6]

There is an assumption inherent in the foregoing discussion which we want to state explicitly. The principle which is used is this:

AXIOM ON COUNTING: Suppose that n *is a counting number and that* d *is a counting number other than zero. Then each set of* n *members can be split into a collection of sets, each having* d *members, and a remainder set which has fewer than* d *members.*

This axiom, applied to objects and to sets of objects, and to sets of sets, underlies the numeration system.

Finally, we have asserted that there is a *unique* decimal numeral for each counting number, and we described this decimal in terms of a counting process with sets. Why is the numeral unique, and does it make a difference which set of objects is chosen? There are other possible difficulties with the discussion. We will consider some of these problems

5. The difference between a number and a numeral is precisely the difference between a person's name and the person. There is really no great difficulty in keeping matters straight. Children learn correct use of the terms just as they learn correct English, by imitating the language of their elders. One should certainly not make a big fuss about it.

6. The verbal names of the smaller numbers are something else; they are semantic accidents. "Seventeen" is no better a name than "ten and seven," and "thirty-seven" is an obvious contradiction of "three tens and seven." "Eleven" and "twelve" are curiosities. "Hundred," "thousand," and "million" are standard names, but "billion" is ambiguous (if we admit that the English are English speaking) and the meaning of "trillion" and so on is completely nonuniform.

again later, after the fundamental operations have been defined and we have further techniques. We have given a rather informal presentation here because children learn about place value and enumeration before they are mathematically equipped to undertake a formal development.

ADDITION

Addition is an operation which to each pair of counting numbers assigns a counting number. It is defined in the natural way. The sum of 4 and 3 is obtained this way: choose a set with 4 members and then a set with 3 members, dump them together, and count. The result is $4 + 3$. There are a few details to clean up. For example: {Joe,Mary,John,Sue} has 4 members and {Mike,Al,John} has three members, but putting these together gives the set {Joe,Mary,John,Sue,Mike,Al,John} which has 6 members but $3 + 4 \neq 6$! (Remember that two sets are the same if each member of one is a member of the other, so the set just described is identical with {Joe,Mary,John,Sue,Mike,Al}.) Moreover, the notion of "putting sets together" needs a little clarification. So we begin by discussing operations and properties of sets.

Two sets are *disjoint* if there is no object which belongs to both. It is clear that in the definition of addition we want to put together *disjoint* sets in order to count and get the sum. Here is a problem to check whether you understand this notion. Suppose a set A is disjoint from a set B, and the set B is disjoint from a set C. Must it necessarily be true that A is disjoint from C? Explain (that is, give an argument as to why this is true, or give an example of sets A, B, and C for which it is not true).[7]

The notion of "putting two sets together" is made precise as follows. The *union* or *join* of two sets A and B, denoted $A \cup B$, is the set of all objects which belong to A or to B (or to both A and B). Thus {a,b,c} $\cup$ {m,n} = {a,b,c,m,n} and {Joe,Mary,John,Sue} $\cup$ {Mike,Al,John} = {Joe,Mary,John,Sue,Mike,Al}. Formally, $A \cup B = \{x: \ x \in A$ or $x \in B\}$, and, pictorially, the union of the sets A and B can be thought of as shown in Figure 8:

Addition is now defined as follows. To find the sum $m + n$ of the numbers m and n, choose a set A which has m members and a set B, disjoint from A, having n members. Then $m + n$ is defined to be $N(A \cup B)$. Thus, to find $2 + 1$ we could notice that {Mark,Iseult} has two members and that the set {Tristram} has one member and is a disjoint from the first set so that $2 + 1 = N(\{\text{Mark,Iseult}\} \cup \{\text{Tristram}\}) =$

7. Looking for an example will be more fruitful.

$N(\{Mark, Iseult, Tristram\}) = 3$. (Of course, we are being much more formal than one would be with children. We should emphasize that the definition of $+$ is manipulative. For a child who knows how to count, the facts that $2 + 1 = 3$ and $7 + 8 = 15$ are experimentally verifiable facts that can be obtained by experiment with a stack of toothpicks.) Notice that $N(A \cup B) = N(A) + N(B)$ if A and B are disjoint. If A and B aren't disjoint, then $N(A \cup B) \neq N(A) + N(B)$.

There is one question about the definition of addition which needs elaboration. Suppose, in computing $m + n$ one person uses disjoint sets A and B and another person uses disjoint sets A^* and B^*. Do they get the same answer? Of course they do, and here is one way to see that this

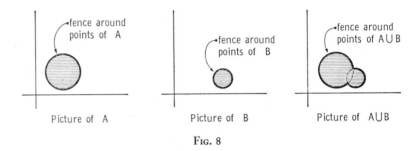

Picture of A   Picture of B   Picture of A∪B

Fig. 8

is the case. Each of A and A^* has m members so A matches A^*, and B matches B^* similarly. Thus, there is a one-to-one correspondence between the members of A and of A^* and also another such correspondence between the members of B and those of B^*. Then each member x of $A \cup B$ can be paired off with a member of $A^* \cup B^*$ (if $x \in A$, pair it to the corresponding member of A^*, and if $x \in B$, pair it to the appropriate member of B^*) and so $N(A \cup B) = N(A^* \cup B^*)$. So the two people got the same answer for $m + n$.

There are several useful general properties of $+$. We list the most important ones.

PROPERTIES OF ADDITION OF COUNTING NUMBERS

1. *Addition is commutative; that is,* m $+$ n $=$ n $+$ m *for all counting numbers* m *and* n.
2. *Addition is associative; that is,* (m $+$ n) $+$ p $=$ m $+$ (n $+$ p) *for all counting numbers* m, n, *and* p.
3. *There is an additive identity; that is, there is a number (namely* 0) *such that* 0 $+$ m $=$ m *for every number* m.

4. *If* m, n, p, *and* q *are counting numbers and if* m < n *and* p < q (*or in fact, also if* p = q), *then* m + p < n + q.

Here is a brief outline of the way these properties can be established. If A and B are sets, then $A \cup B = B \cup A$ because an object belongs to $A \subset B$ if and only if it belongs to A or to B (by the definition of $A \cup B$); this is the case if and only if it belongs to B or to A, which happens when and only when it belongs to $B \cup A$ (by the definition of $B \cup A$). If A and B are disjoint sets, then $N(A \cup B) = N(B \cup A)$ and hence $N(A) + N(B) = N(B) + N(A)$ by the definition of addition. If we choose a set A that has m members, and a set B that has n members, then the last equality becomes $m + n = n + m$. Associativity of $+$ can be proved in much the same way from the fact that $\cup$ is associative (that is, $(A \cup B) \cup C = A \cup (B \cup C)$), and the fact that $0 + n = n$ for all numbers n is true because $\{\} \cup A = A$ for all sets A. The last property takes a little more argument, but it is not difficult. We leave it as a problem for the reader.

It is obvious to us that addition is commutative so that, for example, $4 + 9 = 9 + 4$. But this is not so obvious to a child, and even for an adult, the two questions "What is 7 and 2?" and "What is 2 and 7?" are not equally difficult. Apparently our minds just do not work commutatively, and it takes a lot of exposure to absorb effectively the fact that $+$ is commutative. One reason for this is that we also use another model for addition, which is easiest to describe in terms of the number line. We think of making jumps from a beginning point labeled "o," with successive points labeled according to the number of jumps from "o." To find $2 + 7$, we take 2 jumps, then 7 jumps, and read the label. From this point of view, it is by no means obvious in advance that $2 + 7$ is the same as $7 + 2$. (The pictures in Figure 9 illustrate the two computations.)

The fact that addition is associative is used very frequently. Here is

2

3

an example. If we add the figures in the column 4 from the top we have $2 + 3$, which is 5, and then $5 + 4$ which is 9. Stated more compactly, we compute $(2 + 3) + 4 = 5 + 4 = 9$. If we add from the bottom we have $(4 + 3) + 2 = 7 + 2 = 9$. Notice that these two calculations use different "addition facts," and it is not completely obvious that the answers must always be the same. We can see that the answers must, in fact, be the same without computation if we use commutativity twice

and associativity once, as follows: $(2 + 3) + 4 = 4 + (2 + 3) =$
$4 + (3 + 2) = (4 + 3) + 2$.

The fourth property of addition (that if $m < n$ and $p \leqq q$, then $m +$
$n < n + q$) is frequently used in estimation. For example, one might ask
the question: If I add 728 and 4263, is the answer likely to be around
2500, or would you believe 2 billion, or neither? We could use property
(4) as follows: $700 < 728$ and $4000 < 4263$, so $700 + 4000 = 4700$
$< 728 + 4263$; consequently, 2700 is a bad guess for the sum. On the

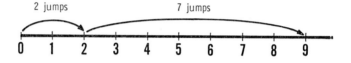

Picture of $2 + 7 = 9$

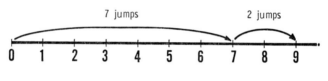

Picture of $7 + 2 = 9$

FIG. 9

other hand, $728 < 800$ and $4263 < 5000$ so $728 + 4263 < 5800$, so 2
billion is not a very good guess either. In fact, the sum must be between
4700 and 5800. (This sort of estimation is easier to think about and even
to talk about than to write about.) Practice with this sort of rough estimation helps to clarify general ideas of magnitude.

AND SUBTRACTION

The operation of subtraction is so closely related to that of addition
that they really cannot be discussed separately. There are several conceptually different ways of describing subtraction, and we begin by discussing these.

The difference $7 - 3$, 7 minus 3, can be obtained as follows: take a
set having 7 members and take away (remove, destroy, or by any means

get rid of) a subset which has 3 members. Count the remaining set (what is left). The number obtained is 7 − 3. In general, to find the difference of counting numbers m and n, where $m \geqq n$: choose a set A such that $N(A) = m$ and a subset B of A such that $N(B) = n$; define the difference set (or remaining set) $A \sim B$ to be $\{x: x \in A \text{ and } x \notin B\}$; and then $m − n = N(A \sim B)$. This is an operational definition, and any child who can count and has a stack of toothpicks or clothespins can verify that 7 − 3 is 4 by experiment. Mathematically, before making this definition, one should be sure that it does not matter just which set A and subset B (having m and n members respectively) that one uses, but this is not hard to see (compare with the same sort of difficulty with the definition of addition). The definition has the advantage that one mathematical fact is operationally obvious: if n is added to the difference, $m − n$, then the result is m. This is true because if we remove a subset B from a set A, leaving a remaining set $A \sim B$, and then put the set B back with the remaining set, then the result is certainly A (that is, if B is a subset of A, then $(A \sim B) \cup B = A$). Consequently we know, for example, that whatever the result is of subtracting 3 from 7, if the answer 7 − 3 is added to 3, then we get 7. Mathematicians say that "subtracting 3 and adding 3 are inverse operations." It is also true that, if we add 3 to any counting number and then subtract 3, the result is the number we started with (because, if A and B are disjoint sets, then $(A \cup B) \sim B = A$).

The operation of subtraction may also be described in terms of addition without mentioning sets. The number 7 − 3 is the answer to the question "7 = 3 + ?" In general, if $n \leqq m$, then $m − n$ is the answer to the question "$m = n + ?$" or $n + \square = m$, or it is the number x such that $n + x = m$. One virtue of this description is that it emphasizes the close relationship between addition and subtraction. The four statements, 7 − 3 = 4, 7 − 4 = 3, 3 + 4 = 7, 4 + 3 = 7, can be thought of as describing the same physical experiment: if a set with 3 members is disjoint from a set with 4 members, then the union of the two sets has 7 members (or in other words: if A, B, and C are disjoint sets having 3, 4, and 7 members respectively, then the union of A and B matches C). It is also clear from this description that "addition facts" and "subtraction facts" are just rearrangements of the same information. Thus, the table presented as Figure 10, which is an addition table, can also be used as a subtraction table. To find the sum of 3 and 4 from this table, we read the entry in the third row and the fourth column. To find 7 − 3 (3 + ? =

7), we look across the 3 row to the 7, and then read the label at the top of the column. It is worth mentioning that the table is symmetric across the downward diagonal line (for example, the entry in the third row and fourth column is the same as the entry in the fourth row and the third column). This is true because addition is commutative.

+	1	2	3	4	5	6	7	8	9
1	2	3	4	5	6	7	8	9	10
2	3	4	5	6	7	8	9	10	11
3	4	5	6	7	8	9	10	11	12
4	5	6	7	8	9	10	11	12	13
5	6	7	8	9	10	11	12	13	14
6	7	8	9	10	11	12	13	14	15
7	8	9	10	11	12	13	14	15	16
8	9	10	11	12	13	14	15	16	17
9	10	11	12	13	14	15	16	17	18

Fig. 10

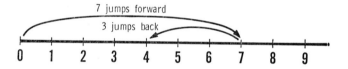

7 jumps forward

3 jumps back

Picture of 7 - 3 = 4

Fig. 11

There is yet another way of describing subtraction by using the number line. For example, to find 7 − 3 we think of taking 7 jumps forward from the label "o" and then 3 jumps backwards, and then reading the label. Figure 11 is an illustration of the process.

Subtraction is an operation which, for pairs of numbers, gives numbers; and we may compare its properties with those of addition. There are some obvious differences. First, addition is defined for every pair of counting numbers, and subtraction is defined only for pairs (m,n) where the second number n is less than or equal to the first number m. Next, subtraction is not commutative; it is not true, for example, that $7 - 3 = 3 - 7$. At the moment, $3 - 7$ is not defined, and even when we get around to assigning a meaning, it is not going to be $7 - 3$. Is subtraction associative? That is, if m, n, and p are counting numbers, is it always true that $(m - n) - p = m - (n - p)$? It is easy to see that this is not the case and that, for example, $(6 - 4) - 2 = 0$ but $6 - (4 - 2) = 4$. (You may wish to convince yourself that $(m - n) - p = m - (n - p)$ only if $n = 0$ and $m \geq n \geq p$.)

There is a property of subtraction and inequality which is very useful in estimation. Suppose m and n are numbers with $m \geq n$ and p and q are numbers with $p \geq q$. Then, if m is at least as large as p and if q is not smaller than n, it will be true that $m - n \geq p - q$. This fact can be proved from the properties of addition and inequality. But if we think about manipulating sets of objects, it is almost obvious that removing fewer than q things from a stack of more than p things leaves more than $p - q$ things. Here is an application of this fact. The difference, $147 - 69$ must be less than $150 - 60$ and greater than $140 - 70$; that is, it must be between 70 and 90.

ALGORITHMS FOR ADDITION AND SUBTRACTION

The Hindu-Arabic system of numeration (naming numbers) turns out to be remarkably convenient for computation, and we want to discuss briefly how computations with addition and subtraction can be done. But let us first be sure we understand just what computation is. From the abstract logical point of view, "computing" $471 + 237$ simply means finding the usual decimal (Hindu-Arabic) name for $471 + 237$; it is just a matter of finding a standard sort of name for a number for which we already have one name, $471 + 237$. There is another way of looking at matters which makes the process sound more interesting. The statement, "Perform the addition: $471 + 237$," perhaps means intuitively something like this: "Consider the following experiment. Count out 471 toothpicks in one stack and then count out 237 toothpicks in another stack. Now predict, mathematically, the result of counting in the usual way the toothpicks in the combined stack." This point of view of computing is probably the most satisfying to most of us. The least satisfying is surely something like the following, which all of us suspect to be happening sometimes. "Computing a sum means writing the numerals and a plus sign on the paper and then, using the rules and the addition facts we memorized, getting an answer."

Let us discuss first a method of computing sums, using the Hindu-Arabic numeration system, or rather, its base five analogue. (The base five numeration system is described in the earlier section, Naming Numbers.) Here is a problem: $24_{five} + 13_{five} = ?$ All that we really need to remember is the meaning of the notation. If we join a set which consists of 2 fives and 4 to a set consisting of 1 five and 3, we surely get a set consisting of $(2 + 1)$ fives and $(4 + 3)$, which is 3 fives and 7. It takes one more step to figure out the base five name for this number. This is easy. Since 7 is 1 five and 2, the number is 3 fives and 1 five and 2 (we are carrying 1!) which is 4 fives and 2 or 42_{five}. Here is another way of showing what is going on. $(2 \times 5 + 4) + (1 \times 5 + 3) = (2 \times 5 + 1 \times 5) + 4 + 3)$ (using commutativity and associativity), which is $(2 + 1) \times 5 + (1 \times 5 + 2)$ (distributing is used), which is $(2 + 1 + 1) \times 5 + 2 = 42_{five}$.

Here is another example. We wish to compute the sum

$$123_{five}$$
$$41_{five}$$
$$412_{five}$$

We remind ourselves what these numerals mean by labeling columns.

fives of fives of fives	fives of fives	fives	ones	
	1	2	3	
		4	1	
	4	1	2	
1				←sum of "fives of fives" column
	1	2		←sum of "fives" column
		1	1	←sum of "ones" column
1	1	3	1	$= 1131_{five}$

After sufficient practice, the part of this computation indicated below the horizontal bar is abbreviated (a notation for carrying is used) so that it might look like the following.

$$
\begin{array}{rcl}
\text{I} \ \ \text{I} \ \ \text{I} & & \leftarrow\text{``carries''} \\
\text{I} \ \ 2 \ \ 3_{\text{five}} & & \\
4 \ \ \text{I}_{\text{five}} & & \\
4 \ \ \text{I} \ \ 2_{\text{five}} & & \\
\hline
\text{I} \ \ \text{I} \ \ 3 \ \ \text{I}_{\text{five}} & &
\end{array}
$$

The same sort of reasoning is carried on for calculations using the decimal system. One can label the columns, reading from the right, with: ones, tens, tens of tens, and so on. ("Ten tens," rather than "hundreds," is probably most suggestive in teaching this process.)

Computing differences is also simple. The problem, $33_{\text{five}} - 12_{\text{five}} = ?$, offers no difficulty whatever, and the problem, $33_{\text{five}} - 14_{\text{five}} = ?$, is only slightly more difficult. Let's think in terms of sets of objects: from a set consisting of 1 five and 4. Think of the first set as 2 fives, and 1 five and 3 (borrow 1). Then removing 1 five from 2 fives leaves 1 five, and removing 4 from a set of 1 five and 3 leaves 4. Consequently, the difference is 1 five and 4, or 14_{five}. The computation might also be arranged in the following form.

five	ones		fives	ones		fives	ones
3	3	or	2	1 3five	or	2	1
							3
1	4		1	4		1	4
1	4		1	4		1	4

There is another method of computation, indicated roughly in the following illustrations. Can you see what is happening and justify the process?

fives	ones		fives	ones			
3	3	or	3	1 3five	or	3	$^{1}3_{\text{five}}$
1	4		1+1	4		1	4five
			1	4		1	4five

There are also other ways of computing differences. We illustrate here by examples a method which reduces each subtraction problem to an addition problem followed (roughly speaking) by subtraction of one. The examples use base ten notation.

$$
\begin{array}{rl}
741 \\
-376 \\
\hline
\end{array}
\quad \text{or} \quad
\begin{array}{rl}
741 \\
+624 \\
-624 \\
-376 \\
\hline
\end{array}
\quad \text{or} \quad
\begin{array}{rl}
741 \\
+\ 624 \\
-1000 \\
\hline
365
\end{array}
$$

$$
\begin{array}{rl}
24,257 \\
-\ 2,944 \\
\hline
\end{array}
\quad \text{or} \quad
\begin{array}{rl}
24,257 \\
+\ 7,056 \\
-\ 7,056 \\
-\ 2,944 \\
\hline
\end{array}
\quad \text{or} \quad
\begin{array}{rl}
24,257 \\
+\ 7,056 \\
-10,000 \\
\hline
21,313
\end{array}
$$

There is one last general remark that needs to be made on computing sums and differences. We have described the process on an intuitive basis, based on a picture of moving sets of objects around. This is really the only way one can discuss the procedure at the stage when children begin learning it. It is possible to reexamine the whole problem after the mathematical machinery of multiplication, perhaps also of exponentiation and so on, is available. The principles involved are quite easy to describe in terms of "expanded notation." A later reexamination in more abstract terms of computing methods (algorithms) for addition and subtraction may deepen a child's understanding of the methods.

MULTIPLICATION

Multiplication is, like addition, an operation which assigns to each pair (m,n) of counting numbers a counting number $m \times n$, their product. There are several ways of describing this operation and we proceed to give informal descriptions before making a formal definition.

The product 3×5 is the number of members in a set which consists of 3 sets of five (3 fives). Consequently 3×5 is the sum of the numbers 5, 5 and 5, which is $10 + 5 = 15$. Alternatively, 3×5 is 3, five times. That is, 3×5 is the number of members in a set which can be split up into 5 subsets, each having 3 members. Consequently 3×5 is the sum $3 + 3 + 3 + 3 + 3$, which is 15. Finally, the number 3×5 can be obtained as follows. Construct a rectangular array of objects, as shown in Figure 12, of 3 rows and 5 five columns. Then 3×5 is the number of members in this array. Notice that this description shows immediately, as indicated in the second and third illustrations (Figure 12), that 3 × 5 can be interpreted as 3 fives or 5 threes, and that all three descriptions give the same result. Each of the descriptions gives a perfectly feasible way for a child who has learned how to count to perform an experiment to find the product of two counting numbers. The descriptions do leave one question open: Does it matter what sets of objects we use in performing the experiment? But this is not a difficult matter to settle.

There is a somewhat more formal description of the product $m \times n$ of m and n. To find the product $m \times n$, choose a set A having m members and a set B having n members. The *cartesian product*, $A \times B$, is defined to be the set of all possible pairs (x,y) with $x \in A$ and $y \in B$.

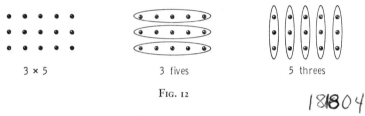

3 × 5   3 fives   5 threes

FIG. 12

(You can obtain a picture of the cartesian product $A \times B$ by thinking of A and B as sets of numbers, so that the pairs (x,y) are points in the coordinate plane. Then the picture of the set $A \times B$ is an array of dots which has n rows and m columns.) The product is the number of members of $A \times B$. (We should check, but do not, that the particular choice of sets A and B does not affect the answer.) Here is an example of how this definition could work. Suppose that m is the number of boys in a classroom and that n is the number of girls, and that we want to find $m \times n$. If we choose A to be the set of boys and B to be the set of girls, then $A \times B$ is the set of all possible couples. For each boy, the set of all couples of which he is a member is clearly in one-to-one correspondence with the set B of girls. Consequently $A \times B$ can be split up into m sets (each consisting of all couples with the same boy as member), each of which has n members; that is, $A \times B$ consists of m sets of n members each. By thinking about the set of couples of which a girl is a member, one can also argue that $A \times B$ consists of n sets, each of which has m members.

The operation of multiplication has several important properties. The following are those most often used.

PROPERTIES OF MULTIPLICATION

1. *Multiplication is commutative; that is* m × n = n × m *for all counting numbers* m *and* n.
2. *Multiplication is associative; that is,* m × (n × p) = (m × n) × p *for all numbers* m, n, *and* p.
3. *There is a multiplicative identity* 1; *that is,* 1 × m = m *for every number* m.
4. *A product* m × n *of counting numbers is* 0 *if and only if either* m = 0 *or* n = 0.
5. *If* m, n, *and* p *are counting numbers, and if* m ≧ 0 *and* p ≧ q, *then* m × p ≧ n × q.

Figure 13 indicates why multiplication is commutative. The point is:

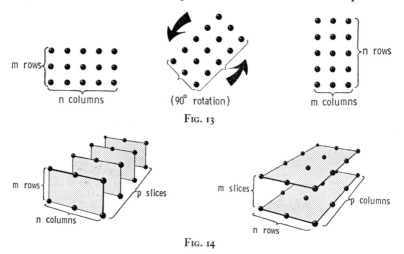

m rows — n columns   (90° rotation)   n rows — m columns

FIG. 13

m rows — n columns — p slices   m slices — n rows — p columns

FIG. 14

if an array of *m* rows and *n* columns is rotated through 90°, it becomes an array of *m* columns and *n* rows, and the number of members in the array is unchanged.

It is also fairly easy to establish associativity. The picture presented in Figure 14 indicates a possible argument. (A more formal way of establishing the argument the picture is supposed to suggest is to show that *A* × (*B* × *C*) matches (*A* × *B*) × *C* for all sets *A*, *B*, and *C*.)

The properties 3 and 4 are easy to see, and it is rather straightforward to establish 5. (If *A*, *B*, and *C* are sets, if *A* is not empty and if *B* is equivalent to a proper subset of *C*, then *A* × *B* is equivalent to a proper subset of *A* × *C*.)

Finally, there is a very important relation between multiplication and addition.

DISTRIBUTIVE PROPERTY: Multiplication distributes over addition in the sense that m × (n + p) = (m × n) + (m × n) *for all counting numbers* m, n, *and* p.

Figure 15 indicates why this is true.

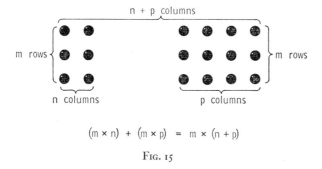

$$(m \times n) + (m \times p) = m \times (n + p)$$

FIG. 15

One may use a similar illustration (Fig. 15) to see that multiplication distributes over subtraction; that is, $m \times (n - p) = (m \times n) - (m \times p)$ whenever m, n, and p are counting numbers with $n \geq p$.

AND DIVISION

Division is an operation which, for certain pairs (n,d) of counting numbers, assigns a counting number $n \div d$, their quotient. The quickest description of division is this: the quotient $n \div d$ of counting numbers n and d is the counting number q (if there is one) such that $q \times d = n$. That is, the quotient $n \div d$ is the answer to the question, ? × d = n. For example, 21 ÷ 3 is 7, because 7 × 3 = 21. Division is related to multiplication in precisely the same way that subtraction is related to addition. A multiplication table can be used to find quotients just as an addition table can be used to find differences. To find the quotient 21 ÷ 3 in a multiplication table one need only look, in the third row, for 21 and then read the label at the head of that column.

There is one inconsistency in the description of division just given. Suppose we seek the quotient, 0 ÷ 0. This is supposed to be the number, is there is one, such that 0 × q = 0. There is such a number; in fact, there is an embarrassment of riches, since 0 × m = 0 for every counting number m! We approach this awkwardness firmly and agree that we will *not* define o ÷ o. This difficulty does not occur in any other case.[8]

There are a few simple facts about division which follow directly from the definition. First, $n \div 1 = n$ for every number n because $1 \times n = n$. Division is not commutative—even when we get around to assigning a meaning to $1 \div 2$, it will not be the case that $1 \div 2 = 2 \div 1$. Division is not associative, as the example, $(16 \div 8) \div 2 = 2 \div 2 = 1$ and $16 \div (8 \div 2) = 16 \div 4 = 4$, shows. If $n \div d = q$, and $n \neq 0$, then $n \div q = d$.

There are other descriptions of division which are conceptually near to applications of the process, and which lend themselves to computation by physical experiment. For example, we describe the quotient $n \div d$ as the number obtained in the following way. Take a set which has n members. Split it into subsets if it is possible; do so, so that each subset has d members. The number of subsets is the quotient $n \div d$. Thus, to find $21 \div 3$, a child might take a stack of 21 toothpicks and count them into stacks of 3. The quotient is the number of stacks. The quotient can then be described as the answer to the questions: How many 3's in 21? How many stacks of 3 can you make from a set of 21 things? How many d's in one n? These questions obviously suggest a physical experiment, and their answers can be considered to be predictions of the result of the experiment. The descriptions of multiplication show that this description of division is the same as saying that $n \div d$ is the answer to the question, $? \times d = n$.

There is another description of division which is, at least operationally, different. Three children are going to divide 21 pieces of candy; how many does each get? The way this is usually done is "one for me, one for you, and one for her, and one for me . . . etc." Getting away from the sticky candy business, the description of $21 \div 3$ being employed is this: if a set of 21 things is split up into 3 equivalent sets, how many members will each set have? Or in general: $n \div d$ is the number of objects in each subset if a set of n objects is split up into d equivalent disjoint subsets. Because multiplication is commutative, this process gives the same result as that described in the previous paragraph.

The number line picture of division seems intuitively nearer the "how many 3's in 21?" approach. Figure 16 indicates the method.

8. If $d = 0$ and $n \neq 0$, then $n \div d$ is supposed to be the number q such that $q \times d = q \times 0 = n$, but this is impossible, so $n \div 0$ is not defined. If $d \neq 0$ and if p and q are both candidates for $n \div d$, that is, if $p \times d = n = q \times d$, then neither p nor q is o and one of them is less than the other, say $p < q$ (trichotomy axiom). But then $p \times d < q \times d$, and this is a contradiction.

Inequalities are used in estimating quotients, much as for differences. The quotient $289 \div 17$ is greater than $280 \div 20$ and less than $290 \div 10$. This fact is a consequence of the properties of multiplication and inequality listed earlier.

——— • ———

There is an extension of the division process which is extremely important, not only in devising algorithms for computing quotients, but also in achieving other purposes. The operation of division gives, for certain pairs (n,d) of counting numbers, a unique number $n \div d$. The process which we now want to describe gives, for every pair (n,d) of counting numbers with $d \neq 0$, a *pair* (q,r) of counting numbers. For want of a better term, we call this operation *partial division*, and we refer

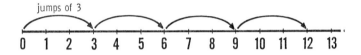

$$12 \div 3 = 4$$

FIG. 16

to the number q as the partial quotient and to the number r as the remainder. If the remainder is 0, then the partial quotient is just the quotient $n \div d$.

For each counting number n and for each number d which is different from 0, the *partial quotient* $[n \div d]$ is the number of d's in n, and the remainder is the number left over. More precisely, to find $[n \div d]$, choose a set A with n members and split it into disjoint subsets, each consisting of d members, as many as possible. The number of subsets is the partial quotient $[n \div d]$, and the number of members of the remainder subset (the members of A which belong to none of these subsets) is the remainder after dividing n by d. For example, if a set of 25 objects is split into sets of 3, there will be 8 sets of 3 and 1 left over. The partial quotient $[25 \div 3]$ is 8 and the remainder is 1. It is clear that $25 = 3 \times 8 + 1$, from the definition of multiplication and addition.

We can also define the partial quotient and remainder directly in terms of multiplication and addition, without mentioning sets. For each counting number n and each counting number d which is not zero, there are numbers q and r with $r < d$ such that $n = d \times q + r$. (See the Axiom on Counting.) The number q is the partial quotient $(n \div d)$, and the number r is the remainder after division by d of n. It is an important fact about counting numbers that the partial quotient and remainder are unique. That is:

PARTIAL DIVISION PROPERTY: If n *and* d *are counting numbers and* d $\neq$ o, *then there are unique counting numbers* q *and* r *such that* r $<$ d *and* n = d $\times$ q $+$ r.

We conclude this section with a rough outline of the argument showing that the numbers q and r are unique. Suppose n is a counting number and $d \neq$ o. According to the counting axiom (see the section on naming numbers), each set having n members can be split into a number of sets, each having d members, and a remaining set which has fewer than d members. This shows that there are numbers q (the number of sets with d members) and r (the number of members of the remaining set) such that $n = d \times q + r$. The only thing that needs to be proved is that the numbers q and r are unique. We must show that if $n = d \times q + r = d \times q' + r'$ with r and r' less than d, then $q = q'$ and $r = r'$. Suppose, for convenience, that $q \geqq q'$ (otherwise, interchange q and q' in the following argument). Then we can show that $d \times q - d \times q' + r = r'$ and hence that $d \times (q - q') + r = r'$. Because $q \geqq q'$, it is true that $r' \geqq r$. Consequently $d \times (q - q') = r - r'$. But $r - r' < d$ because $r < d$, and so $q - q'$ must be o and $q = q'$. So $r - r' =$ o and therefore $r = r'$. Consequently the partial quotient and remainder are unique.

ALGORITHMS FOR MULTIPLICATION AND DIVISION

The Hindu-Arabic numeration system is enormously better than other numeration systems for computations of products and quotients. We describe briefly how these computations can be made.

We first notice how multiplication works out with tens, and tens of tens, and so on. The product 10 $\times$ 10, is ten tens, which is 100. The product 100 $\times$ 10 is ten tens of tens, or 1000 (because multiplication is associative, 10 $\times$ (10 $\times$ 10) = (10 $\times$ 10) $\times$ 10, and we can omit parentheses without ambiguity). Roughly speaking:

$$\underbrace{(10 \times 10 \times \ldots \times 10)}_{m \text{ tens}} \times \underbrace{(10 \times 10 \times \ldots \times 10)}_{n \text{ tens}}$$

$$= \underbrace{(10 \times 10 \times \ldots \times 10)}_{m + n \text{ tens}},$$

or one followed by m zeros multiplied by one followed by n zeros is one followed by $m + n$ zeros.

We next consider multiplication of the sort, 20×400, of numbers whose decimal names consist of all zeros save one digit. Here we use commutativity and associativity of multiplication:

$$20 \times 400 = (2 \times 10) \times (4 \times 100) = 2 \times (10 \times (4 \times 100))$$
$$= 2 \times ((10 \times 4) \times 100) = 2 \times ((4 \times 10) \times 100)$$
$$= 2 \times (4 \times (10 \times 100)) = (2 \times 4) \times (10 \times 100)$$
$$= 8 \times 1000 .$$

In this string of equalities we used the associative law twice, then the commutative law, and then the associative law twice more. (Because it is clear what sort of rearrangements can be made by using these two laws, we shall use them without explicit mention in the rest of this section.)

Finally, the fact that multiplication distributes over addition permits us to compute an arbitrary product as sums of products of the sort just considered. The product $7 \times (43)$ is $7 \times (40 + 3)$, which by the distributive law is $7 \times (40) + (7 \times 3) = 280 + 21 = 301$. More complex multiplications may require several applications of the distributive law. For example:

$$(124) \times (27) = (124) \times (20 + 7) = (124 \times 20) + (124 \times 7)$$
$$= 20 \times (100 + 20 + 4) + 7 \times (100 + 20 + 4)$$
$$= (20 \times 100) + (20 \times 20) + (20 \times 4) + (7 \times 100)$$
$$+ (7 \times 20) + (7 \times 4) .$$

It is clear that this method of computation reduces the calculation of, say, 345×6780 to finding the sum of the products, 300×6000, 300×700, 300×80, 40×6000, 40×700, 40×80, 5×6000, 5×700, 5×80.

The computation of quotients, or of partial quotients, is a straightforward application of the description of division. Suppose we wish to divide 132 by 7. More precisely, we wish to find a partial quotient q and a remainder r such that $132 = q \times 7 + r$. (If $r = 0$, then $q = 132 \div 7$.) One way to proceed is to add 7 to itself successively until the sum is 132 (or is a number differing from 132 by less than 7) and then simply count the number of sevens that have been added up. It is more convenient to modify this procedure by subtracting sevens, or multiples of seven, from 132 until a number less than 7 remains. That is, we try to find numbers q and r with r less than 7 so that $132 - q \times 7 = r$, since this equality happens if and only if $132 = q \times 7 + r$. We do this by subtracting multiples of 7, and the work might be arranged as follows:

$$
\begin{array}{ll}
132 & \\
70 & \text{10 sevens} \\
\hline
62 & \\
56 & \text{8 sevens} \\
\hline
6 &
\end{array}
$$

$$132 = (10 + 8) \times 7 + 6$$

$$[132 \div 7] = 18, \text{ remainder} = 6$$

We give another example of how this procedure works. Suppose we want the quotient, or the partial quotient, $897 \div 37$. The quotient should be less than $900 \div 30$ and more than $800 \div 40$; that is, it should be a number in the twenties. Let us therefore begin by subtracting 20×37.

$$
\begin{array}{ll}
897 & \\
740 & 20 \times 37 \\
\hline
157 &
\end{array}
$$

Estimation can be used to guess the multiples of 37 to subtract. The number of 37's in 157 should be less than $200 \div 30$ and more than $100 \div 40$; that is, the possibilities are 2, 3, 4, 5 and 6 (of course, more careful estimation would reduce the number of possibilities). The calculation below shows the poor guess of 3 being used. Notice that it is not necessary to "start over" after an underestimate. One may simply keep on subtracting multiples and keep track of the multiples subtracted.

$$
\begin{array}{ll}
897 & \\
740 & 20 \times 37 \\
\hline
157 & \\
111 & 3 \times 37 \\
\hline
46 & \\
37 & 1 \times 37 \\
\hline
9 &
\end{array}
$$

$$897 = (20 + 3 + 1) \times 37 + 9$$

$$[897 \div 37] = 24, \text{ remainder } 9$$

PRIMES

There are some interesting and useful facts about the multiplicative structure of counting numbers which we want to point out. Recall that a counting number m is a multiple of another number n if m is equal to the product of n and some counting number k; that is, $m = k \times n$. In this case we say that n is a *divisor* or a *factor* of m. For example, 3 is a divisor of 6, and also a divisor of 12. The set consisting of all possible divisors of 12 is {1,2,3,4,6,12} and every number is a divisor of 0. On the other hand, the only divisors of 13 are 1 and 13.

A *prime* number is a counting number, larger than 1, whose only divisors are 1 and itself. Thus 3 is prime, and 5 is prime, but 35 isn't prime because 1, 5, 7, and 35 are all divisors of 35. Every number can be written as a product of primes—one simply thinks of replacing the number by a product of smaller numbers, and then continuing. For example: $72 = 2 \times 36 = 2 \times 4 \times 9 = 2 \times 2 \times 2 \times 3 \times 3$.

1　2　3　4̸　5　6̸　7　8̸　9̸　1̸0̸　11　1̸2̸　13　1̸4̸　15　1̸6̸　17　1̸8̸

19　2̸0̸　2̸1̸　2̸2̸　23　2̸4̸　2̸5̸　2̸6̸　2̸7̸　2̸8̸　29　3̸0̸　31　3̸2̸　3̸3̸　3̸4̸　3̸5̸　3̸6̸

37　3̸8̸　3̸9̸　4̸0̸　41　4̸2̸　43　4̸4̸　4̸5̸　4̸6̸　47　4̸8̸　4̸9̸　5̸0̸

Fig. 17

The number line gives an easy and instructive way of picturing the primes. The number 2 is a prime, but multiples of 2 by numbers larger than 1 are not, so 4, 6, 8, 10, 12, . . . and so on, are not prime. The number 3 is a prime, but none of the numbers 6, 9, 12, 15, . . . are primes. This suggests a way of picking out prime numbers on the number line. Strike out, on the number line, all multiples (by numbers larger than 1) of 2; then strike out all such multiples of 3; you have now already struck out multiples of 4, but strike out multiples of 5. And so on. This is a systematic way of striking out all numbers which are not prime; those which are left are the primes. Figure 17 shows the process carried out for the first 50 numbers. This process for listing primes is called the *sieve of Eratosthenes*.

It is worth noticing that primes are more common near the beginning of the list, and they seem to be getting sparser toward the end. It seems quite possible, in fact, that we would eventually strike out every number. That is, maybe there are only a finite number of primes. This is not the case—there are infinitely many prime numbers—and the argument to show this is so ingenious and simple that we sketch it in a special case. We show that there is a prime number larger than 100. Let us denote by n number

$$n = (1 \times 2 \times 3 \times \ldots \ldots \times 99 \times 100) + 1,$$

which is the product of all the counting numbers from 1 to 100, plus 1. We assert that every divisor (other than 1) of this number is larger than 100. For example, if 47 were a divisor of n, then, since 47 is also a divisor of $(1 \times 2 \times 3 \times \ldots \times 99 \times 100)$, 47 would be a divisor of $n - (1 \times 2 \times 3 \times \ldots \times 99 \times 100)$. That is, 47 would be a divisor of 1, which is absurd. Consequently every divisor of n is larger than 100, and every number larger than 1 has prime factors.

We have already observed that each number larger than 1 is the product of prime factors. One of the most beautiful theorems of arithmetic states that the prime factors are unique.[9] That is, two people may factor a number into primes in different ways, but they will always get the same list of primes. For example: $36 = 9 \times 4 = 3 \times 3 \times 2 \times 2$ and $36 = 18 \times 2 = 6 \times 3 \times 2 = 3 \times 2 \times 3 \times 2$. (Of course the order in which the primes occur in the lists may be different.)

The uniqueness of factorization of a number into prime factors is a consequence of the fact that if a prime is a divisor of the product of two numbers, then it is a divisor of one of the numbers; that is, if a prime p divides a product $m \times n$, then p divides m or p divides n. Here is a sketch of the proof of this fact. The proof is by contradiction. Assume p divides $m \times n$ but not m or n and that m is the smallest counting number such that, for some n, p divides $m \times n$ but not m or n. We first assert that $m < p$, for otherwise we can find numbers q and r with $r < p$ such that $m = q \times p + r$, whence $m \times n - q \times p \times n = r \times n$, and since p divides the left-hand side, therefore p divides $r \times n$. But m was chosen to be as small as possible; this is a contradiction, and hence $m < p$. Now choose numbers a and t with $t < m$ so that $p = s \times m + t$. Then $p \times n - s \times m \times n = t \times m$, and consequently p divides $t \times m$. This again contradicts the fact that m was supposed to be as small as possible.

CLOCK ARITHMETIC

We are presently going to expand our system of numbers to include numbers other than counting numbers. As a preliminary, to indicate some

9. Notice that, according to our definition of prime, 1 is not a prime. Can you think of a good reason for the fact that we arranged the definition this way?

nice properties that the new system will have that the counting numbers
lack, we want to discuss briefly a new system of numbers, a sort of toy
number system. It is called *clock arithmetic*.

In order to avoid too large a multiplication and addition table, let us
imagine a clock with just five hour labels around the dial. Suppose it is
labeled as shown in Figure 18. We will use this clock to describe two
new operations, called *addition modulo five* and *multiplication modulo five*.
We consider only the numbers that can be read on the clock: 0, 1, 2, 3
and 4. We define $+_5$ as follows: the sum $m +_5 n$ is obtained by starting
the clock at 0, letting it run m hours, then letting it run n hours and
reading the dial. Thus $1 +_5 1 = 2$, $2 +_5 2 = 4$, $2 +_5 3 = 0$, $3 +_5 3 = 1$.
Figure 19 is the addition table for the operation $+_5$.

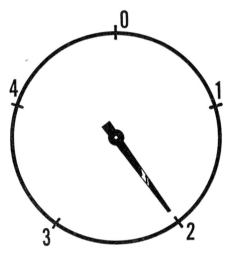

Fig. 18

$+_5$	0	1	2	3	4
0	0	1	2	3	4
1	1	2	3	4	0
2	2	3	4	0	1
3	3	4	0	1	2
4	4	0	1	2	3

Fig. 19

We now have defined the operation $+_5$ for pairs of members of the set $\{0,1,2,3,4\}$. Let us observe some properties. First, there is a $+_5$ identity element, 0; that is, $0 +_5 m = m +_5 0 = m$ for each member m of $\{0,1,2,3,4\}$. Next, the operation $+_5$ is commutative: $m +_5 n = n +_5 m$ for all members m and n of $\{0,1,2,3,4\}$. This can be checked out case by case, or we can notice that the addition table is symmetric across the diagonal. The operation $+_5$ is also associative;[10] we shall not establish this carefully—one could check all the 125 possibilities for m, n, and p for the product $m \times_5 (n \times_5 p)$.

There is one striking difference between the operation $+_5$ on $\{0,1,2,3,4\}$ and the operation $+$ on the set of counting numbers. For each member of $\{0,1,2,3,4\}$, there is a unique member such that the sum of the two is 0. Explicitly, $0 +_5 0 = 0$, $1 +_5 4 = 0$, $2 +_5 3 = 0$, $3 +_5 2 = 0$, and $4 +_5 1 = 0$. Mathematicians describe this fact by saying that every member of $\{0,1,2,3,4\}$ has a $+_5$ *inverse*, or an *inverse with respect to addition modulo 5*. Let us agree that ^5m, to be read as "opposite modulo 5 of m, or negative modulo 5 of m" is the member of $\{0,1,2,3,4\}$ which when added modulo 5 to m gives 0. Thus $^5 0 = 0$, $^5 1 = 4$, $^5 2 = 3$, $^5 3 = 2$, and $^5 4 = 1$. Notice that $^5(^5 m) = n$ for each m; that is, the opposite modulo 5 of each number is itself.

We can also use one of the descriptions of subtraction of counting numbers to define a subtraction modulo 5. The difference $m - n$ of the counting numbers m and n is the number which when added to n gives m; the difference $m -_5 n$ modulo 5 of the members m and n of $\{0,1,2,3,4\}$ is the member of $\{0,1,2,3,4\}$ which when added modulo 5 to n gives m. Thus $1 -_5 4$ is the answer to the question, $? +_5 4 = 1$; that is, $1 -_5 4 = 2$. It is true that any two members of $\{0,1,2,3,4\}$ have a difference modulo 5, and in fact we can compute the difference in terms of opposite modulo 5. Here is the argument: $^5 n +_5 n = 0$, by the definition of opposite modulo 5, therefore $(m +_5 {}^5 n) +_5 n = m$, and consequently $m +_5 {}^5 n$ is the answer to the question, $? +_5 n = m$. Thus $m -_5 n$ is equal to $m +_5 {}^5 n$ for all members m and n of $\{0,1,2,3,4\}$. Any two members of $\{0,1,2,3,4\}$ thus have a difference modulo five. We sometimes say that this system of numbers is *closed under subtraction*.

10. Associativity and other properties of $+_5$ can be proved systematically as follows. Let $R(m)$ be the remainder after partial division of m by 5. Thus $R(27) = 2$, and $R(9) = 4$ (intuitive description: R throws away fives). Then $m +_5 n = R(m + n)$ and $m \times_5 n = R(m \times n)$. These connections between modulo 5 and ordinary addition and multiplication, together with the propositions, $R(m + n) = R(m) +_5 R(n)$ and $R(m \times n) = R(m) \times_5 R(n)$ for all counting numbers m and n, can be used to establish properties of $+_5$ and $\times_5$.

Multiplication modulo 5 is defined as follows. The product modulo 5, $m \times_5 n$, of two members m and n of $\{0,1,2,3,4\}$ is obtained by starting the clock at 0, letting it run n hours, then n more hours, until it has run m hours n times; the reading on the dial is then $m \times_5 n$. Another way of saying the same thing is this: the product modulo 5, $m \times_5 n$, is the remainder after partial division by 5 of the ordinary product $m \times n$. Thus $2 \times_5 4 = 3$ and $4 \times_5 4 = 1$. A multiplication table for $\times_5$ is shown in Figure 20. This multiplication $\times_5$ has many of the properties of ordinary multiplication. In particular, $\times_5$ is commutative and associative, there is a $\times_5$ identity (namely 1), and multiplication modulo 5 distributes over

$\times_5$	0	1	2	3	4
0	0	0	0	0	0
1	0	1	2	3	4
2	0	2	4	1	3
3	0	3	1	4	2
4	0	4	3	2	1

FIG. 20

addition modulo 5. These facts are not hard to establish, and we leave them to the reader. But there is one remarkable property that $\times_5$ possesses that multiplication of counting numbers lacks. Division modulo 5, except by 0, is always possible!

Let us be a little more precise. Following one of the descriptions of division of counting numbers, we define the quotient modulo 5, $m \div_5 n$, to be the number which when multiplied modulo 5 by n gives m; it is the answer to the question, ? $\times_5 n = m$. Thus $2 \div_5 3 = 4$ because $3 \times_5 4 = 2$. In fact, by just looking at the table for $\times_5$ we can obtain a table for $\div_5$ as shown below. We want particularly to call attention to the row in this table (Figure 21) which begins "1." The entries here read: $1 \div_5 1 = 1$, $1 \div_5 2 = 3$, $1 \div_5 3 = 1$, $1 \div_5 4 = 4$. These numbers 1, 3, 2, and 4, are called the *reciprocals modulo 5* of the numbers 1, 2, 3, and 4, respectively. The reciprocal modulo 5 of m is the number which when multiplied modulo 5 by m gives 1; it is the answer to the question, ? $\times_5 m = 1$. Each nonzero number in this system has a reciprocal modulo 5; this fact is sometimes stated as "each nonzero number has a $\times_5$ inverse." Just as subtraction modulo 5 and opposite modulo 5 are related, there is a relation between division modulo 5, and reciprocal modulo 5. This is the relation: the quotient $m \div_5 n$ of m and n modulo 5 is $m \times_5$ (the reciprocal of n modulo 5) for all members m and n of $\{0,1,2,3,4\}$ with $n \neq 0$. A table of reciprocals modulo 5 and a table for $\times_5$ can then be used to obtain a table for $\times_5$.

Summing up our investigation of clock arithmetic, we see that this little number system has the properties of counting numbers, except those involving inequality.[11] It also has properties that the system of counting numbers lacks. Subtraction of any two numbers is always possible in this system, and division is possible except by 0.

$\div_5$	1	2	3	4
1	1	3	2	4
2	2	1	4	3
3	3	4	1	2
4	4	2	3	1

FIG. 21

Our next task is to enlarge the system of counting numbers. In the resulting system—the system of rational numbers—subtraction will always be possible and division, except by 0, will also be possible.

The ideas explored in this section can be pursued further to obtain insight into the structure of counting numbers. The following suggestions are made to the reader who wishes to go further.

There is nothing sacred about the number 5, or at least not very sacred. One may, for example, define $+_4$ and $\times_4$ in the natural way for members of the set $\{0,1,2,3\}$. But notice that $2 \times_4 2 = 0$. Can one be persuaded from this fact, without writing out a multiplication table, that 2 cannot have a reciprocal modulo 4?

Suppose that m is a counting number which is not prime; suppose that $m = n \times p$ where n and p are greater than 1. Then $n \times_m p = 0$. Can one be persuaded in this case that it is impossible for n and p to have reciprocals?

11. We really *have* lost the properties of inequality. You may wish to convince yourself that it is impossible to define $<$ for the members of $\{0,1,2,3,4\}$ so that, if $p < q$ and $m < n$, then $p +_5 m < q +_5 n$.

Suppose that p is a counting number which is prime and that q is one of the numbers $1, 2, \ldots, p - 1$. Think of the row in the table for $\times_p$ corresponding to multiplication by q. Show that no two entries in this row can be equal (one will have to use the fact that p is prime). Then argue that the entries in this row must be just a rearrangement of the numbers $0, 1, \ldots, p - 1$. Finally, use this fact to show that there is a reciprocal modulo p for q.

THE INTEGERS (WHOLE NUMBERS)

We are going to enlarge the system of counting numbers by adjoining some new numbers, the negatives or opposites of the counting numbers. The use of negative numbers is historically quite recent. As late as 1796, William Frend, in a text, *Principles of Algebra*, wrote peevishly about ". . . this strange doctrine of negative quantities, unnecessarily introduced into the otherwise clear and simple science of Algebra or Universal Arithmetick . . .".

Why do we need negatives? Here are a few of the reasons that might be given. Geometrically, we will use negative numbers to label points to the left of 0 on the number line, and later we shall need pairs of numbers, both positive and negative, to label all of the points in the plane. If we label altitudes above sea level with positive numbers, then it is natural to label depths below sea level with negative. If we use positive numbers to denote assets, then negatives are appropriate for debts.

We begin with a description of the integers, which is similar to our description of the counting numbers. Now we consider sets of objects, not arbitrary objects, but just two kinds. To be explicit, suppose that all of the sets consist of balls, some of which are black and some of which are red. Think of the black balls as consisting of matter, and the red balls of antimatter, so that putting one black ball together with one red ball leaves precisely nothing at all. Or, if you prefer, think of black balls as credits and red balls as debts, so that a black and a red cancel each other out. With each set of black balls we associate the number of members of the set. With each set consisting of red balls we associate a new kind of number, called the *opposite* of the number of members, and denoted by the name of the counting number with an opposite sign, " $-$," prefixed. Thus a set of 5 red balls is associated with $^-5$, which is read as "opposite 5." Notice that $^-0 = 0$. An *integer* is a counting number or the opposite of a counting number.

The sum of two integers m and n is defined in this way. Join the set associated with m to the set associated with n. If both matter and anti-matter are present, wait till the mutual destruction is over. The number associated with the remaining set is the sum, $m + n$. Thus $4 + 5 = 9$ because the join of a set of 4 black balls and a set of 5 black balls is a set of 9 black balls; $^-2 + {^-3} = {^-5}$ because the join of a set of 2 red balls and a set of 3 red balls is a set of 5 red balls; $^-6 + 2 = {^-4}$ because the join of a set of 6 red balls and a set of 2 black balls is, finally, a set of 4 red balls; and $93 + {^-93} = 0$.

This description of the addition of integers has several interesting properties. Certainly, for counting numbers, it agrees with the addition we described earlier. It is commutative, essentially by definition. It is also associative, though it is a little more troublesome to go through all the cases of the argument that are necessary to show it. Further, it is always true that $0 + m = m$, whether m is a counting number or the opposite of a counting number. But here is the new phenomenon. Let us agree that the opposite of the opposite of a counting number is the number, so that, for example, $^-(^-5) = 5$. Then, for each integer m, there is an integer ^-m such that $m + {^-m} = 0$. This is true because each integer is associated with a set, and changing the color of the members of the set gives a set, which upon being joined to the original, leaves only the empty set.

We can also define subtraction for every pair of integers. That is, there is always an integer which furnishes an answer to the question, $? + m = n$, for any integers m and n. In fact, it is clear that $n + {^-m}$ is the integer which, added to m, gives n. Consequently, if we define the difference $m - n$ of the integers m and n in the natural way, we have this description of subtraction: To find $m - n$, take the set associated with m, then the set associated with n with the color changed, and join them; the integer associated with the resulting set is $m - n$.

If the above description of the integers and their addition seems unduly fanciful, here is another. (Forget, momentarily, that you have read the preceding description.) Imagine that you are at the bus terminal on a highway running east and west. You want to label all of the mileposts, both to the east and to the west, and you decide to label them with instructions for going from the terminal to the milepost. You decide, then, to label the post one mile to the east as $^+1$, two miles to the east as $^+2$, and so on. Thus, for example, $^+7$ is on the post which is reached by going 7 miles east of the station. The station itself is labeled 0, and points to the west are labeled with an opposite sign to indicate that you go the opposite way from east. Thus ⁻5 is on the milepost 5 miles to the west of the station. Figure 22 indicates how the mile posts would look. Addition is defined as follows. For a pair of each instructions, say ⁻4 and ⁺3, the sum is then the result of following the instruction ⁻4 and then following the instruction ⁺3. That is, "Go 4 miles in the direction opposite to east, and then 3 miles east." Clearly the same result would be obtained by following the single instruction, "Go 1 mile west," or just ⁻1. That is, ⁻4 + ⁺3 = ⁻1. This description of addition might be pictured in Figure 23.

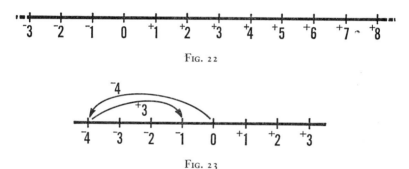

Fɪɢ. 22

Fɪɢ. 23

The milepost (or number line) description of the integers gives the most natural picture of the way we define inequality for integers.[12] Let us agree that an integer m is less than an integer n, or $m < n$, if the label "m" occurs to the left of the label "n." Thus ⁻7 < 0, ⁻8 < ⁻2, and ⁻10,000 < 3. There is also a way of describing inequality in terms of our earlier picture of sets of red and of black balls. To decide which of the integers m and n is smaller, one might take a set that goes with m, then take a set which goes with the opposite of n (change the color), and join them. Then if the result is black, m is the larger, and if the result is red, then n is larger. (One can easily check that this works; think of the black black, black red, red black, and red red cases.) We can summarize these facts as follows:

Call the counting numbers, other than 0, *positive* integers, and call the opposites of the nonzero counting numbers *negative* integers. Then an integer m is greater than an integer n if and only if $m + ⁻n$ is a positive integer.

12. We might conceivably have defined inequality by agreeing that the smaller of two integers is the one which is nearer to 0 on the number line. Can you think of troubles which this definition might cause?

We turn now to the question of how the multiplication of integers would be defined. First of all, we want the multiplication of this new kind of number to agree with the multiplication of counting numbers; that is, if m and n are integers which are also counting numbers, then we want $m \times n$ to be the number of members in an array which has m rows and n columns. But how should we define $^-7 \times 4$ and $^-3 \times {}^-5$? The first of these two questions has one rather simple answer. We should like $^-7 \times 4$ to be opposite 7, taken four times; in other words, it should be the integer that goes with four sets, each of which consists of 7 red balls. In brief, we should like $^-7 \times 4$ to be $^-(7 \times 4) = {}^-28$. More generally, we should like the opposite of a counting number, multiplied by a counting number, to be the opposite of the product of the counting numbers. That is, if m and n are counting numbers, we agree that $^-m \times n$ is to be $^-(m \times n)$. In particular, $^-m \times 0 = {}^-(m \times 0) = {}^-0 = 0$.

We have yet to define the product $^-m \times {}^-n$ of the opposites of two counting numbers m and n. It turns out that we have no choice if we want multiplication to distribute over addition for integers as it does for counting numbers. Here is the argument. If m and n are counting numbers, then $0 = {}^-m \times 0 = {}^-m \times (n + {}^-n) = {}^-m \times n + {}^-m \times {}^-n$ and, since $^-m \times n = {}^-(m \times n)$, we see that $^-(m \times n) + {}^-m \times {}^-n = 0$. Adding $m \times n$ to both sides gives $^-m \times {}^-n = m \times n$. That is, if m and n are counting numbers, then the product $^-m \times {}^-n$ should be $m \times n$.

Here is another way of persuading ourselves that $^-m \times {}^-n$ should be $m \times n$ if m and n are counting numbers. Consider again the number line description of integers. There is a bus station labeled 0 on an east-west highway, the mileposts to the east are labeled $^+1$, $^+2$, and so on, and those to the west are labeled $^-1$, $^-2$, etc. If we agree that a car which is going east at 30 miles per hour has a speed of 30, or $^+30$, and a car going to the west at 40 miles per hour has a speed of $^-40$, then two hours after passing the bus station, the eastbound car is at the milepost 2×30, or $^+60$, and the westbound car is at $2 \times {}^-40$, or at $^-80$. Where was the eastbound car 2 hours before passing the station? Clearly it was at $^-2 \times 30$, and the westbound car was at $^-2 \times {}^-40$, in fact at $^+80$. This situation and related physical problems furnish the principal reasons that we define the product $^-m \times {}^-n$, for counting numbers m and n, to be $m \times n$.

We end this section with a summary statement of some of the important properties of the system of integers. We have not established all of these properties, but there is no great difficulty in seeing why they hold.

SOME PROPERTIES OF THE SYSTEM OF INTEGERS (*Tri-chotomy*): *For each integer, just one of the following three things is true: the integer is positive* (*that is, it is a nonzero counting number*); *the integer is* o; *or the integer is negative* (*the opposite of a nonzero counting number*).

The sum and product of positive integers is positive. One integer is greater than another if and only if their difference is positive.

Addition of integers is commutative and associative. There is a + *identity,* o, *such that* o + m = m *for each integer* m. *For each integer* m *there is a* + *inverse,* ⁻m, *such that* m + ⁻m = o.	*Multiplication of integers is commutative and associative. There is a* × *identity,* 1, *such that* 1 × m = m *for each integer* m. *The product of two integers is* o *if and only if one of them is* o.

Multiplication distributes over addition.

We have tried to arrange the foregoing to point out some similarities and differences between properties of addition and properties of multiplication. Finally, there are some properties which the system of counting numbers possesses which are not possessed by the system of integers. Here is one: every nonempty set of counting numbers has a smallest member. The corresponding statement for integers is false!

THE RATIONAL NUMBERS

We are going to enlarge the number system once more. So far we have been attaching quantitative concepts (numbers) to sets of objects and, in the preceding sections, to sets of two different sorts of objects. We are now going to consider numbers which are suitable for describing parts of objects and new objects which we get by reassembling these parts. In measuring length and area and in many other physical measurement problems, these new numbers occur naturally. These numbers have been used for centuries; they are much older than the Greek civilization. We shall define operations of addition and multiplication for rational numbers and so obtain a number system. This system has the property that each nonzero number has a multiplicative inverse, which is a sort of mathematical analogue to saying that one can divide things up into parts. The name, "rational" number, comes from the word "ratio." It is not supposed to indicate that the only numbers that are not insane are the rational numbers.

Perhaps the easiest way to describe the rational numbers is in terms of the number line. Think of dividing the spaces between the integers into parts of equal length, and then labeling the new points with fractions, as illustrated in Figure 24.

Intuitively, there are two different reasons for labeling the points in the fashion shown. We can think of $\frac{2}{3}$ as two lengths of $\frac{1}{3}$ unit, measured from 0, or we can think of $\frac{2}{3}$ as being one-third of a length of 2 units. That is, dividing a length of 1 unit into 3 parts and taking 2 of them gives the same result as dividing a length of 2 units into 3 parts and taking one of them. If we think of adding $\frac{2}{3}$ to itself 3 times on the number line,

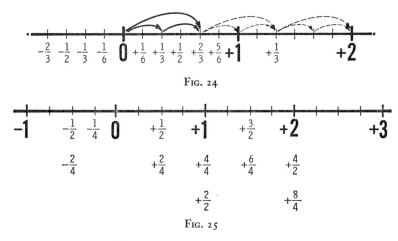

Fig. 24

Fig. 25

that is, finding $3 \times \frac{2}{3}$, then the result is clearly 2. In other words, one answer to the question, $3 \times ? = 2$, is $\frac{2}{3}$. So we can think of $\frac{2}{3}$ as the quotient, $2 \div 3$. Similarly, $-\frac{2}{3}$ can be thought of as $-2 \div 3$.

There is another fact about the labeling of rational numbers which we can see at once from the number line picture. Each of the rational numbers is named by many different fractions.[13] The sketch (Figure 25) shows some of the names of some of the rational numbers.

It is not hard to see how the names shown above for the same number are related to each other. For example, all of the following are the same

13. A *fraction* is a numeral (that is, the name of a number) which is of the special form: a numeral, followed by a division sign, followed by another numeral; or, what is the same thing, a numeral with a bar underneath and a numeral underneath the bar. The one on top is the name of the *numerator* of the fraction, that on the bottom, the *denominator*. Thus, in the fraction

$$\text{``} \frac{4 - 1}{\text{VI}} \text{,''}$$

$4 - 1$ is the numerator and VI is the denominator.

number: $\frac{2}{3}$, $\frac{4}{6}$, $\frac{6}{9}$, $\frac{20}{30}$. The general principle here is quite clear. Stated roughly: Given a fraction, the fraction which results from multiplying the numerator and denominator by the same number is just another name for the same rational number. In general:

If m, n, *and* p *are integers and* n *and* p *are different from zero, then*

$$\frac{m}{n} = \frac{m \times p}{n \times p}.$$

There is a slightly different way to look at this same proposition. If *m* and *n* are integers and *m* $\neq$ o, then *m/n* is the rational number which

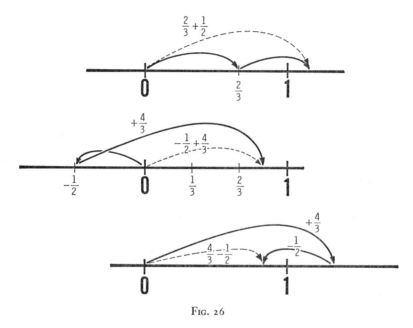

Fɪɢ. 26

is their quotient; that is, it is the answer to the question, ? $\times n = m$. But, if multiplication of rational numbers is to be commutative and associative, then the answer to this question is surely the same as the answer to the question, ? $\times (n \times p) = m \times p$. We will return to this point of view after we describe multiplication of rational numbers.

The usual algorithms for addition and subtraction of rational numbers are easy to explain. The simplest description of the addition and subtraction of rational numbers is by means of the number line. It is precisely the same description as that given for integers. Figure 26 shows examples. It is not entirely obvious from the preceding description just how to compute the sum and difference of rational numbers; more precisely, if we have the fractions which name two rational numbers, how can we find fractions naming their sum and difference? But there is no real difficulty here. It is quite clear from the number line description that, for example, $\frac{2}{8} + \frac{5}{8} = \frac{7}{8}$ and $\frac{7}{9} - \frac{3}{9} = \frac{4}{9}$. In general, there is no difficulty if the two fractions have the same denominator. We use the fact:

If m, n, *and* p *are integers and* n *is different from* o, *then*

$$\frac{m}{n} + \frac{p}{n} = \frac{m + p}{n}.$$

But, simply by renaming the numbers, each such calculation can be reduced to this problem. For example:

$$\frac{2}{3} + \frac{1}{2} = \frac{2 \times 2}{3 \times 2} + \frac{1 \times 3}{2 \times 3} = \frac{4 + 3}{6} = \frac{7}{6}$$

and

$$\frac{5}{7} - \frac{2}{3} = \frac{5 \times 3}{7 \times 3} - \frac{2 \times 7}{3 \times 7} = \frac{1}{21}.$$

We can describe how the multiplication of rational numbers should be defined on the basis of the number line picture. We have seen that $\frac{2}{3}$ can be thought of as $2 \times \frac{1}{3}$, and similarly $\frac{4}{5}$ is $4 \times \frac{1}{5}$. Consequently, if multiplication is to be commutative and associative, we should have $\frac{2}{3} \times \frac{4}{5} = 2 \times \frac{1}{3} \times 4 \times \frac{1}{5} = 8 \times \frac{1}{15} = \frac{8}{15}$. In general:

If m, n, p, *and* q *are integers and* n *and* q *are not zero, then*

$$\frac{m}{n} \times \frac{p}{q} = \frac{m \times p}{n \times q}.$$

There is another description of rational numbers which is intuitively useful. We think of square red cards and square black cards, all of the same size. We now equip ourselves with scotch tape and scissors and adopt the following rules for constructing rectangular cards. We can cut up any square or rectangular card by straight cuts which are parallel to an edge and which divide the card into parts that are of exactly the same shape and size (that are congruent, in the terminology of geometry). We consider all of the rectangular cards that can be obtained by taping cards of the same color together along a common edge. We agree, in much the same fashion as in the description of integers, that black and red annihilate each other. That is, a black card annihilates a red card of the same size and shape, and itself, simultaneously. We now attach a rational number to each of the cards that can be constructed in such a way that if one card can be cut up and reassembled so that it is of the same size and shape as another, then the same number is attached to each. Thus a rational number is associated with a collection of cards, any one of which can be cut up and reassembled to match any other.

We give some examples of cards and of the attached rational numbers (Figure 27). Here is another illustration (Figure 28) showing cards and the rational numbers which are attached to them. (The outline of the unit square is indicated in each case.) The general pattern here is clear.

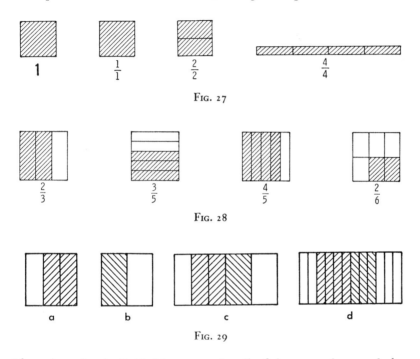

FIG. 27

FIG. 28

FIG. 29

If a unit region is divided into 5 cards, all of the same shape and size, then each of these is attached to the number $\frac{1}{5}$, and a rectangle which consists of three of these is attached to the number $\frac{3}{5}$.

Addition of rational numbers can be described in the same manner as that of integers. For example, in Figure 29 the card **a** can be joined to the card **b**, if they are of the same color, to obtain the card **c**, and the sum of $\frac{2}{3}$ and $\frac{1}{2}$ is the rational number attached to the latter card. It is not hard to find a name for this number, because

$$\frac{2}{3} = \frac{2 \times 2}{3 \times 2} \quad \text{and} \quad \frac{1}{2} = \frac{1 \times 3}{2 \times 3}, \quad \text{and hence} \quad \frac{1}{2} + \frac{1}{3} = \frac{4}{6} + \frac{3}{6} = \frac{7}{6}.$$

Pictorially, we have: card **d**. If cards of opposite colors are joined, then we must wait for the "mutual destruct" mechanism to operate to find their sum.

This description of the rational numbers gives a very nice picture for multiplication. To find, for example, $\frac{2}{3} \times \frac{4}{5}$, we take a card which goes with $\frac{2}{3}$, divide it into 5 congruent parts and recombine 4 of them. Here is a picture (Figure 30). It is almost self-evident from this description that multiplication is commutative (rotate the last picture through 90°) and the following picture (Figure 31) suggests that multiplication distributes over addition.

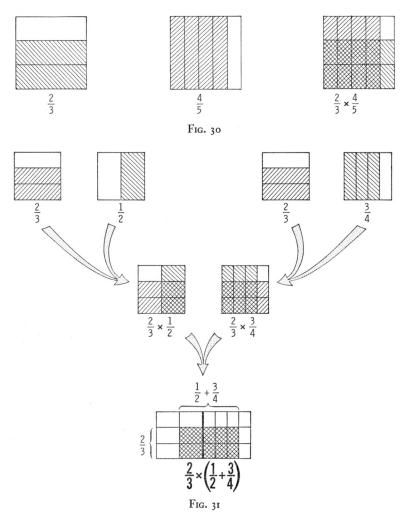

Fig. 30

Fig. 31

Division of rational numbers is defined in terms of multiplication. The quotient,

$$\frac{2}{3} \div \frac{5}{7} \quad \text{or} \quad \frac{\dfrac{2}{3}}{\dfrac{5}{7}},$$

is defined to be the answer to the question, $? \times \frac{5}{7} = \frac{2}{3}$. It is easy to see that there is a rational number which furnishes the answer to this question. Here is one way of seeing this. The number which when multiplied by $\frac{5}{7}$ gives 1 is $\frac{7}{5}$, because $\frac{7}{5} \times \frac{5}{7} = \frac{35}{35}$, and "$\frac{35}{35}$" is just another name for 1. Consequently, if we multiply $\frac{5}{7}$ by $\frac{7}{5}$ and then by $\frac{2}{3}$, that is, by $\frac{7}{5} \times \frac{2}{3}$, the result is certainly $1 \times \frac{2}{3} = \frac{2}{3}$. In other words,

$$\frac{\dfrac{2}{3}}{\dfrac{5}{7}} = \frac{7}{5} \times \frac{2}{3}.$$

There is another way to state the argument. Computing,

$$\frac{\dfrac{2}{3}}{\dfrac{5}{7}} = \frac{\dfrac{2}{3} \times \dfrac{7}{5}}{\dfrac{5}{7} \times \dfrac{7}{5}} = \frac{\dfrac{2}{3} \times \dfrac{7}{5}}{1}$$

which is $\frac{2}{3} \times \frac{7}{5}$ because this quotient is just the number which when multiplied by 1 gives $\frac{2}{3} \times \frac{7}{5}$. In general we see:

If m, n, p, *and* q *are integers and* n, p, *and* q *are different from* 0, *then*

$$\frac{\dfrac{m}{n}}{\dfrac{p}{q}} = \frac{m}{n} \times \frac{q}{p}.$$

It is clear from the preceding that, for every rational number *m/n* other than 0, there is a multiplicative inverse, or reciprocal; that is, a number (namely *n/m*) which when multiplied by *m/n* gives 1.

There is yet another way of thinking about rational numbers which we briefly sketch. We can think of the number $\frac{2}{3}$, for example, as the operation of taking two-thirds of the members of a set. Of course, this operation of taking $\frac{2}{3}$ is not defined for all sets; the set must be one which can be split up into three subsets which are equivalent. Thus $\frac{2}{3}$ of a set consisting of 24 members is (since 24 can be split up into 3 sets, each having 8 members) a set which consists of 2 sets of 8 members, or a set of 16 members. This operation is the same as taking $\frac{4}{6}$ of a set, whenever the set can be split into 6 equivalent subsets.[14] The product of $\frac{2}{3}$ and $\frac{1}{2}$ is the operation of first taking $\frac{2}{3}$ of a set and then taking $\frac{1}{2}$ of the resulting set. It is easy to see that this is the same operation as taking $\frac{2}{6}$ of the set. Addition has a simple description. The operation of taking $\frac{1}{2} + \frac{1}{3}$ of a set is the operation of taking one-half the set, then taking two-thirds the original set, and joining the resulting sets. It is worth noticing that this definition permits one, just by counting and splitting sets into equivalent subsets, to find the sum and product of rational numbers. An algorithm for computation can then be considered to be a method of predicting the outcome of a physical experiment, and the laws which rational numbers obey can be considered to be verifiable physical principles.

In conclusion, we give a summary of some of the most important properties that the system of rational numbers can be shown to have.

Properties of Rational Numbers

The operation of $+$ gives, for every pair (r,s) of rational numbers, a rational number r + s. The operation $+$ is commutative and associative. There is a $+$ identity, o, such that r + o = r for every rational number r. Each rational number r has a $+$ inverse, its negative $^-$r, such that r + $^-$r = o.	*The operation of $\times$ gives, for every pair (r,s) of rational numbers, a rational number r $\times$ s. The operation $\times$ is commutative and associative. There is a $\times$ identity, 1, such that r $\times$ 1 = r for every rational number r. Each rational number r other than o has a $\times$ inverse, its reciprocal, 1/x, such that r $\times$ 1/r = 1.*

Multiplication distributes over addition. Each rational number is just one of the following: positive, negative, or o. The sum and product of positive rational numbers are positive.

DECIMALS

The Hindu-Arabic (decimal) notation, an extraordinarily convenient method of naming counting numbers, can be extended to give names to some of the rational numbers. The idea is simple. We will count not only by ones, tens, tens of tens, etc., but also by tenths, tenths of tenths, and so on. We think of column headings as follows,

---

14. The operation of taking $\frac{3}{2}$ of a set is a little tricky: we split a set into 2 matching subsets, and then take 3 of these. That is, the operation of taking $\frac{3}{2}$ of a set involves creating another "half set."

$$10 \times 10 \qquad 10 \qquad 1 \qquad \frac{1}{10} \qquad \frac{1}{10} \times \frac{1}{10} \qquad \frac{1}{10} \times \frac{1}{10} \times \frac{1}{10}$$

tens of tens   tens   ones   tenths   tenths of tenths

We single out the "ones column" in naming a number by putting a period (decimal point) after the ones digit. Thus 23.4 is $2 \times 10 + 3 \times 1 + 4 \times \frac{1}{10}$. Notice that each successive column is labeled with a number which is $\frac{1}{10}$ that labeling the preceding column. A digit in the tens column names a number which is $\frac{1}{10}$ that given by the same digit in the 10×10 column. The number names we get in this way are *decimal fractions*.

It is convenient to shorten this notation by using exponents. We agree that $10^2 = 10 \times 10$, and $10^3 = 10 \times 10 \times 10$, and more generally that 10^n, for any counting number n, is the number

$$\overbrace{10 \times 10 \times \ldots \times 10}^{n \text{ times}}.$$

In particular, $10^1 = 10$. Notice that if m and n are counting numbers other than o, then $10^m \times 10^n$ is just the product of $m + n$ tens; that is, $10^m \times 10^n = 10^{m+n}$. We can extend this notation to get rid of fractions such as "$\frac{1}{10}$" and "$\frac{1}{10} \times \frac{1}{10}$." We are going to define 10^0, 10^{-1}, 10^{-2}, and so on. How should this be done? The decision which has been made rests on the fact that $10^m \times 10^n = 10^{m+n}$ for positive integers m and n. We want to arrange the definition so that this equality holds for *all* integers m and n, positive or negative or o. In particular, we want $10^m \times 10^0 = 10^{m+0}$, which is 10^m. Consequently, we define 10^0 to be 1. Proceeding, we should like $10^m \times 10^{-m} = 10^{m+-m}$ which is 10^0, or 1. That is, we want 10^m to be $1/10^m$. Thus we define 10^{-1} to be $\frac{1}{10}$, 10^{-2} to be $1/10^2$, and, in general, $10^{-m} = 1/10^m$ for all counting numbers m. It turns out (we shall not give the simple argument needed to establish this fact) that this definition is successful and that $10^m \times 10^n = 10^{m+n}$ for all integers m and n. Thus for example, $10^{-2} \times 10^{-3} = 10^{-2+-3}$ and $10^5 \times 10^{-2} = 10^{5+-2}$.

The numbers 10^3, 10^2, 10^1, 10^0, 10^{-1}, 10^{-2}, . . . and so on, are called *powers of ten*.

If we use the exponent notation we can write 23.4 as $2 \times 10^1 + 3 \times 10^0 + 4 \times 10^{-1}$. Here are more examples: $473.51 = 4 \times 10^2 + 7 \times 10^1 + 3 \times 10^0 + 5 \times 10^{-1} + 1 + 10^{-2}$, $.0004 = 0 \times 10^{-1} + 0 \times 10^{-2} + 0 \times 10^{-3} + 4 \times 10^{-4}$. In general, decimal fractions represent (finite) sums of integer powers of ten each multiplied by one of the numbers 0, 1, . . . , 8, or 9. The exponent notation permits us to compute easily the product of a number by a power of ten. We need only the distributive law and the fact that multiplication is commutative and associative. For example,

$$10^2 \times (234.2) = 10^2 \times (2 \times 10^2 + 3 \times 10^1 + 4 \times 10^0 + 2 \times 10^{-1})$$
$$= 2 \times 10^4 + 3 \times 10^3 + 4 \times 10^2 + 2 \times 10^1 = 23{,}420$$
$$10^{-1} \times (2.3) = 10^{-1} \times (2 \times 10^0 + 3 \times 10^{-1}) = 2 \times 10^{-1} + 3$$
$$\times 10^{-2} = .23$$

Stated roughly: To get the decimal name for the product of a number and a power of ten, say 10^m, just shift the decimal points m places to the right in the decimal name of the number. For example, $10^{-3} \times 234.15 = .23415$ and $10^2 \times .0015 = .15$.

There are two consequences of this "decimal-point shifting" property that we want to point out. First, by multiplying by a suitably chosen power of 10, we can always shift the decimal point so that it sits just to the right of the first nonzero digit. In other words, each decimal fraction represents the product of a number between 1 and 10 and a power of ten. For example: $234.15 = 2.3415 \times 10^2$ and $.0032 = 3.2 \times 10^{-3}$. The scientific name (scientific notation) for a number is the name which is in the form: (decimal name of a number between 1 and 10) $\times$ (power of ten). Scientific notation is almost always used in scientific discussion. It is just simpler to say, for example, that the speed of light is 3×10^{10} centimeters per second than to say that it is $30{,}000{,}000{,}000$ centimeters per second.

It is also possible to draw another consequence from the "decimal-point shifting." Given any decimal fraction (consisting of a finite number of digits) we can, by shifting the decimal point to the right far enough, get the decimal name of a counting number. In other words, if a number has a decimal name with a finite number of digits, then it is a counting number times a power of ten. For example: $3.245 = 3245 \times 10^{-3} =$

$\frac{3245}{10^3}$ and $.0017 = 17 \times 10^{-4} = \frac{17}{10^4}$. In general, the numbers that can be named by decimals with a finite number of digits are just the quotients of counting numbers and powers of ten.

The computation of sums, differences, and products of numbers using decimal fractions is quite straightforward. No new ideas are needed and we do not go into details. There is, however, something new that comes up with division and we want to discuss this.

Recall that (the axiom on counting) if n is a counting number and d is a counting number larger than one, then there are unique counting numbers q and r such that the remainder r is less than d and $n = d \times q + r$. The number q is the partial quotient of n divided by d, and the algorithm for division gives a method of finding q and r. Thus, for example, if we try to divide 32 by 6, we find that $32 = 6 \times 5 + 2$. The computation might be arranged like this:

$$6\overline{/32}$$
$$30 \qquad 5 \times 6 \qquad 32 = 5 \times 6 + 2$$
$$2$$

Here is the point: there is no need to stop the computation at this stage. We might continue as follows:

$$6\overline{/32.}$$
$$30 \qquad 5 \times 6$$
$$2 \qquad\qquad 32 = 6 \times 5.3 + .2$$
$$1.8 \quad .3 \times 6$$
$$.2$$

or we might go further, as follows:

$$6\overline{/32}$$
$$30 \quad \cdots\cdots\cdots \quad 5. \times 6$$

$$2$$
$$1.8 \quad \cdots\cdots\cdots \quad .3 \times 6$$

$$.2$$
$$.18 \quad \cdots\cdots\cdots \quad .03 \times 6$$

$$.02$$
$$.018 \cdots\cdots\cdots \quad .003 \times 6$$

$$.002$$

$$32 = 6 \times 5.333 + .002$$

It seems intuitively obvious that by continuing we can get as small a remainder as we wish! This is in fact the case. We sometimes say that 5.333 is an approximation to $\frac{32}{6}$. In general, it is true that any rational number can be approximated as closely as we wish by numbers of the form (counting number) × (power of ten).

There is another observation that we want to make about the preceding process. It is perfectly obvious that $\frac{32}{6}$ wants to be 5.3333333333 . . . . . . and so on, with the "threes" continuing forever. That is, the decimal name for $\frac{32}{6}$ should be an infinite (nonending) decimal. More generally, the division algorithm gives us a way to assign to each positive rational number (i.e., each quotient of nonzero counting numbers) a decimal expansion which may or may not have a finite number of digits.

There is one other curious fact about the preceding computation. The decimal for $\frac{32}{6}$ has a remarkably unimaginative pattern; it just goes on with "threes" forever. If we try another example, for instance $\frac{19}{11}$, we find that the decimal expansion is 1.727272727272727272 . . . . and it just goes on repeating "72." (Do this computation for yourself and you'll see why.) Such a decimal is called a *repeating decimal*. That is, a repeating decimal is one which, perhaps after some initial digits, consists of a single pattern of digits repeated over and over.

It seems possible that every rational number is represented by a repeating decimal. It turns out that this is the case. We shall not go into the argument in detail, but we do want to suggest the reason this happens. Think of performing the division algorithm to find the decimal expansion for $\frac{38}{79}$. Think of the usual abbreviated form of presenting the calculation, and think of the remainders you get after each subtraction. What are the possible remainders? They are just the numbers 0, 1, 2, 3, ... 77, 78 (actually, the remainders are these numbers multiplied by powers of ten). What happens when the same remainder occurs twice? Can you think of a reason why the decimal expansion for $\frac{38}{79}$ should repeat?

One might very well ask whether *every* repeating decimal can be gotten as the decimal expansion for some rational number. Let us indicate by an example why this is, in fact, the case. Suppose we are given the decimal expansion: 341.21212121212121212 . . . . with "12" repeated forever. The trick is this. Let us call the number this decimal represents n, and then observe that whatever n is, the decimal expansion for 100 × n should be 34121.212121 . . . . Thus we have

$$100 \times n = 34121.21212121 \ldots \ldots$$
$$n = 341.21212121 \ldots \ldots \ldots$$

Subtracting, we get $99 \times n = (34121 - 341)$, and therefore we should have n equal to the quotient

$$\frac{(34131 - 341)}{99}.$$

This sort of argument can be used to show generally that every positive rational number can be represented by a repeating decimal, and that every repeating decimal represents a rational number.

What, if anything, is represented by a decimal which doesn't repeat? For example, suppose we describe a decimal as follows: after the decimal point, put a "1," then a "0," then a "10," then a "100," and so on. This decimal does not repeat and so it does not come from the division algorithm for a quotient of counting numbers. Does it represent any number?

In later mathematical study, we shall find that such decimals represent numbers of a new kind. The system of rational numbers will be enlarged to include these new numbers, and it will turn out that each of these has a decimal representation which will be a repeating decimal if and only if the number is rational. The enlarged system will be called the system of "real numbers" (the adjective "real" is a heritage from medieval metaphysics; it was not conceived possible that numbers other than these could exist).

There is a last question which we can discuss. Why should we bother with real numbers? Are not the rational numbers enough? One answer to this question goes back to the Greek mathematicians. Among the many properties of the real number system that the system of rational numbers fails to possess is the following: There is a real number whose square is 2. If one believes everything that has been said in this section, he can convince himself of this fact by recalling that the algorithm for computing square root which he has been taught gives him a way of computing the decimal corresponding to the square root of 2. On the other hand, an argument[15] constructed by the Greeks shows that there are no counting numbers m and n such that

$$\frac{m}{n} \times \frac{m}{n} = 2.$$

15. Here is a brief indication of an argument which shows that it cannot happen that $(m/n \times m/n) = 2$ for counting numbers m and n. The proof is by contradiction. Suppose that $(m/n \times m/n) = 2$, or, what is the same thing, that $m \times m = 2 \times n \times n$. Now look at the prime factorization of $m \times m$, and of $2 \times n \times n$. Persuade yourself that $m \times m$ is the product of an even number of prime numbers and that $2 \times n \times n$ is the product of an odd number.

Part II

A$_{LGEBRAIC}$ S$_{YSTEMS}$

RICHARD A. DEAN

In this part of the chapter we shall take an algebraic look at some common mathematical systems appearing explicitly or implicitly in many secondary mathematical curricula.

First, here is a blueprint for any mathematical system. A mathematical system consists of the following:

1. A set of elements
2. Some (or no) operations under which the set is closed
3. Some (or no) relations which are defined on the elements of S
4. The laws or axioms which govern the operations and relations and which serve to characterize the system
5. As many properties or consequences of these axioms (4) as can be proved

In one notable case, which we shall study later, there is a vital interrelation between two such systems. In that situation one system "operates" on the other; together they make a vector space.

GROUPS

One of the simplest and perhaps the most basic algebraic system is that of a group. Here are some examples of groups.

Example 1. The symmetries of an equilateral triangle. Consider the equilateral triangle of Figure 1. A symmetry of the triangle is any mapping of the triangle into itself which preserves distance. We may rotate the triangle 120° in either direction about its center, or we may reflect the triangle about any one of its bisectors, *A*, *B*, *C*. Having performed one symmetry, we may perform another. It turns out that there are just six symmetries (including the one which does nothing but leave every point fixed!). The elements of the group are the symmetries. The operation on the set S of symmetries is that of performing one symmetry after another—that is, composition of symmetries.

130

The requirement that distance be preserved means that the distance between two points after the symmetry mapping must be the same as before. Now, since each point of the triangle is to be mapped into some point of the triangle, and distance is to be preserved, it is not too difficult to see that each vertex must be mapped into itself or another vertex. This

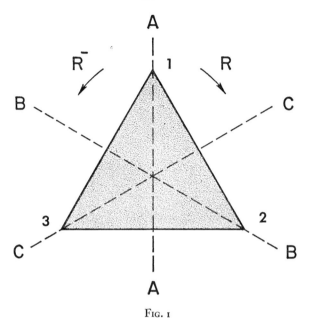

Fig. 1

in fact gives a nice way of describing the effect of any symmetry. Number the positions of the vertices 1, 2, 3, as shown in Figure 1. Now, for example, to record the symmetry of a rotation of 120° in the clockwise direction, we write

$$\begin{matrix} 1 & 2 & 3 \\ 2 & 3 & 1 \end{matrix}$$

to indicate that the vertex in position 1 is mapped into the vertex in position 2, and so on. In this way we can list all the symmetries

$$I = \begin{pmatrix} 1 & 2 & 3 \\ 1 & 2 & 3 \end{pmatrix}, \quad \text{the identity symmetry}$$

$$R = \begin{pmatrix} 1 & 2 & 3 \\ 2 & 3 & 1 \end{pmatrix}, \quad \text{the rotation of 120° clockwise}$$

$$R^- = \begin{pmatrix} 1 & 2 & 3 \\ 3 & 2 & 1 \end{pmatrix}, \quad \text{the rotation of 120° counterclockwise}$$

$$A = \begin{pmatrix} 1 & 2 & 3 \\ 1 & 3 & 2 \end{pmatrix}, \quad \text{the reflection about bisector } A$$

$$B = \begin{pmatrix} 1 & 2 & 3 \\ 3 & 2 & 1 \end{pmatrix}, \quad \text{the reflection about bisector } B$$

$$C = \begin{pmatrix} 1 & 2 & 3 \\ 2 & 1 & 3 \end{pmatrix}, \quad \text{the reflection about bisector } C.$$

The result of first performing symmetry R and then A is $\begin{pmatrix} 1 & 2 & 3 \\ 3 & 2 & 1 \end{pmatrix} = B$, which we write as $RA = B$.

Exercise 1: Fill in the table of Figure 2 with all possible combinations of the symmetries of the triangle.

	I	R	R̄	A	B	C
I	·					
R				B		
R̄						
A						
B						
C						

Fig. 2

Exercise 2: Compute in this way all the symmetries of the square.

Example 2. The rigid transformations of the plane. The elements of the group are the transformations. It turns out that these can be described by translations, rotations, and reflections of the plane. Again the operation is that of *composition* in which one transformation is performed after another. This group is very important in the study of geometry. In particular, many important geometric properties, such as congruence, can be studied from the group point of view. Indeed, two geometric shapes are congruent if and only if one can be transformed into another by an element of this group.

Example 3. The integers. Here the group operation is addition.

Example 4. The nonzero rational numbers. Here the operation is multiplication.

Example 5. The nonzero elements in mod 5 arithmetic. Here the operation is multiplication. Refer to the table on page 109 about "clock arithmetic."

The formal definition of a group now follows.

A *group* is a nonempty set S and a binary operation (here denoted (o)) defined on S so that

(1) S is closed under (o), and the operation (o) is associative.

(2) There is an element e such that $e \, o \, s = s \, o \, e = s$ for all $s \in S$.

(3) If e is an element satisfying (2), then for all elements $s \in S$ there exists t such that $s \, o \, t = t \, o \, s = e$.

An element e satisfying (2) is called an *identity* element. We can prove some elementary results which help to clarify the axioms.

Property 1. The identity element is unique.

Proof. If e and f are identity elements, then

$$e \, o \, s = s \, o \, e = s \quad \text{for all } s \in S \quad \text{and}$$
$$f \, o \, s = s \, o \, f = s \quad \text{for all } s \in S.$$

Set $s = f$ in the first and $s = e$ in the second to obtain

$$e \, o \, f = f \, o \, e = f \quad \text{and} \quad f \, o \, e = e \, o \, f = e .$$

Thus $f = e \, o \, f = e$.

An element t such that $s \, o \, t = t \, o \, s = e$ is called an *inverse* for s.

Property 2. For each s there is only one inverse element.

Proof. Suppose $s \, o \, t = t \, o \, s = e = r \, o \, s = s \, o \, r$.

Then $t = t \, o \, e = t \, o \, (s \, o \, r) = (t \, o \, s) \, o \, r = e \, o \, r = r$.

The unique element which is the inverse of s is denoted by s^{-1} (or sometimes by $-s$). In example 1, the identity is I, and the inverses of the elements are as follows: The inverse of R is $R-$ and, conversely, every other element is its own inverse.

In example 2, the identity element is 0 and the inverse at a is $(-a)$.

In example 3, the identity element is 1 and the inverse of a/b is b/a.

Exercise 3: Prove that every equation $a \, o \, x = b$ has a unique solution.

Groups are encountered explicitly or implicitly in almost every mathematical situation. They made their historical debut in the study of the theory of equations. Abel (1902–1949) and Galois (1811–1832) used them to determine which equations had solutions which could be expressed in terms of radicals.

Here is still one more example which is amusing because the group turns out to be exactly like example 1.

Example 6. Let S be the set of six functions

$$I: \ I(x) = x$$

$$R: \ R(x) = \frac{1}{1-x}$$

$$-R: \ R(R(x)) = \frac{1-x}{-x}$$

$$A: \ A(x) = \frac{1}{2}$$

$$B: \ A(R(x)) = 1 - x$$

$$C: \ A(-R(x)) = \frac{-x}{1-x}$$

The operation is that of composition of functions as we have indicated in the definitions of $-R$, B, and C.

As example 1 shows, the group operation is not commutative. In example 1, $RA = B$ while $AR = C$. However, there are many cases as seen in examples 3, 4, and 5 which are commutative. These groups are called *abelian* in honor of Abel.

Definition. An abelian group is one in which $x \ o \ y = y \ o \ x$ for all $x,y \in S$.

FIELDS

The concept of a field and the field axioms are the cornerstone of high school algebra. The notion of a *field* is a generalization or abstraction of the system of rational numbers. A leisurely discussion of the field axioms appears on page 124. Using the group concept, we can give a telegraphic statement.

A *field* is a set S having at least two elements, which is closed under two operations, customarily denoted by $(+)$ and $(\cdot)$ and called *addition* and *multiplication*, respectively, such that

(1) Under $(+)$ the set S is an abelian group. (The identity element is called "zero", denoted 0, and the inverse of a, by $-a$.)

(2) Under $(\cdot)$ the set of nonzero elements of S form an abelian group. (The identity element is called "one," denoted 1. The inverse of a is denoted by a^{-1}.)

(3) The distributive law $a \cdot (b + c) = (a \cdot b) + (a \cdot c)$ holds for all $a,b,c \in S$.

Example 7. The integers mod 2. The set $S = \{0,1\}$ and addition and multiplication are defined by the tables

+	0	1
0	0	1
1	1	0

·	0	1
0	0	0
1	0	1

Example 7 is a popular one because it is the basic internal arithmetic used in some computers. Example 7 generalizes to the integers mod p where p is any *prime*. The operation tables are computed by ordinary arithmetic modified only when the sum (or product) exceeds p, in which case the sum (or product) is divided by p and the *remainder* is entered on the table. For example, in the integers mod 11, we have $9 \cdot 7 = 8$ since $9 \cdot 7 = 63$ and $63 = 11 \cdot 5 + 8$. Multiplicative inverses can be found from the Euclidean algorithm. For example, in the integers mod 11, to find 9^{-1}, that is, to find a solution to $9x = 1$, we solve in the integers $9x + 11y = 1$. Thus

$$9 \cdot 5 + 11(-4) = 1 \quad \text{and so}$$
$$9 \cdot 5 = 1 \ (\text{mod } 11), \text{ or } 9^{-1} = 5.$$

It is important to do the arithmetic modulo a *prime*. If a prime is not chosen, then a field will not result because some nonzero elements will not possess multiplicative inverses. For example, in the integers mod 6, there is no solution to $2 \cdot x = 1 \ (\text{mod } 6)$. The case $p = 5$ appears explicitly on page 117.

Example 8. Real numbers of the form $a + b\sqrt{2}$ where a and b are rational numbers. Thus $(1 + 3\sqrt{2})(2 + 5\sqrt{2}) = 36 + 12\sqrt{2}$ and $(1 + 3\sqrt{2})^{-1} = -(1 - 3\sqrt{2})/17$.

This generalizes to the set of numbers of the form $a + b\sqrt{d}$ where d is a fixed rational number and a and b are any rational numbers. Indeed, in a similar fashion you can show that

$$S = \{a + b\sqrt[3]{2} + c\sqrt[3]{4} \text{ where } a,b,c \text{ are rational}\}$$

is a field. The tricky part is to produce the multiplicative inverse.

Other examples of fields which we shall now discuss in more detail are the real numbers and the complex numbers. First, however, we must discuss the relation of "order" on the rational numbers.

RATIONAL NUMBERS AND ORDER

An important additional feature of the field of rational numbers is *order*, the relation of "less than," or "greater than." This notion has already been discussed in some detail on pages 84–86, and now we shall simply list the defining properties for an order relation on a field.

Definition. A field F is said to be ordered by a relation, usually denoted by $\leq$, if and only if the relation satisfies:

1. $a \leq a$ for all a in F.
2. $a \leq b$ and $b \leq a$ always implies $a = b$.
3. $a \leq b$ and $b \leq c$ always implies $a \leq c$.
4. For any two numbers, a and b, either $a \leq b$ or $b \leq a$.
5. Whenever $a \leq b$, then $a + c \leq b + c$.
6. Whenever $a \leq b$ and $0 \leq r$, then $a\,r \leq b\,r$.

Here is one of the consequences of these axioms.

Theorem. If a field is ordered, then $x^2 \geq 0$ for all x.

Proof. Either $0 \leq x$ or $0 \leq -x$. Why? Apply (6) to conclude $0 \leq x^2$ or $0 \leq (-x)^2$, and since $x^2 = (-x)^2$, the conclusion holds.

Exercise 4. Verify that if for rational numbers we define $a/b \leq c/d$ if and only if $a\,d \leq b\,c$, then the rationals are ordered.

Exercise 5. Verify that there is only one way to order the rationals if we require that for any two integers a, b, then $a \leq b$ as rational numbers if and only if $a \leq b$ as integers. Show that another ordering is possible for the rationals if this condition is dropped.

Not every field can be ordered by a relation satisfying all the properties listed above. For example, the finite field of the integers mod 2 cannot be ordered. A more significant and important example is the field of complex numbers. If you stop to think about it, you have never seen "inequalities" like $1 + i < 2i$. More of that later.

There is an intimate connection between the rational numbers and geometry. We associate each rational number with a point on the number line. These points can be constructed by straightedge and compass once a point corresponding to 0 and one corresponding to 1 have been chosen. This is a familiar exercise from high school geometry. In what follows we shall refer to rationals both as numbers and as points on a number line. It is important for us to recall now that this process seems to fill up the line. Indeed, just by using a pencil you can make enough dots representing rational numbers to give the appearance of a solid line.

Mathematically this is expressed by saying that the rational numbers are *dense*. One attribute of this property is that between any two rationals there is another rational. Indeed, $(a + b)/2$ is a rational if a and b are rationals and it lies between a and b as shown in Figure 3. Another attribute of the density of the rationals is that given any point on the number line, there is a rational number as close to it as you please. If P is the point, then for all integers n there is a rational number r such that the distance from P to r is less than $1/n$, as indicated in Figure 4.

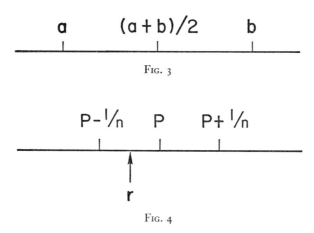

FIG. 3

FIG. 4

We know that certain points on the number line cannot be labeled by rational numbers. For example, we can construct a square of side 1 unit and then lay off its diagonal (of length $\sqrt{2}$) on the number line (see Figure 5). The point P cannot be assigned a rational number. This is so because it was shown earlier (page 128) that $\sqrt{2}$ is not a rational number. To find a mathematical system rich enough to provide names for all points on the number line and to reflect the arithmetic operations implied by the geometry, we must construct a larger system.

THE REAL NUMBER SYSTEM

The rigorous construction of the real numbers is not a truly difficult task, but it is lengthy. There is not space here to give even an intuitive sketch of the entire process. We shall discuss the two chief ways of going about the construction, cite references, and conclude with the fundamental property of the real number system. Each method of construction employs one of the key properties of the real numbers.

The first method of construction stems from and yields the usual decimal notation. Consider the numbers

$$a = .125$$
$$b = .125125125 \quad \text{(the repeating decimal)}$$
$$c = .1250125001250001250000125000001250000001\,25 \dots$$

The number a is rational. Indeed, $a = 125/1000 = 1/8$. The number b is rational since, among other things, it is a repeating decimal. To express

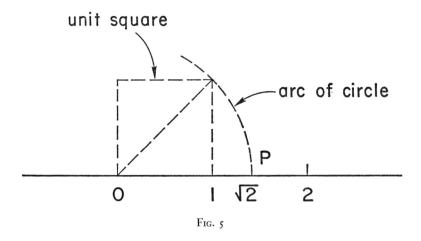

unit square

arc of circle

P

O   1   √2   2

F$_{IG}$. 5

b as the quotient of two integers, we note that $1000b = 125 \cdot 125125$ and thus $1000b - b = 125$. So $999b = 125$; hence $b = 125/999$. This trick works for any repeating decimal and is discussed on page 129.

We can also obtain b as a sequence of closer and closer approximations by *rational* numbers.

First approximation:

$$b_1 = .1 \qquad\qquad = 1/10.$$

Second approximation:

$$b_2 = .12 \qquad\qquad = 1/10 + 2/100$$
$$\text{etc.} \quad b_3 = .125 \qquad\qquad = 1/10 + 2/100 + 5/1000$$
$$b_4 = .1251 \qquad\qquad = 1/10 + 2/100 + 5/1000 + 1/10000$$
$$b_5 = .12512 \qquad\qquad = b_4 + 2 \cdot 10^{-5}.$$
$$\text{etc.}$$

Here is another approximating sequence:

$$B_1 = .125 \qquad = 125 \cdot 10^{-3}$$
$$B_2 = .125125 \qquad = 125 \cdot 10^{-3} + 125 \cdot 10^{-6}$$
$$B_3 = .125125125 = B_2 + 10^{-9}$$

etc $\quad .$

$$B_n = B_{n-1} + 125 \cdot 10^{-3n} \text{ and so on } .$$

This last sequence $\{B_n\}$ leads to the infinite series

$$b = \sum_{n=1}^{\infty} 125 . 10^{-3n}$$

which is a geometric series and the sum can be determined. Indeed, b is the limit of the sequence $\{B_n\}$. The number b is also the limit of the sequence $\{b_m\}$ which too can be expressed as an infinite series, although not a geometric one. We emphasize again that the numbers B_n and b_m are rational numbers.

This sequential point of view is the only way the number c can be viewed. It is not a rational number for it does not "repeat." The numbers $1,2,5$ which reoccur are separated by longer and longer strings of zeros. Here is the approximating sequence for c:

$$c_1 = .1 \qquad = 1/10 \quad = 10^{-1}$$
$$c_2 = .12 \qquad = 12/100 = 10^{-1} + 2 \cdot 10^{-2}$$
$$c_3 = .125 \qquad = 10^{-1} + 2 \cdot 10^{-2} + 5 \cdot 10^{-3}$$
$$c_4 = .1250 \qquad = 10^{-1} + 2 \cdot 10^{-2} + 5 \cdot 10^{-3} + 0 \cdot 10^{-4}.$$
$$c_5 = .12501 \quad = 10^{-1} + 2 \cdot 10^{-2} + 5 \cdot 10^{-3} + 0 \cdot 10^{-4} + 1 \cdot 10^{-5}.$$

$$c_n = \sum_{k=1}^{n} x_k \, 10^{-k}$$

where the coefficients x_k are as indicated in the suggestion of the definition for c. The limit of the sequence of rational numbers, $\{c_n\}$, is c. Alternatively, we could have written the sequence as the infinite series

$$\sum_{k=1}^{\infty} x_k 10^{-k} .$$

This development of the real numbers uses infinite sequences of rationals to *represent* numbers. The special type of sequence used is called a *Cauchy sequence* after Cauchy (1789–1857), who was one of the first to recognize its importance in analysis. The sequences we have seen are examples of Cauchy sequences. It is clear even from these examples that a real number may be represented by several different sequences. This is one of the technical difficulties of this presentation. It turns out, however, that we can prove the important theorem.

Theorem. For every real number between 0 and 1 there is always one approximating sequence of the form

$$\left\{\sum_{k=1}^{n} e_k \, 10^{-k}\right\} = \sum_{k=1}^{\infty} e_k \, 10^{-k} \quad \text{where} \quad 0 \leq e_k \leq 9 \, .$$

This sequence is, of course, the decimal expansion for the real number. By adding an appropriate integer, we can obtain for every real number a decimal representation. Even these sequences are not unique since, for example, .999 and 1.000 are different sequences for 1.

Each decimal sequence yields a procedure for locating a point on the number line. Each successive decimal (term of the infinite series) gives a new approximation to the location of the number within a smaller interval.

Example 9. To locate c on the number line we would proceed as indicated in the sequence of enlargements shown in Figure 6.

The full story of the development of the real numbers through the use of sequence can be found in Feferman, *The Number Systems.*[1]

The other development of the real numbers is known as the "completion by cuts" which is attributed to Dedekind (1831–1916). The idea of this construction is essentially geometric and succeeds because it can identify the holes left on the number line after the rationals have been located. Each hole is "filled" by a new number. Since the rationals are dense, it seems plausible that if there is a point not named by a rational, then with respect to that point the set of rational numbers has been bisected—cut in two. We illustrate this with $\sqrt{2}$. Whatever point is named by $\sqrt{2}$, it seems reasonable that there should be a set of rationals greater than $\sqrt{2}$, and all the rest should be less than $\sqrt{2}$. This

1. S. Feferman, *The Number Systems* (San Francisco: W. H. Freeman & Co., 1964).

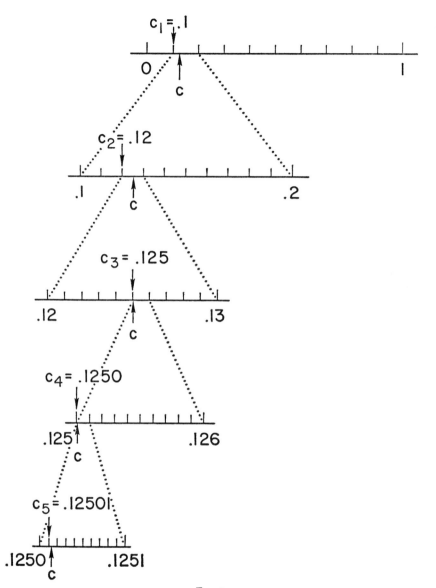

Fig. 6

bifurcation or cutting of the rational numbers into two nonempty disjoint sets somehow must identify $\sqrt{2}$. Specifically let

$$G = \{r : r^2 \geq 2 \text{ and } r \text{ rational}\} \quad (\text{``}G\text{''} \text{ stands for ``greater.''})$$

$$L = \{r : r^2 < 2 \text{ and } r \text{ rational}\} \quad (\text{``}L\text{''} \text{ stands for ``less.''})$$

Clearly G and L are nonempty and disjoint while $G \cup L$ equals the set of all rational numbers. Moreover, every element of G is greater than every element of L.

In the Dedekind cut procedure, the real numbers come into one-to-one correspondence with such pairs of subsets of rational numbers. This construction is given in detail in Landau, *Foundations of Analysis*.[2]

In this all-too-brief account of methods of construction of the real numbers, we have simply tried to indicate how real numbers can be identified with points on a line. Many technical problems await us; in particular, operations of addition and multiplication must be defined so that they are consistent with those of the rational numbers and so that all the field axioms are satisfied. The most significant difference between the rational numbers and the real numbers is discussed in the next section.

THE FUNDAMENTAL PROPERTY OF THE REAL NUMBERS

However, if the construction of the real numbers is made from the rational numbers, a mathematical system results which is

1. a field that contains the rational numbers as a proper subsystem,
2. ordered by ($\leq$) so that the order properties listed under the rational numbers hold for all real numbers, and in which
3. the least upper bound property holds.

It is property (3) which distinguishes the real numbers from all other systems. The least upper bound property says this:

If S is a nonempty subset of real numbers for which there is at least one number which is larger than all numbers in S, then there is a least (smallest) number which is larger than all numbers in S. To repeat more precisely: An upper bound for S is a number which is greater than or equal to each number in S. The *least* upper bound for S is an upper bound that is less than all other upper bounds for S. The least upper bound for S may be a member of S.

2. Edmund G. H. Landau, *Foundations of Analysis* (Translation: Bronx, N.Y.: Chelsea Publishing Co., 1963).

To illustrate this principle, we shall use it to show that in the set of real numbers there exists a square root for 2. To begin with, let

S = the set of all rational numbers r such that $r^2 < 2$.

There is at least one number which is larger than all the numbers of S. We need only exhibit one whose square is larger than 2; it is not hard to show that $2^2 = 4 > 2$. Indeed,

Lemma 1. Any positive number k such that $k^2 \geq 2$ is an upper bound for S.

Proof. If $0 < k < u$, it follows that $k^2 < u^2$. On the other hand, if r is in S, then $r^2 < 2$; hence if r is in S, and $2 \leq k^2$, then $r \leq k$.

The least upper bound property now guarantees that S has a least upper bound which we denote by b. We shall now prove that $b^2 = 2$. First we need one other principle about least upper bounds.

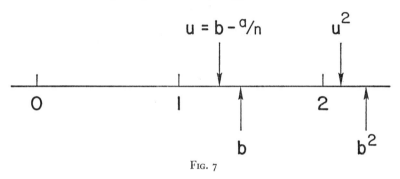

FIG. 7

Lemma 2. If $v < b$, then there exists a number r in S such that $v < r \leq b$.

Proof. If $v < b$, then v cannot be an upper bound for S, since b is the *least* upper bound for S. But this means that there is some r in S such that $v < r$ and $r \leq b$ since b is an upper bound for S.

The proof now follows in two stages.

Stage 1. We prove that $b^2 \leq 2$.

Suppose to the contrary that $b^2 > 2$. We shall show that there is a positive number, u, less than b, whose square exceeds 2. Thus by Lemma 1, u would be an upper bound for S, but less than b—a contradiction.

Let $a = b^2 - 2 > 0$. Choose a positive integer n so that the following two conditions are satisfied:

$$n > 2b, \text{ or equivalently } 1 > 2b/n \text{ and so that}$$
$$n > a/b, \text{ or equivalently } b - a/n > 0 .$$

These choices are illustrated in Figure 7. Let $u = b - a/n$.

Now compute:

$$u^2 = (b - a/n)^2 = b^2 - 2ba/n + a^2/n^2$$
$$= b^2 - a + a - 2ba/n + a^2/n^2$$
$$= b^2 - a + a(1 - 2b)/n) + a^2/n^2 > b^2 - a = 2.$$

Thus $u^2 > 2$.

Stage 2. We prove $b^2 \geq 2$.

Suppose to the contrary that $b^2 < 2$. We construct a rational number t such that $b < t$ and yet $t^2 < 2$. This implies that b is not an upper bound for S—a contradiction.

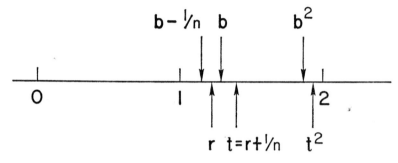

Fɪɢ. 8

Let $c = 2 - b^2 > 0$, or $2 = c + b^2$. Choose a positive integer n such that the following three conditions are satisfied:

$$n > 1/b \quad \text{and so} \quad b - 1/n > 0,$$
$$n > 4b/c \quad \text{and,}$$
$$n^2 > 2/c.$$

By Lemma 2 there is a rational number r in S such that

$$0 < (b - 1/n) < r < b.$$

Let $t = r + 1/n$. We have $b < t$ as illustrated in Figure 8. We compute:

$$t^2 = (r + 1/n)^2 = r^2 + 2r/n + 1/n^2$$
$$< b^2 + 2b/n + 1/n^2 \quad \text{(since } 0 < r < b)$$
$$< b^2 + c/2 + c/2 \quad \text{(by choice of } n)$$
$$< b^2 + c = 2.$$

Thus $t^2 < 2$.

Our proof is completed by putting the results of stages 1 and 2 together; $b^2 = 2$.

The least upper bound principle is very important. As we said, it characterizes the real numbers. It can be used to prove these important theorems about continuous functions:

1. Every continuous function on a closed interval assumes its maximum value.
2. If a continuous function f is defined on closed interval $[a,b]$ and changes sign (say $f(a) f(b) < 0$), then there is a number c such that $a < c < b$ and $f(c) = 0$.
3. Every polynomial of odd degree has a real zero.

. . . And on and on into calculus!

Blockbuster: Prove, from the axioms for the real numbers, that between every pair of real numbers there is both a rational and an irrational number.

THE COMPLEX NUMBERS AND PLANE VECTORS

After developing the real numbers, the next larger number system which is discussed is the complex numbers. In the real numbers $r^2 \geq 0$ for all real numbers, r, and indeed the sum of nonzero squares is nonzero. Thus the equation $x^2 + 1$ has no solution in the set of real numbers. The complex numbers are a field in which this equation has a solution. One solution is denoted traditionally by i. The other solution is then $-i$.

There are several standard motivations for the complex numbers, and each has its own merits. We shall not detail any of these constructions. Ultimately they all boil down to the important one-to-one correspondence between a point in the plane whose real coordinates are (a,b) and the complex number $a + bi$. This correspondence is indicated in Figure 9.

Points in the plane also denote vectors, and the addition of complex numbers is the same as the addition of vectors.

Definition of addition:

For vectors: $(a,b) + (c,d) = (a + c, b + d)$.

For complex numbers: $(a + bi) + (c + di) = (a + c) + (b + d)i$.

Figure 10 shows the parallelogram law.

Physical forces are added in this way and so the complex numbers become a mathematical model for forces acting in a plane. This fact has tremendous import in the natural sciences.

We could digress to develop vectors and vector spaces at this point. For high school mathematics there is some point in doing this because

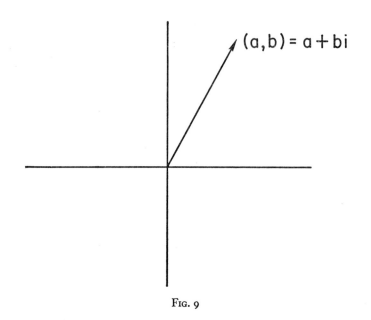

Fig. 9

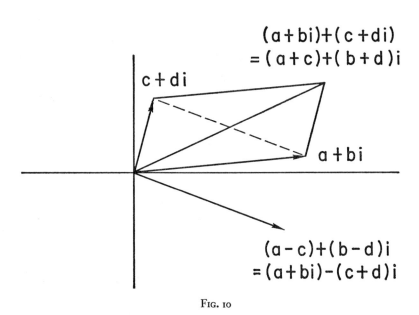

Fig. 10

the material on vectors can be viewed very simply in a geometrical context. Pursuing complex numbers frequently leads to deep questions in analysis which are harder to handle. However, since we are looking at number systems, it seems natural to complete our description of complex numbers now. In any event, complex numbers should be presented in a highly geometric context.

For mathematics, the vitally important fact is that a multiplication can be defined on these plane vectors (or complex numbers) so that they become a field. Incidentally, this is unique in mathematics. No larger vector space with real coordinates can be made into a field.

Definition of multiplication:

$$(a + bi) \cdot (c + di) = (ac - bd) + (ad + bc)i$$

Motivation for this definition comes from pretending that the distributive, commutative, and associative laws hold for complex numbers and that $i^2 = -1$. Thus,

$$(a + bi)(c + di) = (a + bi)c + (a + bi)di = ac + bic + adi + bidi$$
$$= ac + bdi^2 + bic + adi$$
$$= ac - bd + (ad + bc)i.$$

However, if we *define* multiplication and addition, we are obliged now to prove all the field axioms. This is a very easy but laborious task and we shall omit it. Every student of mathematics should do it once (and only once) in his lifetime! It is important to note that real numbers are a subsystem of the complex numbers by the identification of a with $(a, 0) = a + 0i$.

There is a geometric interpretation for multiplication which is very important. To make this connection, we introduce the notion of the length or modulus of a complex number.

Definition of length:

$$|a - bi| = \sqrt{a^2 + b^2}$$

The real number $\sqrt{a^2 + b^2}$ is the length of the vector (a, b); it is the distance from the origin to the point (a, b). See Figure 11. Since vector addition (and subtraction) follow the parallelogram law, we can express the distance between complex numbers:

Distance $[(a + bi), (c + di)] = |(a + bi) - (c + di)|$
$$= \sqrt{(a - c)^2 + (b - d)^2}$$

The *argument* of the complex number $a + bi$ is the measure of the angle the vector (a,b) makes with the positive x-axis. This is shown in Figure II. Thus

$$(a,b) = a + bi = \sqrt{a^2 + b^2} \; (\cos \theta, \sin \theta)$$
$$= \sqrt{a^2 + b^2} \; (\cos \theta + i \sin \theta)$$

where θ is the argument of the complex number $a + bi$.

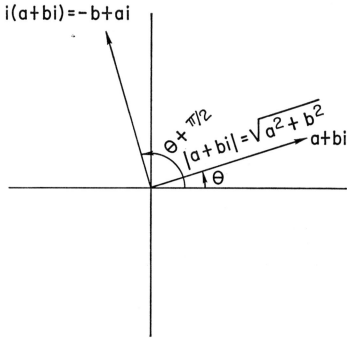

FIG. II

We can now explain multiplication geometrically:

1. The modulus of the product $(a + bi)(c + di)$ is the *product* of the moduli of the factors $(a + bi)$ and $(c + di)$.

2. The argument of the product $(a + bi)(c + di)$ is the *sum* of the arguments of the factors $(a + bi)$ and $(c + di)$.

These facts are readily verified from the definitions and some elementary trigonometry identities. It is handy to know that these can be used in reverse order. For example, to rotate a vector or complex number by 90 degrees counterclockwise, just multiply it by i. (See Figure II.)

While no brief account of the complex numbers can begin to do justice to the wealth of material that becomes available with their use, it may be meaningful to list three significant features of the complex numbers.

Theorem 1. The complex numbers cannot be ordered so that the laws of an ordered field hold. (Hint: Should $i > 0$ or should $i < 0$? Whichever, $i^2 > 0$, or $-1 > 0$. Similarly, $1 > 0$; but then $-1 + 1 = 0 > 0$. Tilt!)

Theorem 2. All the zeros of all polynomials (with real or complex coefficients) are complex. (This is a deep theorem and depends on rather sophisticated arguments.[3])

Corollary: Every polynomial with real or complex coefficients can be factored into a product of factors of degree 1 in the field of complex numbers:

$$a_0 + a_1 x + a_2 x^2 + \ldots + a_n x^n = a_n(x - c_1)(x - c_2) \ldots (x - c_n).$$

Theorem 3. The complex numbers are the only finite dimensional vector space over the reals on which a multiplication can be defined so that the resulting system is a field. (This is in fact a result of Theorem 2. It means that the program of building bigger number systems to solve equations, or to find points on a line or in a plane, is over!)

Exercise 6.

Prove (using complex numbers) that the diagonals of a parallelogram bisect each other.

Give geometric interpretation for the set of complex z such that

1. $|z - i| \leq 2$
2. $|z - i| \leq |z - 1|$
3. $|z - i| + |z + i| = 4$.

VECTOR SPACES

This mathematical system is more complicated than any of the others we have examined because it involves the interaction of two systems. At the same time this complexity is reflected in a wide variety of applications. For this reason a study of vector spaces is very important.

The simplest case involving vectors usually occurs in a discussion of signed numbers. As shown in Figure 12a, we can present negative numbers from the point of view of vectors on a line. Vectors are used to indicate repeated combinations of signed numbers as shown in Figure 12b. It is clear even at this stage that a vector somehow tells something of direc-

3. See, for example, R. M. Redheffer, "What! Another Note Just on the Fundamental Theorem of Algebra," *American Mathematics Monthly*, LXXI (1964), 180–85.

tion and magnitude. Direction and magnitude of what? It is of a displacement or translation of the line.

We have seen that complex numbers may be thought of as vectors in the plane or 2-space. In doing so, we identify a point with a vector and with a complex number. By attaching an arrow to the number $\alpha = a + bi$ as in Figure 13, we seem to be giving the complex number α direction and magnitude. It too may be thought of as a displacement of the plane;

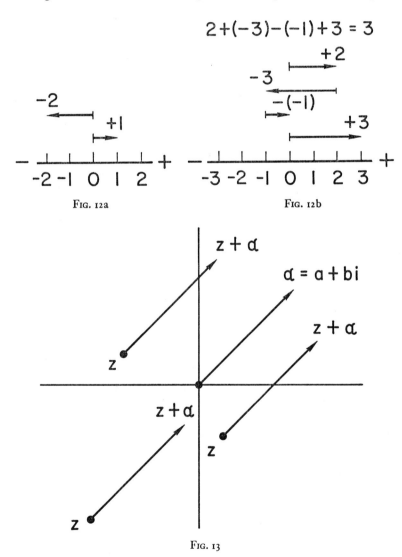

$$2+(-3)-(-1)+3 = 3$$

$+2$

-3

$-(-1)$

$+1$ $+3$

-2

$-2\ -1\ \ 0\ \ 1\ \ 2$ $-3\ -2\ -1\ \ 0\ \ 1\ \ 2\ \ 3$

Fig. 12a   Fig. 12b

$z + \alpha$

$\alpha = a + bi$

$z + \alpha$

z

$z + \alpha$

z

$z + \alpha$

z

Fig. 13

it is the displacement or translation which sends every complex number z into $z + a$. The single number a, or equivalently the image of the origin under this translation, contains all the information we need about the displacement. Consequently it is correct, and in many cases more convenient, to consider the vector as a point in some space.

The study of vector spaces naturally breaks up into two parts:

1. A study of vector spaces themselves. This includes a statement of the axioms and the elementary consequences. This part of the study treats the topics of linear dependence and independence, basis, subspaces, inner (or dot) products, and other geometric aspects.

2. A study of a class of functions from one vector space to another. The class of functions singled out for study is the class of linear transformations. This part of the study introduces matrices to facilitate algorithms for computation and to describe explicitly these linear functions. Here too is a proper place to introduce determinants.

One of the fundamental applications of vector spaces is the study of systems of linear equations. For simplicity, consider a single equation like

$$2x + 3y - z = 0.$$

A solution consists of three numbers; for example, if $x = -1$, $y = 1$, and $z = 1$, then

$$2(-1) + 3(1) - (1) = 0.$$

The solution may be written concisely as an ordered triple $(-1,1,1)$ where we employ the usual convention that the first number is to be substituted for x, the second for y, and the third for z. Another solution is $(-3,2,0)$. The two *fundamental observations* are these:

1. Two solutions can be added or subtracted to obtain a third solution.

Example:

$$(-1,\ 1,\ 1) + (-3,\ 2,\ 0) = (-1 + (-3),\ 1 + 2,\ 1 + 0)$$
$$= (-4,\ 3,\ 1) \text{ is a solution.}$$

2. Any solution can be multiplied by a constant to obtain another solution.

Example:

$$\pi(-1,\ 1,\ 1) = (-\pi,\ \pi,\ \pi) \text{ is a solution.}$$

From observation (1) we can conclude that the *solutions* form an abelian group under the operation $(+)$ defined by adding the respective numbers in the triples.

From observation (2) we conclude more—that we can multiply a solution by any real number and obtain a solution.

The solutions are called *vectors;* the operation (+) is called *vector addition;* the multiplication is called *scalar multiplication.*

A triple of numbers also represents a point in 3-space. The operations we have been describing show that we can make space into a mathematical system with the operations of vector addition and scalar multiplication.

As we said, there are many examples where the crucial information is carried by an ordered set of numbers and where it makes sense to add sets and/or multiply through by a scalar factor. Probably the most common example and certainly one of great importance in the applied fields is that of physical forces. What is important for physics is that two forces add like vectors—that is, by adding their respective components. Similarly, when a force is multiplied by a constant, its components are multiplied by this same constant. Geometrically, this results in the parallelogram law for addition of vectors. In this way, space becomes a mathematical model for physical quantities.

VECTOR SPACE AXIOMS

We begin by studying the blueprint for vector spaces. A vector space over a field F is:

1. An abelian group V. The elements of V are called vectors, the group operation is written (+), the identity element is denoted by O. (In this chapter we shall use capital letters to denote vectors.)

2. There is defined an operation, called scalar multiplication, between the elements of the field F and V. (This operation is usually denoted simply by juxtaposition. We shall use lowercase letters to denote the elements of F.) The axioms for scalar multiplication are these: For all r,s in F and all A,B in V:

2.1 $r(sA) = (rs)A$,

2.2 $(r + s)A = rA + sA$

2.3 $r(A + B) = rA + rB$

2.4 $1A = A$.

Example 10. Let R be the field of real numbers, and let n be fixed positive integer. Let V be the set of all n-tuples of real numbers. Thus typical vectors have the form

$$(a_1, a_2, \ldots, a_n) .$$

Vector addition and scalar multiplication are defined component-wise by

$$(a_1, a_2, \ldots, a_n) + (b_1, b_2 \ldots, b_n)$$
$$= (a_1 + b_1, a_2 + b_2, \ldots, a_n + b_n)$$
$$r(a_1, a_2, \ldots, a_n) = (ra_1, ra_2, \ldots, ra_n).$$

Exercise 7. In $V_n(R)$ it is easy to see that $OA = O$. Prove this for all vector spaces.

This example can be varied in two ways. One is by varying the choice of n. When $n = 1$, V is indistinguishable from the field of real numbers R. When $n = 2$, V is the plane; when $n = 3$, V is a model of our three-dimensional world.

The notation for this example is reasonably standard. This vector space is expressed as $V_n(R)$ or just V_n. The subscript n indicates how many components there are to each vector, R denotes the field of real numbers and tells us that the components themselves are real numbers.

This example can also be varied by replacing the field R by another. For example, if F is the field of two elements O, 1 with mod 2 addition and multiplication, then $V_2(F)$ consists of these four vectors:

$$(0,0) \quad (0,1)$$
$$(1,0) \quad (1,1).$$

Blockbuster: Define a multiplication of vectors in $V_2(F)$ so that together with vector $(+)$ the system becomes a field.

Example 11. The solutions of $2x + 3y - z = 0$. Note that these solutions are vectors in V_3, and yet not all vectors of V_3 are solutions. Hence this example does not fall under the category of the preceding one since it does not consist of *all* triples of real numbers. This is an example of a subspace of V_3.

Definition. A subset W of a vector space V is called a *subspace* of V if W satisfies all the axioms for a vector space, using the vector operations defined on V. Thus W is a vector space itself, and because it uses the operations of V, it is called a subspace of V. It is easy to see that a subset W of V is a subspace if and only if it is closed under the operations of addition and scalar multiplication.

Exercise 8. Show that the solutions for $2x + 3y - z = 1$ are not a subspace of V_3. Show that all solutions of this equation have the form $(-1, 1, 0) + A$ where A is a solution of $2x + 3y - z = 0$.

Here are three more examples of subspaces:

Example 12. Let A be a fixed vector in V. Let $L(A) = \{rA:r \text{ in } R\}$. This is subspace. If $A \neq 0$, then $L(A)$ is the line through A. (See Figure 14.)

Example 13. Let A and B be vectors in V_3. Let $L(A,B) = \{rA + sB:r,s \text{ in } R\}$. If A and B are not colinear, then $L(A,B)$ is the plane determined by the lines $L(A)$ and $L(B)$. (See Figure 14.)

Example 14. This example generalizes the previous two. Let S be a set of vectors in a vector space V. The set $L(S) = \{\Sigma r_i S_i : r_i \text{ in } R, \text{ and } S_i \text{ in } S\}$, which is the set of all finite linear combinations of vectors in S, is a subspace of V. $L(S)$ is called the linear span of S. If W is a subspace of V, and S is a subset of W such that $L(S) = W$, then W is said to span W.

DEPENDENCE, INDEPENDENCE, BASIS

The most important ancillary concept in the study of vector spaces themselves is the notion of *linear dependence*. This concept is defined for a set of vectors, and it means that the vectors are related in a simple way.

Definition. A finite set $D = \{D_1, D_2, \ldots, D_m\}$ of vectors in V is called linearly dependent if and only if there exist scalars $r_1, r_2, \ldots, r_m$, *not all zero*, such that

$$r_1 D_1 + r_2 D_2 + \ldots + r_m D_m = 0 .$$

Linear dependence means that one of the vectors in D can be expressed as a linear combination of the others. Since not all of $r_1, r_2, \ldots, r_m$ are zero, let us suppose for specificity that $r_1 \neq 0$, then

$$D_1 = - 1/r_1(r_2 D_2 + \ldots + r_m D_m)$$
$$= -r_2/r_1 D_2 - r_3/r_1 D_3 - \ldots - r_m/r_1 D_m .$$

The negation of dependence is independence:

Definition. A finite set $J = \{J_1, J_2, \ldots, J_n\}$ of vectors in V is called linearly independent if and only if it is not dependent.

This means that whenever

$$s_1 J_1 + \ldots + s_m J_m = 0 ,$$

then

$$s_1 = s_2 = \ldots = s_m = 0 .$$

Example 15. The set of vectors $\{(-1,1,1), (-3,2,0), (0,1,3)\}$ is linearly dependent since

$$3(-1,1,1) + (-1)(-3,2,0) + (-1)(0,1,3) = (0,0,0) .$$

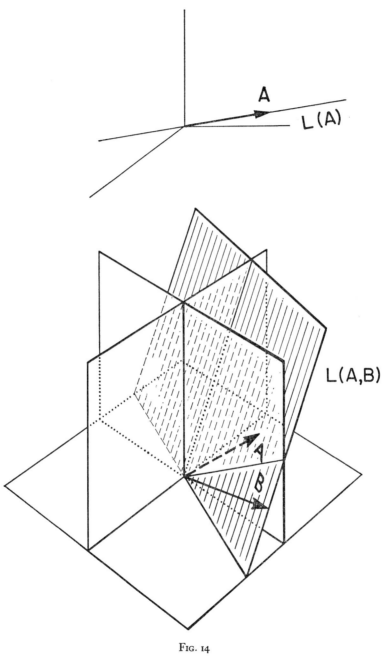

L(A)

L(A,B)

Fig. 14

On the other hand $\{(-1,1,1),\ (-3,2,0)\}$ is independent since

$$s(-1,1,1) + t(-3,2,0) = (-,\ -,\ s) = (0,0,0)$$

implies that $s = 0$ and this in turn implies that $t = 0$.

In a very real sense, an independent set of vectors is an economical set since no vector can be expressed in terms of another. Let us see how this works.

Suppose we want to express in some compact way all solutions of a system of equations. For simplicity look again at

$$2x + 3y - z = 0 .$$

This equation has an infinite number of solutions. One way to see this is to verify that $(-r,r,r)$ is a solution for every real r. If we select one of these, say, $(-1,1,1)$, then all the others $(-r,r,r) = r(-1,1,1)$. Thus for economy it suffices to list just $(-1,1,1)$. Another solution different from these is $(-3,2,0)$. We saw above that $\{(-1,1,1),\ (-3,2,0)\}$ was a linearly independent set. Thus this set contains two essentially different solutions for the equation.

Are there others? How many linearly independent solutions are there for the equation $2x + 3y - z = 0$? It turns out that there are no others independent from those two. To prove this, note that $z = 2x + 3y$ and so all solutions must have the form

$$(x,\ y,\ 2x + 3y)$$

and we have

$$(x,y,2x + 3y) = (2x + 3y)(-1,1,1) - (y + x)(-3,2,0) .$$

Thus the set $(-1,1,1)$, $(-3,2,0)$ is precisely what is needed to express all solutions, and it is an economical set for no one of the vectors in it would yield all other solutions as linear combinations. This is an important example of the concept of a *basis* of a vector space.

Definition. A *basis* for a vector space V is a set B of vectors such that
1. $L(B) = V$. (The linear span of B is the whole space V.)
2. B is linearly independent.

Condition (1) insures that B generates all vectors in V. Condition (2) says that all vectors in B are essential; none can be deleted without affecting the space spanned.

There are many bases for a vector space V.

Example 16. The vector space of solutions for $2x + 3y - z = 0$ has, among others, these two bases:

$$\{(-1,1,1), (-3,2,0)\} \quad \text{and} \quad \{(1,0,2), (0,1,3)\} \, .$$

This second basis comes from the general solution $(x, y, 2x + 3y)$ by setting $x = 1$, $y = 0$ for the first vector and setting $x = 0$, $y = 1$ for the second.

The significant invariant property associated with all bases for a vector space is their number.

Theorem. Every vector space V has a basis, and the number of elements in each basis is the same. This number is called the dimension of V.

Example. The dimension of V_n is n. In view of this theorem we need only exhibit a basis for V_n. It is easy to see that a basis is provided by the usual "unit vectors":

$$E_1 = (1,0,0, \ldots , 0)$$
$$E_2 = (0,1,0, \ldots , 0)$$
$$E_3 = (0,0,1, \ldots , 0)$$
$$\vdots$$
$$E_n = (0,0,0, \ldots , 1) \, .$$

Corollary. If V has finite dimension n, then every set of more than n vectors is linearly dependent.

There is an important application of this theorem to the solutions of systems of linear equations.

Theorem. If the number of unknowns m exceeds the number of equations n, then the system

$$a_1 x_1 + b_1 x_2 + \ldots + d_1 x_m = 0$$
$$a_2 x_1 + b_2 x_2 + \ldots + d_2 x_m = 0$$
$$\vdots$$
$$a_n x_1 + b_n x_2 + \ldots + d_n x_m = 0$$

has a nontrivial solution, i.e., one in which some $x_i \neq 0$.

Proof. First we write this system as a vector equation. Let $A = (a_1, a_2, \ldots , a_n)$, $B = (b_1, b_2, \ldots , b_n), \ldots , D = (d_1, d_2, \ldots , d_n)$ so that the system of equations may be written

$$A x_1 + B x_2 + \ldots + D x_m = 0 \, .$$

Now the existence of a nontrivial solution is precisely the statement that the set of m vectors $\{A, B, \ldots, D\}$ is linearly dependent. Since each of these vectors is in V_n which has dimension n, the linear dependence of the set of vectors now follows because there are m vectors in the set and $m > n$.

There are many applications of vectors to geometry. The most important concept in this application is the notion of "dot product" between vectors. This real valued product is used to define length and angles in V_n.

Definition. If A,B are in V_n, say

$$A = (a_1, a_2, \ldots, a_n) \quad \text{and} \quad B = (b_1, b_2, \ldots, b_n),$$

then we define the "inner" or "dot" product to be

$$A \cdot B = \sum_{i=1}^{n} a_i b_i = a_1 b_1 + a_2 b_2 + \ldots + a_n b_n.$$

Here is a list of the basic facts about dot products which you can verify in the two dimensional (V_2) case by means of diagrams and elementary geometry.

1. $A \cdot B$ is an element of the field.
2. $A \cdot B = B \cdot A$ for all A,B.
3. $A \cdot A \geq 0$ and $A \cdot A = 0$ if and only if $A = 0$.
4. $rA \cdot B = r(A \cdot B)$.
5. $(A + B) \cdot C = A \cdot C + B \cdot C$.
6. $|A \cdot B|^2 \leq (A \cdot A)(B \cdot B)$.
7. Length of $A = \sqrt{A \cdot A}$.
8. $A \cdot B = \sqrt{(A \cdot A)} \sqrt{(B \cdot B)} \cos \theta$.

Property (8) is used as the definition of the cosine of the angle between two vectors in V_n when $n \geq 3$. Thus it gives a way of defining the angle between two vectors. $A \cdot B$ is the length of the projection of A on B as shown in Figure 15.

LINEAR TRANSFORMATIONS AND MATRICES

To complete the study of vector spaces, we turn to a study of a useful class of functions defined from one vector space to another. To be specific, we study functions T from V_n into V_m such that

1. $T(A + B) = T(A) + T(B)$ for all A,B in V_n.
2. $T(rA) = rT(A)$ for all A in V_n and all real numbers r.

Such functions are called *linear transformations* because they "transform" or "map" the space V_n into the space V_m and because every line in V_n is transformed into a line in V_m.

Exercise 9. Show that if T is a linear transformation, then

$$T(O) = O .$$

In most applications $n = m$ and we shall restrict this account to this case, and indeed most of our examples will be for the case $n = m = 3$.

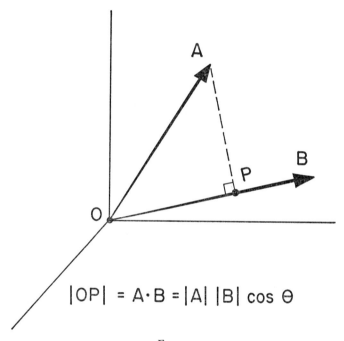

$$|OP| = A \cdot B = |A| \, |B| \cos \theta$$

Fig. 15

Example 17. An example of a very common linear transformation from V_2 into V_2 is given by the rotation of t degrees as follows:

$$T(x,y) = (x \cos t + y \sin t, \ -x \sin t + y \cos t)$$

or, as it more familiarly appears in books on analytic geometry,

$$x' = x \cos t + y \sin t$$
$$y' = -x \sin t + y \cos t .$$

An important consequence of (1) and (2) is that to completely determine T we need to know the values for T only on a basis for V. For example, consider the basis for V_3 given by the unit vectors

$$E_1 = (1,0,0), \ E_2 = (0,1,0), \ \text{and} \ E_3 = (0,0,1) \, ,$$

and suppose that T maps V_3 into V_3. Now if A is in V_3, we have

$$A = a_1 E_1 + a_2 E_2 + a_3 E_3$$

and hence

$$T(A) = T(a_1 E_1) + T(a_2 E_2) + T(a_3 E_3)$$
$$= a_1 T(E_1) + a_2 T(E_2) + a_3 T(E_3) \, .$$

Thus, in this case, T is completely determined by knowing the three
vectors

$$T(E_1) = (t_{11}, \ t_{12}, \ t_{13})$$
$$T(E_2) = (t_{21}, \ t_{22}, \ t_{23})$$
$$T(E_3) = (t_{31}, \ t_{32}, \ t_{33})$$

so that

$$T(A) = (a_1 t_{11} + a_2 t_{21} + a_3 t_{31}, \ a_1 t_{12} + a_2 t_{22} + a_3 t_{32},$$
$$a_1 t_{13} + a_2 t_{23} + a_3 t_{33}) \, .$$

Several important things are derived from this computation. The first
is that there is a one-to-one correspondence between transformations and
arrays of numbers

$$T = \begin{bmatrix} t_{11} & t_{12} & t_{13} \\ t_{21} & t_{22} & t_{23} \\ t_{31} & t_{32} & t_{33} \end{bmatrix}$$

which is established by interpreting the first row of the array as the
image, $T(E_1)$ of E_1 under the transformation T, and so on. A change in
the transformation necessitates a change in the array and conversely.

Such an array is called a *matrix*. The one just constructed is called the
matrix of the transformation T. Because of the one-to-one correspondence, we shall use the same letter to denote both the transformation and
its matrix. This can be confusing, but as long as the basis (in our case
E_1, E_2, E_3) is understood, no confusion will result. Of course, if the basis
is changed, the matrix associated with T will change even though the
transformation does not! This study is an important part of the theory
of matrices but one which we cannot sketch here.

In general, a matrix M is an array of n rows and m columns of numbers. The element in the pth row and qth column is denoted by m_{pq}.

Example 18. Here is a 4 × 3 matrix. In it $m_{23} = 0$

$$\begin{bmatrix} 1 & -1 & 2 \\ 3 & 2 & 0 \\ \pi & 8 & -7 \\ 4/3 & 5 & \sin 2 \end{bmatrix}$$

The second inference from the calculation for T is that it suggests a very convenient algorithm which can replace or serve as a mnemonic device for the calculation. Watch:

$$T(A) = T(a_1,a_2,a_3) = \overrightarrow{(a_1,a_2,a_3)} \;\; \begin{bmatrix} t_{11} & t_{12} & t_{13} \\ t_{21} & t_{22} & t_{23} \\ t_{31} & t_{32} & t_{33} \end{bmatrix}$$

$$= (a_1 t_{11} + a_2 t_{21} + a_3 t_{31}, \text{ etc , etc})!$$

The arrows are to indicate how to form the *first* coordinate of $T(A)$. Simply move across the vector A and down the *first* column of the array, multiplying corresponding coordinates and adding. To find the second coordinate of $T(A)$, use the second column; to find the *third* coordinate, use the *third* column. This process is called a "row-column" multiplication.

Exercise 10. Show that $N = \{A : T(A) = O\}$, the set of vectors transformed into the zero vector, is a subspace of V_n.

Show that $N = O$ if and only if T is a one-to-one mapping.

The third consequence of this calculation is the beautiful relation which occurs when transformations are performed one after another. To see what happens, suppose that T and S are linear transformations each mapping V_3 into V_3. We describe them by their matrices:

$$T : V_3 \rightarrow V_3 \qquad T = \begin{bmatrix} t_{11} & t_{12} & t_{13} \\ t_{21} & t_{22} & t_{23} \\ t_{31} & t_{32} & t_{33} \end{bmatrix}$$

$$S : V_3 \rightarrow V_3 \qquad S = \begin{bmatrix} s_{11} & s_{12} & s_{13} \\ s_{21} & s_{22} & s_{23} \\ s_{31} & s_{32} & s_{33} \end{bmatrix}$$

Now what is $S(T(A))$? What is the matrix that corresponds to the linear transformation which is the result of first applying T and then S, that is, the composition $S \cdot T$? We need to determine the effect of the composition on the basis E_1, E_2, E_3. Well,

$$T(E_1) = (t_{11}, t_{12}, t_{13}). \text{ So } S(T(E_1)) = S(t_{11}, t_{12}, t_{13})$$

$$= (t_{11}, t_{11}, t_{13}) \quad \begin{bmatrix} s_{11} & s_{12} & s_{13} \\ s_{21} & s_{22} & s_{23} \\ s_{31} & s_{32} & s_{33} \end{bmatrix}$$

$$S(T(E_1)) = (t_{11}s_{11} + t_{12}s_{21} + t_{13}s_{31}, \; t_{11}\,s_{12} + t_{12}s_{22} + t_{13}s_{32},$$
$$t_{11}s_{13} + t_{12}s_{23} + t_{13}s_{33}) \; .$$

We have computed $S(T(E_1))$ and so this vector constitutes the *first* row of the matrix corresponding to the composition of the two transformations. We can compute the matrix TS (first T, then S) by simply writing the scheme above with the second and third rows of T under the first and carrying out a "row-column" multiplication. In the diagram below, the arrows indicate how to compute the element in the second row and third column of the matrix TS. Note that we use the second row of T and the third column of S.

$$\begin{array}{ccc} T & S & TS \end{array}$$

$$\begin{bmatrix} t_{11} & t_{12} & t_{13} \\ t_{21} & t_{22} & t_{23} \\ t_{31} & t_{32} & t_{33} \end{bmatrix} \begin{bmatrix} s_{11} & s_{12} & s_{13} \\ s_{21} & s_{22} & s_{23} \\ s_{31} & s_{32} & s_{33} \end{bmatrix} = \begin{bmatrix} r_{11} & r_{12} & r_{13} \\ r_{21} & r_{22} & r_{23} \\ r_{31} & r_{32} & r_{33} \end{bmatrix}$$

The first row of the product, (r_{11}, r_{12}, r_{13}), has been calculated above as $S(T(E_1))$. The element r_{23} in the second row and third column is

$$r_{23} = t_{21}s_{13} + t_{22}s_{23} + t_{23}s_{33} \; .$$

Example 19.

$$\begin{array}{ccc} T & S & TS \end{array}$$

$$\begin{bmatrix} 0 & 1 & 3 \\ -1 & -2 & 3 \\ 0 & 1 & -1 \end{bmatrix} \begin{bmatrix} 2 & 1 & -1 \\ -2 & -1 & 1 \\ 3 & 0 & 1 \end{bmatrix} = \begin{bmatrix} & | & | \\ \hline & | & 2 \\ \hline & | & | \end{bmatrix}$$

To find the element in the second row and third column

$$(-1 \quad -2 \quad 3) \begin{pmatrix} -1 \\ 1 \\ 1 \end{pmatrix} = (-1)(-1) + (-2)(1) + (3)(1) = 2 \; .$$

Exercise 11. Complete the computation of TS in the above example. After you are done, verify that $S(T(1,1,1)) = (13, -1, 6)$ in two ways. First calculate $T(1,1,1)$, then $S(T(1,1,1))$, using both matrices T and S. Then use the matrix product TS of example 18 to calculate by the rule

$$(1,1,1) \begin{bmatrix} & | & | \\ \hline & | & 2 \\ \hline & | & | \end{bmatrix} = (13, -1, 6) \; .$$

MATRICES

The set of $n \times n$ matrices form a mathematical system themselves of considerable importance. The entries in the matrix may be taken from any field, although we shall assume here that all numbers are real numbers. Part of the reason is that matrices mirror exactly the linear transformations of V_n into itself. In this way they tell us a great deal about geometry. This study is particularly important because when $n \geq 4$, it is almost the only tool we have for studying geometry! Another reason for its importance is that every finite group has a model consisting of matrices of suitable size. But even apart from these applications, matrices form a system which is of interest for its mathematical beauty, its difficulty, and its reluctance to surrender all its mysteries.

The work with compositions of transformations motivated a definition for the product of matrices by use of the "row column" product.

$$
\overset{T}{\begin{bmatrix} p^{\text{th}} \text{ row} \\ \longrightarrow \end{bmatrix}} \overset{S}{\begin{bmatrix} q^{\text{th}} \\ \text{column} \\ \downarrow \end{bmatrix}} = \overset{TS}{\begin{bmatrix} r_{pq} \end{bmatrix}}
$$

The element in row p and column q of TS is

$$
r_{pq} = \sum_{k=1}^{n} t_{pk} s_{kq} .
$$

Exercise 12. Prove that those 3×3 matrices T such that $T(A) = O$ if and only if $A = O$ form a group under multiplication.

Prove that a matrix C satisfies $CT = TC$ for all 3×3 matrices if and only if

$$
C = \begin{bmatrix} c & o & o \\ o & c & o \\ o & o & c \end{bmatrix} .
$$

If C is the matrix above, relate the entries in CT to those in T. Matrices are added easily under an entry by entry rule:

$$
\overset{T}{[t_{pq}]} + \overset{S}{[s_{pq}]} = \overset{T+S}{[(t_{pq} + s_{pq})]}
$$

Exercise 13. Prove that all the field properties hold except that:

1. Multiplication is not commutative.
2. Not every nonzero matrix has a multiplicative inverse.

Exercise 14. Show that a 3×3 matrix T has a multiplicative inverse if and only if $(a_1, a_2, a_3)\ [T] = (0,0,0)$ implies $(a_1, a_2, a_3) = (0,0,0)$.

An ancillary notion to the theory of matrices is that of the determinant of an $n \times n$ matrix. The determinant is a function, denoted *det*, from the set of $n \times n$ matrices into the real numbers. Thus $\det(T)$ is a real number. It is possible to identify this function by a few of its key properties, and this approach is taken by some authors. We shall give here definitions for the cases $n = 2$ and $n = 3$. The case $n = 2$:

$$\det(T) = \det \begin{bmatrix} t_{11} & t_{12} \\ t_{21} & t_{22} \end{bmatrix} = t_{11}t_{22} - t_{12}t_{21}.$$

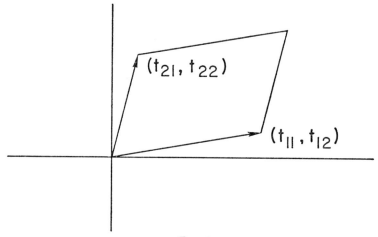

FIG. 16

It is important to note that $|\det(T)|$ is the area of the parallelogram whose sides are the vectors (t_{11},t_{12}) and (t_{21},t_{22}) as shown in Figure 16. Thus $\det(T) = 0$ if and only if the rows (or columns) are linearly dependent.

The case $n = 3$:

$$\det(T) = \det \begin{bmatrix} t_{11} & t_{12} & t_{13} \\ t_{21} & t_{22} & t_{23} \\ t_{31} & t_{32} & t_{33} \end{bmatrix}$$

$$= t_{11} \det \begin{bmatrix} t_{22} & t_{23} \\ t_{32} & t_{33} \end{bmatrix} - t_{12} \det \begin{bmatrix} t_{21} & t_{23} \\ t_{31} & t_{33} \end{bmatrix} + t_{13} \det \begin{bmatrix} t_{21} & t_{22} \\ t_{31} & t_{32} \end{bmatrix}.$$

It is important to note that $|\det(T)|$ is the volume of the parallelopiped generated by the three row vectors of T. Thus $\det(T) = 0$ if and only if the rows (or columns) of T are dependent. (See Figure 17.) It is often

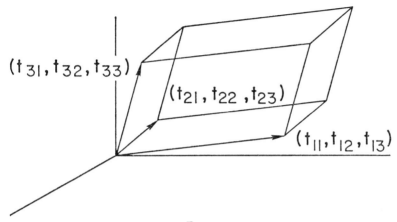

$$(t_{31}, t_{32}, t_{33})$$

$$(t_{21}, t_{22}, t_{23})$$

$$(t_{11}, t_{12}, t_{13})$$

FIG. 17

important to calculate determinants and there are many tricks available. Most of these tricks make use of the following properties:

1. The value of a determinant is changed in sign if two rows (or columns) are interchanged.
2. The value of a determinant is unchanged if the scalar multiple of one row is added to another row. A similar result holds for columns.
3. The determinant of the identity matrix $\begin{bmatrix} 1 & 0 \ldots 0 \\ 0 & 0 \ldots 1 \end{bmatrix}$ is 1.
4. If the matrix has two identical rows (or columns), then its determinant is zero.
5. If a row (or column) is multiplied by a real number r, the value of the determinant is multiplied by r.

Exercise 14. Show that the following are equivalent:

1. $\det(T) \neq 0$.
2. $T(A) = O$ if and only if $A = O$.
3. The system of equations $(x_1, x_2, x_3)\, T = (0,0,0)$ has only the trivial solution $(x_1, x_2, x_3) = (0,0,0)$.
4. The rows of T are linearly independent.
5. The columns of T are linearly independent.

There are many more fascinating things about matrices, linear transformation, and determinants. There are applications to calculus, economics, and physics, to mention only three wide-ranging topics. A few interesting treatments of this topic are listed in the following bibliography.

BIBLIOGRAPHY

1. FINKBEINER, DANIEL T. *Introduction to Matrices and Linear Transformations.* 2d ed. San Francisco: W. H. Freeman & Co., 1966.
2. HALMOS, PAUL R. *Finite-Dimensional Vector Spaces.* 2d ed. Princeton, N.J.: D. Van Nostrand Co., 1958.
3. MARCUS, MARVIN. *Basic Theorems in Matrix Theory,* Superintendent of Documents, U.S. Government Printing Office, Washington, D.C. (15 cents).
4. SEARLE, SHAYLE R. *Matrix Algebra for the Biological Sciences.* New York: John Wiley & Sons, 1966.
5. STOLL, ROBERT R., and WONG, EDWARD T. *Linear Algebra.* New York: Academic Press, 1968.

CHAPTER IV

Geometry and Measurement

H. STEWART MOREDOCK

Introduction

One of the most spectacular and significant developments that has occurred recently in the school mathematics curriculum has been the incorporation of a considerable amount of geometric material throughout the program. Only a few years ago practically all of the geometry being taught was concentrated at the tenth grade. Now it is being taught systematically at all levels and, surprisingly, is being accepted by everyone concerned.

Why has a systematic treatment of geometry and measurement been so readily accepted in the elementary and junior-high grades? In general it has been found that geometry offers a new and exciting dimension to the conventional arithmetic program. Some of the beneficial results of introducing geometry earlier are as follows:

1. A deeper understanding on the part of the students of the structure of their physical space
2. A strengthening of the arithmetic program in providing geometric models for the arithmetic processes
3. A more fundamental development of the nature of measurement and the measuring process
4. A closer relation of the mathematics program with the science program in the earlier grades

In this chapter, the content of the geometry and measurement program at the various grade levels will be examined, and a rationale will be offered for what is being done and for what is being proposed for the program.

Geometry in the K-VI Program

The geometry studied in the K-VI grades is often called "informal geometry." The "informal" is not to be taken in any casual or sloppy sense but to indicate that the geometry is *not* formal or deductive. To move the axiomatic or deductive treatment of tenth-grade geometry down into the early grades would of course be disastrous.

One of the major objectives of the geometry program at this level is to enable students to analyze more deeply the geometric structure of their physical environment. The emphasis is upon exploring and identifying geometric ideas drawn from surrounding objects. The work of Piaget has served as a helpful guide in developing the kinds of activities with physical objects from which the geometric ideas are abstracted and in suggesting the sequence of these activities.

The first attempts at introducing geometry into the K-VI program were quite timid. Usually only a small separate section at the end of each text was devoted to geometry. The content was mainly definitional in nature with attention given mainly to the correct representation of points, lines, and planes, and the proper naming of segments, rays, and angles.

Geometry now has been brought into the mainstream of the program. The number line, rectangular arrays, and other geometric models have been found useful in developing the properties and algorithms of the operations with numbers. Also geometry emerges in the elementary school science program in the study of the physical characteristics of objects.

We shall examine now the highlights of an informal geometry program. In this sketch we shall see that the program is not casual or haphazard but that there is a sequence of ideas which must be carefully followed.

SHAPES AND PRIMITIVE CONCEPTS

The first phase in the informal geometry program is the study of the shapes of such objects as balls (spheres), boxes (rectangular prisms), cans (cylinders), and blocks (cubes). The children get the feel of flat and rounded surfaces, and of edges and corners (vertices). Rectangles, squares, triangles, and circles are first encountered as shapes rather than as drawings on a sheet of paper. There is a kinesthetic as well as a visual introduction to the common geometric figures. Throughout the informal geometry program the geometric ideas are formulated from and related to physical objects, but during this first phase special emphasis is given to studying the geometric properties of physical objects.

After the common geometric figures have been introduced in a general sort of way, the next step is to develop some ideas which can be used to analyze these figures.

The idea of a *point* is fundamental to any analysis of a geometric figure. At the elementary level, a point is usually interpreted as an exact location and it is represented by a dot and named by a capital letter. *Space* then becomes *the set of all points,* and therefore all geometric figures are formed as sets of points which are subsets of space.

It has already been pointed out that many geometric figures such as squares and rectangles should be seen first as shapes of flat sides of such objects as boxes, table tops, and walls. Flat surfaces, when thought of as extending outward in all directions without ending, suggest sets of points called planes. The figures formed as flat shapes can be analyzed in a plane as represented by drawings on a sheet of paper.

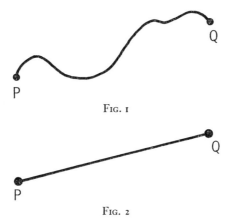

FIG. 1

FIG. 2

From the outlines of shapes, we form the idea of a *curve*. At the elementary level most of the study is focused on curves that lie in a plane. Therefore a curve in a plane is introduced as a set of points suggested by a tracing of a pencil made on a sheet of paper without lifting the pencil from the paper. At this stage the term "path" is used interchangeably with curve in order to relate the idea to its physical origin. Also since curves or paths may be "wiggly or straight," it is more meaningful to the students to talk about straight paths than straight curves. Furthermore, at this level we can talk in a natural way about curves or paths that "cross," that "pass through" a point, or that "connect" points.

The drawing (Figure 1) represents a path or a curve which connects points P and Q in a plane. P and Q are endpoints of the curve. It is a "simple" curve or path because it does not cross itself.

The concept of a path or curve can now lead to the development of the idea of a line segment and a line (Figure 2).

There are many paths that connect P and Q but there is only one unique straight path that has P and Q as endpoints. This unique straight path is called a line segment and is labeled $\overline{PQ}$. If the straight path is continued in both directions without ending, it is called a line. Consequently the line is determined by the two points P and Q, and is labeled $\overleftrightarrow{PQ}$.

Straightness is a physical property of a tightly drawn piece of string and of the edges of such objects as a ruler, a box, and a sheet of paper. Straightedges are used in drawing representations of lines and segments. The physical concept of straightness is used to provide plausibility for the geometrical concept that any two points in space determine a line. *Flatness* is also a physical property of such objects as table tops, floors, and window panes which gives rise to the idea of a plane. Together the physical ideas of straightness and flatness give credence to the geometric concept that if two points of a line lie in a plane, then the entire line lies in the plane. In other words, a "straight" line lying in a "flat" plane will never part company.

INCIDENCE PROPERTIES

The way in which we relate points, lines, and planes to each other is fundamental to our concept of space. We have already accepted some statements which begin to characterize our abstract geometric model of physical space. For example, we have agreed that any two points determine a line, and that if two points of a line lie in a plane then the entire line lies in the plane. There are other statements of this type which are called properties of incidence and are explored in the informal geometry program.

Two lines may intersect or may not intersect. If they intersect, in how many points may they intersect? If they intersect in two or more points, then they are the same line because two points determine a single unique line. This leads us to the fact that if two lines intersect, they intersect in exactly one point called the point of intersection.

If two lines do not intersect, are they parallel? Not necessarily. In the drawing of a box (Figure 3), the two lines $\overleftrightarrow{AB}$ and $\overleftrightarrow{CF}$ do not intersect and they are not parallel. Since $\overleftrightarrow{AB}$ and $\overleftrightarrow{CF}$ are not in the same plane and do not intersect, they are called "skew lines." The two lines $\overleftrightarrow{AB}$ and $\overleftrightarrow{CD}$ however do lie in the same plane and they do not intersect. Therefore they are "parallel lines." The possibilities then for two lines are: (*a*) they intersect in exactly one point, (*b*) they are parallel, or (*c*) they are skew.

What are the possible situations for a line and a plane? The children can explore this question using a pencil and a sheet of paper. One possibility is that the line and the plane do not intersect and are therefore parallel. Another possibility is that the line "pierces" or intersects the plane in exactly one point. If the line intersects the plane in two or more points, then the line lies in the plane by previous agreement. Thus there are three possibilities for a line and a plane.

There are many planes that can pass through two points, or the line determined by the two points. However, there is only one plane that can pass through these two points and another point not on the line of the

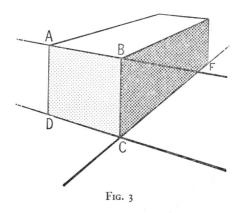

FIG. 3

two points. Children can explore this phenomenon using three finger tips representing three non-collinear points in space, and a piece of cardboard, which can always be pressed against the three fingertips. Therefore a plane is determined by any three non-collinear points in space. A plane can also be determined by two intersecting lines or by a line and a point not on the line.

Two planes may intersect or they may not intersect. If they do not intersect, then they are parallel planes. Is it possible for two planes to intersect in exactly one point? For example, two sheets of paper can be held so that the corner of one sheet touches the surface of the other sheet. We have agreed, however, that the plane represented by the sheet of paper does not stop at the corner but continues without ending in all directions. Thus if two planes intersect, they intersect in a line. If the intersection of a pair of planes consists of a line and one or more points not on the line, then by previous agreement they are the same plane. These relationships can be studied by examining such objects as boxes where the intersection of two faces can be seen as an edge and where parallel faces can be identified.

This completes the introductory development of the primitive concepts of point, line, and plane which are the basic ingredients of geometric analysis. At first these concepts will be given a great deal of physical content by the children because they will have difficulty in idealizing points and comprehending the infinitude of lines and planes. The abstractness of these concepts will develop with their use and with the maturity of the children. It is important that the properties of incidence be studied throughout the school mathematics curriculum at the maturity level of the children because these properties refine the concepts of point, line, and plane so that they may be used effectively to analyze geometric figures.

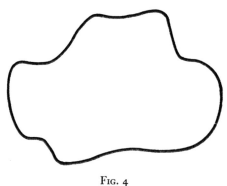

FIG. 4

CURVES AND POLYGONS

Curves in a plane may be simple or non-simple. We have already noted that simple curves are the ones that do not cross themselves. Curves may also be closed or open. A closed curve is one that can be traced by starting at a point and returning to that point.

Simple closed curves in a plane such as the one represented in Figure 4 are of special importance because most of the figures studied at this level are of this type.

A simple closed curve can be used to introduce the important idea of *separation* since children can readily identify points that are inside, outside, and on a simple closed curve. A simple closed curve separates the plane into two disjoint parts— the interior and the exterior. The curve itself is called the *boundary* and belongs to neither part. A *region* is formed by joining a simple closed curve and its interior.

Any path which connects a point in the interior and a point in the exterior must cross the simple closed curve. It may also be noted that a line separates a plane into two disjoint parts called *half-planes* or *sides*, and any path connecting points on opposite sides must cross the line. With this background, it is possible to show why such figures as segments and simple open curves do not separate a plane. Also, it is possible to develop a way for determining if two points are on the same side of a line. If the segment having these two points as endpoints does not intersect the line, then the two points are on the same side of the line.

The stage is now set for introducing the *polygon*. A simple closed curve consisting of segments such as the one shown in Figure 5 is called

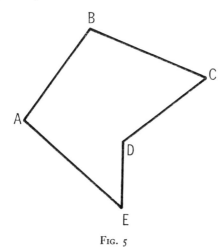

Fig. 5

a polygon. The segments are the sides and the endpoints of the segments are the *vertices*. A polygon can be designated by the letters for its vertices. Polygons are classified by the number of sides they have: triangles—3 sides, quadrilaterals—4 sides, pentagons—5 sides, and so on.

Since a polygon is a simple closed curve, it has an interior and an exterior. A polygon together with its interior forms a polygonal region. This enables us now to designate and study such regions as triangular and rectangular regions. Polygonal regions may be *convex* or *non-convex*. If for every two points in the interior of a polygon the segment having these points as endpoints is contained in the interior, then the polygonal region is convex. The polygonal region shown above is not convex because there is a segment whose endpoints are in the interior, but the segment itself is not contained in the interior.

Most of the polygons studied at the elementary level are polygons whose regions are convex. Triangles, the simplest form of polygon, are formed by any three non-collinear points in space and always form convex regions. The common forms of quadrilaterals such as squares, rectangles, parallelograms, rhombuses, and trapezoids all form convex regions.

We have seen now the sequence of ideas that leads to the development of a polygon. At first glance, it is rather surprising to find how much is involved in forming the idea of a polygon. This background development must be done carefully so that polygons may be adequately analyzed later.

ANGLES

There is another geometric figure which has not yet been introduced but which plays an important part in the analysis of polygons. It is the *angle*.

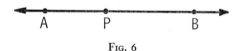

$$A \qquad P \qquad B$$

Fig. 6

In order to develop the idea of an angle, it is necessary to look again at a line and note the separation properties of a point on a line. In Figure 6, point P separates the line $\overleftrightarrow{AB}$ into two disjoints parts called *half-lines*, where P does not belong to either half-line. Points A and B lie on opposite half-lines; therefore P is between A and B. Point P together with the half-line containing B forms the ray $\overrightarrow{PB}$. Point P is the vertex of the ray, and in naming the ray, the vertex is named first. The joining of the half-line containing A with point P forms the ray $\overrightarrow{PA}$: The two rays $\overrightarrow{PA}$ and $\overrightarrow{PB}$ are called *opposite rays*. A ray can be determined by any two points in space, one of which is designated as the vertex.

Rays may be used to indicate directions from a location. For example a certain ray may indicate North, and another, Southwest. Two opposite rays then indicate opposite directions from their common vertex. Thus a line may be oriented in two different ways by taking either direction indicated by a pair of opposite rays on the line as positive.

In our physical environment there are many things that suggest the idea of a ray. We think of a light ray as starting from a light source (vertex) and heading out in some direction without ending. In navigation and surveying a ray is suggested by a line of sight or bearing. A ray can also be suggested simply by a pointing finger. From these and other examples children may develop initially the idea of a ray.

An angle is formed by the union of two non-collinear rays having a common vertex. The angle shown in Figure 7 is formed by the two rays $\overrightarrow{AB}$ and $\overrightarrow{AC}$ and it is labeled $\angle BAC$. The rays are the sides of the angle and the vertex is point A which is named in the middle.

An angle can show how two directions are related at a location. For example in the drawing above, $\overrightarrow{AC}$ could represent the heading of a ship, and $\overrightarrow{AB}$ could represent the bearing of a lighthouse from the ship. The angle $\angle BAC$ shows the relation of these two directions at the ship. Many other examples could be provided to help children develop the idea of an angle.

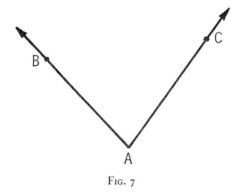

FIG. 7

Any three non-collinear points in space with one designated as the vertex determines an angle. These same three points also determine a plane. Therefore we can speak of the plane of the angle.

The plane of an angle is separated by the angle into two disjoint parts called the interior and exterior, with of course the angle belonging to neither part. In Figure 8 the half-plane of $\overleftrightarrow{PR}$ containing Q has been shaded in one direction and the half-plane of $\overleftrightarrow{PQ}$ containing R has been shaded in another direction. The part where the two shadings cross is the interior of $\angle QPR$. Another way of determining the interior of $\angle QPR$ is to draw the segment $\overline{QR}$. The points between Q and R lie in the interior of the angle. Two angles having a common vertex and a common side and whose interiors do not overlap are called adjacent angles. The angles, $\angle AOB$ and $\angle BOC$, shown in Figure 9, are a pair of adjacent angles.

Shown in Figure 10 are two non-collinear segments $\overline{AB}$ and $\overline{BC}$ having a common endpoint. It is often convenient to think of the angle $\angle ABC$

formed by these two segments even though the rays $\overrightarrow{BA}$ and $\overrightarrow{BC}$ forming the angle are not shown. This permits us to talk about angles of triangles, of parallelograms, and of other kinds of polygons later.

Thus far we have been developing geometric concepts without involving measurement. This part of the informal geometry program is

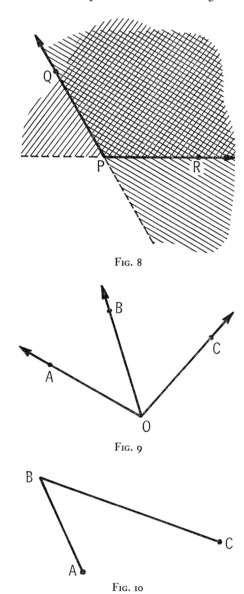

Fig. 8

Fig. 9

Fig. 10

called *non-metric geometry*. These non-metric ideas could be pursued further, but we would soon go beyond the comprehension level of the children in the K-VI grades.

CONGRUENCE

We turn now to the metric geometry portion of the program. The key
that opens the door to metric geometry is congruence. We shall examine
how the concept of congruence is developed and how it is used in measurement and in the development of important geometric ideas.

In general, two geometric figures are congruent if they have the same
size and shape, or, in other words, if one is the exact copy of the other.
A key property of our space is that it is "homogeneous"; it is everywhere the same. Therefore figures may be copied freely everywhere. In
our present day technology, our copy machines, plastic molds, and assembly lines are continuously producing congruent objects.

This global view of congruence, however, is not very helpful in analyzing the congruence of figures. By focusing simply on the congruence of
segments and angles, a considerable amount of analysis and development
can be done. We shall look at the part of this development that is done
at the elementary level.

At the beginning, congruence is given an operational definition. Two
segments are congruent if a copy of one may be made to fit exactly on
the other. The children can be shown how to construct segments congruent to a given segment by marking the edge of a sheet of paper, or by
spreading a compass to match to the endpoints of the given segment and
using the marked edge or the compass spread to draw the congruent segment. Exactness, of course, is impossible but these activities convey the
meaning of congruent segments. The notation is also introduced. If the
two segments $\overline{AB}$ and $\overline{CD}$ are congruent, we write $\overline{AB} \cong \overline{CD}$.

The same development used for congruent segments is applied to
angles. Two angles are congruent if a copy of one can be made to coincide with the other. The checking and constructing of congruent angles
is a bit more complicated than it is for segments. At first the children
might draw a copy on a tracing sheet placed over the given angle and then
move the sheet to the desired location for checking or drawing another
congruent angle. Another way would be to place the center of a circular
cardboard disc at the vertex of the given angle as shown in Figure II
and mark the edge of the disc to match the sides of the angle. Then the
marked disc could be used for checking or constructing a congruent

angle. This use of the disc would lay the groundwork for ruler and compass construction of congruent angles and for the development of the protractor which would come later.

With congruence of angles we are set now to develop the idea of a right angle. The drawing (Figure 12) shows a wire bent to form a right angle, ∠*ABC*. There is a way of testing to see if the bent wire forms a

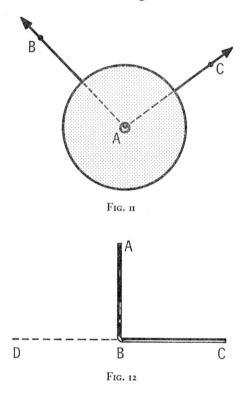

Fig. 11

A

D   B   C

Fig. 12

right angle. Hold $\overline{AB}$ fixed and flip $\overline{BC}$ over to the dotted segment $\overline{DB}$. If *D*, *B*, and *C* are collinear, then ∠*ABC* is a right angle.

Another model of a right angle can be made by paper-folding as illustrated in Figure 13. First the paper is folded to form the folded edge $\overline{DC}$. Then the paper is folded so that $\overline{DB}$ coincides with $\overline{BC}$, forming the dotted segment $\overline{AB}$. This forms the right angle, ∠*ABC*.

These experiences with constructing physical models of right angles suggest a way to develop a definition of a right angle. The two angles shown in Figure 14, ∠*AOB* and ∠*BOC*, are adjacent angles with common side $\overrightarrow{OB}$ and their other sides as opposite rays $\overrightarrow{OA}$ and $\overrightarrow{OC}$. If ∠*AOB* and $\angle BOC$ are congruent, then they are right angles. *Perpendicularity* is a concept that follows immediately from the concept of a right angle. If two lines intersect in such a way that a right angle is formed, then the two lines are perpendicular. Physical examples of perpendicularity are everywhere within easy reach for the children to explore this concept.

Armed with the concepts of congruent segments, congruent angles, right angles, perpendicularity, and the previously developed concept of

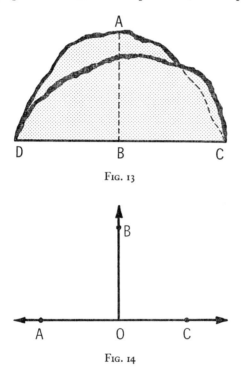

Fig. 13

Fig. 14

parallelism, the children may resume their analysis of geometric figures. At the elementary level, this analysis consists mainly of using these concepts in an exploratory way to classify certain figures and to list their properties. The formal development of these properties is done later.

We shall list some of the classifications and properties of figures that are explored and identified at this level. Triangles with at least two congruent sides are *isosceles* and the angles opposite these two congruent sides are congruent. Triangles with three congruent sides are *equilateral* and their angles are congruent. A parallelogram is a quadrilateral whose opposite sides are parallel. The opposite sides and opposite angles of a parallelogram are also congruent. A rectangle is a parallelogram whose angles are all right angles. A square is a rectangle whose four sides are congruent. A rhombus is a parallelogram whose four sides are congruent. These concepts can now be used in identifying the distinguishing features of such solids as cubes, boxes, and pyramids and in constructing paper models of these solids.

Further informal exploration can be provided with the introduction of *diagonals*. At first, diagonals may be defined for quadrilaterals as segments having opposite vertices as endpoints. The children can then examine the diagonals of different kinds of quadrilaterals to determine which types have congruent diagonals and which ones have perpendicular diagonals.

MEASUREMENT OF LENGTH

We come now to measurement in the development of which, we shall find, congruence plays a key role. Measurement is essentially a process

FIG. 15

of assigning numbers to compare some common attribute of objects. This means that measurement involves a certain kind of activity and should be learned as such. There is, however, a sequence of ideas and related activities that underlies the process which will be discussed at this time. We shall focus first on the measurement of the length of objects. The simplicity of the length concept makes it ideally suited for analyzing the underlying ideas of the measurement process.

The first stage in the measurement of length is the procedure for the direct comparison of lengths. The drawing (Figure 15) shows the comparison of the lengths of two bars a and b by matching the left ends of the bars. Since the right end of bar a falls on bar b, the length of a is shorter than the length of b. There are three possible outcomes for a comparison of lengths: (a) shorter than, (b) longer than, and (c) the same. This result is similar to the trichotomy law for numbers. If for some reason it is impossible to line up the objects as shown above, then the length of one object can be marked on the edge of a sheet so that it can be transferred to the other object.

The *transitive* property applies to the length relations. For example, if the length of a is shorter than the length of b and the length of b is shorter than the length of c, then by transitivity we may conclude that the length of a is shorter than the length of c. The relation "having the same length" is an equivalence relation and therefore partitions the objects into equivalence classes. Any object of an equivalence class can serve as a representative of that class. The activity in this first stage highlights the fact that objects may be completely ordered according to their length. This is a necessary requisite for length or any other attribute to be measured.

The next stage consists of exploring the additive nature of length. The lengths of two or more objects can be combined into a single length. For example, the ends of bar a above can be marked on the edge of a sheet. Then with the mark for the right end of a matched with the left end of b, the right end of b is marked on the sheet. The space between the marks on the sheet for the left end of a and the right of b represents the combined length of a and b. This procedure may be continued to com-

FIG. 16

bine several lengths into one length, and furthermore these combined lengths may be compared with each other, as was shown for single lengths.

The procedure of combining lengths can be applied successively to a single object by "stepping off" or "marking off" end to end the length of the object along a line. In the drawing (Figure 16), the length of a is "marked off" along the length of b as shown. In this way the length of a is being used as a unit of measure. Since the length of b is equivalent to about 5 lengths of a, then the measure of b is 5. Children should have the experience of using arbitrary units and deciding whether or not the last length marked off should be counted. They should also explore the fact that a given object can have different measures of length when different units are used.

The marking off of a unit length on each object being measured should soon become a monotonous chore for the children. Therefore, the convenience of having a unit length already marked off along a line should lead to the development of a scale as shown in Figure 17. The endpoints of the segments congruent to the unit segment are marked with numerals to facilitate the counting of unit lengths. The construction of scales using different units is a fundamental activity which should not be bypassed by the students. These scales lead to the development of the number line, and they are used in the construction of rulers.

The third and final phase of developmental activity in the measurement of length consists of using the scales and rulers just developed. In the drawing (Figure 18), the shaded portion of the scale shows the part that is closer to 6 than to either 5 or 7. Since the right ends of bars *a* and *b* fall within the shaded part of the scale, the measure for both bars is 6. Obviously the bars have different lengths but they have the same measure

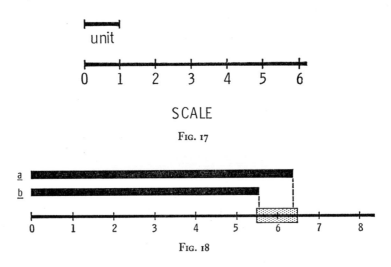

Fig. 17

Fig. 18

since they are being measured to the nearest unit. This shows the approximate nature of the physical process of using a scale or ruler in measuring to the nearest unit.

The concept of *precision* arises in attempting to reduce the difference in length that objects may have and yet have the same measure. A closer or more precise measurement requires the use of a smaller unit of measure. This becomes visually apparent when the shaded portion of the scale dwindles in size as a smaller unit is used. Thus, precision of measurement is determined by the size of the unit used. Later, students will learn that the difference between the true length of an object and its stated measurement is called the *error of measurement*. The greatest possible error, which is one-half the unit employed, is used to indicate the precision of measurement.

When arbitrary units are used, the communication of the measurements is severely limited. As soon as this is realized, attention is directed to standard units which have widespread use. Both the British-American and metric systems are studied, and lately an increasing amount of attention is being given to the metric system. In both systems, smaller units are obtained by subdivision. In the British-American system, there is no simple uniform method for converting from one unit to another as there is in the metric system, which employs a simple base-ten conversion. There is a close relation between the base-ten place-value system and the metric system which should be developed for the students. The process of measuring to the nearest unit is applicable to standard units as well as to arbitrary units. In the study of the metric system, there needs to be a more conscious development of experiences to make the metric measures more meaningful to the students. This development is not so crucial for the British-American system because the measures in this system are encountered daily.

Measurement provides the link between the mathematical systems and the physical world. Therefore measures have a key role in the applications of mathematics and are used in computations. Since the measures used in computations are approximate, the general rule needs to be stated that the results of the computation should not be more precise or accurate than the measures used in computation.

In metric geometry the measures of the abstract figures are often declared to be exact, with the realization, of course, that this is in reality impossible but permissible in an ideal or abstract sense. For example, in defining a circle to be the set of points in a plane having the same distance from a point called the center, the distance is taken to be exact. We may consider then a circle whose radius has a measure of exactly 5. Usually, when an exact measure is used, the unit of measure is immaterial and not mentioned.

The distinction between theoretical and actual measurement should be made clear, and the students should know at any moment which kind of measurement is being used in the discussion. This is particularly important since computation with approximate measures is quite different from that with theoretically exact measures.

The assignment of an exact measure to the length of a segment establishes a functional relation between segments and non-negative numbers. A very valuable opportunity is provided in the study of measurement to develop and reinforce the important idea of a *function*. To emphasize this functional relation, the following functional notation is often used.

"m($\overline{AB}$)" means "the measure of segment *AB*."

"d(AB)" means "the distance between points A and B."

The underlying idea for this functional relation and, in fact, the idea which authorizes the use of exact measures is the existence of a one-to-one correspondence between the set of real numbers and the set of points on a line. This existence is taken as an axiom in geometry and is often called the "ruler axiom."

The sequential development of the ideas and procedures for measuring length has been outlined fairly completely because it serves as a prototype for the measurement of other geometric quantities. As a result,

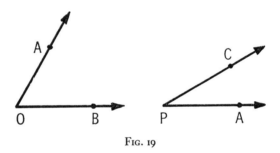

FIG. 19

the forthcoming discussion of the measurement of angles, area, and volume is considerably reduced because reference is made continually to the development for measuring length.

MEASUREMENT OF ANGLES

The angles $\angle AOB$ and $\angle CPA$ (Figure 19) can be compared by placing a copy of $\angle CPA$ on $\angle AOB$ so that the side $\overrightarrow{PA}$ coincides with side $\overrightarrow{OB}$ and $\overrightarrow{PC}$ lies in the *A*-side of $\overrightarrow{OB}$. Since the side $\overrightarrow{PC}$ falls in the interior of $\angle AOB$, then $\angle CPA$ is smaller than $\angle AOB$. If the side $\overrightarrow{PC}$ had fallen on $\overrightarrow{OA}$ or had fallen in the exterior of $\angle AOB$, then $\angle CPA$ would have the same size as or would be larger than $\angle AOB$. Thus we have the same trichotomy of possible outcomes for comparing angles as we had for comparing segments. In the measurement of angles, there is an additive property similar to the one stated for segments. The sum of the measures of the two adjacent angles shown in Figure 20, $\angle AOB$ and $\angle BOC$, is equal to the measure of $\angle AOC$.

The unit angle shown in Figure 21 can be used to measure ∠*AOB* as follows:

The arc of a circle is drawn with center at *O*. Starting with side $\overrightarrow{OB}$, a copy of the unit angle is used to mark off along the arc adjacent angles congruent to the unit angle. The marks on the arc are numbered to show how many unit angles are used. This shows that the measure of ∠*AOB*

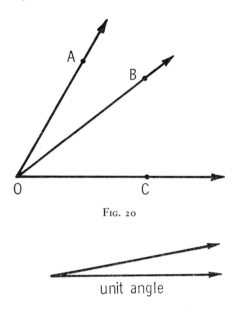

FIG. 20

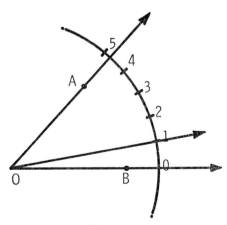

FIG. 21

to the nearest unit is 5, since by the additive property the measure of ∠AOB is the sum of the measures of the unit angles. Scales such as the one shown in Figure 22 can be developed by students and used for measuring angles.

Following this scale construction experience with arbitrary unit angles, the standard degree unit is introduced along with the protractor.

Measures can now be used to identify and to classify angles. The small letter a indicates the measure of the angle shown in Figure 23. The angle

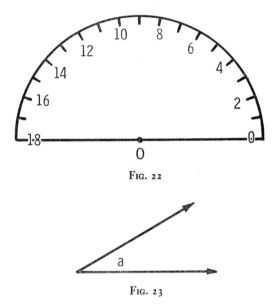

FIG. 22

FIG. 23

is identified as " ∠a" meaning "the angle whose measure is a." Therefore $m(\angle a) = a$. Congruent angles have the same exact measure. This can be stated as follows: ∠a ≅ ∠b if and only if $a = b$.

The measure of a right angle is defined to be 90 degrees (exactly). Angles whose measures are less than 90 are called *acute*, and those whose measures are greater than 90 are called *obtuse*. Zero degree angles and 180 degree angles or "straight angles" are eliminated by the definition of an angle as being a figure consisting of two non-collinear rays with a common vertex. Two adjacent angles having sides which form a line as shown for ∠a and ∠b in Figure 24 are called *supplementary*. In this case, $a + b = 180$. Generally any two angles, adjacent or not, having measures whose sum is 180 are called supplementary. If the sum is 90, they are called *complementary*.

The model shown below (Figure 25), consisting of sticks represented by $\overline{AB}$, $\overline{AC}$, and $\overline{BD}$ hinged at A and B, can be used to explore the relation between supplementary angles and parallel lines.

If the model is set so that $\angle a$ and $\angle b$ are right angles, then $\overleftrightarrow{AC}$ and $\overleftrightarrow{BD}$ are parallel. In this case $a + b - 180$. This illustrates that two lines perpendicular to the same line are parallel. Now if $\angle a$ is set on the model as shown above, what would be the setting of $\angle b$ so that $\overleftrightarrow{AC}$ and $\overleftrightarrow{BD}$ are

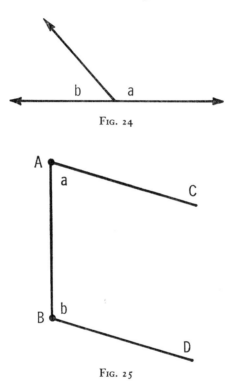

FIG. 24

FIG. 25

parallel? Various settings and measurements would lead the students to accept the following: $\overleftrightarrow{AC}$ and $\overleftrightarrow{BD}$ are parallel if and only if $\angle a$ and $\angle b$ are supplementary.

A 1-degree arc is defined as $\frac{1}{360}$ of a circle, which provides us with a means of measuring arcs of circles in terms of arc degrees. An angle whose vertex is at the center of a circle such as $\angle AOB$ shown in Figure 26 is called a *central angle*. There is an important relation which students can explore between the measure of a central angle and the measure of the arc "cut off" by the sides of the angle. For example, if $m(\angle AOB)$

= 40°, then the measure of both arc *AB* and arc *CD* in arc degrees is 40. This provides a meaningful background for the development of the concepts of latitude and longitude.

Area is related to the size of a simple closed region in a plane. Two regions such as the regions I and II shown in Figure 27 can be compared as follows: A copy of region II is made from a piece of cardboard and placed on region I. Since the copy of region II can be made to fit within the boundary of region I by cutting and refitting where necessary, the area of region II is less than the area of region I. In comparing areas of regions, there is the usual trichotomy of possible outcomes: less than,

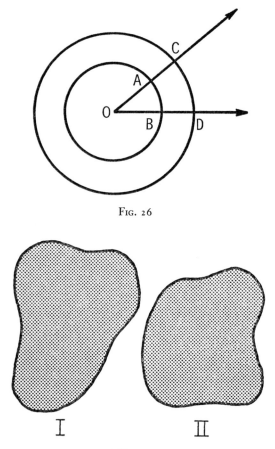

Fig. 26

Fig. 27

greater than, and same size. The additive property also applies to area measurement. The area measure of the union of two regions is equal to the sum of the area measures of the two regions. The additive property is implicitly used in the cutting and refitting of copies of regions which represent what is called the *decomposition* of regions. Furthermore, congruent regions have the same area measures.

The assigning of a number to indicate the magnitude of the area of a region involves establishing a unit region which is in the form of a square. Graph paper is especially convenient for the early stages of measuring

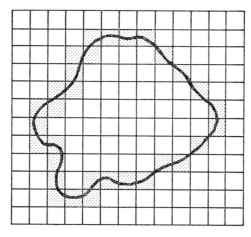

Fig. 28

areas because the unit square regions are already marked off. The area of the region shown in Figure 28 using the unit squares provided by the graph paper is found as follows.

The number of unit squares lying completely within the boundary is 44. The number of shaded unit squares which are crossed by the boundary is 31. Then the area of the region is between 44 and 75 square units. Precision can be improved by using a smaller unit square region. This procedure for finding area is important because it provides the generality for the measurement of area and it shows in a different way the approximate nature of the measurement process.

In order to simplify the computation of area at the introductory level, the rectangular regions are conveniently dimensioned so that they may be completely "covered" by an exact whole number of unit squares. The dotted lines for the rectangular region in Figure 29 show the "fitting" or "tiling" of unit square regions. The length and width are measured in the same units that form the unit squares. If the length measure is ℓ and the width measure is w, then the number of unit squares is ℓw. This leads to the formula for the area of a rectangular region.

$$A = \ell w .$$

The area formula can also be justified when the length and width of the rectangular region are not a whole number of units. The unit squares

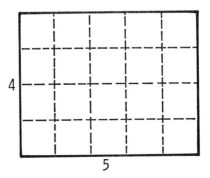

FIG. 29

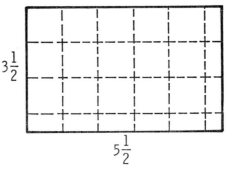

FIG. 30

are simply scaled down to the fractional part of the unit used in measuring the length and width. For example, if the dimensions of a rectangular region are $5\frac{1}{2}$ by $3\frac{1}{2}$ units as shown in Figure 30, then one can count 15 whole square units, 8 half square units, and 1 quarter square unit. This makes a total of $19\frac{1}{4}$ square units, which is the product of $5\frac{1}{2}$ and $3\frac{1}{2}$. The effect on the computation of areas of rectangular regions of having approximate measures instead of exact measures is developed in the later grades.

The students are next introduced to the idea that the diagonal of any rectangle, including a square, divides the region into two congruent parts. This can be explored by cutting a rectangular piece of cardboard along a diagonal, as shown in Figure 31, and fitting the pieces exactly on each other. The area of the rectangular region $ABCD$ is bh. Then the area of the right triangular region ABC is $\frac{1}{2}bh$.

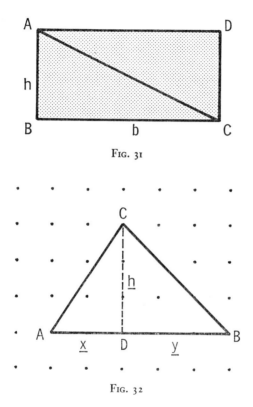

Fig. 31

Fig. 32

The dots in the drawing below represent the vertices of a "covering" of non-overlapping unit squares. $\triangle ABC$ is drawn so that its vertices fall on the dots. The base b of $\triangle ABC$ is $x + y$, and the height is h as shown.

The area of the right triangle (Figure 32) $\triangle ADC$ is $\frac{1}{2}xh$, and the area of the right triangle $\triangle BDC$ is $\frac{1}{2}yh$. Then the area of $\triangle ABC = \frac{1}{2}xh + \frac{1}{2}yh = \frac{1}{2}(x + y)h = \frac{1}{2}bh$.

The area of the obtuse triangle $\triangle ABC$ (Figure 33) equals the area of right triangle $\triangle DBC$ minus the area of right triangle $\triangle DAC$. Then the area of $\triangle ABC = \frac{1}{2}(b + x)h - \frac{1}{2}xh = \frac{1}{2}bh + \frac{1}{2}xh - \frac{1}{2}xh = \frac{1}{2}bh.$ These examples show the general pattern of how students may verify the area formula for triangles. In each case, the students would use the numerical measures of length shown by the dots instead of using the letters.

A physical model of the drawings above can be made by taking a flat piece of board and driving nails in partway at the location of the dots. Rubber bands stretched around the nails can represent various triangles. Using this device, which is often called a "geo-board," the students can very quickly construct a triangle and compute its area and thereby develop and verify the area formula for any triangle. Using different rubber bands, they may construct different triangles having the same base

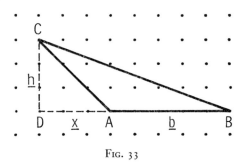

FIG. 33

and height and verify that they have the same area. Exploration of the effect on the area of a triangle if its base or height is doubled or halved may also be made. The use of the geo-board may also be extended to explore the areas of polygons of various shapes.

VOLUME

The measurement of *volume* is developed in the same fashion as was the measurement of area. A unit cube is developed from a unit length, and space is "filled" with the non-overlapping unit cubes. At the elementary level, computation of volume is limited to box-shaped figures (right rectangular parallelopipeds).

These box-shaped figures may be formed by stacking unit cubic blocks as shown in Figure 34. The volume of the box is determined by counting the unit cubes which exactly fill the box. The number of unit cubes in each horizontal layer is ℓw, and the number of layers is h. Hence the number of unit cubes or volume V is given by the following formula,

$$V = \ell w h$$

This formula can be verified for fractional units in the same way as was done for the area formula earlier.

The various units of liquid volume such as pints, quarts, and gallons are introduced at the elementary level. The activities at this level are aimed at familiarizing the students with the units and teaching them to convert from one unit to another. The same is true for units of weight, time, and temperature.

Metric units are getting both more extensive and more intensive treatment in the elementary grades because of the growing importance of

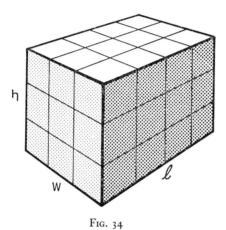

FIG. 34

these units. Students can become familiar with these units by estimating the size of objects in metric measures and by showing objects which they think have certain metric dimensions. They are introduced to the simple base-ten system of converting from one metric unit to another. This can reinforce their understanding of the base-ten positional system. They can also see the interrelation between metric measures of volume, weight, and liquid volume. For example, a liter has a volume of 1000 cubic centimeters or 1 cubic decimeter and has the volume of 1 kilogram of water at maximum density. With these experiences, the students will see why the metric system has been adopted by scientists everywhere and why it is gaining widespread acceptance throughout the world.

Geometry Program in Grades VII–IX

Geometry has recently been given a very significant and prominent role in the junior-high mathematics program. This can easily be verified by examining mathematics texts being currently used in Grades VII through IX. Formerly, the geometry at this level consisted mainly of mensuration of areas, volumes, perimeters, surface areas, and angle measures of various geometric figures. Now the trend is to build on the informal geometry of the elementary grades a sequential program which is deductive in character but which still retains the flavor of physical space geometry.

The rationale of the geometry program at the junior-high level is essentially the same as that for the elementary grades with the emphasis being somewhat changed, however. This shift in emphasis is reflected in the following list of main objectives for the program:

1. To refine the qualitative knowledge of physical space geometry obtained in the elementary grades.
2. To organize this knowledge deductively in short sequences and as families of properties.
3. To relate these geometric concepts to other aspects of the mathematics program.

Most of the concepts introduced in the informal geometry of the elementary grades are also covered again at the junior-high level, but they are treated more intensively and extensively. In general, the definitions are stated more precisely, and more technical terminology and notation are used. Also, more attention is given to making the structure more explicit in sequencing the axioms and theorems, and more proofs are developed at this level than at the elementary-grade level. At the same time, constant reference is made to the physical sources of geometric ideas, and geometry is developed as a mathematical model of our physical space.

The concepts of incidence separation, betweenness, orientation, convexity, and related ideas which are basic to the structuring of space have already been discussed here in connection with the elementary grade program. Consequently, this survey of the junior-high mathematics program will be devoted to the new concepts that are introduced at this level and to some of the deductive sequences that are studied.

CONGRUENCE AND RIGID MOTIONS

A considerable amount of the geometry at the junior-high level involves the concept of congruence. In fact, it could be identified as the central theme of the geometry program at this level. As in the elementary grades, congruence is at first given an operational definition. Two figures that have the same size and shape are said to be congruent. In other words, two figures are congruent if a copy of one made on a sheet of tracing paper can be fitted exactly on (can coincide with) the other.

Two congruent triangles I and II are shown in Figure 35. There is a motion of the tracing sheet so that a copy of triangle I moves from a fitting

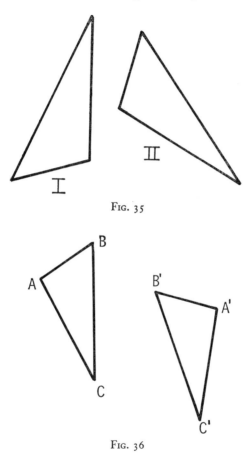

Fig. 35

Fig. 36

on triangle I to a fitting on triangle II. For this motion, the image of triangle I is triangle II. There is another motion in which the image of triangle II is triangle I. In this way, the study of motions which always result in congruent images is introduced. Such motions are called *rigid motions*. Since points have images for these motions, a convenient way of naming image points is developed. For the motion shown in Figure 36, the image of $\triangle ABC$ is $\triangle A'B'C'$ in which the image of A is A'

(read *A* prime) and so on. This lays the groundwork for developing the idea of corresponding vertices for congruent triangles. Also the students will note that for a copy of △*ABC* to fit on △*A'B'C'*, it is necessary to flip over the tracing sheet.

With the aid of a tracing sheet, the students can now explore a variety of rigid motions. In the first place, they soon find that a rigid motion in a plane is determined by three non-collinear points *A*, *B*, and *C* and their images *A'*, *B'*, *C'* so that △*ABC* and △*A'B'C'* are congruent. Students also are led to discover that once a rigid motion has been defined in a

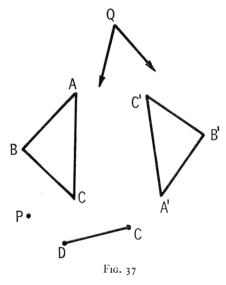

FIG. 37

plane, then each point and therefore each figure in the plane has an image. For example, for the rigid motion defined by △*ABC* and its image △*A'B'C'* (Figure 37), the students are asked to find the images of such figures as point *P*, ∠*Q*, and $\overline{DC}$, using a tracing sheet. Later, the motion of the tracing sheet is de-emphasized and a motion is seen as a particular correspondence of points known as a *mapping* or a *transformation* of the plane.

The key feature of a rigid motion is the fact that distances are preserved. In other words, for any two points *A* and *B* (and their images *A'* and *B'* for a rigid motion), the distance between *A'* and *B'* is the same as the distance between *A* and *B*. Later the students will learn that these rigid motions or transformations are called *isometries*. In the meantime, the students should explore not only the fact that rigid motions preserve

distance but also the fact that they preserve such properties as parallelism and collinearity. It should also be noted that for rigid motions, the
images of lines are lines, of circles are circles, of angles are angles, and
so on.

The students are now ready to study some special results of rigid motions. There is of course the motion in which each point in the plane is its
own image. This is called the *identity motion*. For the motion shown in

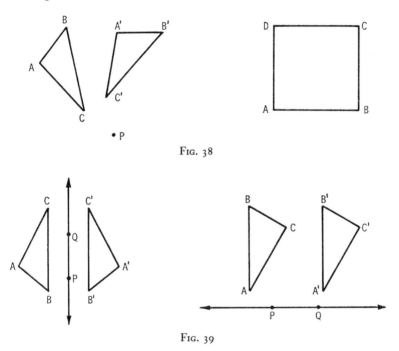

FIG. 38

FIG. 39

Figure 38, point P is its own image and is called a *fixed point*. For the
square shown at the right, students are asked to describe some motions
in which the square is its own image. A figure which is its own image for
a motion is said to be *invariant* for that motion.

For the motion shown at the left in Figure 39, the line $\overleftrightarrow{PQ}$ is invariant
and each point of the line is a fixed point. For the motion shown at the
right, the line $\overleftrightarrow{PQ}$ is invariant but the points on the line are not fixed. The
image of each point on the line, however, lies on the line. This shows
two ways in which a figure may be invariant for a motion. The students
should do a considerable amount of wide-ranging exploration of the many
possible results of rigid motions.

BASIC TYPES OF RIGID MOTIONS

There are three basic types of rigid motions which are helpful in analyzing rigid motions. The first type of motion is called a *slide* or *translation*. In the diagram below (Figure 40), the image of △*ABC* is found as follows: Copy △*ABC* and the dotted line, and mark the tail point of the arrow on a tracing sheet. Slide the tail mark to the arrow tip, keeping the tracing of the dotted line on the arrow. The copy of △*ABC* is now at the location of the image △*A'B'C'*.

A slide or translation is a rigid motion in which the distance from each point to its image is the same and in the same direction. Therefore a slide

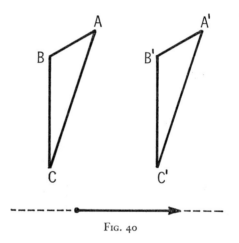

Fɪɢ. 40

is determined by a single point and its image. A slide can be shown by a slide arrow by letting the length of the arrow represent the distance and the arrowhead indicate the direction from each point to its image. There are many different slide arrows that show the same slide. The students should explore many different situations related to slides. They should note for what slides a line is invariant, and they should observe that, if a line is not invariant for a slide, then its image is another line parallel to it.

The next basic type of rigid motion is called a *flip* or *reflection*. In the diagram (Figure 41), the image of △*ABC* is found as follows. Copy △*ABC* and the dotted line ℓ with point *P* on a tracing sheet. Flip over the sheet so that the mark for *P* falls on *P* and the tracing of ℓ lies on ℓ. The copy of △*ABC* now locates the image △*A'B'C'*. The triangle △*A'B'C'* is called the reflection image of △*ABC* in line ℓ. The line ℓ is called the reflection line and point *P* is a reference point for using the tracing sheet. Each point on the reflection line is fixed for the reflection. The students later learn that the reflection line is the perpendicular bisector of a segment connecting a point and its image. In the diagram above, if the sheet is folded along the dotted line ℓ, then $\triangle ABC$ and $\triangle A'B'C'$ will coincide. Thus reflections may be explored through paperfolding. Also, if a mirror is placed along line ℓ, the reflection of $\triangle ABC$ in the mirror is seen to be located at $\triangle A'B'C'$.

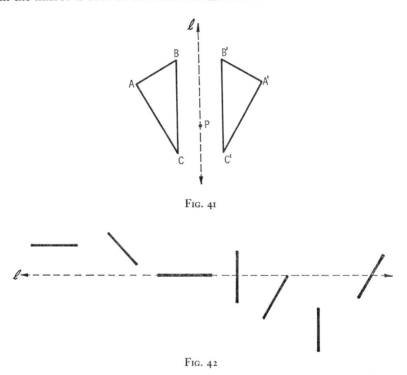

FIG. 41

FIG. 42

The students should now observe the reflections of figures with regard to different reflection lines or to different positions relative to a reflection line. For example, they should find the reflections of various segments in different relative positions to a reflection line as shown in Figure 42. The students should also find reflection lines for which certain segments, lines, and different polygons are invariant. For example, the isosceles triangle $\triangle ABC$ shown in Figure 43 is invariant for the reflection line ℓ shown. A reflection line for which a figure is invariant is called a line of symmetry for the figure. This introduces the study of symmetry, which is an important part of the junior-high geometry program. When various types of polygons are studied, their symmetry properties should be studied along with their other properties.

The third type of rigid motion is called a *turn* or *rotation*. The image of △*ABC* shown in Figure 44 is obtained as follows. On a tracing sheet copy △*ABC* and $\overline{OD}$. Hold the mark for point *O* fixed and turn the sheet so that the tracing of $\overline{OD}$ falls on $\overline{OE}$. The copy of △*ABC* now shows the location of △*A'B'C'*. Point *O* is the *turn center* or *center of rotation*. The curved arrow with its tail and tip segments at *O* shows the amount and direction of the rotation.

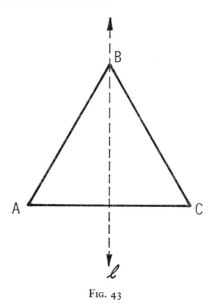

FIG. 43

Rotations may have two directions, clockwise and counterclockwise, and they are usually counterclockwise unless otherwise indicated. Some standard turns are shown in Figure 45. The *full turn* is the same as the *identity motion*. For rotations that are not the identity motion, the center of rotation is the only fixed point. There are many different curved arrows at a center of rotation which show the same rotation.

In their explorations of rotations, the students will find that the distance of a point and its image from the center of rotation is the same and that each point and its image may be connected by the arc of a circle with its center at the center of rotation. Consequently, a circle is invariant for any rotation about its center. Students should continue their explorations by finding a rotation in which a segment or a line is invariant and one in which for a pair of parallel lines each is the image of the other. Also, they should examine many different figures which are invariant for certain rotations.

Any rigid motion in a plane may be analyzed in terms of the three basic types of motions—translations, reflections, and rotations—either used singly or in combination. This study of the composition of motions may be introduced to students in the following way: Show them two congruent Diagrams I and II (Figure 46). Ask them to describe ways in which Diagram II may be obtained as an image of Diagram I, using only translations, reflections, and rotations. The students will probably find that there are many different ways.

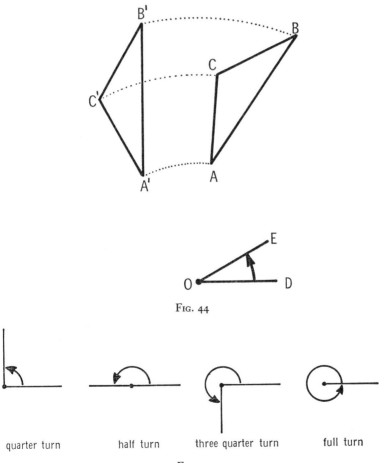

Fig. 44

quarter turn   half turn   three quarter turn   full turn

Fig. 45

This study of "motion" geometry provides a wealth of material which requires student involvement and therefore should be of great interest to the students. This exploratory work with motions should provide a deeper understanding of congruence since the images for these motions are always congruent to the original figures. Furthermore, in the study of the various types of geometric figures, these motions add a new dimension by providing an opportunity to examine the invariance properties of these figures for certain motions. Of course the topic of transformations of the plane is an important part of geometry, and the study of motions provides the necessary background for this topic. It should be noted

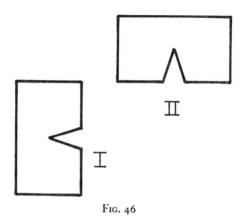

Fig. 46

here that the study of motions provides an opportunity to strengthen the function concept because the point-image correspondence is one to one.

VECTORS

The introductory development of translations (slides) provides an excellent background for a later study of *vectors*. In the exploratory work with translations, it was noted that there were many arrows having the same length and direction which denoted the same translation. Therefore it was only necessary to select a representative arrow to show a translation. This representative arrow suggests the idea which is called a vector. We shall name the vector by a single letter with an underbar $\underline{a}$ (Figure 47).

In mathematics, a translation is a certain correspondence of points with their images. In physics, a translation is interpreted as a displacement or a change of position of objects or particles. The vector $\underline{a}$ shown in Figure 47 may be interpreted as a *displacement* of a certain distance and direction. When a displacement shown by vector a is applied to an object at A_1, its new position will be at A_2 (Figure 48). Displacement is considered to be a vector quantity in physics. Some other vector quantities are *force*, *velocity*, and *acceleration*. These concepts are increasingly being studied in science programs at the junior-high level; therefore there is an increasing need for the study of vectors at this time.

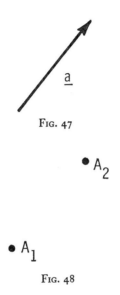

FIG. 47

• A_2

• A_1

FIG. 48

The equality of vectors a and b as displacements means that each object is displaced the same by a as by b. Also, if just one object is displaced the same by a as by b, then $a = b$.

Let vector a be a displacement which displaces an object from A to B. Then there is a displacement which displaces the object from B back to A. This displacement is represented by a vector that is the opposite of a and is denoted by $-a$. Note that $-(-a) = a$.

Displacements can be used to motivate the addition of vectors. We shall interpret the expression $a + b$ to mean the result of applying displacement a to an object, then applying b to the object. This can be pictured as in Figure 50.

The vector $a + b$ is called the *sum* (or sometimes *resultant*) of the vectors a and b. The students should verify that if an object is given a displacement from A to B (shown by a vector a) followed by a displacement from B to C by a vector $\underline{b}$, then the object will be given a displacement from A to C as shown by the vector $\underline{a} + \underline{b}$.

The fact that vector addition is commutative and associative should be explored and verified. The zero vector $\underline{O}$ is motivated by the addition

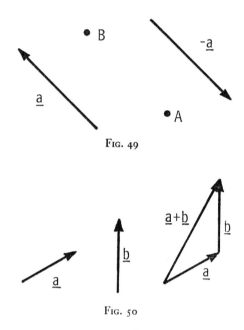

FIG. 49

FIG. 50

of a vector and its opposite. In summary, vector addition has the following properties:

1. $\underline{a} + \underline{b}$ is a vector (closure)
2. $\underline{a} + \underline{b} = \underline{b} + \underline{a}$ (commutative)
3. $(\underline{a} + \underline{b}) + \underline{c} = \underline{a} + (\underline{b} + \underline{c})$ (associative)
4. the zero vector $\underline{O}$ exists such that $\underline{a} + \underline{O} = \underline{O} + \underline{a} = \underline{a}$
5. for each vector $\underline{a}$, the opposite $-\underline{a}$ exists such that $a + (-a) = (-a) + a = \underline{O}$

These are the properties for a mathematical system called a *commutative* (or *abelian*) *group*. These properties make the addition of vectors structurally the same as the addition of integers, rationals, or reals. This may be the first time that students have encountered a mathematical system for something other than numbers, and therefore this should be exploited here.

The subtraction of vectors can be related to addition. Subtracting a vector $\underline{b}$ is the same as adding its opposite $-\underline{b}$. In other words,

$$\underline{a} - \underline{b} = \underline{a} + (-\underline{b}) \ .$$

The term "scalar" refers to a number that is an element of a field (rationals or reals), and the term probably stems from the fact that these numbers were considered to be the results of scale readings. A distinction is made in science between scalar quantities and vector quantities.

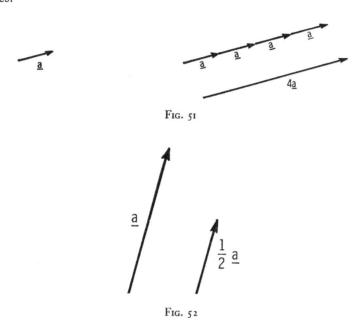

FIG. 51

FIG. 52

Scalar multiplication is an operation that combines scalars and vectors and it can be introduced in the following way (Figure 51). Consider $\underline{a} + \underline{a} + \underline{a} + \underline{a}$. The vector $\underline{a} + \underline{a} + \underline{a} + \underline{a}$ is given the name $4\underline{a}$. In the same way, vectors such as $5\underline{a}$, $7\underline{a}$, and $13\underline{a}$ can be shown. In Figure 52 is shown a way of introducing the vector $\frac{1}{2}\underline{a}$, which has one-half the length of the arrow for the vector $\underline{a}$. In a similar fashion, vectors such as $\frac{2}{3}\underline{a}$ and $1\frac{7}{5}\underline{a}$ can be shown. Negative scalars can be introduced as indicating opposites. For example, $(-2)\underline{a}$ is the product of (-2) and $\underline{a}$, and is interpreted as the opposite of $2\underline{a}$. In other words,

$$(-2)\underline{a} = -(2\underline{a}) \ .$$

We shall therefore write $-2\underline{a}$ which can be interpreted either way. Thus for any scalar k, an element of a field, and for any vector $\underline{v}$, an element of an additive commutative group, the product $k\underline{v}$ has been formed and interpreted.

The properties of scalar multiplication may now be examined. Using drawings, the students should explore the following properties for scalars k, m and vectors $\underline{u}$, $\underline{v}$, $k(\underline{u} + \underline{v}) = k\underline{u} + k\underline{v}$, $(k + m)\underline{v} = k\underline{v} + m\underline{v}$, $(km)\underline{v} = k(m\underline{v})$. They should also note that $1\underline{v} = \underline{v}$, $0\underline{v} = \underline{0}$, and $k\underline{0} = \underline{0}$. These properties complete a mathematical system which is called a *vector space*.

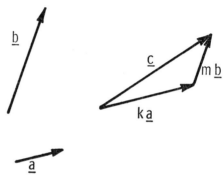

FIG. 53

There is a relation between scalar multiplication and parallelism which the students should observe. Two non-zero vectors $\underline{a}$ and $\underline{b}$ can be represented by parallel arrows if and only if $\underline{a} = k\underline{b}$ or $\underline{b} = k\underline{a}$ for some scalar k. This should be developed intuitively with numerical examples and drawings.

With scalar multiplication and its relation to parallelism, the students are ready to investigate the fact that any vector $\underline{c}$ can be expressed in terms of two non-zero non-parallel vectors $\underline{a}$ and $\underline{b}$. For example, in Figure 53 it is shown that scalars k and m can be found for a vector $\underline{c}$ such that $\underline{c} = k\underline{a} + m\underline{b}$ for the given vectors $\underline{a}$, $\underline{b}$ in a plane. This is sometimes called decomposing a vector in terms of two given vectors. The students now should be shown two unit vectors $\underline{i}$ and $\underline{j}$ (Figure 54) that are perpendicular and asked to express several vectors in terms of $\underline{i}$ and $\underline{j}$. This experience should come after they have encountered the rectangular coordinate system so that they can see the similarity between this vector system and the coordinate system.

The applications of vectors are plentiful and should be used throughout the study of vectors at the junior-high level. There are some problems involving the effect of wind velocity on airplanes in flight, the effect of currents on ships, and the analysis of components of forces that are quite appropriate at this level. These problems involve graphical solutions of triangles and would provide a deeper understanding of properties of triangles.

MEASURES

At the junior-high level, the distinction between metric geometry, which involves numbers as measures, and non-metric geometry, which

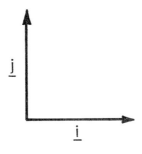

FIG. 54

does not involve measures, is made more explicit. The metric part of the program comes after the study of the structural properties of space and begins with the development of measures for segments.

Before measures are assigned to segments, it is assumed first that there is a one-to-one correspondence between the set of points on any line and the set of real numbers. For each point there is exactly one number, and for each real number there is exactly one point on the line. This assumption is often called the "ruler postulate." To establish a one-to-one correspondence for any given line, it is necessary to select two different points on the line and assign o to one point and 1 to the other point. The rest of the pairings of numbers and points are automatically taken care of with this assignment of o and 1. Furthermore, this assignment orients the line and establishes a positive and negative direction for the line. The direction from 0 to 1 is positive and from 1 to 0 is negative. The real number assigned to a particular point on the line is called the *coordinate* of that point, and the point assigned to a particular number is called the *graph* of that number. When a one-to-one correspondence is established for a line, the line is said to be "coordinatized," and this same one-to-one correspondence can be extended to all lines.

We are now ready to assign a measure to a segment $\overline{AB}$ on a coordinatized line ℓ (Figure 55). Endpoint A has coordinate a and endpoint B has coordinate b as shown at the left. The distance between A and B, or the length of $\overline{AB}$, is the absolute value of the difference between the real numbers a and b. If we write "$m\overline{AB}$" to mean "the measure of $\overline{AB}$," then we have the following result:

$$m\overline{AB} = |a - b| .$$

Measures are therefore non-negative real numbers. The use of the small letter m emphasizes the function idea of assigning a unique measure to

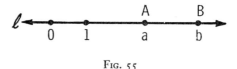

FIG. 55

a segment for a given coordinatization. Later the m is dropped and the measure of $\overline{AB}$ is indicated simply as AB or with a small letter such as a.

Students are already familiar with the coordinatized line in the form of a number line, which was introduced in the elementary grades. Intuitively, the coordinatized line becomes an abstract idealized ruler used for assigning exact measures to segments.

The ruler postulate brings the real number system with all its properties into the geometry development, and therefore it is a very powerful postulate. Congruence of segments can now be defined in the following manner:

$$\overline{AB} \cong \overline{CD} \text{ if and only if } m\overline{AB} = m\overline{CD} .$$

The ruler postulate induces an order for the points on a line. If point P is between points A and B, then $m\overline{AB} = m\overline{AP} + m\overline{BP}$. If $m\overline{AP} = m\overline{BP}$, then P is the midpoint of $\overline{AB}$. Any line, segment, or ray passing through midpoint P is called a bisector of $\overline{AB}$. For any three points A, B, and C

$$m\overline{AC} \leq m\overline{AB} + m\overline{AC} .$$

This last statement is called the *triangle inequality*. If the coordinate of *A* is *a* and that of *B* is *b* on a coordinatized line *ℓ* shown in Figure 56, then we have the following results. The graph of:

$$\{x : b \leq x \leq a\} \text{ is } \overline{AB}$$
$$\{x : x \leq a\} \text{ is } \overrightarrow{AB}$$
$$\{x : x > b\} \text{ is half-line } BA.$$

There is a postulate which is often called the *protractor axiom* that provides measures for angles. This axiom states that there is a one-to-one

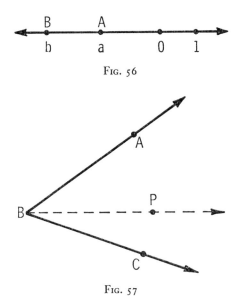

FIG. 56

FIG. 57

correspondence between the set of angles and the set of real numbers between 0 and 180. The measures are called *degrees*. Intuitively, the protractor axiom establishes a one-to-one correspondence between the set of points on a semicircle and the set of real numbers, $\{x : 0 \leq x \leq 180\}$. The semicircle becomes an abstract idealized protractor used to assign a measure to any angle ∠*ABC* which is designated *m*∠*ABC*. Angles are congruent if and only if they have the same measures. Furthermore, if *P* is a point in the interior of an angle ∠*ABC* as shown in Figure 57, then *m*∠*ABC* = *m*∠*ABP* + *m*∠*CBP*.

If *m*∠*ABP* = *m*∠*CBP*, then $\overrightarrow{BP}$ is a *bisector* of ∠*ABC*.

The students are reminded that a pair of angles such as ∠*ABP* and ∠*CBP* which have a common side and vertex and non-overlapping interiors are called adjacent angles. Any pair of angles having measures whose sum is 180 is a pair of supplementary angles. Furthermore, a pair of supplementary angles that are congruent are right angles.

Two non-adjacent angles determined by two intersecting lines are called *vertical angles*. The proof that any pair of vertical angles such as $\angle x$ and $\angle y$ in Figure 58 are congruent requires measures. It can be shown that $x = 180 - z$ and $y = 180 - z$, therefore $x = y$. If two lines ℓ and m intersect so that a right angle is formed, say $\angle a$, then the two lines are perpendicular (Figure 59). We write $\ell \perp m$. The students can

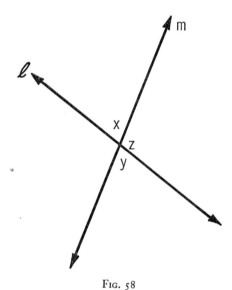

Fig. 58

show that the angles $\angle b$, $\angle c$, and $\angle d$ are also right angles. Using rigid motions, it can be pointed out that two lines are perpendicular if each is invariant for the reflection in the other.

There are many other metric concepts besides bisectors, supplementary angles, congruence of vertical angles, and perpendicularity, which require measures for their definition and development. A circle, for example, is defined metrically as a set of points equidistant from a single point. There are also the metric ideas related to parallels and transversals, and the metric properties of various geometric figures. Before these concepts can be developed adequately, it is necessary to have available the congruence properties of triangles.

TRIANGLE CONGRUENCE

Congruence for triangles has already been developed in connection with rigid motions. In a rigid motion, the vertices of a triangle $\triangle ABC$ are matched with those of its congruent image, $A'B'C'$. This can be extended to the general idea that there is a correspondence of vertices for any pair of congruent triangles which can be indicated by the order of naming the vertices in the congruence statement. For example, in the statement $\triangle ADC \cong \triangle SRT$ the following correspondence of vertices is

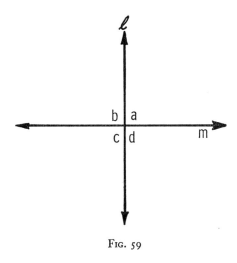

FIG. 59

indicated: $A \leftrightarrow S$, $D \leftrightarrow R$, and $C \leftrightarrow T$. This leads then to the following congruence of corresponding angles and sides:

$$\angle A \cong \angle S \quad \overline{AD} \cong \overline{SR}$$
$$\angle D \cong \angle R \quad \overline{AC} \cong \overline{ST}$$
$$\angle C \cong \angle T \quad \overline{DC} \cong \overline{RT}$$

In general, two triangles are congruent if and only if there is a correspondence of vertices such that the corresponding parts are congruent. A great deal of experience should be provided for the students to identify correspondences of vertices and corresponding parts from given congruence statements and pairs of congruent triangles.

With this background, students are ready to explore shorter ways of determining if two triangles are congruent. The best procedure is to involve the students in copying triangles by using a ruler and a protractor.

In Figure 60 is shown $\triangle ABC$ and $\overline{A'B'}$ so that $\overline{AB} \cong \overline{A'B'}$. Ask the students to find ways of locating C' above $\overline{A'B'}$ so that $\triangle A'B'C' \cong \triangle ABC$. One way of locating C' is shown in Figure 61. Using a protractor, a ray is drawn so that $\angle A' \cong \angle A$. With a ruler, C' is located on the ray so that $\overline{A'C'} \cong \overline{AC}$. After completing $\triangle A'B'C'$, a tracing sheet may be used to check that the two triangles are congruent. This leads to the SAS (side, angle, side) congruence property of triangles. Two tri-

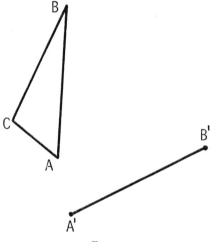

Fig. 60

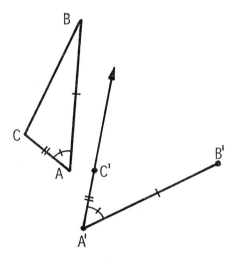

Fig. 61

angles are congruent if two sides and the included angle of one are congruent to two sides and the included angle of the other. In the same fashion, the other ways of locating C' lead to the ASA (angle, side, angle) and the SSS (side, side, side) congruence properties of triangles.

PERPENDICULARITY AND PARALLELISM

Armed with the three congruence properties for triangles, the students may now develop proofs of the congruence of certain parts of geometric figures. For example, in Diagram I of Figure 62 they can prove that any point P on a perpendicular bisector ℓ of $\overline{AB}$ is equidistant from A and B. In

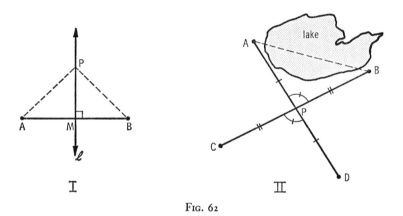

I   II

FIG. 62

Diagram II, they can show that the distance from A to B across a lake can be found by measuring the distance from C to D. Students will need careful guidance in developing proofs. At first they can complete outlines of proofs before they are turned loose to construct proofs on their own. However, before they can go much further in developing proofs of properties of figures, they are going to have to examine the structure of parallelism.

Using the protractor axiom and triangle congruence, it can be proven that for a point P and a line ℓ in a plane there is one and only one line through P perpendicular to ℓ (Figure 63). This statement enables us to prove that two lines perpendicular to the same line are parallel. Line ℓ is perpendicular to lines m and n. Suppose m and n are not parallel and meet at some far distant point P. Then there would be two lines through P perpendicular to ℓ, which cannot be. Therefore m and n are parallel. We write $m | | n$.

Another proof can be given using rigid motions. For the reflection in line ℓ above, point P has an image P' on the other side of ℓ. By the separation property of a line in a plane, P and P' are distinct points. Then there are two lines m and n through two points P and P'—a situation which is contrary to the fact that only one line can pass through two

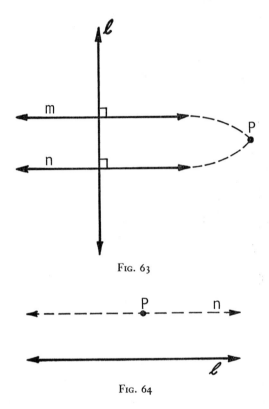

Fig. 63

Fig. 64

points. Therefore m and n are parallel. It is important to use rigid motions throughout whenever possible to strengthen the development of geometric ideas.

Using a ruler and a protractor, the students can now draw a line n through a point P not on line ℓ that is parallel to ℓ (Figure 64). First they draw a line m through P perpendicular to ℓ. Then they draw n perpendicular to m at P. The question now arises: Is line n the only line through P parallel to ℓ? It may come as a surprise to the students that, after centuries of struggling with this question, it was finally shown that no answer could be proven but that some assumption would have to be made.

This activity led to the development of some non-Euclidian geometries. In Euclidean geometry, however, the following assumption is made which is called the *parallel postulate*. For a line ℓ and a point P not on ℓ, there is only one line through P parallel to ℓ.

With the parallel postulate, it is possible to prove that if $m||n$ and $\ell \perp n$, then $\ell \perp m$ (Figure 65). Suppose m is not perpendicular to ℓ. Then let p be a line, $p \perp \ell$ at B. But p would be another line parallel to n through B, and this cannot be. Therefore, m must be perpendicular to ℓ. The students are now ready to consider the following situation. In Figure 66, $m||n$, $p||q$, and $a = 90$. The students can easily prove now that $\angle b$, $\angle c$, and $\angle d$ are also right angles. A quadrilateral such as $ABCD$

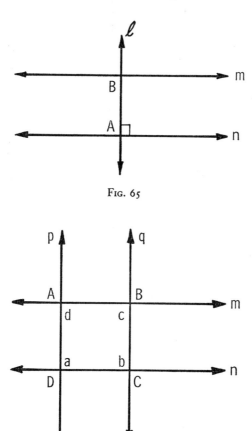

FIG. 65

FIG. 66

whose angles are all right angles is a rectangle. Using triangle congruence, it can be proven that the opposite sides of a rectangle are congruent.

Transversal t intersects parallel lines m and n at A and C, forming the alternate interior angles $\angle a$ and $\angle b$ (Figure 67). $\overline{AB}$ and $\overline{CD}$ are drawn

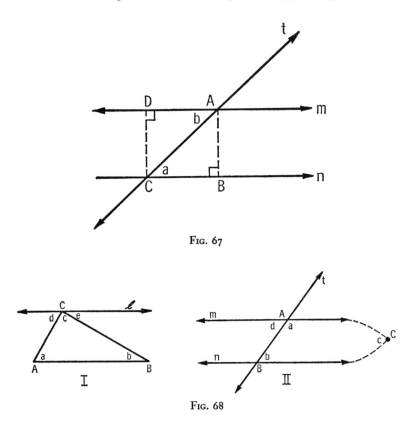

FIG. 67

FIG. 68

perpendicular to m and n, forming rectangle $ABCD$. Using the SSS property, it follows that $\angle a \cong \angle b$. The students may now continue by showing that, for any two parallel lines and a transversal, the pairs of corresponding angles are congruent and the pairs of interior angles on the same side of the transversal are supplementary.

Before the converses of the above statements are considered, it would be helpful to have available the fact that the sum of the measures of the angles of a triangle is 180. This can be proven with the aid of Diagram I (Figure 68) in which line ℓ is drawn through C parallel to $\overline{AB}$. The students can easily show that $a + b + c = 180$. In Diagram II (Figure 68) it is given that the alternate interior angles $\angle b$ and $\angle d$ are congruent. Are m and n parallel? Suppose they are not and they meet at some distant point C. Then $a + b + c = 180$. But $a + d = a + b = 180$. So C must equal zero and this cannot be. Therefore m and n are parallel.

In the study of parallelism, we see that the students can participate in the development of a carefully structured sequence of ideas. Also there are many applications of parallelism which can be explored by the students. A classic example is the use of parallelism by Eratosthenes about 2200 years ago to determine the circumference of the earth—with surprisingly accurate results.

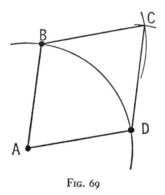

FIG. 69

ANALYZING GEOMETRIC FIGURES

With the powerful tools of the congruence properties of triangles and the ideas related to perpendicularity and parallelism, the students are ready now to analyze the properties of some geometric figures. The rectangle and some of its properties have already been introduced because they were helpful in the development of parallelism. The rhombus is next to be studied because its properties are especially applicable to compass and straightedge constructions.

A rhombus is a quadrilateral with all its sides congruent (Figure 69). The students may get acquainted with a rhombus by constructing one. Start with a point A as center and draw an arc. With any two points B and D on the arc as centers, draw arcs with the given radius intersecting at C. The quadrilateral $ABCD$ is a rhombus. The students may also construct a rhombus with a given angle, or with a given diagonal, or with some given condition.

Using triangle congruence, it can be proven that each diagonal of a rhombus bisects the opposite angles. This justifies the construction of the bisector of an angle, $\angle A$, shown in Diagram I (Figure 70). Since $\overline{AD}$ is a diagonal of the constructed rhombus $ABCD$, then $\overline{AD}$ bisects $\angle A$.

It can also be proved that the diagonals of a rhombus are perpendicular bisectors of each other. This then justifies the construction of the perpendicular bisector of a segment $\overline{AB}$ shown in Diagram II (Figure 70). $\overline{AB}$ and $\overline{CD}$ are diagonals of the constructed rhombus $ADBC$. In this way, students see the justification of the various compass and straightedge constructions.

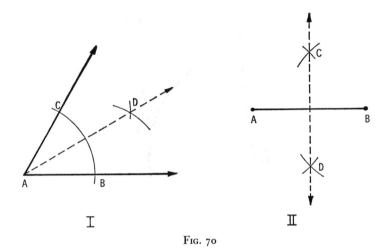

I   II

FIG. 70

The analysis of figures continues by proving the various properties of parallelograms. By way of summary, the students check to see which of the following properties are true for all parallelograms, all rectangles. all rhombuses, and all squares.

1. Opposite sides are parallel
2. Opposite sides are congruent
3. Opposite angles are congruent
4. Neighboring angles are supplementary
5. All angles are right angles
6. Diagonals bisect each other
7. Diagonals are congruent
8. Diagonals bisect opposite angles
9. Diagonals are perpendicular
10. All sides are congruent

The students should discover that a square has all ten properties and that there are quadrilaterals which have none of the above properties. They should also explore which properties automatically follow from a given property. For example, if the diagonals of a quadrilateral bisect each other, what other properties does the quadrilateral have?

The symmetry properties of figures should also be studied at this time. If a figure is invariant for a reflection in a line, then the line is a line of symmetry for the figure. Paper-folding is helpful in the early exploratory stages of finding lines of symmetry for figures. The figures may be classified by the number of symmetry lines they have. In connection with symmetry, the medians, angle bisectors, altitudes, and perpendicular bisectors of triangles should be explored because sometimes they are lines of symmetry. Rotational symmetry of figures should also be examined. For example, a parallelogram is invariant for a half-turn about the intersection of its diagonals. In all this work with symmetry, the students should be given opportunity to use their compasses and straightedges for finding images of points and figures for rigid motions in place of using tracing sheets. Also, the study of rotational symmetry may be extended to include a consideration of inscribed and circumscribed figures.

To conclude this survey of the geometry program for Grades VII through IX, a few additional topics will be mentioned. The area and volume formulas can be studied again, but this time the formulas can be derived for the various regions, using triangle congruence and some simple algebra. The concept of *similarity* for triangles, especially right triangles, can be introduced and explored, using ratios. This study may include some of the trigonometric ratios and also the development of the Pythagorean rule for right triangles.

As a final topic, mention should be made of relating geometry to the coordinate plane. The coordinatized line came into being with the ruler axiom. With two perpendicular coordinatized lines as axes, a coordinatized plane can be established in which there is a one-to-one correspondence between ordered pairs of real numbers and points in the plane. Equations for lines, segments, rays, and half-planes can be developed. Also, students may explore rigid motions in the coordinate plane and develop coordinate rules for points and their images. For example, for a counterclockwise quarter turn f, the coordinate rule for the image of a point $P(x,y)$ can be expressed as a function

$$f : (x,y) \rightarrow (-y,x) \ .$$

For a reflection g in the y-axis, the function would be

$$g:(x,y) \rightarrow (-x,y) \ .$$

In this way students may begin to see the power of coordinate notation and to understand that rigid motions are transformations of the plane.

Geometry in the Senior High School

An appraisal of the geometry program which is evolving at the elementary and junior-high levels reveals that, when this program is realized, it will have a profound effect on the geometry offered in the tenth grade and in the later grades. Most of the content of the conventional tenth-grade geometry of a few years ago will be removed from its isolation at this level and diffused throughout the lower levels with varying degrees of informality and rigor.

Some of the goals that are considered significant for the geometry program at the senior-high level are listed below.

To provide opportunity for:

1. Acquiring a systematically organized body of geometric knowledge of physical space
2. Developing deductive thinking
3. Developing inductive and creative thinking
4. Gaining insight into axiomatics and the construction of mathematical models
5. Mastering a variety of approaches to geometry
6. Relating geometric content to other parts of mathematics and preparing a foundation for further study of mathematics.

The first objective has already been noted as an important goal for the geometry program in the elementary and junior-high grades. Some attention is given to this objective at the senior-high level, since the organization of geometric content is more complete at this level and it is knowledge that is basic for performance in the practical arts. There is, however, a shift of emphasis to other objectives for the program.

Geometry is generally recognized as an ideal subject in which to stress deductive reasoning. For centuries it has served as a model of a deductive structure of ideas, and its content offers a rich variety of logical form. It is a subject that has been completely axiomatized; its content has a great deal of intrinsic interest because of its relation to physical space; and its concepts are relatively free of emotional "hang-ups" and biases which plague the content of other subjects. Furthermore, the students should be ready for this type of reasoning after having had some ex-

posure to developing short deductive sequences in the junior-high program. For these reasons the goal of deductive thinking is an important
one at this level.

Experience has shown that the objective of developing deductive
thinking is a difficult one to achieve. Quite often in the past, this objective degenerated into the memorization of proofs. Recently, as a result
of attempts to correct the defects in the logical structure of Euclidean
geometry, this objective got bogged down in a fetish of symbolism and
overconcern with small details. Continuous efforts need to be made to
achieve a better balance between the requirements of rigor and the interests and maturity of the student. The logic that is involved in developing a deductive structure must be seen first as "common sense" by
the students before it takes the form of formal symbolic logic. Also,
certain gaps in the deductive structure should be allowed to remain (or
should be assumed to be filled) if the filling would be tediously lengthy
for the students. On the other hand, the development should not become
sloppy and dishonest. Some very careful tightrope walking needs to be
done in attaining this goal.

The objective of developing inductive and creative thinking is an important one for the geometry program. Provision should be made for
students to use their "hunches" and make some guesses on the basis of
their observations. These guesses should then be tested to see if they
fit into the structure. This process allows for student involvement and
participation which is so vital to effective learning. Too often, geometry
is presented as a formidable "untouchable" structure. In geometry there
is a wealth of material that can be used to develop inductive thinking
and tax the ingenuity of the student.

Throughout the elementary and junior-high grades, geometry is developed as a mathematical model of physical space. Certain geometric
concepts are seen as idealizations of certain physical objects, and the relations among the concepts closely resemble the relations among the
physical objects. At the senior-high level, after Euclidean geometry has
been studied fairly comprehensively, the nature and construction of a
mathematical model can be explored with the students. This objective
may be achieved by noting that there are other very respectable mathematical models of space, which are known as non-Euclidean geometries.
These other models may be pursued briefly to show the important role
of axioms in the construction of these models. This should lead to an
appreciation of the dependency of a model upon the choice of axioms.

The axioms which are common to these geometries should be noted as well as the axioms which serve to distinguish one geometry from another. A brief study of certain finite geometries may also be helpful in providing some insight into how mathematical models are designed.

APPROACHES TO GEOMETRY

There are different approaches to geometry and it is important that the senior-high geometry program provide an opportunity for the students to master these approaches or techniques. Some of these approaches are listed below and they will be discussed in more detail later.

Synthetic.—This is the name given to the approach used by Euclid and found in the conventional geometry texts. In this approach, a complex structure of geometry is formed from a rather complicated set of axioms. It is the approach most familiar to everyone.

Coordinate.—In this approach, geometry is studied algebraically by means of coordinate systems. The logical foundations for this approach are essentially those of algebra. This study leads to the development of analytic geometry.

Transformations.—This approach has already been discussed at the junior-high level in connection with rigid motions or isometries. At the senior-high level, geometry may be studied through an algebra of transformations.

Vectors.—In the junior-high program, vectors were introduced as an outgrowth of translations and certain physical quantities. Now, vectors can be used to develop geometry through the use of vector algebra. This approach is coordinate-free and leads to the development of the vector space, which is an important part of mathematics.

It is important that geometry not be developed in isolation from the rest of mathematics but that its ideas be related and integrated into the mainstream of mathematics. Some of the approaches listed above are especially suited for achieving this objective and for preparing students for further study in mathematics.

Obviously, the task of accomplishing all of the goals that have been listed is a formidable one. The spreading of geometry instruction throughout the various school levels will be of some help when it has been effected. The existence of the variety of approaches to geometry listed above and the possible combinations of these approaches considerably complicate the problem of curriculum-planning for the geometry program at the senior-high level. Mention has already been made of the forthcoming impact of the junior-high program. Because of these complexities and uncertainties, the shape of the future senior high school geometry program is quite unclear at this time.

It is certain, however, that each of the approaches listed above, individually or in some combination, will have an important bearing on the future program. Consequently the geometry programs which embody each of these programs will be examined briefly.

SYNTHETIC GEOMETRY

The content of this program has already been described in connection with the elementary and junior-high programs. It is the conventional tenth-grade geometry program of today; however, its dominance at the senior-high level will very likely decrease as its content is incorporated into the lower-level programs.

The content of the synthetic geometry program provides a starting point for any overall school geometry program. Its concepts and relationships are fairly easily grasped since they are closely related to physical space. Consequently the development of the other approaches is dependent upon an understanding of the content of this program.

During the past decade a great deal of effort has been made to correct the omissions and weaknesses of Euclid's axioms, thereby putting the conventional program on an axiomatic basis that is more in line with today's requirements. There have emerged out of these efforts to "clean up" Euclid essentially two types of high school synthetic geometry programs. One type follows basically the Hilbert axiom system. In this system the primitive concepts are point, line, betweenness, and congruence. The axioms are grouped as axioms of incidence, of betweenness (or order), of congruence, of continuity, and the parallel axiom. The axioms of continuity consist of the Archimedes postulate and the completeness postulate which permit the introduction of measurement and the coordinatized line, but these have a minor role in the program.

The other type of synthetic geometry program follows the axiom system developed by Birkhoff. In this system the primitive concepts are point, line, distance, and angle. The metric postulates contain the ruler and protractor axioms which have been discussed previously, and they are used to establish the betweenness and congruence concepts. It has been found that the metric postulates are readily acceptable to high school students. Furthermore, the metric foundation provides a very efficient means of developing the traditional content of geometry. As a consequence, the Birkhoff type of programs are receiving widespread favor and acceptance throughout the country. Both the Hilbert type and Birkhoff type of programs use a substantial amount of sophisticated symbolic equipment made available by set theory in order to sharpen the development of the geometric concepts.

These recent changes in the conventional program have not been made without dissent or reservations. The matter of the amount of rigor is still a hotly debated item. It is likely that some reasonable compromise program will evolve from the experiences with these changes. It is also likely that some shortened compact form of the synthetic program will be an important part of the senior-high geometry program.

COORDINATE GEOMETRY

The coordinate approach begins with a coordinate system on a line which is a one-to-one correspondence between the line and the set of real numbers which relates distances between points on the line and differences between numbers. Two points determine exactly one coordinate system, and any two coordinate systems on a line are related affinely. Rays and segments are subsets of lines and can be described by means of a coordinate system. Betweenness and midpoints of segments can also be described using coordinates. The protractor axiom is used in the same way as the ruler axiom to establish a ray-coordinate system for angles.

There follows next a synthetic development of the definitions and properties of various angles, including right angles and perpendicularity, triangle congruence properties and their use, the parallel postulate and its consequences, and similarity leading to the Pythagorean theorem. This synthetic development leads to the establishing of the Euclidean plane.

The Euclidean plane is coordinatized in the usual manner, using a pair of coordinatized perpendicular lines called the x- and y-axes so that there is a one-to-one correspondence between the plane and the set of ordered pairs of real numbers. The distance formula for any two points in the plane is developed using the Pythagorean theorem.

For any points $P_1(x_1,y_1)$ and $P_2(x_2,y_2)$

$$P_1P_2 = \sqrt{(x_2 - x_1)^2 + (y_2 - y_1)^2} \, .$$

The formula for the midpoint of a segment immediately follows from the distance formula. After exploring the pattern of coordinates of points on a line, the slope of a line is defined and its consequences explored. This leads to the development of the equations on a line of the two-point form and the point-slope form. This development usually makes use of the set-builder notation and parameters. The concept of *slope* is used to develop conditions for perpendicularity and parallelism for oblique lines. If m_p and m_q are the slopes of lines p and q, then

$$p \perp q \text{ if and only if } m_p \cdot m_q = -1, \text{ and}$$

$$p \,|\,|\, q \text{ if and only if } m_p = m_q .$$

Coordinates can now be used to develop proofs of some of the theorems in geometry. In constructing proofs using coordinates, the students should learn to set up coordinate systems which simplify the expressions involving coordinates. They can prove, for example, that if a segment joins the midpoints of two sides of a triangle, its length is $\frac{1}{2}$ the length of the third side. They can also prove theorems about the concurrence of angle bisectors and perpendicular bisectors of sides of triangles and many of the properties of special kinds of quadrilaterals. Students should also learn when to use coordinates and when to use other ways of proving theorems. Coordinate systems can be developed in three-dimensional space, and the coordinate method can be applied to problems in three-dimensional situations.

The development outlined above can be varied in different ways. For example, the coordinatized line can be used to coordinatize the affine plane. After the various theorems of affine geometry have been developed, a perpendicularity relation can be introduced on the affine plane, which leads to the Euclidean plane and the theorems that are particular to it.

With this background in coordinate geometry and with further work in algebra, a student would be ready to study analytic geometry during the latter part of the senior-high program.

TRANSFORMATION GEOMETRY

A transformation of a plane is a one-to-one correspondence of the set of all points of a plane onto itself. Consequently, for a given transformation, each point P in a plane has a unique image P' in the plane, and also P itself is the image of some unique point. In the transformation approach, geometric figures and their images are studied and their geometric properties are compared.

The concept of transformation provides a central and unifying idea for geometry in the same manner as the concept of a function does for analysis. By considering such properties as collinearity, distance, perpendicularity, orientation, and angle measure, transformations are analyzed and classified in terms of the geometric properties that are left unchanged. This leads to an organization of geometric material into different kinds of geometry.

The transformations most appropriate for the secondary level are those in which it is required that distances be invariant. In other words, for any two points A and B, and their images A' and B' for the transformation, the distance between A and B is the same as that between A' and B'. These distance-preserving transformations are called isometries, and they have been introduced as rigid motions at the junior-high level.

At the senior-high level, isometries are now analyzed more deeply. In preserving distances it can be shown that isometries also preserve all the geometric properties except orientation. Isometries which preserve orientation are often called displacements. In general, isometries preserve size and shape, which means that, for an isometry, each figure has a congruent image. As a result, the study of isometries can be introduced through the use of tracing sheets as described for the junior-high level.

The use of isometries can provide a much deeper study of congruence than the older practice of using superposition. Isometries provide a more generally unifying and logically acceptable approach to congruence. Instead of building the idea of congruence from the congruence of segments to the congruence of triangles to the congruence of polygons and polyhedra, this approach deals with the congruence of all figures simultaneously. Furthermore, the study of isometries can reinforce the idea of a function and can provide for an extensive study of symmetry. Let line s and point A be given as shown in Figure 71. The reflection in line s shall be denoted by M_s. Since s is the perpendicular bisector of $\overline{AA'}$, then A' is the image of A for the reflection in s. This is written

$$M_s(A) = A'.$$

Also, the image of A' is A, and this is written

$$M_s(A') = A.$$

Two intersecting lines a and b and point A are shown in Figure 72. A_1 is the image of A for the reflection M_a. Hence $M_a(A) = A_1$. A_2 is the image of A_1 for the reflection M_b. Hence $M_b(A_1) = A_2$.

These two reflections M_a and M_b can be combined and written as follows:

$$M_b M_a(A) = M_b(M_a(A))$$
$$= M_b(A_1) = A_2 .$$

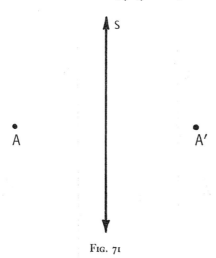

FIG. 71

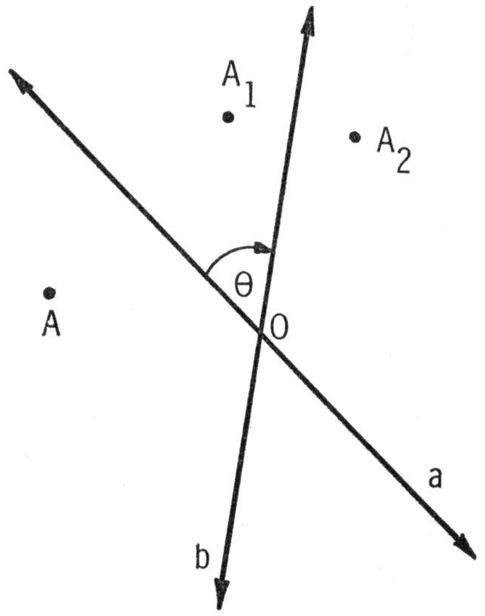

FIG. 72

This notation M_bM_a is read from right to left and means "first M_a, then M_b." For the combined transformation M_bM_a, the image of A is A_2, and is written as follows: $M_bM_a(A) = A_2$. The students will find that the transformation M_bM_a is the clockwise rotation about point O with an angle of rotation 2θ. In general, $M_bM_a \neq M_aM_b$. However, if $M_bM_a = M_aM_b$, then $a \perp b$.

For the line s and point A shown in Figure 71, it is noted that $M_sM_s(A) = A$. When the reflection M_s is performed twice, the result is the

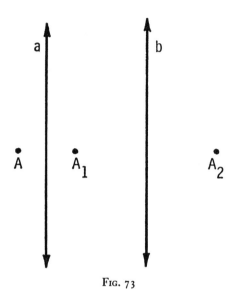

FIG. 73

identity transormation, I. In other words, $M_sM_s = I$. If the correspondence between points for a given transformation Q is reversed, the inverse transformation Q^{-1} is obtained. It follows then that

$$QQ^{-1} = Q^{-1}Q = I.$$

Consequently the reflection M_s is its own inverse, $M_s^{-1} = M_s$.

Two parallel lines, a and b, and point A are shown in Figure 73. $M_a(A) = A_1$ and $M_b(A_1) = A_2$. M_bM_a is A_2. $M_bM_a(A) = A_2$.

If the distance between the lines a and b is d, then the distance between A and A_2 is $2d$. For the transformation M_bM_a, the distance between any point P and its image P' is $2d$ and in the same direction. Thus M_bM_a is a translation.

The development shown above for reflections can be continued leading to the development of an algebra of isometries. The algebraic operations for isometries result in a mathematical system called a *group*. In this way students may classify and relate the different kinds of isometries and see how they behave structurally. Also it is worthwhile for the students to study the isometries using a coordinate plane.

After examining the isometries, the students are ready to study other kinds of transformations. It has already been noted that isometries preserve both the shape and size of geometric figures. If the requirement that a transformation preserve size be dropped but that shape be retained, then we are led to a study of *similarity transformations*. In these transformations, all lengths are decreased or increased in the same ratio but the shapes are unchanged. The students can continue to determine what specific properties are invariant for the similarity transformations. Other kinds of transformations are those which do not preserve size or shape but which do preserve collinearity and parallelism. These transformations are called *affine transformations* and may also be studied briefly at the senior high school level.

VECTOR GEOMETRY

The vector approach to Euclidean geometry generally takes its departure from a study of translations. As noted previously, a translation is determined by an arbitrary point P and its image P'. This pair of points determines a distance and direction which can be represented by an arrow leading from P to P'. For a given translation, the arrows from points to their images are equivalent, and the equivalence class of arrows is called a vector, which can be represented by any one of the arrows. In this way, each translation is associated with a vector and vice versa.

It is important to note that there are two fundamental types of objects involved in this approach: (*a*) points in a plane or space and (*b*) vectors as translations. We shall speak of a translation T with vector $\overrightarrow{v}$ which operates on points A, B, C, etc. Any ordered pair of points (A,B) determines a translation which is sometimes denoted as $\overrightarrow{AB}$. The ordered pair (A,A) defines the zero vector $\overrightarrow{o}$. It is essential that, in relating points and vectors, the fundamental distinction between points and vectors be carefully maintained.

Translations are combined by vector addition, which is defined by the following triangle addition rule (see Figure 74). This has already been explored at the junior-high level using tracing sheets. It is noted that vector addition is

commutative, $\quad \vec{a} + \vec{b} = \vec{b} + \vec{a}$

and

associative, $\quad (\vec{a} + \vec{b}) + \vec{c} = \vec{a} + (\vec{b} + \vec{c})$.

The zero vector $\vec{o}$ is the identity element for vector addition:

$$\vec{a} + \vec{o} = \vec{o} + \vec{a} = \vec{a} .$$

Also, each vector $\vec{a}$ has an inverse $- \vec{a}$ such that $\vec{a} + (- \vec{a}) = \vec{o}$ (Figure 75). Then the set V of vectors with vector addition + form a commutative or abelian group.

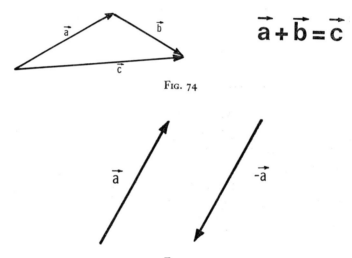

FIG. 74

FIG. 75

Scalar multiplication is introduced next and the development described in the junior-high program is reviewed. The scalars here are elements of the real number system R, and scalar multiplication associates each scalar $k \in R$ and vector $\vec{v} \in V$ with the vector $k\vec{v} \in V$. Scalar multiplication has the following properties: For each j, $k \in R$ and $\vec{u}$, $\vec{v} \in V$

$$k(\vec{u} + \vec{v}) = k\vec{u} + k\vec{v} \qquad (j + k)\vec{v} = j\vec{v} + k\vec{v}$$
$$(j \cdot k)\vec{v} = j(k\vec{v}) \qquad\qquad 1\vec{v} = \vec{v} .$$

These properties complete the development of a vector space.

In applying vectors to geometry, it is convenient to express certain geometric concepts and relations vectorially. For non-collinear points A, B, C, D in a plane,

$$\overrightarrow{AB} = k\overrightarrow{CD} \text{ means that } \overline{AB} \parallel \overline{CD} \text{ and } \overleftrightarrow{AB} \parallel \overleftrightarrow{CD}.$$
$$\overrightarrow{AB} = \overrightarrow{CD} \text{ means that } \overline{AB} \cong \overline{CD} \text{ and } \overline{AB} \parallel \overline{CD}.$$

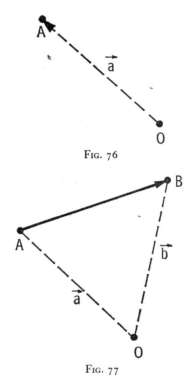

FIG. 76

FIG. 77

A plane π with an arbitrary origin o is denoted by π_0 (Figure 76). For any point A in π_0, there is the vector $\overrightarrow{OA}$ which is designated as $\overrightarrow{a}$. The vector $\overrightarrow{a}$ is called the position vector of A. Likewise for any translation in π_0 with vector $\overrightarrow{v}$, there is a unique point A in π_0 such that $\overrightarrow{OA} = \overrightarrow{v} = \overrightarrow{a}$. This establishes a one-to-one correspondence between the set of points in π_0 and the set of vectors as translations in π_0.

Any vector $\overrightarrow{AB}$ in π_0 can be expressed in terms of the position vectors $\overrightarrow{a}$ and $\overrightarrow{b}$ as shown in Figure 77:

$$\overrightarrow{a} + \overrightarrow{AB} = \overrightarrow{b}$$

therefore,

$$\overrightarrow{AB} = \overrightarrow{b} - \overrightarrow{a}.$$

The midpoint M of a segment $\overline{AB}$ in π_0 can be expressed in terms of the position vectors $\vec{a}$, $\vec{m}$, and $\vec{b}$, as shown in Figure 78:

$$\vec{m} = \vec{a} + \tfrac{1}{2}\overrightarrow{AB}$$
$$= \vec{a} + \tfrac{1}{2}(\vec{b} - \vec{a})$$
$$= \tfrac{1}{2}(\vec{a} + \vec{b})$$

In general, for the plane π_0, we can think of the position vectors without drawing them (Figure 79). For example, $\vec{d} - \vec{b}$ is the expression

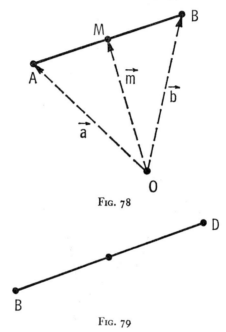

FIG. 78

FIG. 79

for the vector $\overrightarrow{BD}$, and $\tfrac{1}{2}(\vec{b} + \vec{d})$ is the position vector of the midpoint of $\overline{BD}$.

Shown in Figure 80 is an example of using vectors to prove a geometric theorem.

Given: parallelogram $ABCD$.

Prove: the diagonals bisect each other.

Proof:

1. $\overrightarrow{AB} = \overrightarrow{DC}$ since $AB \cong DC$ and $\overline{AB} \parallel \overline{CD}$
2. $\vec{b} - \vec{a} = \vec{c} - \vec{d}$ substitution
3. $\vec{b} + \vec{d} = \vec{a} + \vec{c}$ add $\vec{a}$ and $\vec{d}$ to both sides
4. $\tfrac{1}{2}(\vec{b} + \vec{d}) = \tfrac{1}{2}(\vec{a} + \vec{c})$ multiply both sides by $\tfrac{1}{2}$.

Then the position vectors for the midpoints of $\overline{BD}$ and $\overline{AC}$ are the same.

Sometimes it is not necessary to use position vectors in the proofs (see Figure 81).

Given: quadrilateral $ABCD$

Points P, Q, R, S are midpoints of $\overline{AD}$, $\overline{DC}$, $\overline{CB}$, and $\overline{AB}$ respectively.
Prove: $PQRS$ is a parallelogram.

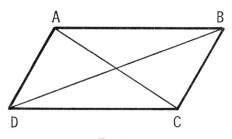

Fig. 80

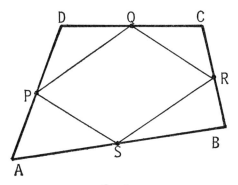

Fig. 81

Proof:
1. $\overrightarrow{PD} = \frac{1}{2}\overrightarrow{AD}$, $\overrightarrow{DQ} = \frac{1}{2}\overrightarrow{DC}$, $\overrightarrow{SB} = \frac{1}{2}\overrightarrow{AB}$, $\overrightarrow{BR} = \frac{1}{2}\overrightarrow{BC}$ by hypothesis
2. $\overrightarrow{PQ} = \overrightarrow{PD} + \overrightarrow{DQ} = \frac{1}{2}(\overrightarrow{AD} + \overrightarrow{DC})$
3. $\overrightarrow{SR} = \overrightarrow{SB} + \overrightarrow{BR} = \frac{1}{2}(\overrightarrow{AB} + \overrightarrow{BC})$
4. $\overrightarrow{AD} + \overrightarrow{DC} = \overrightarrow{AB} + \overrightarrow{BC}$ because each is equal to $\overrightarrow{AC}$
5. $\overrightarrow{PQ} = \overrightarrow{SR}$ by substitution
6. $\overline{PQ} \cong \overline{SR}$ and $\overline{PQ} || \overline{SR}$
7. Therefore $PQRS$ is a parallelogram.

Perpendicularity is introduced through the concept of the *inner product* or *dot product* of two vectors. We shall denote the magnitude or length of a vector $\vec{a}$ by $|\vec{a}|$. If the angle between two vectors $\vec{a}$ and $\vec{b}$ is θ, then the inner product of $\vec{a}$ and $\vec{b}$ is

$$\vec{a} \cdot \vec{b} = |\vec{a}| \cdot |\vec{b}| \cos \theta .$$

If $\vec{a}$ and $\vec{b}$ are not zero, then

$$\vec{a} \perp \vec{b} \text{ if and only if } \vec{a} \cdot \vec{b} = 0 .$$

The inner product can now be used in geometric proofs involving perpendicularity.

Further work in vector geometry can be done with the study of linear combinations of vectors leading to linear dependence and independence and to bases of vector spaces. Later in the senior-high program it would be possible to study linear transformations in general, using matrices and linear algebra.

SUMMARY

The future shape of the geometry program in the senior high school is quite obscure at the moment. However, it is possible to predict that, with more of synthetic geometry being studied at the elementary and junior-high levels, less time will be devoted to synthetic geometry at the tenth grade. This will provide more room for the other approaches to geometry. At first, there will be units of these other approaches introduced in the program, which will be revised and expanded with experience.

For the synthetic approach, there are the following programs: (*a*) the conventional geometry programs, (*b*) the recently developed "clean Euclid" programs of the Hilbert type and Birkhoff type, and (*c*) the non-Euclidean geometries. Then there are the programs which make extensive use of algebraic techniques: (*a*) the coordinate geometry program, (*b*) the transformation geometry program, and (*c*) the vector geometry program.

It would be advantageous at this point to match the various programs with the objectives stated at the beginning of this section on the senior high school level. For this purpose, a matrix is presented below which may be useful to persons studying the various types of geometry programs. Check marks may be used to indicate programs that are especially suited for meeting particular objectives.

PROGRAM	OBJECTIVE					
	Physical Space	Deductive Thinking	Inductive and Creative	Axiomatics and Models	Variety of Approaches	Future Study
Conventional geometry						
"Clean-Euclid" Hilbert type						
"Clean-Euclid" Birkhoff type						
Non-Euclidean geometry						
Coordinate Geometry						
Transformation Geometry						
Vector Geometry						

To anyone using this chart, it should be apparent that no single program will do the job of accomplishing all of the objectives.

CHAPTER V

Functions

R. CREIGHTON BUCK

Introduction

One powerful research technique which has been responsible for many advances in mathematics in labeled *abstraction*. This term denotes the specific analytic process which examines a number of different mathematical problems or theories and recognizes that each contains a common pattern or structure, which is then pulled out (abstracted) and made the subject of independent study. When this process is successful, the new mathematical entity thus created turns out to be present in an unrecognized form in a multitude of other situations; its study brings about a coherence and simplicity of viewpoint which did not exist before and leads to discoveries about the entity that make possible major advances in mathematics.

Two such concepts are *set* and *function*. In terms of the long span of the history of mathematics, both have emerged very recently.[1] It is therefore not at all surprising that the general concept of function, as well as an explicit mention of set theory, did not appear in school mathematics until the last decade. For example, the last NSSE yearbook to treat mathematics (*The Teaching of Arithmetic*, 1951) does not contain a reference to either "set" or "function." In contrast, here is an excerpt from an outline of the mathematics curriculum, K-VI, which is part of the 1967 "Report of the Cambridge Conference on Teacher Training." Referring to a chart which displayed the basic topics in the curriculum, together with their interrelations, the authors said:

1. Some of the basic ideas of set theory are implicit in Aristotle but did not achieve maturity until almost 1900. Similarly, no single author or moment of time can be credited with the "invention" of the function concept; Tom Hawkins suggests the period 1860–1915, although some aspects appear as early as 1650. See Tom Hawkins, *The Development of the Modern Theory of Integration* (Madison: University of Wisconsin Press, 1969).

Some of the most important items are deliberately omitted from the diagram, not because they are unimportant, but, on the contrary, because they should be nearly ubiquitous. Chief among these are the concepts of FUNCTION and SET, which should be used throughout the development wherever natural examples and uses occur. By Grade 6, both the words *function* and *set* (and the ideas behind them) should be established firmly and correctly as natural parts of the pupil's mathematical language.[2]

Some critics have failed to understand the reasons which lie behind the introduction of new concepts into the mathematical curriculum. One statement from the 1963 "Report of the Cambridge Conference" speaks to this point:

Contemporary mathematical research has given us many new concepts with which to organize our mathematical thinking; it is typical of the subject that some of the most important of these are very simple. Concepts like set, function, transformation group, and isomorphism can be introduced in rudimentary form to very young children, and repeatedly applied until a sophisticated comprehension is built up. We believe that these concepts belong in the curriculum not because they are modern, but because they are useful in organizing the material we want to present.[3]

The basic idea of *set* is such a concept. It is already implicit in our language in the form of the collective noun. It is present when we classify anything or describe one of its properties. It is even more in evidence when we mention relationships between properties or classifications. It was therefore to be expected that the language and some of the tools of set theory should have found a ready (and at times an overenthusiastic) reception by both textbook writers and teachers.

The concept of function is more subtle, both in its nature and in the role which it plays in the curriculum. Even the prestigious "Report of the Commission on Mathematics" failed to treat the concept adequately. The resultant misunderstanding is clearly visible in many presentations of the "new" mathematics, although not in those that have been developed by classroom teachers and educators with support and advice from professional research mathematicians.

The purpose of the present article is to focus on the function concept, to describe several of its aspects, and to chart some of its appearances

2. *Goals for Mathematics Education for Elementary School Teachers* (Cambridge Conference on Teacher Training [Boston: Houghton Mifflin Co., for Educational Development Center, Inc., 1967]), p. 98.

3. *Goals for School Mathematics* (Report of the Cambridge Conference on School Mathematics [Boston: Houghton Mifflin Co., for Educational Services, Inc., 1963]), p. 10.

in the mathematics curriculum. At the start, we shall rely upon examples; the modern concept of function will not emerge in its final form until the end of the chapter, where we enter more deeply into the technical background.

Function as "Rule"

Perhaps more than other scientists, mathematicians tend to use everyday words, investing them with specific technical meanings which have little if any connection with their common meanings. For example, each of the words "integrate," "differentiate," "ring," "field," "group," "ideal," and "radical" are technical mathematical terms. This is also the case with the word "function"; its common meaning as a noun is "role" or "capacity" or "performance."

Perhaps the synonym that comes closest to expressing the mathematical meaning of function is "rule" or "algorithm." Any situation in which a specific process exists that can be applied to any number in a certain set, and which yields numbers, can be described by means of a particular function. Thus, the rule "square it" corresponds to a particular function S which applied to 3 yields 9, applied to $\frac{1}{2}$ yields $\frac{1}{4}$, and applied to -2 yields 4. The function here is the specific instructions which say: "Take the given number and compute its product with itself."

In this initial approach to the concept of function, students are asked to imagine a specific function as a machine whose mechanism is concealed within a box that has two openings, one for the input and one for the output. (See Figure 1.) If a number is dropped into the "input" funnel, a number will emerge from the "output" spout—the result of the operation that the function was designed to do to the input number.

A different and more complicated function is described by:

Q: Take the given number, add 3, double the result, add 4, and then divide by 2.

If we were to "drop 4 into the input funnel" of this function, the output will be 9, as we see by carrying out the instructions. Likewise, if Q is applied to 2, the result will be 7.

If one had to work solely with such verbal descriptions of functions, it would be very difficult to make much progress. Indeed, this was one of the severe handicaps that faced mathematical scholars prior to the fifteenth century when the use of standard symbols became more common. As a first step, we may use letters or other symbols to denote certain specific functions. This we have already done above, using S for the "square it" function, and Q for the function of the previous paragraph. A special convention is adopted; if F is the name of a specific function, then $F(2)$ will indicate the number that results from applying the function F to the number 2. Thus, we might say

S applied to 5 yields 25

or

$$S(5) = 25$$

In the same way, we observed above that $Q(4) = 9$ and $Q(2) = 7$.

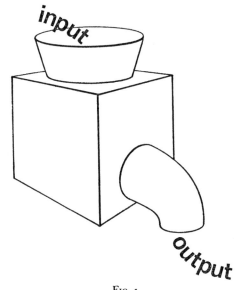

Fig. 1

To see that this agrees with common practices, consider the square root function, usually denoted by $\sqrt{}$. Here, we could write

$$\sqrt{}(49) = 7$$

$$\sqrt{}(100) = 10$$

although it is also common to write $\sqrt{49} = 7$ and $\sqrt{100} = 10$.

The name of a function can also be a combination of letters, as in "sin," "cos," "log"; for example, we recognize the statement

$$\log (2) = .30103$$

to mean that the logarithm function, applied to 2, yields .30103.

Associated with any function is a specific set of numbers called its "domain." These are merely the numbers to which the function may be applied, according to the given instructions. Since any real number may be multiplied by itself, the domain of the function S is the set of all real numbers. In contrast, since no negative real number has a real square root, the domain of the function $\sqrt{}$ consists of all the real numbers greater than or equal to 0.

Special symbolic notations are also used to help in describing specific functions. The "square it" function S can be described by the display

$$\square \rightarrow \square \times \square$$

and the more complicated function Q by the display

$$\square \rightarrow \{2 \times (\square + 3) + 4\} \div 2$$

In each of these, the $\square$ is to be filled by a numeral and the result of the operation calculated arithmetically. Thus, to find $Q(3)$, we have

input
$$\boxed{3} \rightarrow \{2 \times (\boxed{3} + 3) + 4\} \div 2$$
$$= \{2 \times 6 + 4\} \div 2$$
$$= \{12 + 4\} \div 2$$
$$= 16 \div 2 = 8$$

Another more common practice is to use x (or some other convenient letter) as a place-holder variable, instead of the box. We then say that the function in question is described by a formula. For example, the function Q might be described by the formula:

$$Q: \qquad x \rightarrow \{2(x + 3) + 4\} \div 2$$

or by

$$Q(x) = \{2(x + 3) + 4\} \div 2$$

One reason for the use of formulas, rather than words, is that it is possible to develop convenient procedures for working with formulas, which, therefore, make it easier to work with functions.

This is easy to illustrate. We say that two functions are the same if they accomplish exactly the same results. If the two functions were F and G, then we would write $F = G$ if and only if their domains are the same and $F(a) = G(a)$ for every choice of the number a; F and G have the same outputs when any number in the domain is used as input.

Now consider the function H described by the display:

$H:$ $\square \rightarrow \square + 5$

or, equivalently,

$$H(x) = x + 5 .$$

It is easy to see that $H(1) = 6 = Q(1)$, $H(2) = 7 = Q(2)$, $H(3) = 8 = Q(3)$, and $H(4) = 9 = Q(4)$. Can we show that in fact $H = Q$? We cannot test each of the infinite collection of possible input numbers. Instead, we use elementary algebra to see that

$$
\begin{aligned}
Q(x) &= \{2(x + 3) + 4\} \div 2 \\
     &= \{(2x + 6) + 4\} \div 2 \\
     &= \{2x + 10\} \div 2 \\
     &= x + 5 = H(x) .
\end{aligned}
$$

Almost all the routine work in elementary algebra is merely practice in learning to work with functions and in showing that certain formulas define the same function. This is precisely the content of such assertions as

$$x + 2 = 2 + x$$
$$x^2 - 4 = (x - 2)(x + 2)$$

and even

$$(a^2 x^3 y^4)(b\ x\ y^2) = a^2 b x^4 y^6 .$$

It should also be pointed out that a great many important mathematical discoveries are often demonstrations that two complicated formulas (or rules) which had been studied independently turn out to describe exactly the same function.

Functions in the Classroom

How do these ideas appear inside the classroom? Perhaps several hypothetical scenes will suggest some of the possibilities.

A teacher has been reviewing with her pupils addition of (small) whole numbers. At this point, she chooses to help them take a first step toward the conceptualization of the process of addition itself, on a non-verbal level. [In our terminology, she wishes to create familiarity with functions such as the function g defined by $g(x) = x + 2$.]

She will first have the pupils calculate the sums

$$1 + 2 =$$
$$4 + 2 =$$
$$5 + 2 =$$

and others. She will then use the phrase:

the function called "adding two"

and immediately introduce the diagram

$$\square \rightarrow \square + 2$$

At the same time, to reinforce and to help visualize the idea that the process of adding two has an existence as an entity, she will move to the number line that is part of the permanent display in the classroom

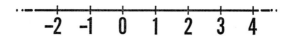

and, on this, will interpret the box diagram above as "moving 2 to the right" or "jumping up 2." This may be done by asking questions such as:

If I add 2 to this number, where will I get to?
If I start at 6, and add 2, where will I be?

If the number line has (as it should) the negative numerals -1, -2 -3, etc., marked to the left of 0, then she may also ask for the results of adding 2 to -2, or to -1, or even to -3. After this has been done on the number line, the results may be written either as

If I add 2 to 6, I get 8
If I add 2 to -3, I get -1
If I add 2 to 0, I get 2

or as

$$6 + 2 = \quad 8$$
$$-3 + 2 = -1$$
$$0 + 2 = \quad 2$$

keeping in mind the diagram

$$\square \rightarrow \square + 2$$

A similar "game" is then played with the function "add 3," diagrammed as: $\square \rightarrow \square + 3$. The teacher will speak of this as: the function called "adding 3," and she will point out that the two functions are different. [Note that she will have used the term *function* without an explicit definition; this is analogous to using the word "fruit" when speaking of apples and oranges. A child cannot learn *fruit* without experience with apples, oranges, etc., nor can he learn *function* without examples. Much learning arises from context. Note, however, that the teacher has not used the notation $g(2)$ or $g(x)$.]

At some future time, the teacher may also discuss the function called "subtracting 3" and point out that it reverses the effect of "adding 3" when used on the number line.

At another time, the teacher may look at the function description:

$$\square \rightarrow 2 + \square$$

and, by working with examples, arrive at the agreement that this function is the same as "adding 2" because of the commutativity of addition. Note also that this new function looks quite different from "adding 2" when examined on the number line, since we would now start from 2 and move various distances to the right.

Among experienced educators, Max Beberman (UICSM), Robert Davis (Madison Project), and David Page (ESI, now EDC) have been quite successful in introducing an understanding of the function concept early in the school curriculum. One of their pedagogical experiments is especially interesting.[4] The teacher may tell his pupils that he has a certain function in mind and they are to guess what it is. They may give him any number, and he will apply his function to their number and tell them the result. All of these pairs are written on the blackboard and serve as the data from which the children must deduce the formula for the teacher's function. As an illustration, the students may have elicited the following information:

2	5
4	9
1	3
11	23

As the store of information about the function increases, students will become sure that they know what the teacher's function is. The teacher will test the students, not by asking for a formula or for a verbalized description of the rule, but merely by giving *them* a number and seeing

4. *Goals for Mathematics Education for Elementary School Teachers, op. cit.*

if they can come up with the same result that his function gives. Finally, after more and more of the pupils seem to have discovered the rule, he will display it; in the case we have illustrated, he will write down:

$$\square \ \rightarrow \ 2 \ \square \ + \ 1$$

In addition to being exciting teaching, this "guess my function" game gives them practice in arithmetic, experience in reasoning from data, and help in learning to handle the function concept. Moreover, following the spiral pattern which seems to have become one of the major ingredients in the new curricula, the teacher can return to this procedure in successive years, working with more and more complicated functions until, in senior high, one reaches the general topic of curve fitting.

This section would be incomplete without a brief mention of computers and the present and future relevance of computing to school curricula. The writer leaves to others (if they choose) to discuss the technological and vocational aspects, including the possibilities that are latent in computer-assisted instruction. What is relevant here is the close relationship between the concept of *function* and the object known as a *computer program*. The latter can be regarded as a set of abbreviated instructions which, when furnished to the computer together with whatever input data is needed, generates the elaborate sequence of actions that the computer is expected to perform, including the preparation and printing of the final output. The nature of the task done by the computer depends upon the particular computer program that has been fed into it, so that a general purpose computer can behave in an infinite number of essentially different ways.

In numerical work, one thing that a computer is often called upon to do is to calculate the values $F(c)$ of some very complicated function F for certain choices of the numbers c. The computer program will then comprise a description of the function F, in the form of detailed instructions that tell the computer how to behave so as to *be* the function F. Thus some aspects of the concept of function are contained in the general notion of a program. Not all computer programs can be regarded simply as descriptions of numerical functions, for some are collections of instructions which also contain instructions for modifying these instructions; some of the analogies between this and biological mechanisms such as DNA and the genetic code are among the more exciting aspects of the applications of this branch of mathematical science.

It should be added that some of the recent text materials prepared by the School Mathematics Study Group for the elementary school and for Grades VII and VIII introduce functions and some of the techniques being developed by computer scientists in a very imaginative and satisfactory way.

Function as Graph

Sometimes the most useful way to present a specific function F is to give a complete tabulation of its values, listing each number c in its domain, and with it, the corresponding value of $F(c)$. When it is either impossible or impracticable to list all the numbers in the domain of a function, it may be quite sufficient to list only those that most frequently arise in applications of the function. Thus, if one is interested in the function f given by the formula

$$f(x) = x^2 + x$$

it may be quite sufficient to have the table:

$x =$	o	.1	.2	.3	.4	.5	.6	.7	.8	.9	1.0
$f(x) =$	o	.11	.24	.39	.56	.75	.96	1.19	1.44	1.71	2.0

In many cases, such tables provide the only way that most people encounter certain functions; this is true of the logarithm function and of many of the specialized functions tabulated in chemistry handbooks. For the businessman, this may also be true in the case of the *interest tables*, which are merely convenient displays of the more frequently used values of certain functions which yield the total return of an investment when the interest rate and the number of years are given.

The information about a function which is contained in a partial tabulation of its values can also be displayed graphically, and in this form it can be even more useful in understanding the nature and properties of a particular function. The idea which makes this display possible, and which constitutes another of the fundamental concepts in mathematics, is commonly credited to René Descartes (ca. 1637); this is the realization that, with respect to an origin and a pair of coordinate axes, each point in the plane can be associated uniquely with an ordered pair of real numbers, and conversely. (See Figure 2.) With this in mind, we can then take any table of values for a function, and use each input entry x for

the first coordinate of a point and the output entry $f(x)$ as the second
coordinate. In this way, we will obtain a collection of points in the plane,
one for each tabulated value of the function. In Figure 3, we have done
this for the table presented above. We can now imagine doing this for
every possible input value x; the resulting points will fill in between those
we already had and will result in the smooth curve shown in Figure 4. This

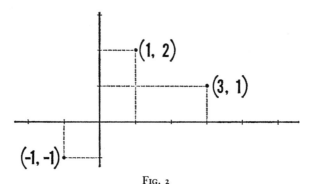

FIG. 2

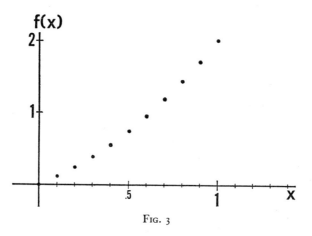

FIG. 3

curve is called the *graph* of the function f. Different functions will have
different graphs, and one of the basic topics in the study of functions is
to learn how to interpret graphs and to recognize properties of functions
from information contained in their graphs.

This aspect of functions is so important, and so much a part of the
everyday uses of mathematics, that it must be started very early in a
pupil's education. It may occur first in a segment devoted to science or

to social studies rather than to mathematics, but this can be an asset. The following illustration shows how a single classroom activity can be used over a period of weeks to build pupil understanding of the concept of function and graph.

The needed equipment consists of an outdoor thermometer recording the temperature of a scale from −20 to 100 and some large sheets of

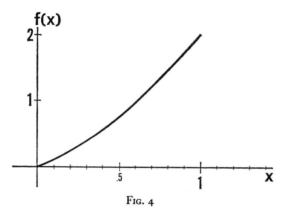

FIG. 4

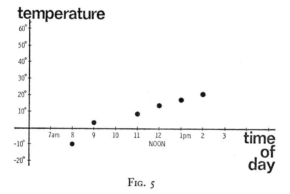

FIG. 5

paper. The first step is to have students observe the outside temperature at selected moments of the class day and record these observations by marking a point corresponding to the ordered pair (time, temperature). After this has gone on for some days, the students will have become adept at producing charts similar to that shown in Figure 5. The teacher now points out: "We didn't measure the temperature at 10 o'clock, or at 3 p.m. Do you think we could guess what it was?" After recording several guesses, she may then reveal that she did check the temperature herself and record the true value. This then leads at once to the question of how they would record the information if they had the temperature at shorter intervals of time and what the result would look like. For several days this is done, and the result is first a graph with closely spaced dots and then a smooth curve running from 8 a.m. through 3 p.m.

The teacher then asks: "What do you think the temperature graph would look like if we took the temperature all night long?" Each pupil draws a graph showing what he thinks the curve will look like, and the pupils' curves are then compared the next day with the true curve as obtained from either local weather-station data or newspaper reports. Comparison of these twenty-four-hour graphs for different days gets across, in a very concrete way, the fact that two functions can be different and also builds skill in interpreting graphs of functions.

In later grades, the examples and purpose of the study can become more sophisticated. Suppose that the students have been measuring and recording as a graph the number pairs (L, T), where L is the length of a pendulum and T is its period in seconds. From this graph, what can be said about the function g which calculates T from L by $T = g(L)$? From their experience with graphs of specific functions, they may decide that the graph they are dealing with looks like the graph of a function such as square root, and thus be led to the conjecture that the relationship between L and T is given by $T = c\sqrt{L}$ and then to an empirical determination of the value of c. Such experiences lead pupils to an understanding of the mathematical nature of "physical laws," namely, that these laws are assertions that there exist functions which relate the values of certain measurable quantities in nature.

The General Concept of Function

Until now, all examples of functions have been simple numerical ones, having values that are numbers and a domain that consists of numbers. No such restriction is part of the concept of function; indeed, many important functions have nothing to do with numbers. In order to explain this, we must gradually enlarge the concept of function.

As a first step, let us observe that many common functions have as their domain not individual numbers but pairs of numbers. For example, the ordinary process of addition can be regarded as a function which operates on pairs of numbers, to yield a single number, their sum. The corresponding mental image should be a box with *two* input funnels, and one output spout.

Again, the standard formula for the volume of a cone

$$V = \tfrac{1}{3}\pi R^2 H \qquad R = \text{radius}, \ H = \text{height}$$

describes a function of "two variables," meaning that if we assign numerical values to both R and H, we can calculate the corresponding value of V. This same function is sometimes described by the display

$$\triangledown, \square \rightarrow \tfrac{1}{3}\pi \triangledown^2 \square \qquad \begin{array}{l} \triangledown = \text{radius} \\ \square = \text{height} \end{array}$$

where we have used different shaped boxes to distinguish between the one to be filled by the radius of the cone and the one to be filled by the height of the cone. This device is so clumsy that one turns very quickly to the use of letters, as above.

There is no limit to the number of separate variables that may be involved. For example, the formula for calculating the resistance of a number of different resistances, connected in parallel, is given by:

$$R = \cfrac{1}{\dfrac{1}{R_1} + \dfrac{1}{R_2} + \dfrac{1}{R_3} + \cdots + \dfrac{1}{R_n}}$$

where R_k is the resistance of the k-th resistance.

The conventional notation for indicating the number of variables (number of input funnels) is illustrated as follows. If we use the letter v for the function which calculates the volume of a cone, we would write

$$V = v(R,H) = \tfrac{1}{3}\pi R^2 H$$

It is important to note that $v(2,3)$ and $v(3,2)$ are different numbers; the former is $\tfrac{1}{3}\pi (2)^2 3 = 4\pi$ and the latter is $\tfrac{1}{3}\pi (3)^2 2 = 6\pi$.

If we use T as the function which yields the total resistance for a parallel circuit of four resistances, we would write

$$R = T(R_1, R_2, R_3, R_4) = \cfrac{1}{\dfrac{1}{R_1} + \dfrac{1}{R_2} + \dfrac{1}{R_3} + \dfrac{1}{R_4}}$$

We can also adapt the "$\rightarrow$" convention by describing each of these functions by

$$v: \qquad (R,H) \ \rightarrow \ \tfrac{1}{3}\pi R^2 H$$

and

$$T: \qquad (R_1, R_2, R_3, R_4) \qquad \cfrac{1}{\dfrac{1}{R_1} + \dfrac{1}{R_2} + \dfrac{1}{R_3} + \dfrac{1}{R_4}}$$

The next larger leap in understanding occurs when it is realized that a function of one or more variables can in fact be regarded as a function of one variable (a machine with a single input, rather than one with many). This realization comes as soon as it is seen that we can in fact treat an assembly of numbers such as the ordered pair (R,H) or the ordered quadruplet (R_1, R_2, T_3, R_4) as a single entity. This is the essence of Descartes' discovery of analytical geometry; we can, for example, think of the pair $(3,5)$ as represented by a point in the plane, and an ordered quadruplet such as $(2, 4, 7, 5)$ as represented by a point in four-dimensional space. These functions then revert to the type we have discussed before in that they have a *single* input funnel; the difference is that they are constructed to accept a more complicated input, an ordered sequence of numbers instead of a single number.

This is a difficult transition for many children and indeed for some adults. Nevertheless, the realization that a complex composed of many measurements or specific attributes can be treated and thought of as though it were a single point is one which has made possible some of the basic advances in physics, economics, and psychology, as well as in mathematics. On one extreme, we are able to lump together into one single vector all of the components which reflect the responses of an individual to a battery of psychological tests, thus studying a collection of individuals as an assemblage of points in a multidimensional space. In another direction, we can represent the entire state of the national economy by a single point and follow the changes in the economy by watching the motion of the point.

In this way, some of the most complex situations in which people are interested can be simplified and rendered possible of study. The problem of achieving a satisfactory definition of human intelligence can be reformulated in terms of the creation of a suitable numerical-valued function, whose domain is the set of psychological vectors. The problem of achieving a better measure of the health of the economy becomes that of choosing the correct function on the set of points which comprise the possible states of the economy.

At this stage, it is now possible to make the final step of abstraction and formulate the general concept of *function*. For this purpose, we must have two sets, A and B. The elements in these sets may be anything at all; neither has to be numbers. A function on A to B, often denoted by a statement such as

$$f : A \rightarrow B$$

is a rule by which we assign to each member of the set A some member of the set B. If a is in A, then $f(a)$ denotes the member of B that corresponds to a. We also speak of A as the *domain* of the function f and say that f takes its values in the set B. The mental picture is still the same; a box with an input funnel and an output spout. The difference now is that the nature of the input and of the output is unrestricted.

When this stage is reached, a student suddenly realizes that there are functions wherever he looks and that a great deal of his time in school (and out of it) has been spent in learning to work with certain specific functions. Several examples may be helpful.

In the experience of students, the process of *measurement* becomes one of the most pervasive sources for functions whose domain of definition is non-numerical. In the concept of "length," they have seen a function L_{in} which assigns to any physical stick S its length $L_{in}(S)$ in inches. They have also used the function L_{yd} which assigns to a stick S its length $L_{yd}(S)$ in yards. Each of these functions has for its domain the collection of physical objects that can be measured, and its values are non-negative numbers. The relations between the units "yard" and "inch" can be stated in terms of the two functions as the equation

$$L_{in} = 36 \, L_{yd}.$$

In the same way, any specific unit of weight gives rise to a specific weight function W; the function W_g, applied to a quantity Q of material, yields the number $W_g(Q)$ which is the weight of this material in grams. In some cases, physical measurement leads to a function of several variables. Thus, we can define $d_{ft}(P,Q)$ to be the distance, measured in feet, between two locations P and Q on the earth; the function d_{ft} is then a number-valued function whose domain is the collection of all pairs of locations on the earth.

When the process of using a tape measure or a scale is looked at more closely, objections can be raised to the model presented above, for functions have to be uniquely determined while measurement seems to be inherently ambiguous and indeterminate. One approach is to say that there *is* a length function L which will give the accurate true value of the length $L(S)$ of a specific stick S, but we can calculate only an approximation to its value. (Analogy: $\sqrt{2}$ is the exact value, but we can calculate only an approximation such as 1.41421.)

Another approach, more popular with recent treatments, is to associate a measurement function F with each specific procedure for measuring the quantity involved, and then to allow the values of F to be intervals of numbers, rather than a single number. For example, if F_1 is the length function associated with a yardstick, and F_2 that associated with a steel tape, then we might have $F_1(S) = [23\frac{5}{8},24]$, while $F_2(S) = [23\frac{11}{16},23\frac{13}{16}]$. In this way, it is possible to incorporate into a measurement function some of its error behavior as well. (Some recent school texts have included a treatment of some aspects of "interval arithmetic" as a practical tool in working with measurement and estimation.)

Many other examples could be given to show the utility of functions whose domain or whose set of values is non-numerical. In talking about simple logic, "truth value" becomes a function V whose domain is the set of meaningful statements and whose values are the letters T and F. If β is a statement, then $V(\beta) = T$ when β is true, and $V(\beta) = F$ when β is false. In advanced geometry, the geodesics on a curved surface are the curves of shortest length joining two points. This can be formulated in terms of functions by inventing a function G whose domain is the collection of pairs of points P, Q on the surface and whose values are curves on the surface, such that $G(P,Q)$ is the geodesic joining P and Q.

The role that functions play in mathematics is so extensive that it is impossible to give any summary that is both brief and adequate. There is no branch of mathematics whose developments since 1800 can be studied in their present form without an understanding of the general function concept. This is even more true when it comes to the applications of mathematics to physical problems. As an illustration, there is a whole class of problems in which the objective is to solve a set of equations to determine an unknown function. (This is analogous to the simple algebraic problem of solving for the unknown numerical quantities in an algebraic equation, but since the unknown is now a *function*, the techniques are vastly more complex. Simple examples of this would be the solution of differential equations, of partial differential equations, and of functional equations.)

In algebra, the study of isomorphism and homomorphism between structures is exactly the study of certain types of functions. In geometry and topology, the concepts of congruence, of symmetry, and of homomorphism and continuous deformation are intrinsically questions dealing with restricted classes of functions. In modern analysis, one of the most actively growing fields of research in the past forty years has been the study of functions whose domain is itself a class of functions; integration and differentiation are two simple examples of such functions.

The Axiomatic Approach

In the preceding pages, there has been much discussion of the function concept, many illustrations of functions and their use, but nowhere a formal *definition* of function. Instead, the term "function" has been applied to specific examples and the reader has been left to infer meaning from context. (Of course, it is not a formal definition to equate "function" with "rule" if the latter is then left undefined.) The purpose of this section is to discuss some of the pedagogical and mathematical aspects of this approach, with the hope of clarifying some of the problems that have arisen in connection with the "new" mathematics in the classroom situation.[5]

Let us first point out that one cannot define something except by reference to something else. This means that any subject must admit undefined terms or must be entirely described within some other theory, which in turn must have undefined elements or must be entirely described in terms of . . . (and so on). This classical example of infinite regression, applied to mathematics, shows that we must adopt some starting point and that the elements of this basis will contain undefined terms. The choice of such a basis must be subjective and guided by such criteria as aesthetics, economy, usefulness, and tradition. In practice, there is no unique starting point; what is selected as a basic undefined term in one axiomatic structure in mathematics may become definable in another. A simple example is geometry. In the Euclidean framework, point and line are undefined, as are such phrases as "lie on," "determined by," and "parallel." In analytical geometry, each of these is defined in terms of the real numbers. A *point* becomes an ordered pair (a, b) of real numbers, and a line is the set of all points (x,y) where the coordinates x and y satisfy an equation such as $Ax + By + C = 0$. However, note that we have not defined "real number," "ordered pair," "set," or "satisfy."

The history of mathematics of the past century shows an increased awareness of the use of undefined terms and a much greater analysis of the underlying philosophical problems. In the period from 1880 to 1920,

5. See also R. C. Buck, "Goals for Mathematics Instruction," *American Mathematical Monthly*, LXXII (1965), 949–56; R. L. Wilder, "The Role of Instruction," *Science*, CLVI (1967), 605–10, and "The Role of Axiomatics in Mathematics," *American Mathematical Monthly*, LXXIV (1967), 115–27; *Proceedings of the Preliminary Meeting on College Level Mathematics* ([Katada Report, 1964] Japanese International Printer, 1965); *Role of Axiomatics and Problem-Solving in Mathematics* (Conference Board of the Mathematical Sciences [Boston: Ginn & Co., 1966]).

much attention was given to the possibility of creating a single axiomatic structure within which all mathematics could be defined and explained. It was at once perceived that this Adamic structure must embrace an axiomatization of logic itself, and the first major fruit of this intensive introspection was the treatise *Principia Mathematica*, by Whitehead and Russell. Unfortunately, the entire project—launched with such hope—found itself wrecked on certain rocks which were discovered in the years between 1910 and the present, and a theorem of Gödel shows that the original goal was inherently too ambitious.[6]

One result of the study of the foundations of mathematics was the development of *set theory*. It had been observed that much of classical mathematics made constant (and uncritical) use of terms such as "the set of all . . .", ". . . is a member of the class of all . . .", and the like. When these were subjected to intensive analysis, a systematic structure was created based on a limited number of axioms, which—together with the axioms of logic—was hoped to be powerful enough to serve as the basis for all mathematics. If this were to be the case, then it would have to be possible to *define* the concept of function within this new system in terms of the ideas of set theory alone. (Please note that the reasons are philosophical and not pedagogical.) The problem was solved successfully between 1910 and 1915 in the following way.

First, we observe that all the information needed about a function is contained in its graph. If we know all the points (x,y) which are related by the equation $y = f(x)$, then we know the function f completely; for, if we are asked to apply f to a specific input c, we need only find the pair (x,y) whose first member is c and then read off the second member.

This observation enables us to reduce the notion of a function formally to that of a certain sort of set:

A function is a set of ordered pairs (x,y) *which has the special property that no two pairs occur which have the same first member, but different second members.*

The reason for this restriction lies in the fact that $f(c)$ is unique; it is the result which the function f yields when applied to the input c. Thus, there cannot be in its graph two different points, each of which has the same first member c.

The statement above does not answer the problem completely, since it in turn contains an unexplained term, "ordered pair (x,y)," as well as

6. Wilder, "The Role of Axiomatics in Mathematics," *op. cit.*, pp. 115–27.

such phrases as "first member" and "second member." By a very ingenious device, Norbert Wiener found that it was possible to reduce these concepts to the primitive concepts of set theory; he defined the ordered pair (a,b) to be

$$\{\{\{a\}, \phi\}, \{\{b\}\}\}$$

At this point, it should be recognized that this solution, while of philosophical importance and an intellectual achievement of high merit, is a tour de force. The significance of this for the development of mathematics is minor, and the ability to recast the concept of function within the axiomatic theory of sets is a fact which most mathematicians would seldom use. As a pedagogical device, its use is strictly limited; in teaching, the basic problem is to choose the most appropriate way to build understanding and skill in the use of functions. Experience seems to show that the "a function is a class of ordered pairs" approach is one which imposes severe limitations upon the student and provides a poor preparation for any further work with functions, either in school or later.

In this connection, the distinguished American mathematician Saunders MacLane has pleaded:

By an historical accident, arising from late 19th century preoccupations with sets, most Foundations of Mathematics make the notion of "set" the primitive one, with "function" derivative. In these "classical" foundations, ordered pairs are defined, in wholly artificial fashion, by constructions on sets, while each function is (artificially) identified with its graph.

For economy, it may be well to deal with just a single primitive notion (say that of set). For *effectiveness in teaching* mathematics, it would be more in order to follow a balanced approach, using the intuitions of both "set" and function. Unfortunately, recent American reformers of elementary mathematics teaching have been over-zealous in propagandizing the notion of set. This has led to elementary books grossly over-emphasizing sets (and logic). This overemphasis should be reversed; for example, one should no longer preach that a function *is* a certain sort of set of ordered pairs.[7]

It should be observed that it is at this point that the 1959 "Report of the Commission on Mathematics" is weakest.[8] The entire treatment of the function concept was confined to about a page, and the "class of ordered pairs" approach was adopted in order to subsume "functions" under a more general setting to emphasize the importance of the notion of sets. This report, intended for mathematically sophisticated readers, did

7. *Proceedings of the Preliminary Meeting on College Level Mathematics, op. cit.*, p. 69.

8. *Report of the Commission on Mathematics*, College Entrance Examination Board, 1959.

not contain a full treatment since it was assumed that their mathematical backgrounds made this unnecessary. Some texts, attempting to follow the Commission Report, based their whole treatment of functions upon the ordered-pair formulation, thus presenting a singularly narrow and not very useful approach. Fortunately, under the leadership of some of the curriculum study groups, and spurred by criticism by scientists and mathematicians, a more valid and representative treatment of the function concept is now becoming available.

The ability to make subtle distinctions seems to be dependent upon maturity. There seems to be ample evidence that there is something called "concept readiness" and that refinements of viewpoints may be meaningless to students until a certain threshold has been reached. This readiness factor is evident in geometry classes where teachers find that some students are much more ready than others to discuss the formal deductive structure of geometry and the necessity for *proof* of results which they have already come to believe, such as the statement that a circle separates the plane into two regions. A similar problem arises in connection with the need for precision in definitions. Most students, for example, will be quite content with their intuitive understandings of the concept of whole number and will see little reason to refine this further by means of set theory; indeed, to do so at the wrong time is to replace something with which they are quite secure by an involved and unmotivated construction which uses concepts and terminology that are strange. (The definition referred to is that in which the whole number associated with a set of objects is *defined to be* the collection of all sets that are isomorphic to the given set.)

The writer feels that a similar remark must be made about the concept of function. For most students, the intuitive understanding which is acquired by working with numerous examples provides an ample and satisfying basis upon which to build; it is not until later that the question of a possible formal definition of the term "function" arises. However, this is a specific matter that should be studied on its own.[9]

Research Topics

There are many aspects of the teaching of mathematics for which tradition or the mathematical organization of the material would suggest one course, but for which recent study would suggest an alternate. The

9. R. L. Wilder, "The Role of Intuition," *op. cit.*, pp. 605–10, and "The Role of Axiomatics in Mathematics," *op. cit.*, pp. 115–27.

entire area of elementary analysis and the role of functions is one in which much work remains to be done if teachers are to receive adequate guidance. Most of the obvious questions remain unanswered. In this final section, a few of these will be identified. An additional reference, and one to be recommended to anyone concerned about the philosophy of education, is the extraordinarily stimulating paper, "Mathematics Teaching—with Special Reference to Epistemological Problems."[10] This paper, by Professor Davis, is enlivened by a discussion of many of his own experiences with children and with the presentation of the function concept in the early grades.

As a first suggestion, the author of this chapter feels that there are many questions dealing with the process of abstraction and with that of concept formation which should be explored and for which the notion of *function* could serve as a focus. In one direction, one might simply seek to determine the stage of learning at which it becomes possible for a student to recognize correctly a wide range of instances of the abstract concept of function. In another, the central problem would be to determine when the student reaches the point at which functions acquire the same concrete or tangible quality of existence that is possessed by, for example, the whole numbers. Both of these are appropriate areas for elementary education. On a more advanced level, it would be interesting to explore the stages through which a student goes in acquiring an intuitive familiarity and security with the concept of multidimensional spaces and the ability to treat a complex of numbers as the coordinate description of a single point in a space of high dimension. Finally, there should be a study in depth of the development of critical judgment as it appears in the change of attitude toward a postulational system— specifically, at what stage is a student ready to question the foundations of a subject and those things he has been led to accept?

On the pedagogical side, there are many areas that should be examined. More attention should be given to the exploitation of number lines with points to the left of the origin marked as -1, -2, -3, etc., in the earliest grades. Many have also suggested that the early introduction of simple decimals to label intermediate points will build early familiarity with the notation and better prepare students for later encounters. (As a suggestion, one might *start* with two place decimals such as 2.50, 2.75, etc.,

10. Robert Davis, "Mathematics Teaching—with Special Reference to Epistemological Problems," (Report on the Conference on Needed Research in Education [Athens: University of Georgia Press, 1968]).

since these are already part of their environment.) It would then be possible to look at simple functions such as

$$\square \rightarrow \square + 3$$

and, on the number line, lead students to guess the appropriate value for 2.50 + 3, 3.75 + 3, and even −1.5 + 3.

Again, we have given an illustration of the use of a physical problem (temperature measurement and prediction) to help teach the concept of function, graph, continuity, and rate of change. Intuitively, this procedure should produce better learning, and there should be transfer of skills and understanding from this illustration to other situations; this, of course, should be tested. Again, other examples such as this one should be constructed. (David Hawkins has devised many in his study of mathematics learning through science.)

Functions may be described in ways other than formulas, tables, or graphs. One way is by *recursion*. Suppose that we write:

$$F(1) = 3$$

$$F(n + 1) = 1 + 2F(n) \qquad n = 1, 2, 3, \cdots$$

From this, it is possible to calculate the values of F. Thus, $F(2) = 1 + 2F(1) = 1 + 2 \times 3 = 7$, $F(3) = 1 + 2F(2) = 1 + 2 \times 7 = 15$, and so on. In this particular case, there is a simple formula for $F(n)$ which makes it possible to calculate $F(5)$, for example, without having to calculate $F(4)$ first, namely

$$F(n) = 2^{n+1} - 1$$

However, with slightly more complicated recursions, there is no simple formula for F. For example, if we write

$$F(0) = 1$$

$$F(1) = 2$$

$$F(n + 1) = F(n) + F(n - 1) \qquad n = 1, 2, 3, \cdots$$

then, as before, we can calculate all the values of F that we might desire. Thus,

$$F(2) = F(1) + F(0) = 2 + 1 = 3$$

$$F(3) = F(2) + F(1) = 3 + 2 = 5$$

$$F(4) = F(3) + F(2) = 5 + 3 = 8$$

There is also a formula for F by which one might calculate $F(5)$ without having to have calculated all the previous values of F, but no student is going to guess it!

$$F(n) = \frac{5 + 3\sqrt{5}}{10}\left(\frac{1 + \sqrt{5}}{2}\right)^n + \frac{5 - 3\sqrt{5}}{10}\left(\frac{1 - \sqrt{5}}{2}\right)^n$$

Nevertheless, the simple recursion process provides one with a complete algorithm for computing the values of F. This suggests two questions which might be studied: (a) Can we use such recursively defined functions to study the ability of students to see the implications of formulas? (b) Can we find at what stage in his mathematical development a student begins to question the right to say that a recursion *defines* a function?[11]

Finally, study should be given to the possibility of presenting some aspects of approximation theory and "curve fitting," if it can be shown that this too increases the concrete quality of functions.

11. In explanation of (b), see R. C. Buck, "Mathematical Induction and Recursive Definitions," *American Mathematical Monthly*, LXX (1963), 128–35.

CHAPTER VI

Issues in the Teaching of Mathematics

STEPHEN S. WILLOUGHBY

In human affairs, there seems to be a tendency to swing from one extreme to another. Often, having swung violently between two extremes, man finds himself coming to rest somewhere in the middle, like a pendulum that has stopped oscillating. In mathematics education, this pendulum-like action has occurred with respect to many issues. In this chapter we will examine some of those issues.

Is There a Best Method of Teaching Mathematics?

Although there appears to be no clear, unambiguous evidence supporting one teaching technique over another, there is some evidence to support the contention that a teacher who is skilled in a non-teacher-directed technique is also quite skilled in a teacher-directed situation, while the converse is not true. Thus, the teacher who uses non-directed techniques fairly often is probably a better teacher whether the technique itself is good or not. In all probability, the technique used should depend on the characteristics of the children involved (age, background, mental maturity, etc.), the nature of the subject matter to be taught, the teacher, and other factors. At present, there is no clear research evidence to suggest when a particular technique is more appropriate, but there does seem to be general agreement that for young children a non-directed method is quite often very effective, while for older students the question is more controversial.

The use of various teaching aids also provokes considerable discussion. In light of the evidence that elementary school children are in a concrete reasoning stage rather than a formal abstract reasoning stage, most mathematics educators believe that it is desirable to use large amounts of manipulative materials with young children.

This same principle would apply to children who are older but who still have not fully entered the abstract reasoning stage. On the other hand, many teachers believe that it is undesirable to encourage the continued use of concrete aids beyond the time when they are actually needed by the child. Thus, the child should constantly be encouraged to give up his aids as soon as he can comfortably do so—or perhaps even a little earlier.

There are many aids which teachers may use in the classroom. Computer-assisted instruction, programed texts, movies, film strips, etc. have all gained their advocates. In general, it seems fair to say that none of these aids will ever replace the teacher or even replace all of the other aids. However, each has its value in helping the teacher to do a better job of teaching some children. More information on some of these aids can be found in chapters iv and xi of this yearbook.

For many years, educational researchers have been aware of something known as the "Hawthorne effect." Essentially, this principle asserts that, whenever an experimenter tries something new, the new procedure is likely to be more effective than the old technique, no matter what the relative merits of the two techniques may be. The reason for this greater effectiveness is that, when people realize that they are part of an experiment and that somebody is consciously trying to improve their lot, they do better. This phenomenon has resulted in some curious research findings—findings that the most incredible sorts of techniques are better than traditional ones. Of course, if the new techniques become the traditional ones after a few years, then the *old* traditional techniques will appear to be new techniques and can then be shown to be better than the old experimental (or new traditional) techniques.

For the teacher, it is always important to examine new research findings in light of the question of whether proper control was provided to avoid the Hawthorne effect. However, even though the Hawthorne effect does make life difficult for educational experimenters and interpreters of educational research, it suggests an excellent opportunity for classroom teachers. If any kind of experiment seems likely to be effective, then teachers should try, experimental techniques in their own classrooms—not primarily because they want to produce more knowledge about how children learn, but rather because any change made is likely to improve the education of the particular children the teacher is teaching. The pendulum mentioned in the first paragraph of this chapter *should* keep swinging. Even if we appear to be merely oscillating at times, coming back to a teaching technique that was discarded a few years earlier, there is reason to believe that the very act of changing will improve the educational process. Thus, it may be that change for the sake of change is really desirable. Of course, educators should try to use their best judgment, as well as results of the best available research findings, in making the decision as to which technique to try next.

Need Each Item of Knowledge and Skill Be Taught as a Separate Independent Unit of Learning?

From the time that Plato recommended the study of mathematics as a prerequiste for the study of philosophy to the present, there has been a general belief that studying mathematics is good for the mind, independent of any useful aspects the mathematics may have. This point of view seems to have been particularly well entrenched shortly before the turn of the present century. Several experiments during the late 1800's and early 1900's suggested, however, that learning mathematics does not necessarily make one more logical in other fields. In fact, there was even a question raised as to whether there is any transfer of learning between two branches of mathematics unless the two branches have large numbers of what Thorndike called "identical elements."

Thorndike developed his own ideas on the teaching of arithmetic in *The Psychology of Arithmetic*, published in 1922. In Thorndike's approach to the teaching of arithmetic, the underlying structure of the mathematics itself was essentially of no importance. Rather, he believed, the specific facts that would be useful to an individual should be determined, and then these facts should be taught to him by a stimulus-response method. The pupil should react to a particular stimulus with a particular response, thus building up a bond between the two. By this reasoning, the stimulus "$5 + 2$" should elict the response "7" as should the stimulus "$2 + 5$." That there is some connection between the two stimuli would be something the pupil might discover on his own at a later time, but there should be no serious attempt on the part of the teacher to teach him this general relationship nor to use it in helping to build the bonds.

Thorndike's psychological theories were derived both from his work with human beings and from his work with animals. He, like other stimulus-response psychologists after him, did a considerable amount of work with lower animals and extrapolated some of the results to human beings. Although the methods of these psychologists have been effective in getting both lower animals and human beings to respond with "correct" answers, there are many educators who have reservations about such methods for teaching people. Furthermore, later evidence has suggested that there can be considerable transfer of understanding between different situations if the first learning situation emphasizes general understanding rather than rote memory. Judd was one of the early psychologists to produce evidence along these lines, and numerous later experiments supported the contention that, when children master general principles, there can be a very high degree of transfer.[1]

To What Extent Can Children Learn Mathematics As They Should Know It by Engaging in Rote Learning?

Virtually everyone who consciously addresses himself to the question of whether it is better for a child to understand mathematical concepts or to commit verbalizations of the concepts to memory agrees that understanding is important and desirable. During the recent "revolution" in school mathematics, this point of view became so prevalent that in some instances textbooks provided substantial material to help children understand a concept, but virtually no practice or drill work to help them become adept at using it. Available evidence suggests that a child can understand without becoming adept in using the particular skill involved (addition of fractions, for example), but if the skill is one in which he ought to become proficient, practice or drill will be needed. On the other hand, if drill is used without understanding, retention does not seem to be as great, and, of course, the learning of a skill involving the same understanding but different sorts of symbols will be more difficult if the understanding has not been developed.

A great deal of actual teaching does not appear to give much importance to understanding. This is true not only of "traditional" classes in which, for example, learning the multiplication table by

1. See chapter ii for a much more complete discussion of transfer.

rote is emphasized, but also of "modern" classes in which the commutative, associative, and distributive laws are learned by rote. In fact, a great deal of mathematics is now (and always has been) taught and learned by rote. Although many educators would probably say that this rote procedure is unfortunate, there seems to be no clear evidence that *all* children should learn all mathematics first through understanding and then become adept at the skills and verbalizations. In fact, it seems distinctly possible that, for many children, understanding may come more appropriately *after* or *during* acquisition of the skills and of the ability to verbalize. Although there are many strongly held opinions on this subject, there seems to be little clear evidence regarding which children should learn which mathematics in which ways.

Recognizing the need for drill raises the question of which methods of administering the drill are most effective. Evidence seems to suggest that drill on a particular subject should be spread out over a fairly long period of time to be most effective. That is, if children are going to spend two hours drilling on a particular skill, the drill will be more effective if the two hours are spent in eight fifteen minute sessions over a period of several weeks rather than in one two-hour session. In fact, there is even some evidence which suggests that leaving a subject for several weeks and then returning to it is more effective than studying it entirely on successive days.

Evidence also supports the commonsense notion that motivated drill is more effective than unmotivated drill. Unfortunately, the method of motivating particular children is not always clear. Some children will be motivated if real life problems involving the skill are introduced, while others would much prefer to have the skill enmeshed in a game situation (competitive or not, depending on the child). There is also some evidence to suggest that (*a*) keeping the child informed as to his progress towards acceptable competence in a particular skill, and (*b*) letting him know clearly why the skill is going to be needed, help to motivate him.

To What Extent Does Understanding Promote or Hinder Learning?

As indicated in the previous section, understanding generally appears to promote retention of the learning of a concept and may also help in the learning of similar concepts. However, there are circumstances under which an overemphasis on what appears to be understanding may be actively harmful. For example, if a person has learned a particular algorithm for an operation (such as the standard algorithm for division) and then is asked to learn a more complex algorithm that emphasizes understanding (the subtractive method of division), the procedure is likely to be both confusing and irritating to him. If, on the other hand, the algorithm emphasizing understanding is taught first, and it is then shown that the second algorithm is simply a short cut for the first, the procedure seems to be beneficial.

There are also times when "understanding" does not mean the same thing for a child as for an experienced mathematician. For example, approaching integers as ordered pairs of natural numbers is an excellent way to show that the system of integers is consistent if the system of natural numbers is also consistent. However, the argument involved here is appropriate to graduate study in mathematics, not to junior high school mathematics. The junior high school pupil can probably understand the integers through their relation to the real world more readily than through a formal deductive system.

Similarly, a complete understanding of Euclidean plane geometry (along the lines proposed by Hilbert) or of the notion of limits would tend to be so difficult to achieve that the development of such understanding would be likely to prevent the student from ever reaching the interesting and useful parts of geometry and calculus. In cases of this sort, an intuitive understanding can be developed early in the study of the subject, and, if a more complete understanding is desired, the subject can be reconsidered after the student has developed more mathematical maturity.

When Are Children Ready To Learn a Given Segment of Mathematics?

The answer to this question is far more complex than it might appear to be on the surface. Although it is true that textbook writers, curriculum makers, and others have been proceeding for many years as though they knew the answer to this question, present evidence suggests that it is not possible to provide any sort of simple answer to the general question. A major reason for this is that different children obviously become "ready" for a given topic at different times. This is true not only with regard to chronological age, but also with regard to development in other respects. For example, one child may be ready to begin reading before he is ready to add and subtract whole numbers or to throw and catch a ball; another child may be ready to play ball first, add and subtract next, and read last; while others may be ready for these activities in still different orders.

Even within the broad area of mathematics, different people apparently become ready for various activities in different orders. Some people seemingly can visualize and reason about geometric figures before they are able to generalize using algebraic symbols, while others will be ready for these activities in reverse order.

The reasons for this disparity among different persons in readiness for a particular activity are not entirely clear. Undoubtedly one of the reasons is biological—individuals (even brothers) differ from each other at birth and will naturally find different learning styles more appealing. A second reason has to do with a person's environment. Because of various activities a person may have carried out in the past, he may or may not have become ready to attempt a particular activity. A twenty-year-old man who has grown up on an island where there are no mechanical appliances, for example, is not likely to be as ready to drive an automobile as is a man of similar physical and intellectual ability who has grown up in a twentieth-century industrialized society. In this case, if we wished to teach the non-industrialized man to drive a car, it would be desirable to expose him first to a large number of experiences with mechanical things—most notably, with automobiles.

In a similar way, if a child has not had any experiences with numbers and groups of things that are counted, he is not as likely to be ready to learn arithmetic as a person who has had these experiences. Thus, many people have suggested from time to time that it is possible to provide children with certain experiences which will prepare them to learn a given activity. For example, if we wish a child to learn how to prove a mathematical proposition, we could encourage him to carry on arguments that will convince others that he is right about both mathematical and non-mathematical propositions. We could also see to it that he is provided with an opportunity to listen to such arguments carried on by others.

However, there are obviously some limitations to what can be done in providing experiences that prepare a person to learn a given subject. For example, there are few people who would think it was worthwhile to provide a child with many mechanical experiences in his first years so that he would be ready to start learning to drive a car at the age of three. Even if the car could be reconstructed to accommodate his small physical stature, there is some reason to suppose that three-year-olds *ought* not to be driving automobiles. By the same token, even though it may be possible to provide children with experiences that will enable them to learn to carry out formal abstract mathematical proofs at the age of six years, there are many people who believe that it is more important to teach other things to young children.

Thus, the answer to the question of when children are ready to achieve particular learning will vary with the child and his experiences. Although it is possible to provide a child with experiences that will get him ready to learn a particular subject, this may or may not be desirable. Presumably, it is desirable for the teacher, through his own observations and through the use of the various more formal instruments that have been developed, to find out as much as possible about the readiness of each child for subjects that are about to be taught; and, if certain children are not ready, they should probably be exposed to appropriate experiences to make them ready before the subject itself is taught to them.

Is There a Danger of Pacing Instruction Too Rapidly?

Throughout the history of mathematics education in this country, there has been a tendency to teach particular topics to children at an ever earlier age. As late as 150 years ago, it was common to find arithmetic being taught in college. Of course, as various subjects have been taught to ever younger children, the character of these subjects has changed somewhat, but the overall trend towards teaching certain subjects earlier is unmistakable. Until recently, for example, it was common to think of elementary school mathematics and arithmetic as synonymous. In the past two decades, however, it has become increasingly common to find other mathematical subjects being taught in the elementary school as well. Geometry is one of the most important of these subjects, but there are also some elementary algebra, some probability and statistics, some simple number theory, and even an introduction to computer science being taught in the elementary school.

As these new or more advanced subjects enter the elementary school, there are several important facts to remember. First, the process of introducing new topics will be difficult for the teacher. This is partially because a person who has been out of school for some time often has difficulty learning new subjects, and partially because the teacher will have relatively little experience on which to depend in making decisions. If a six-year-old child has trouble seeing that the area of a three-by-four square is twelve, is this because he does not understand conservation of matter (for the continuous case this appears to be more difficult than with the discrete case), is it because he cannot count, or is it because he just does not happen to be interested? Someone is going to have to make a decision as to what to teach and how to teach it. Unfortunately, many topics find their way into school textbooks without first having been tried in the classroom, thus making the teacher's life more difficult. It is also important to remember that, even if the idea has been tried with children, the teacher's pupils may be different from those on whom the idea was tried.

A second fact to remember is that not everything that *can* be taught to children *should* be taught to them. Many people are very much impressed when they discover that children can learn advanced mathematical ideas at a very early age, and some of these persons have therefore jumped to the conclusion that it is good to teach these ideas to children as early as possible. At present, we have very little evidence regarding the long-range effect of such teaching on the majority of children. The final decision as to (*a*) what should be taught, (*b*) how it can be taught, and (*c*) to which children it is profitable to teach it, must be made by mathematicians, mathematics educators, psychologists, and school teachers working together.

In the secondary schools it has become common to combine the seventh- and eighth-grade materials into a one-year course for better mathematics students, with the idea of having them complete a year of calculus before the end of high school. Again, it is not clear that this is a desirable practice. One natural question to ask about this procedure is why it is possible for one group of children to learn twice as fast as the other for only one year. Since it is known that testing procedures are not entirely reliable and, furthermore, that children change in their relative abilities and interests, it seems that a procedure in which the accelerated group and the regular group did not proceed at such radically different rates for such a short period of time might be more appropriate.

Even more important, however, is the question of whether it is desirable to rush through the curriculum with the intent of completing a year of calculus before the end of high school. Teachers have complained that many of their better students stop taking mathematics as soon as they have enough to satisfy the entrance requirements of the college of their choice even when they complete that amount a year earlier because of acceleration. Perhaps the act of accelerating the learning of mathematics has had the effect, in some cases, of reducing interest in it. Again, there is no clear evidence as to which students can and should learn which mathematics at a given time, but there is some reason to suppose that acceleration, by itself, is not necessarily always good. Information from a recent international study in mathematics education suggests that interest in mathematics and the desire to take more mathematics are highest in those countries where the early learning of mathematics proceeded at the most leisurely pace—the data is neither conclusive nor even unambiguous with regard to this issue, but it does appear that there is a real danger of pacing instruction too rapidly.

To What Extent, and in What Sense, Does "Discovery" Play a Useful Part in Learning?

In recent years, there has been a controversy over various methods of teaching, with the "discovery" method of teaching receiving particular attention. Although there are many strong opinions as to whether the discovery method is the best one to use, it is very difficult to find a satisfactory statement of what *the* discovery method is. There are those who think of the discovery method as one in which the teacher leads the pupil through a series of questions to which the pupil needs only to answer "yes" or "no" in order to arrive at an important truth after a certain number of questions. This system is exemplified in some of Socrates' teachings as reported by Plato. The experience that many teachers have had with this system is that, while children can take each individual step correctly, they are unable to understand the whole process after they have finished, or even to repeat the reasoning at a later time. The student quite often has the feeling that he has been trapped by this system rather than that he has learned from it. Furthermore, in a typical classroom situation, it often happens that one or two students do most of the "discovering."

Another form of the discovery method occurs when a teacher presents his pupils with a particular situation and encourages them to think about it and draw certain kinds of conclusions from it. Presumably, the kinds of situations differ depending on the maturity of the children, the subject matter being taught, and the other conditions existing at the time. For example, with very young children, who have had little exposure to the concept in question, the situation presented by the teacher would probably involve concrete objects (or the teacher would encourage the children to use concrete objects in drawing their conclusions). For children who are more familiar with the concept being considered, less reliance on concrete objects and more reliance on some sort of abstract reasoning might be encouraged. Presumably, different children in the same class might be encouraged to proceed in different ways—depending on their state of maturity with respect to the given concept.

A far more radical notion of the discovery approach has the teacher asking the children what they want to learn as of the moment and then proceeding from there. This laissez-faire technique seems so inefficient, in terms of the vast amounts of knowledge available and the presumed superior knowledge of the teacher and of curriculum makers, that relatively few educators accept the procedure in this form. On the other hand, there are many who believe that it is desirable for the teacher and his students to attack a problem together, especially when neither knows the answer. Although this practice may not be an efficient way for the student to acquire knowledge, the process involved is likely to be very educational. The way in which the teacher and students make mistakes and correct them is likely to be as instructive as is the actual information acquired.

Unfortunately, because of the many differing definitions of "discovery" and because of the fact that virtually every advocate of a particular type of discovery would contend that the procedure ought to change with the maturity of the pupils and other conditions, it is difficult to assess the merits of "the discovery method" of teaching mathematics as compared with others. As suggested in the first section of this chapter, there is some evidence that a teacher who can use a non-directed technique can also do well in a teacher-directed situation, and it seems reasonable to suppose that those teachers are most effective who change their methods with the situation and use a variety of techniques.

When and How Can Emphasis Be Placed on Proof?

A very informal introduction to the concept of proof can start as early as the child understands a subject well enough and is sufficiently mature to be willing to try to convince others by rational argument rather than by bellowing or by placing complete reliance on authority. For different children this more rational approach may occur at different ages, but present information suggests that most children are not ready for any great emphasis on proof until the age of ten or twelve.

As children move from the elementary school to the junior and senior high school, they develop a greater interest in logically convincing others that what they believe is true. Even many elementary school children reveal a tendency in this direction, but it is common for the child to rely on authority at early ages. He will argue that something must be true because a parent or a teacher says it must be true. As children begin to revolt against authority, they begin to develop their powers of persuasion to the extent that they can carry on something that begins to look like proof.

The proof of a junior high school pupil is not likely to look very much like the proofs one sees in a geometry class. In fact, the statement-reason type of proof that one finds in geometry has very little similarity to proofs seen anywhere else—including more advanced mathematics classes. Most people prove their beliefs by carrying out an argument (in paragraph form rather than in statement-reason form) which they believe is going to convince their listener. If the proof does convince the listener, it is a satisfactory proof for its purpose and, if it does not, it is unsatisfactory. Proofs are not really used to discover *truth;* they are used to convince somebody that a certain proposition is true—or, more correctly, that if certain accepted propositions are true, then the proposition in question is also true. However, as one well-known mathematician has been heard to say, Goliath with a proof is no match for David with a counterexample. No matter how good a proof appears to be, there may be a flaw in it.

In teaching children to use proofs and abstract reasoning, it is therefore desirable for the teacher to encourage them to make up their own arguments rather than to try to follow some given model of proof. If the teacher sees some flaw in the proof, he may try to produce a counterexample, or he may check with the children themselves to see if others are convinced by the proof of the prover. In situations like this, it is desirable for the teacher to conceal his beliefs, since the children will tend to accept his authority rather than think for themselves. The teacher may challenge a statement he believes to be true and defend one he believes not to be true, thus encouraging the children to think for themselves.

Should We Stress the Theoretical or the Applied Aspects of Mathematics?

Mathematics was first developed as a useful system for solving certain problems that could not be solved by other means, or that were very complicated to solve by other means. In the hands of the ancient Greeks, it became a highly theoretical subject that was less and less practical in a strictly utilitarian sense. It is true that Archimedes, one of the greatest mathematicians of all time, was able to combine the theoretical and practical sides of mathematics to produce many useful machines as well as physical principles, but generally the Greek mathematicians seem to have thought of mathematics as a beautiful, abstract, semi-religious study that had little practical relation to the mundane world around them.

In the mathematics education of this country, the split between the useful and the theoretical has been an important issue at various times. Generally, it has been agreed that arithmetic should be taught because it is likely to be useful. Unfortunately, the examples chosen for textbooks have often had little to do with adult life, much less with the life of children, but at least it was generally believed that children should learn arithmetic because it is useful in the everyday life of adults. In secondary school mathematics, on the other hand, the desirability of teaching useful mathematics has not been so widely accepted. For many years, geometry was thought of as something people should study in order to improve their ability to reason. Outstanding mathematicians, such as John Perry of England and E. H. Moore of the United States, criticized school geometry and other parts of school mathematics for not being sufficiently applied and suggested specific changes that they believed would be desirable. After these recommendations were made (in the late 1800's and early 1900's), the curriculum in England did begin to include more applied mathematics, but relatively little movement in that direction has occurred in the United States.

Since the Second World War, and more particularly since the Russians orbited their first satellite, there has been a great increase of interest in mathematics throughout all segments of the population. During this time, there has been a drastic rise in the number of children taking mathematics and in the level of mathematics they are taking in schools. This can be seen in the recent study of the Survey Committee of the Conference Board of the Mathematical Sciences,[2] in which it is reported that, between 1960 and 1965, the number of entering freshmen who were able to begin with analytic geometry and calculus more than doubled. From the same source, it can be seen that in the ten-year period from 1955 to 1965, the number of bachelor's degrees awarded to mathematics majors and statistics majors increased more than fivefold (4,034 to 21,270). Similar gains obtained for higher degrees in mathematics.

For many reasons, the school mathematics that has been created in response to this increased interest (now known as "the new mathematics") has tended to be rather abstract. This has been partially a reaction to some of the "social arithmetic" which preceded the "revolution" (especially in the junior high school), partially a response to the fact that abstract mathematical systems have turned out to be very useful to physicists and applied mathematicians (as models for situations that occur in the real world), and partially due to the fact that it is very difficult to find really good applied

2. John Jewett and Clarence B. Lindquist, *Aspects of Undergraduate Training in the Mathematical Sciences,* Report of the Survey Committee of the Conference Board of Mathematical Sciences, CBMS, 1967.

problems that fit naturally into school mathematics. Morris Kline, one of the most prominent critics of the "new mathematics," objects to the modern programs largely because of their lack of application and relation to the real world. Several of the more prominent school mathematics projects (SMSG and the Cambridge Conference on School Mathematics, for example) have begun to make serious efforts to increase the use of physical applications in the teaching of school mathematics. As such projects move forward, it can be assumed that better textbooks with more emphasis on applied mathematics will become available. Certainly, the ultimate goal of mathematics education for most children is to make the mathematics useful to them in some sense, but the method of achieving this goal is not entirely clear.

Is There Any Justification for Expecting All Children To Attain the Same Standards of Performance?

The fact that there are individual differences among people—mental and psychological as well as physical—has probably always been recognized. The extent of the differences in mental characteristics has become clearer and has had a greater influence on education in this country since the widespread use of aptitude and achievement tests, beginning about 1920. Educators now generally accept the proposition that there ought to be some differentiation in instruction in light of the recognized differences in ability, experience, and learning styles of the pupils. Chapter xi of this yearbook is devoted to such differentiation of instruction.

In spite of the widespread acceptance of the doctrine of individualization of instruction, actual practice in the schools does not appear to emphasize such individualization very heavily. This is especially true in the upper elementary grades and in the secondary schools, contrary to what one would expect if appropriate individualization were the rule throughout the schools. It is very common to find that, in the early elementary grades of a school system, the teacher encourages different children to work at different speeds and at differing degrees of depth, but, in the same system, the children are all expected to proceed at the same rate after the fifth (or some other) grade. Of course, if children really do proceed at differing rates in the early grades, it could be assumed that by the age of ten or twelve the differences would be so great that it would be nearly impossible for them to be kept together, studying the same subjects at the same speed. In fact, many children apparently begin to find mathematics and other subjects less enjoyable and less comprehensible at about this age.

There are many possible explanations for this lack of differentiation in higher grades. It seems to be partially due to a difference in philosophy (especially between elementary and secondary school teachers); partially due to the fact that as children grow older the differences are magnified and therefore more difficult to deal with; and partially due to an increased emphasis on subject matter and the need to "succeed" before proceeding to the next subject.

On the surface, it would appear that differentiation of instruction for different children would be desirable, but there is some evidence to suggest that it may not be as desirable as many educators believe. It is well known and has been substantiated by many research findings that if a child knows that a certain level of proficiency is expected of him, he will produce accordingly. Thus, if instruction is differentiated in such a way that a child who is slightly behind is made to believe that he does not have to produce much in order to satisfy the teacher, he is likely to end up even further behind. Differentiation, then, should not mean that precisely the same things are done by all children but simply at a slower rate by certain children. Rather, appropriate experiences should be provided for each child, depending on his particular characteristics. Furthermore, it may be desirable to set fairly high standards for all children who have any chance of meeting them—this may be particularly true of children from so-called "deprived" backgrounds who are likely to have ability but are simply lacking certain kinds of experiences.

Since all people have some need for certain abilities such as the ability to solve problems involving simple arithmetic, it is probably reasonable to expect all children to become reasonably proficient in those abilities, even if they obtain the required proficiency at different times. For other skills and concepts, however, the need may not be as universal, and it may be justifiable to allow certain children to become less proficient than other children in these. However, it is important that the teacher not underestimate the potential of any individual child and thus lower his self-concept.

How Can We Motivate Reluctant Learners?

Clearly, the answer to this question depends to a large extent on the answer to the question: "Why is the learner reluctant?" In the case of some children, there is a feeling that learning everything possible in school will be of little value because they will never be able (for some extraneous reason such as skin color, name, or religion) to use the knowledge and ability they have. In such cases, it will be difficult for the individual teacher to solve the problem without the aid of society generally, since the child is so clearly right. However, conditions are changing, and it is becoming easier and easier to find people of virtually every ethnic background in positions which allow them to use their schooling. In many cases, the teacher will find that such people are quite enthusiastic about coming to the school and speaking to groups of students. Encouraging such activities may be the best way for the teacher to reach children who are reluctant to learn because of real or supposed prejudice.

Other children look at the material they are expected to learn in school and realize that it has so little relation to reality that it is not likely to do them any good to learn it—except to raise their grade point average. For many children the artificial incentive of grades is not effective. One partial solution to this problem is to make the curriculum more relevant. In different situations, the teacher may have more or less freedom to try to make the curriculum more meaningful. If the individual teacher does not have such freedom, he may be able to encourage group activity among the teachers that will lead to a more realistic curriculum. One way to make the curriculum more appropriate is to encourage the students themselves to provide the class with good problems—these may become as artificial as the textbook problems, but they can be useful in adding some interest—and a store of good problems might be built up over several years and shared among several teachers. In communities where high school graduates are likely to be looking for work within the community, it is also possible to get potential employers to provide the school with problems they would like employees to be able to solve. It is also possible that the teacher, by using some imagination, may come up with subjects that will be of great interest to some of the pupils. Probability and statistics, for example, can be very interesting to many children, both because of their relationship to certain kinds of games, and because these subjects play such an important role in many aspects of society today.

It is important for the teacher to remember, however, that when a child asks, "What use is this stuff?" he is not necessarily looking for a lecture on how the subject might be used by some hypothetical professional person, but rather he is likely either to be asking how it relates to his personal life, or (even more likely) he is telling the teacher that he does not really understand the subject. The teacher may answer the question in whatever way seems appropriate at the time, but he should think of the question as a warning signal that the pupil is having some sort of trouble with the topic being questioned. It may be possible to solve his problem by simply explaining some of the difficult mathematical points; it may be possible to relate the subject to the child's life; it may be desirable to stop teaching the subject; or perhaps some combination of responses may be appropriate.

Some children find it difficult to learn because of conditions in their home or neighborhood. It is unrealistic to give large homework assignments to a child who has no place to do such work. If a family of eight is living in a two-room apartment, it is not likely that a child in the family will be able to find a nice, quiet, well-lit desk on which to do his work. In such instances, assuming the teacher is unable to do anything that might change the home conditions, he might try to make facilities available in the school in which children can work, or he might allow a larger amount of time in class for them to do their "homework."

Undernourishment will have a very undesirable effect on a child's ability to learn, and the teacher may or may not be able to change the situation. In some cases, the lack of proper nourishment is not due to poverty, but rather to lack of knowledge and interest. In such cases, it may be possible to help children through science or health classes to learn more about nutrition. Of course, in the instances of poverty, school-lunch programs may be of some help, but the teacher may find that he is able to do little without major help from society at large—in such instances, the teacher can simply do his best to be understanding and helpful.

Often, attitudes of other people affect a student's desire to learn. In some cases, friends and family do not think learning is important, or they are actively opposed to it. In some instances, it may be possible for the teacher or a guidance counselor to change the attitude or influence of the people who are doing the damage, but this tends to be a very difficult job. Working directly with the student will usually be easier, though in the long run perhaps less effective.

It is clear that the teacher will find it difficult to motivate all reluctant learners by his activities within the classroom, but there are many things which the teacher can do within the classroom that will be of some help. First, the teacher himself should have respect for the subject being learned and for the pupils learning it. Second, he should go out of his way to find out more about the pupils and to use examples that will be of interest to them. Third, if he cannot make the subject intrinsically interesting to all the children, he should try to add excitement by means of games (e.g., contests, "find the missing number from these clues," various mathematical games put out by commercial companies, etc.), story-telling from the history of mathematics, field trips to places where mathematics is being used, and other activities. Even if he uses all of the best suggestions available, however, the teacher who is able to motivate all of his pupils for any major portion of a school year is a most unusual person.

What Is the Function of the Textbook or of Detailed Courses of Study in Guiding Teachers?

Many textbooks are apparently written with the belief that the teachers who will be using them have little knowledge of the subject matter, less knowledge of how to teach it, and very little time to prepare class activities. Unfortunately, one or more of these assumptions is quite often true. Assuming, however, that the teacher is competent and does have time to do a reasonable amount of planning, should he deviate widely from the text materials or course guides in order to provide better individualization for his pupils and a richer experience for them, or should he stick closely to the prescribed program in order to assure a higher degree of continuity as the children proceed through school?

Assuming the school system is large enough to require the teaching of mathematics in the same grade by several teachers, the argument for sticking reasonably close to a prescribed syllabus is a very strong one. There can be found many instances of children who have been exposed to an introduction to a particular topic (for example, sets) seven or eight times but who have never gone deeply into the subject. Sometimes this superficial repetition is the result of poor overall planning, but it is often caused by teachers who have decided that it would be fun to teach a particular topic and who have done so without consideration of an overall plan. In any large system, the teachers should get together under the leadership of the appropriate official (mathematics coordinator, department chairman, curriculum coordinator, etc.) and decide what mathematics a child ought to know when he leaves a particular grade. Then the individual teacher should feel obligated to pass along to the next teacher information regarding what specific parts of the expected mathematics certain children have not yet mastered. In general, the teacher should not encourage children to delve deeply into subjects usually reserved for later grades until they have mastered the material for their own grade.

This does not mean that a teacher should be restricted to a day-to-day lesson plan made up by some authority, nor does it suggest that teachers should feel obligated to cover every page of a textbook in the usual order. Just as there are individual differences among children, there are individual differences among teachers as well. Classroom teachers should be given as much freedom as possible to develop appropriate programs for all the children they are teaching. These programs may involve using several different textbooks within the same class, or even different books for an individual pupil at different times; it may mean that at times no textbook at all is used for certain children; other materials, or perhaps no commercially prepared material at all, may be appropriate. However, the teacher should have some overall, community-wide plan in mind as he guides individual children through their study of mathematics, and he should report to the next teacher any major deviations from such a plan.

In this chapter many questions have been discussed which are often asked by classroom teachers. The discussions have not provided definitive answers but have attempted to consider some prevalent views regarding these issues. In the long run, each teacher must develop his own philosophy of teaching and make his own decisions in light of that philosophy. However, exposing oneself to some of the questions asked by others and some of the answers provided by others should help a person to be a better teacher.

Suggested Sources for Further Information

It would be impossible to list even the titles of the many important works on the teaching of mathematics that have appeared in the recent past. However, for the interested reader, we list here a few important sources of further information. Each of these sources will lead to large numbers of other sources if the reader wishes to pursue the matter further.

1. *The Arithmetic Teacher.*—This is one of the two official journals of the National Council of Teachers of Mathematics. Articles on the teaching of mathematics from prekindergarten through the eighth grade appear in this journal along with reviews, research articles, official notices of the NCTM, and other information which is important to persons interested in the teaching of mathematics below the high school level.

2. *The Mathematics Teacher.*—This is the secondary school counterpart of *The Arithmetic Teacher*. Every secondary school teacher of mathematics who wishes to remain abreast of recent developments in his field should have access to this journal and to other publications of the NCTM. More information about one or both of these journals and about other NCTM materials can be had by writing to the National Council of Teachers of Mathematics, 1201 Sixteenth Street, N.W., Washington, D.C. 20036.

3. *SMSG Newsletter.*—This is a periodic summary of the latest activities of the organization that has been in the forefront of curricular changes in mathematics for the past decade. An individual may receive this by writing to School Mathematics Study Group, School of Education, Cedar Hall, Stanford University, Stanford, California 94305.

4. *The Continuing Revolution in Mathematics.*—This is the title of an issue of *The Bulletin of the National Association of Secondary School Principals*, Volume 52, Number 327, April, 1968. It has been

reprinted as a separate pamphlet by the National Council of Teachers of Mathematics.

This publication presents a collection of articles by outstanding mathematics educators regarding the changes that have occurred, that are occurring, and that may be expected to occur in the teaching of mathematics in this country. Included are case histories of the change that has occurred in certain specific school systems, as well as information on slow learners, mathematically talented students, changes in college mathematics, the relation between science and mathematics, teaching methods, staffing problems, materials, and other topics that will be of interest to teachers and administrators.

5. *Administrative Responsibility for Improving Mathematics Programs.*—This is the Report of the Joint Project on the Administration of Mathematics Programs of the American Association of School Administrators, the Association for Supervision and Curriculum Development, the National Association of Secondary School Principals, and the National Council of Teachers of Mathematics, Washington, D.C., 1965.

Planning, organizing, implementing, and evaluating curricular changes are discussed. The bibliography is helpful to specialists as well as to general administrators. A copy may be obtained from any of the participating organizations for fifty cents.

SPECIAL PROBLEMS

CHAPTER VII

Teacher Education

ROY DUBISCH

Introduction

In discussing the training of teachers of mathematics in the United States, we will make consistent use of the classification system developed by the Teacher Training Panel of the Committee on the Undergraduate Program in Mathematics (CUPM), a committee of the Mathematical Association of America. This classification system is as follows:[1]

LEVEL I. *Teachers of elementary school mathematics.*
This level consists of teachers confronted with the problem of presenting the elements of mathematics (arithmetic and the associated material now commonly taught) in grades K through 6. (The committee recognizes that special pedagogical problems may be connected with grades K through 2, and so a special program may be appropriate for teachers of such grades.)

LEVEL II. *Teachers of the elements of algebra and geometry*
Included here are teachers who are assigned the task of introducing preliminary material prior to the formal year courses in algebra and geometry. These preliminary materials are now commonly presented to most students in the early junior high school grades; they are often introduced to the better students in the upper elementary school grades.

LEVEL III. *Teachers of high school mathematics.*
These teachers are qualified to teach a modern high school mathematics sequence in grades 9 through 12.

LEVEL IV. *Teachers of the elements of calculus, linear algebra, probability, etc.*
This is a mixed level, consisting of teachers of advanced programs in high school, junior college teachers, and staff members employed by uni-

---

1. *Recommendations for the Training of Teachers* (Revised, December, 1966; Committee on the Undergraduate Program in Mathematics, Mathematical Association of America [Berkeley, Calif.: Distributed by the CUPM Central Office, 1966]), p. 7.

versities to teach in the first one or two years. These teachers should be qualified to present a modern two-year college mathematics program.
LEVEL V. *Teachers of college mathematics.*

These teachers should be qualified to teach all basic courses required in a strong undergraduate college curriculum. . . .

The main part of our discussion appears under the next four major headings of this chapter and will be concerned with the undergraduate training of teachers at Levels I-III with particular attention to Level III. The first of these four sections, the one immediately following the Introduction, will describe briefly the situation prior to 1961; the next section will outline the CUPM recommendations; and the following two will respectively (*a*) survey the present situation and (*b*) discuss deficiencies in the present program and attempt some predictions as to future developments.

Under the two following major headings will be considered graduate work for teachers at (*a*) Levels I-III and (*b*) Levels IV and V. The final section will be concerned with the problems of in-service education.

The Situation Prior to 1961

Any discussion of teacher training must take into account the fact that schools will frequently allow the teaching of a subject by a person with no special training in that subject. The view that "anybody can teach mathematics" has had wide acceptance in the past and has not entirely disappeared at the present time. Thus, the existence of excellent teacher training programs in mathematics in a certain state by no means leads to the conclusion that all mathematics courses in the state are taught by graduates of such programs. In any school there are likely to be older teachers with outdated training; and a coach, with no more than two years of high school mathematics, may still be "filling in his schedule" by teaching a mathematics class.

With this caution in mind, let us look briefly at teacher training in mathematics in 1960—the year before the publication of the CUPM report, the 1966 revision of which has already been referred to.[2] There were (and still are) great variations in programs throughout the country. What we will describe generally are "average" programs, with some attention to extremes.

Level I. Precollege mathematics.—Perhaps one year of algebra and

2. *Ibid.*

one year of geometry in high school (but frequently only a "general math" course in place of algebra and geometry) was provided at this level. No actual college mathematics courses were required; usually only a course in methods of teaching arithmetic made up the average program. Such a course would normally have a small amount of mathematical content but would concentrate on the mechanics of teaching. At best, one would find an elementary school teacher who, because she liked mathematics, took three or four years of high school mathematics and perhaps even a year of college (pre-calculus) mathematics.[3]

Level II.—This was not generally recognized as a special category.

Level III.—There have always been great variations at this level even when one leaves out of consideration the coaches, the home economics teachers, etc., who have taught some mathematics. On the one hand, there have been teachers with weak teaching majors which involved no mathematics at a level higher than first-year calculus; and, on the other hand, there have always been a few top-quality persons with strong majors from first-rate institutions who have chosen the teaching of secondary mathematics as a career.

An "average" teacher with a major in mathematics usually had a rather minimal major based on the same kind of mathematics courses taken by students who were not preparing for teaching. In semester hours his program in the 1950's typically would have been as follows:

Pre-calculus mathematics	6
Calculus	8
Theory of equations	3
College geometry	3
Differential equations	3
Electives (history of mathematics, mathematics of finance, theory of numbers, advanced calculus)	6–9

In addition, it is perhaps appropriate to note that, in 1960, with the rich opportunities of mathematics majors for industrial employment and the numerous fellowships and assistantships available to them for graduate study, the prospective teacher was more likely to be a "C" student than an "A" student.

3. Arden K. Ruddell, Wilbur Dutton, and John Reckzeh, "Background Mathematics for Elementary Teachers," in *Instruction in Arithmetic* (Twenty-fifth Yearbook, National Council of Teachers of Mathematics [Washington: the Council, 1960]), pp. 296-319.

As inadequate as these teacher preparations were for the mathematics curricula of the late 1960's, they were, in a sense, by no means entirely inadequate for most pre-1960 curricula. These earlier curricula, by and large, stressed *mechanics* rather than *understanding* so that they could be presented in a routine fashion by someone with a very limited understanding of basic principles. Indeed, early experience with "up-grading" institutes in the years just preceding large-scale changes in textbooks pointed up the difficulty of preparing teachers in advance of the changes. Most of the teachers coming to these early institutes (e.g., 1957 and 1958) simply could not relate what they were studying to their future teaching. And, on the other hand, the most successful institutes in the early 1960's were those which concentrated on a careful examination of specific high school texts and teacher's manuals such as those produced by the School Mathematics Study Group (SMSG).

The CUPM Recommendations

There have been in the past (and there are now) many groups and individuals concerned with the improvement of school mathematics and the training of teachers of mathematics. However, there is no question but that the group having the greatest influence on curriculum reform has been SMSG under the leadership of Professor E. G. Begle. For this reason we can take 1958—when SMSG first came into existence—as a dividing line between "old mathematics" and "new mathematics." The impact of SMSG was, of course, a gradually developing one. The first trial of SMSG materials occurred in 1958–59 at the seventh- and eighth-grade levels. From that time on, development of a series of texts (including various alternatives, supplementary materials, etc.) continued in a systematic fashion until a complete SMSG series from K-XII was available in 1967.

Very early, however, in the history of SMSG, it was realized that the majority of mathematics teachers were ill-prepared to teach from the texts that SMSG was producing. Thus, as early as 1959, SMSG produced books suitable for in-service training of teachers and encouraged the development of summer and academic-year institutes for teachers.

Such in-service, "remedial"-type teacher education has played an essential role in the implementation of improved mathematics programs in the schools. It soon became transparently evident, however, that we were in the ridiculous position of graduating certified teachers with majors in mathematics whose first assignment needed to be to attend a summer institute to learn about the "new" mathematics! Reform in the training of teachers of mathematics was clearly needed.

Just as in curricular reform, many individuals and groups have been concerned with changes in teacher training. But just as SMSG has been the dominant influence in school curricula reform in mathematics, so has the Committee on the Undergraduate Program in Mathematics (CUPM) been the dominant influence in the improvement of teacher preparation. Its recommendations[4] for Level I-III training have been widely endorsed and are as follows (a course as referred to in these recommendations is a three-semester-hour course or equivalent):

RECOMMENDATIONS FOR LEVEL I
(Teachers of elementary school mathematics)

As a prerequisite for the college training of elementary school teachers, we recommend at least two years of college preparatory mathematics, consisting of a year of algebra and a year of geometry, or the same material in integrated courses. It must also be assured that these teachers are competent in the basic techniques of arithmetic. The exact length of the training program will depend on the strength of their preparation. For their college training, we recommend the equivalent of the following courses:

(A) A two-course sequence devoted to the structure of the real number system and its subsystems.
(B) A course devoted to the basic concepts of algebra.
(C) A course in informal geometry.

The material in these courses might, in a sense, duplicate material studied in high school by the prospective teacher, but we urge that this material be covered again, this time from a more sophisticated, college-level point of view.

Whether the material suggested in (A) above can be covered in one or two courses will clearly depend upon the previous preparation of the student.

We strongly recommend that at least 20 per cent of the Level I teachers in each school have stronger preparation in mathematics, comparable to Level II preparation but not necessarily including calculus. Such teach-

4. *Recommendations for the Training of Teachers, op. cit.*

ers would clearly strengthen the elementary program by their very presence within the school faculty. This additional preparation is certainly required for elementary teachers who are called upon to teach an introduction to algebra or geometry.

RECOMMENDATIONS FOR LEVEL II
(Teachers of the elements of algebra and geometry)

Prospective teachers should enter this program ready for a mathematics course at the level of a beginning course in analytic geometry and calculus (requiring a minimum of three years in college preparatory mathematics). It is recognized that many students will need to correct high school deficiencies in college. However, such courses as trigonometry and college algebra should not count toward the fulfillment of minimum requirements at the college level. Their college mathematics training should then include:

(A) Three courses in elementary analysis (including or presupposing the fundamentals of analytic geometry). This introduction to analysis should stress basic concepts. However, prospective teachers should be qualified to take more advanced mathematics courses requiring a year of calculus, and hence calculus courses especially designed for teachers are normally not desirable.

(B) Four other courses: a course in abstract algebra, a course in geometry, a course in probability from a set-theoretic point of view, and one elective. One of these courses should contain an introduction to the language of logic and sets. The Panel strongly recommends that a course in applied mathematics or statistics be included.

RECOMMENDATIONS FOR LEVEL III
(Teachers of high school mathematics)

Prospective teachers of mathematics beyond the elements of algebra and geometry should complete a major in mathematics and a minor in some field in which a substantial amount of mathematics is used. This latter should be selected from areas in the physical sciences, biological sciences, and from the social studies, but the minor should in each case be pursued to the extent that the student will have encountered substantial applications of mathematics.

The major in mathematics should include, in addition to the work listed under Level II, at least an additional course in each of algebra, geometry, and probability-statistics, and one more elective.

Thus, the minimum requirements for high school mathematics teachers should consist of the following:

(A) Three courses in analysis. These should be at least at the level of courses 1, 2, 4 of the CUPM report *A General Curriculum in Mathematics for Colleges* (1965).[5]

(B) Two courses in abstract algebra. The courses should include linear algebra as well as the study of groups, rings and fields. The courses 3 and 6 of the GCMC report are suitable [see footnote 5].

(C) Two courses in geometry beyond analytic geometry. These courses should be directed at a higher understanding of the geometry of the school curriculum.

(D) Two courses in probability and statistics. These should be at least at the level of 2P and 7 of the GCMC report, and should be based on calculus.

(E) In view of the introduction of computing courses in the secondary school, a course in computer science is highly recommended. For example, the course described on p. 27 of the GCMC report and in the CUPM report *Recommendations on the Undergraduate Mathematics Program for Work in Computing* (1964),[6] or the course "Introduction to Computer Science" described in the revised *Recommendations on the Undergraduate Mathematics Program for Engineers and Physicists* (1967).[7]

(F) Two upper-class elective courses. A course in the applications of mathematics is particularly desirable. Other courses suggested are, introduction to real variables, number theory, topology, or history of mathematics. Particular attention should be given here to laying groundwork for later graduate study.

One of these courses should contain an introduction to the language of logic and sets, which can be used in a variety of courses.

In addition to the broad outlines for teacher training presented above, CUPM has developed more detailed course outlines,[8] and has also emphasized that the spirit in which the courses are taught is of

5. *A General Curriculum in Mathematics for Colleges* (Committee on the Undergraduate Program in Mathematics, The Mathematical Association of America [Berkeley, Calif.: Distributed by CUPM Central Office, January, 1965]).

6. *Recommendations on the Undergraduate Mathematics Program for Work in Computing* (Committee on the Undergraduate Program in Mathematics, Mathematical Association of America [Berkeley, Calif.: Distributed by the CUPM Central Office, May, 1964]), p. 27.

7. *Recommendations on the Undergraduate Mathematics Program for Engineers and Physicists* (Revised, January, 1967; Committee on the Undergraduate Program in Mathematics, Mathematical Association of America [Berkeley, Calif.: Distributed by the CUPM Central Office, January, 1967]).

8. See *A General Curriculum in Mathematics for Colleges, op. cit.*; *Recommendations on the Undergraduate Mathematics Program for Work in Computing, op. cit.*; *Recommendations on the Undergraduate Mathematics Program for Engineers and Physicists, op. cit.*; *Course Guides for the Training of Teachers of Junior High and High School Mathematics* (Committee on the Undergraduate Programs in Mathematics, Mathematical Association of America [Berkeley, Calif: Distributed by CUPM Central Office, June, 1961]).

prime importance. They point out, for example, that presentation should relate the mathematics studied to the content of secondary school mathematics rather than emphasizing preparation for more advanced study.

Considerable time has elapsed since CUPM first published (1961) outlines[9] for some of the recommended courses. More recently, as seen in the 1966 revision of the recommendations, it has made reference to course outlines available in other CUPM recommendations (for example, the GCMC report). In actual practice, the course offerings are heavily conditioned by the books available—many of which mention in their preface (correctly or incorrectly) that they follow the CUPM recommendations. For this reason it seems appropriate to consider the present state of affairs rather than to give further details of the CUPM recommendations at this point.

The Present Situation for Levels I–III

LEVEL I

In 1961 there were really no texts which came at all close to the CUPM recommendations for Level I. Now there are at least a dozen for course A, with new ones still being published, and revisions of some of the "pioneers" have begun. Texts for courses B and C have just begun to appear.

A preliminary draft of the CUPM course guides was followed by a revised version in 1968.[10] A comparison of this revision with the textbooks written for course A, as well as comparisons among the various texts, reveals very considerable differences in regard to level and style of presentation. On the other hand, most of the topics considered are fairly standard—sets and operations with sets, numeration systems, whole numbers, integers, rational numbers, real numbers—the essential idea being to lead the students to an understanding of the basic concepts underlying the arithmetic of the elementary school. In addition, many of these texts include a chapter on geometry in lieu of a separate course C.

9. *Course Guides for the Training of Teachers of Junior High and High School Mathematics, op. cit.* See also first edition, 1961.

10. *Course Guides for the Training of Teachers of Elementary School Mathematics* (Revised, 1968; Committee on the Undergraduate Program in Mathematics, Mathematical Association of America [Berkeley, Calif.: Distributed by CUPM, 1968]).

Before considering courses B and C, let us look at the amount of college mathematics currently being required of elementary education majors. The two tables below show a dramatic change in the last few years.[11]

Actually, the situation is even more encouraging than the figures

TABLE 1

NUMBER OF SEMESTER HOURS OF MATHEMATICS RE-
QUIRED OF ELEMENTARY EDUCATION MAJORS
FOR GRADUATION BY AMERICAN COLLEGES

HOURS	NUMBER OF COLLEGES		PERCENTAGE OF COLLEGES	
	1962	1966	1962	1966
0.............	173	75	22.7	8.3
1–2...........	39	29	5.1	3.2
3–4...........	308	345	40.4	38.3
5–6...........	209	339	27.4	37.6
7–8...........	17	63	2.2	7.0
9–10.........	11	40	1.4	4.4
11–12.........	5	10	0.7	1.1
Total........	762	901	99.9	99.9

TABLE 2

CHANGES IN THE NUMBER OF SEMESTER HOURS OF MATHEMATICS
REQUIRED BY COLLEGES OF ELEMENTARY EDUCATION MAJORS
FOR GRADUATION OVER THE PERIOD 1962–1966

CHANGE IN HOURS.......	+12	+10	+8	+7	+6	+5	+4	+3	+2	+1	0	−1	−2	−3	−4	−5	−6
NUMBER OF COLLEGES....	2	1	3	2	40	19	27	152	41	34	343	9	9	34	2	3	4

indicate. The 1966 survey also indicated that many colleges are planning to increase their requirements soon, and other colleges pointed out that many of their students take Level I elective courses. Furthermore, as the CUPM report states: "Even the fact that some of the correspondents indicated acute embarrassment in reporting how little mathematics their colleges require is a hopeful sign!"[12]

11. The two tables are drawn from *Forty-one Conference on the Training of Teachers of Elementary School Mathematics: A Summary*. (Committee on the Undergraduate Program in Mathematics, Mathematical Association of America [Berkeley, Calif.: Distributed by CUPM, June, 1966]).

12. *Ibid.*

As encouraging as these figures are, however, they do indicate that there is not much of a move toward the twelve-hour requirement recommended by CUPM. Indeed, some of the above six-hour-requirement figures reported are somewhat misleading in the sense that they include a course or courses required of all students as general education rather than courses specifically designed to be of maximum benefit to the prospective elementary school teacher. Thus, in terms of the present situation, there is no great point in discussing details of the courses B and C of the CUPM Level I recommendations. They will, however, be considered again in the next section, in which deficiencies in the present programs will be examined.

LEVEL II AND LEVEL III

There is still very little in the way of programs specially designed for Level II teachers. There has been very widespread acceptance of the basic principles of the CUPM Level III recommendations—although, as in the case of Level I, the interpretations of the recommendations vary considerably. Let us consider the recommended courses in order.

(A) *Three courses in analysis.*—CUPM has not recommended any special version of this standard sequence for teachers. The requirement for this sequence (essentially analytic geometry and calculus) is quite universal. The levels of the courses naturally vary from college to college. However, the emphasis on underlying ideas—so especially important for the prospective teacher—is generally common today.

(B) *Two courses in abstract algebra.*—The requirement of at least one course in abstract algebra for a mathematics major is almost universal today, and most colleges require two. The CUPM course guides suggest considering the elementary aspects of fields, rings, integral domains, and groups in the first course with special emphasis on the ring of integers, the field of rational numbers, the field of real numbers, the field of complex numbers, and the integral domain $F[x]$ of polynomials over a field.[13] These topics are certainly considered in all of the numerous books written for a first course in abstract algebra. Frequently, however, the course provides only a rather

---

13. *Course Guides for the Training of Teachers of Junior High and High School Mathematics, op. cit.*

hurried treatment of such basic concepts as mathematical induction and the construction of the rational number system and tends to rush on into the discussion of more esoteric and, from the standpoint of the high school teacher, less useful topics. Furthermore, there is frequently little or no attempt made to relate the material of the course to the teaching of secondary school algebra.

Similar comments apply to the second-semester course on linear algebra (or to a year course which presents linear algebra first or in a mixture with other topics). The basic recommended topics of vector spaces, linear transformations, and linear systems are standard in any course in linear algebra.

Three additional topics are listed in the CUPM outlines, however, which are not commonly covered in courses in linear algebra. Considered briefly, these are (*a*) vector geometry, (*b*) linear programing, and (*c*) game theory.

In summary, we may conclude that recommendation B is substantially being met in terms of topics covered, but that there are frequently deficiencies in regard to emphasis on topics and in relating them to the structure of high school mathematics.

(*C*) *Two courses in geometry beyond analytic geometry.*—The recommendations here are very specific: "These courses should be directed at a higher understanding of the geometry of the school curriculum." Since the "geometry of the school curriculum" is almost entirely Euclidean geometry in the form of some modification of Euclid's presentation, this means that much of the content of these courses should be concerned with the foundations of Euclidean geometry (both in the "synthetic" approach used in almost all high school geometry texts prior to 1960, and in the "metric" approach, now quite popular, used in the SMSG *Geometry*).[14] The other two topics suggested by CUPM for discussion are (*a*) the constructions possible with ruler and compass and (*b*) other geometries as compared to Euclidean. Under (*b*) would come a brief introduction to projective geometry and finite geometries and a very considerable discussion of non-Euclidean geometries based on a consideration of the role of the parallel postulate in Euclidean geometry.

The basic problem in implementing this portion of the CUPM recommendation is that, in contrast to the recommended algebra

14. *Geometry* (Pasadena, Calif.: A. C. Vroman & Co., 1961).

courses, the recommended geometry courses do not correspond to a standard geometry sequence required of (or even recommended for) non-teaching majors. The three traditional undergraduate courses in geometry have been advanced Euclidean geometry (usually offered under the title of "college geometry"), projective geometry, and solid analytic geometry. Another fairly common offering has been non-Euclidean geometry and, more recently, differential geometry. Today, solid analytic geometry has largely disappeared (with the bare essentials incorporated into the analytic geometry-calculus sequence) and the college geometry course is less commonly offered than it was ten years ago.

In rather few schools, however, do we find a year sequence in geometry closely paralleling the CUPM recommendations. The basic reasons are not hard to find. First of all, geometry is simply not, at the present time, as much in the mainstream of mathematics as are, for example, algebra and analysis. Thus, colleges which must limit their offerings will naturally tend to limit them in the area of geometry rather than in more "essential" areas. Secondly, the kind of geometry that is of maximal current research interest (e.g., convexity and differential geometry) is not the kind of geometry that is as closely related to the present secondary school curriculum as is the geometry of the CUPM recommendations. In particular, the importance of a study of the foundations of Euclidean geometry is near zero except for prospective teachers of Euclidean geometry. (In contrast, almost any first-year sequence in abstract algebra is likely to have considerable in common with the CUPM-recommended sequence for prospective teachers.)

(D) *Two courses in probability and statistics.*—The suggested course outline for this sequence is similar to that suggested in *A General Curriculum in Mathematics for Colleges* (see footnote 5) for all mathematics majors. This requirement seems to be fairly adequately implemented.

(E) *A course in computer science.*—This recommendation did not appear in the 1961 report. Such a course is by no means universally offered and is certainly not a part of a teaching major in many schools at the present time—not even in those schools which have adopted the 1961 recommendations.

(F) *Two upper-class elective courses.*—These are generally required, however, with wide latitudes in selection being allowed.

Finally, for Level III, CUPM points out the desirability of a "methods" course which would deal with such items as:

1. The objectives and content of the many proposals for change in our curriculum and texts.
2. The techniques, relative merits, and roles of such teaching procedures as the inductive and deductive approaches to new ideas.
3. The literature of mathematics and its teaching.
4. The underlying ideas of elementary mathematics and the manner in which they may provide a rational basis for teaching.
5. The chief applications which have given rise to various mathematical subjects. (These applications will depend on the level of mathematics to be taught and are an essential part of the equipment of all mathematics teachers.)

Such a course is commonly required, and texts have recently become available that are fairly appropriate for meeting the objectives of such a "methods" course.

Deficiencies in Present Undergraduate Programs

In the CUPM recommendations, we find the cautionary note ". . . the recommendations are minimal in nature. . . . It is expected that as high school curricula are strengthened, these minimal recommendations will be revised."[15]

In considering deficiencies in present programs, then, let us begin by considering the extent to which these *minimal* recommendations are being carried out and the trends toward reaching these minimal goals. Then we will consider likely changes in the recommended course structure. Finally, we will consider other needs in teacher training which are, at most, touched on lightly in the CUPM recommendations.

The 1966 situation in regard to Level I has already been indicated in Table 1. All indications point to an almost universal establishment of a five-six-hour or more requirement by about 1970. At the same time there will be an increase in the number of colleges (or state certification regulations) requiring more than six hours. The writer doubts, however, that the per cent of colleges requiring more than six hours of mathematics for Level I will rise above 25 per cent and probably not more than 5 per cent will require the full twelve hours.

15. *Recommendations for the Training of Teachers of Mathematics* (rev.), *op. cit.*, p. 5.

At the same time there will be an increasing number of Level I teachers who will elect stronger preparation in mathematics (comparable to Level II preparation except not necessarily including calculus). CUPM (see earlier section) has advocated that at least 20 per cent of the Level I teachers in each school have such a stronger preparation. If more colleges offered such a CUPM-type sequence for prospective elementary school teachers as, for example, a minor, the author thinks that perhaps 10 per cent of elementary majors might be attracted into such a program. At the present time, however, the only mathematics courses beyond Level I courses that are likely to be available to the elementary major are Level III courses with a calculus prerequisite. For this reason, it appears that the minimum required Level I courses are the most that we can expect of all but a handful of elementary school teachers.

What about likely changes in the recommended minimal program? First of all, in the face of the extreme difficulty of getting colleges to move beyond the six-unit, two-course requirement, it seems highly unlikely that there will be any significant amount of agitation for requiring more than twelve hours of college mathematics for Level I.

Secondly, the present Level I course recommendations are based largely on an elementary-secondary mathematics background of traditional mathematics. Thus, for example, the 1967 texts available for the Level I courses in the real number system include quite detailed discussions of such topics as the algebra of sets and numeration systems, which are really covered quite adequately in modern elementary-secondary texts. Similarly, much of the algebra and geometry in the other two CUPM-recommended Level I courses is a repetition of contemporary algebra and geometry courses at the secondary level. One may predict that, in the near future, many colleges will offer a six-hour package, based on a modern elementary-high school mathematics background, which will provide adequate coverage of the CUPM-recommended Level I topics.

Thirdly, there have already been calls for a considerable upgrading of the present CUPM recommendations. Thus, for example, *Goals for Mathematical Education of Elementary School Teachers*[16] calls for the same twelve-hour requirement of CUPM but proposes a se-

16. *Goals for Mathematical Education of Elementary School Teachers* (Report of the Cambridge Conference on Teacher Training [Boston: Houghton Mifflin Co. for Education Development Center, Inc., 1967]).

quence closer to the present CUPM Level II than to the present CUPM Level I. Actually, several alternative programs are proposed in this volume but all of them include—in addition to the study of the real number system—(*a*) a considerable amount of geometry from the transformational point of view, (*b*) a certain amount of abstract algebra (especially matrices as related to transformations), (*c*) topics in probability and statistics, and (*d*) intuitive differential and integral calculus.

The argument for such a considerably increased mathematics requirement for elementary school teachers is, of course, that the elementary school mathematics curriculum of the future will demand such a background of the teachers. In the words of *Goals*: "The UICSM [University of Illinois Committee on School Mathematics] and SMSG courses, which the visibly awed public has lumped together as 'new math,' may in a very few years seem tame indeed when compared with the mathematical fare of quite young children."

There is certainly no question that the mathematics of the elementary school will increase in sophistication, but many signs indicate that the changes for the average school and for the average child will not be as great as *Goals* and other reports indicate. It seems much more likely that, for quite some time, the major effort will be to improve and publish both content *and* methods of presentation of material at roughly the present level—for both children and their teachers.

This is not to say that experimentation with more sophisticated elementary school curricula will not take place. Indeed, programs of considerably more depth than the ones commonly used today will undoubtedly be available for the superior students in many schools. Futhermore, some school systems will undoubtedly develop and use materials of considerably more sophistication than the average. In such situations, teachers will be needed with the level of training indicated in the *Goals* report. But, to repeat, this writer does not see the need for a large number of such highly trained elementary school teachers in the next decade. Furthermore, if the elementary school mathematics curriculum does indeed develop throughout the country along the lines indicated in various reports,[17] it is likely that schools

17. See *Goals for Mathematical Education of Elementary School Teachers*, *op. cit.*; *Goals for School Mathematics* (Report of the Cambridge Conference on School Mathematics [Boston: Houghton Mifflin Co. for Educational Services,

will be forced to abandon the self-contained classroom above the second or third grade as far as mathematics is concerned.

Now let us turn to a consideration of Level II. Probably the most spectacular improvement in the K-XII mathematics curriculum in recent years has been at the seventh- and eighth-grade levels. The traditional programs have been such a dull mixture of arithmetic review and boring applications that almost any change would have been an improvement! The changes that have been made, however, have made severe demands on Level II teachers and, as mentioned before, there has been little attention to the development of programs for Level II. Instruction of seventh- and eighth-grade mathematics is largely in the hands of teachers with, at most, Level I training. (At the ninth-grade level, one is more likely to find teachers with something like Level II training or even Level III training, especially if the school system involves a IX-XII high school.)

School administrators are generally well aware of the need for better-prepared mathematics teachers at the junior high level and, frequently, assign teachers with Level III preparation to junior high schools. Most mathematics teachers, however, prefer a senior-high over a junior-high assignment and, given the current shortage of mathematics teachers, are likely to be able to move out of the junior high school after two or three years.

There is, then, a real need for active programs of Level II training, but few exist today and there are no real signs of many developing in the near future. The basic reason for this is that the Level II training, intermediate as it is between that of Level I and Level III, simply does not fit either most certification patterns or most major-minor baccalaureate requirements. Most junior high school teachers of mathematics can expect to teach only mathematics if they are qualified and, hence, will normally take their major in mathematics— which then brings them to Level III. On the other hand, junior high school teachers who teach only an occasional mathematics class are unlikely to have anticipated this possibility by taking Level II training.

Even if it were possible to persuade a significant number of prospective teachers to undertake Level II training, there would still be the problem of finding institutions which offer Level II programs. We have already pointed out that many colleges experience difficulty in setting up Level III programs because some of the suggested sequences for teachers (notably the geometry sequence) do not fit too well into the various mathematics programs designed for other than the prospective teacher. Some of the Level II courses, however, represent much more of a misfit. In particular, a single course in algebra and a single course in geometry are recommended for Level II in contrast to the two-course sequences in both algebra and geometry for Level III. Now, even if quite adequate Level III algebra and geometry sequences exist in a college, it does not follow at all that one can obtain satisfactory Level II courses. Indeed, it is difficult to imagine a two-semester algebra sequence in which the first semester would provide an adequate Level II preparation. Thus, specially designed courses are indicated for Level II—and specially designed courses for certain groups of students are never very popular with mathematics departments and are virtually impossible for small departments.

We may conclude that it would probably be wise to avoid putting substantial effort into the development of Level II programs and to concentrate on the improvement of Level I and Level III programs.

Now let us consider Level III. Statistics on the implementation of the CUPM recommendations at Level III are not as readily available as they are for Level I. Various conferences on the problem as well as a sampling of college requirements indicate a substantial implementation of the CUPM Level III recommendations. If deficiencies exist, they are most likely to be (for reasons discussed previously) the lack of a course in foundations of geometry and of a course in computer science. However, even though the Level III requirements at a particular college may appear to be identical with the CUPM recommendations, appearances can be deceiving. For example, a course in abstract algebra may (very properly from the point of view of the prospective Ph.D. in mathematics) spend very little time in examining the characteristic properties of the rational number field, the real number field, and the complex number field. From the point of view of the Level III teacher, however, a thorough treatment of the complex number field and its subfields is absolutely basic.

As is the case in Level I, changes in Level III training in the future will be heavily influenced by changes in the mathematics curriculum of the schools. If, for example, as many people predict, calculus becomes a standard offering in high schools, it is obvious that the high school teacher will need more work in analysis than is presently included in the CUPM Level III program. (Possibly, however, this additional preparation may be included in a year of post-graduate work that is becoming more and more a requirement for permanent certification.)

In any event, there are bound to be a certain number of changes in Level III programs because of the fact that a non-trivial part of the present recommended program is essentially remedial or review work in terms of the better, contemporary elementary and secondary mathematics programs (for example, discussions of set notation and the axioms for an ordered field). We can, therefore, certainly expect some tightening up of the basic courses—especially those in algebra and geometry. The recommended computer course will also become more common. The greatest change is likely to be in the geometry sequence. Present-day secondary school geometry courses (modeled, for example, on either of the two SMSG geometry texts[18]) provide a background which should lead to a briefer treatment of the foundations of Euclidean geometry than has been possible in the past. This will provide time for a greater consideration of some of the more dynamic aspects of geometry of current interest—especially transformation geometry and convexity.

Regardless, however, of how closely the syllabi for teacher-training courses match the most carefully prepared recommendations of the most highly qualified committees, there are still likely to be serious deficiencies in teacher training at all levels. It is becoming increasingly clear that it is not sufficient to recognize the desirability of special courses for teachers; we must also recognize the need for special procedures in the teaching of such courses. Three aspects of this problem are as follows:

1. There is a great need to relate more closely what is being studied to problems of teaching elementary and secondary school mathematics. For example, it is not enough to present a satisfactory definition of polynomials as, for example, infinite dimensional vectors with all but a finite number of components equal to zero. In order for this to be really meaningful in terms of teaching beginning algebra,

---

18. *Geometry, op. cit.; Geometry with Coordinates* (Pasadena, Calif.: G. C. Vroman & Co., 1964).

we need to point out the considerable deficiencies in more elementary "definitions" of polynomials.

2. Closely related to the need just described is the need to provide for a discussion of teaching methods along with content, rather than a study of content and methods in separate courses. For example, a proof of the ring property, $(-a)(-b) = ab$, becomes much more meaningful in the light of a discussion of ways of presenting this property of the real or rational number systems at various grade levels.

3. Somehow we must come to grips with the fact that a "C"-level understanding of a topic by a teacher may be worse than no understanding at all. For example, a somewhat muddled presentation of a proof by induction in a college mathematics class may, by usual grading standards, be entitled to a "C" grade. A prospective teacher, however, who passes the course with such a performance is all too likely to provide us with a second generation of students whose initial understanding of proof by induction is badly muddled.

Here, of course, the writer is not insisting on a miraculous, 100 per cent understanding of all topics studied by the prospective teacher. There is no need, for example, for him to have perfectly in mind a proof of Lagrange's theorem for groups. But there are many aspects of the mathematics a prospective teacher studies for which we should not be satisfied with a "C"-level understanding.

Increasingly, people are finding out that none of the good new mathematics curricula are proof against the incompetent teacher. Indeed, it is far easier to distort and destroy a carefully structured mathematics program than a routine, drill-oriented program so typical of the past. Unless we look beyond the syllabi of teacher-education programs, it seems certain that we will encounter increasing difficulty in implementing improved curricula in the schools.

Graduate Study for Teachers at Levels I–III

In this section we are concerned with formal, sequential-type graduate study in contrast to occasional in-service courses or institutes, which will be discussed in the concluding section of this chapter.

First of all, there really is no point in discussing graduate programs in mathematics for Level I or even for Level II. One can only hope that a reasonable graduate program for Level I and Level II teachers will allow the possibility of their taking for graduate credit some additional work in mathematics at a level appropriate for them. The remainder of this section, then, will be concerned with formal graduate programs for Level III (and, to some extent, Level IV and V) teachers.

In considering graduate programs for Level III teachers we must first acknowledge the existence of "supplementary" programs at the master's degree level. These are of two basic types.

One type takes a person with a liberal arts background and a major in mathematics and, in a year or two (frequently through an internship program), provides the necessary professional education background for a teaching certificate. Frequently, the degree of Master of Arts in Teaching (MAT) is awarded along with the certification. A typical program of this kind is that of Harvard where the requirements for the degree involve a two-year program, beginning with a seven-week summer session in which supervised teaching is done in the morning and in which the afternoons are devoted to planning and evaluation. The course work consists of

Introduction to Education..................	6 hrs.
Educational Psychology...................	3
Mathematics courses......................	6
Curriculum and Methods in Mathematics.....	6
Course in anthropology, history, philosophy, or sociology............................	3
Elective.................................	3
	27 hrs.

and the program includes a year of internship earning nine hours of credit.

The second type of supplementary degree usually involves a certified teacher with a background of a weak major in mathematics and three or more years of teaching experience. Frequently, the work for such a degree is taken in summer sessions or in summer or academic-year institutes sponsored by the National Science Foundation. The M.A. (or MAT) program for such a student will typically involve mainly mathematics courses at the level of the CUPM-recommended, upper-division courses together with a very small amount of graduate mathematics courses and a seminar on the curriculum. Frequently, some or all of the courses are specially designed for teachers. The program may or may not involve an expository thesis, and it may involve no courses in education or, at most, a very limited number of courses.

Supplementary programs of the two types just described are, unfortunately, still needed. An increasing number of students, however, are getting their baccalaureate degrees with CUPM Level III preparation—and more. What is available to them for graduate work? And what is available as additional mathematics training for those persons obtaining either one of the supplementary-type master's degrees?

The answer—at most universities—is course work designed to lead to a traditional graduate degree in mathematics. Now it is certainly not in any way harmful for a high school teacher to take, for example, a graduate-level sequence in algebra similar to that taken by the prospective Ph.D. in mathematics. But one can certainly argue, first of all, that a good deal of the material in traditional graduate sequences in mathematics is of very limited value to the high school teacher in his own teaching. Second, there are certainly many aspects of mathematics of great importance to the high school teacher that are not considered in a traditional graduate sequence of mathematics courses (for example, historical and recreational aspects, relation of advanced mathematics to elementary mathematics, etc.). Finally, relatively few present-day high school teachers have the mathematical ability to cope with graduate mathematics courses that are designed primarily for potential Ph.D.'s in mathematics. (And this is *not* a shameful fact. Teaching secondary school mathematics effectively does not demand the specialized skills of a research mathematician and, on the other hand, does demand many other vital skills which a suitable graduate program should attempt to improve.)

Now there is an increasing number of universities that do offer reasonable graduate-degree programs for teachers that build upon a CUPM-level preparation in mathematics (frequently through a separate department of "mathematics-education"). These programs are mixtures of mathematics and education. They vary from a program of mathematics courses identical with those for the research Ph.D. plus two or three education courses and with an expository rather than a research thesis—to programs with a heavy concentration on education and little additional mathematics. Examples of these two extremes are the respective programs leading to a Ph.D. in mathematics education at Yeshiva University and to the Ed.D. at the University of Washington. The Yeshiva degree differs from the traditional doctorate in mathematics essentially only in requiring nine credits in education and psychology and in the substitution of an expository thesis for the standard research dissertation. On the other hand, the Ed.D. at the University of Washington simply requires the completion of twenty quarter-hours of approved work in an area outside education, and this outside area could, of course, be mathematics. (Most of such hours in mathematics would probably be at the 400 senior-graduate level—rather than at the strictly graduate 500 level). The total degree requirements for the Ed.D. involve a minimum of ninety-six quarter-hours beyond the master's degree, of which thirty are devoted to the dissertation.

In between these extremes one can find as degree requirements just about every possible combination of education courses, mathematics courses, and mathematics-education courses. In general, considerable latitude is allowed in the course program, and there are few course requirements specifically mentioned. Thus, for example, the *Florida State University Graduate Bulletin* simply states that a minimum of one-third of the graduate course work for a doctorate in mathematics education must be in education (including courses in mathematics education such as curriculum studies and the like).

According to a survey made by W. W. Hamilton in his 1967 doctoral dissertation at North Texas State University, the average program for the Ph.D. or Ed.D. in mathematics education consists of ninety semester hours including ". . . forty to forty-eight hours in mathematics; eighteen to twenty-four hours in education, and permitting a dissertation consisting of research in the teaching of mathematics, research in mathematics, or statistical, historical, or expository research."[19]

In looking over graduate programs in mathematics or mathematics education that have been specifically designed for teachers, one cannot avoid getting the impression that, in general, their content has been determined more by expediency and the intricacies of local

19. William W. Hamilton, "Doctoral Programs in Mathematics and Education As Related to Instructional Needs of Junior Colleges and Four Year Colleges," Unpublished doctoral thesis, North Texas State University, Denton, Texas, 1967. For details concerning existing programs in mathematics education, see also Clarence B. Lindquist, *Mathematics in Colleges & Universities* (U.S. Office of Education Circular No. 765, 1965—OE-56018).

university politics than by a careful analysis of the needs of the candidate in his profession as a teacher. It seems essential that serious consideration be given to the question of the composition of graduate programs of maximum usefulness for teachers of mathematics at all levels.

In the design of such maximally effective programs, the following essential points should be kept in mind:

1. The typical graduate student in mathematics education is undoubtedly someone who has not had formal course work in mathematics for three to ten years—and who has had little time and opportunity for informal study. It is inevitable that he will be rusty in certain areas—especially in those which have experienced rapid change. He should be given an opportunity to undertake, with graduate credit, a certain amount of course work devoted to the review and updating of previous course work. (A similar need for review is also frequently met by a Ph.D. returning for further study—e.g., on an NSF Faculty Fellowship. Such a person, however, is not concerned with further degrees or even graduate credit and can, without difficulty, sit in on graduate or even undergraduate courses for review purposes.)

2. The CUPM-recommended preparation for secondary school teachers demands rather little in the way of analysis courses. Surely, however, a person obtaining any advanced degree in mathematics should be prepared to teach first-year calculus (whether in college or in advanced-placement high school courses). Hence, a graduate program in mathematics for teachers should include courses in analysis at least to the level of an introductory senior-graduate-level real variables course. Again, however, graduate credit should be given for junior-level analysis courses lying between the CUPM-required analysis courses and this senior-graduate-level course.

3. Ample opportunity should be afforded (graduate credit problems again) for the teacher-graduate student to broaden his horizons by taking courses in areas of mathematics that he may previously have neglected—for example, history of mathematics, number theory, logic, computer programing, linear programing, and so on. A broad knowledge of basic mathematics is surely of more importance to the secondary school or undergraduate-college teacher than is extensive specialization.

4. At least one course in curriculum development should be a part

of the program (perhaps offered by the education department or jointly by the mathematics and education departments if a mathematics-education department does not exist at the university).

5. A reading course in "recreational" mathematics should be part of the program.

6. A low-level, mathematics-"research" seminar should be required (problem-solving at the level of problems in the *American Mathematical Monthly, Mathematics Magazine*, and similar journals).

7. A seminar on expository writing would be profitable.

8. Some study of cognitive processes in the area of mathematics would be appropriate—for example, a study of the work of Piaget, Bruner, etc. (offered by education or psychology departments).

9. A *limited* amount of regular (i.e., pre-Ph.D.) courses in mathematics should be required.

No thesis is suggested for the master's degree although a certain amount of writing would be required under items 5 to 7. The Ph.D. (or Ed.D. or Doctor of Arts—or whatever the title) should certainly require a thesis. In some cases, a suitable thesis would be directed toward research in education somewhat as in the typical Ed.D. program.[20] In the author's opinion, however, it would be a serious mistake not to permit a "project"-type thesis such as the development of curricular materials (together with testing and rewriting), historical studies, translations, and the like.

Training for Teachers at Levels IV and V

The CUPM recommendations for teachers at Level IV (lower-division mathematics) embrace basically a *strong* master's degree which, in turn, is based on a strong undergraduate mathematics major. In particular, course work should include full-year courses in at least two of the areas of modern algebraic theory, analysis, and geometry from a topological point of view. In each case, the course should be a bona fide graduate course based solidly on a prerequisite of a junior-senior-level course in the subject. In addition, CUPM recommends at least one semester of teaching a class in undergraduate mathematics under the close supervision of an experienced teacher.

20. For a general discussion of graduate work in education, see *The Graduate Study of Education* (Report of the Harvard Committee [Cambridge: Harvard University Press, 1965]).

For Level V (teachers of the first four years of college mathematics), CUPM suggests essentially course work at the level of the doctorate together with seminars and reading courses designed to acquaint the student with research and the relation of his graduate work to undergraduate instruction. In particular, the recommendations call for completing the third of the three basic courses required for Level IV and for a second year of graduate study in at least one of these three fields ". . . as well as additional graduate courses in mathematics representing areas of special interest to the faculty."[21]

The CUPM recommendations by no means suggest that the attainment of a Ph.D. is not a desirable goal for Level V teachers, but simply suggest that the non-thesis course program described above will provide an adequate preparation for undergraduate teaching. Clearly these Level IV and V recommendations are by no means entirely unrelated to the doctoral programs discussed in the preceding section for Level III teachers. A doctoral program in mathematics education of the kind suggested in a preceding section, Graduate Study for Teachers at Levels I-III, should certainly provide training adequate for Level IV teaching. It would even provide, if the graduate mathematics component were reasonably strong, a sufficiently strong background for teaching in the mathematics-education area in a university.

In-service Education

Most recent in-service education in mathematics at all levels has been very much remedial in nature. Thus, for example, it has not been uncommon to have a college offer a Saturday-morning class for high school teachers for which the basic text was one commonly used in "modern" mathematics programs at the senior level in high school. In terms of time involved, such "courses" have varied from two or three late-afternoon sessions (sometimes run by book salesmen) to academic-year institutes.

In any event, there is no need here to attempt to describe the content of such remedial in-service courses since their general purpose has been to provide the equivalent of the preservice training that we

21. For further details, see *Qualifications for a College Faculty in Mathematics* (Report of the Ad Hoc Committee on the Qualifications of Teachers, Committee on the Undergraduate Program in Mathematics, Mathematical Association of America [Berkeley, Calif.: Distributed by CUPM, January, 1967]), p. 10.

have been describing. The methods and means employed have been as varied as the needs of the students: late-afternoon classes offered by the school district using its best-qualified staff as teachers; university or college extension classes; Saturday, summer, and academic-year institutes; films; TV programs; and correspondence courses.[22]

The need for such remedial in-service work is, unfortunately, still very real but, fortunately, is diminishing somewhat. The need now is to develop systematic procedures for in-service work designed to maintain competence. In the words of CUPM, ". . . continued intellectual and professional growth is essential to continued competence as a teacher . . . the difficulties involved in upgrading many of our present teachers and in stimulating continued growth in others provide some of the most important and pressing problems faced by the mathematical community."[23]

22. See example, *Inservice Education of High School Mathematics Teachers* (U.S. Office of Education Bulletin 1961, No. 10—OE-29022).

23. *Qualifications for a College Faculty in Mathematics, op. cit.,* p. 15.

CHAPTER VIII

Applications of Mathematics

H. O. POLLAK

Applications and the Classroom

In this chapter, we are going to examine in some measure the nature of applications of mathematics and how such applications relate to the teaching of mathematics. The problem is a rather complex one, and the subject is so beset with various misconceptions and intuitive prejudgments that we must think our way through the issues rather carefully. It would, of course, be logical to begin with as precise a definition of applications of mathematics as is possible. However, our contact with problems of mathematics education during recent years has somewhat converted us to the spiral method of teaching, and this method tends to suffer from attempts at becoming too precise too early. Our plan, therefore, is to make a modest beginning and to return to the problem many times.

What do we mean by applications of mathematics? It is clear that the phrase connotes a connection of mathematics with something else. More than that, there is the implication that this is a useful connection, that something of "practical" value might be expected to come of it. For the recipient of the mathematics, applications of mathematics typically serve three relatively distinct ends: (*a*) They may illumine situations in everyday life, (*b*) they may help in the development of some other discipline, or (*c*) they may be of value in some other branch of mathematics. For our present purposes, we shall exclude applications of one branch of mathematics to another and concentrate on applications to real life and to other disciplines. There is a broad range of depth and seriousness to applications of both kinds, and a still broader range of material that currently passes in mathematics textbooks for applications of mathematics.

The first and most obvious kind of application of mathematics is an immediate use in everyday life. It is important to realize that not only arithmetic but also algebra, geometry, probability, statistics, and, in fact, most of elementary and secondary mathematics are likely to be involved. It is also interesting that such everyday applications may be either exact or approximate in character. When we check the computation of the sales tax, try to figure out how much paint it will take for the living room, refigure a recipe for a different number of people, try to build or to move a bookcase, buy a rug of the right size, win a little money at poker, or plant tomatoes, we are using mathematics in "everyday" life. Problems of this kind quite naturally also appear in our textbooks. Here are some examples of perfectly sensible everyday problems taken from texts that happen to be in my office.

Mr. Twiggs changed the price of potatoes in his store from 4½¢ a pound to 3 pounds for 14¢.

(a) Did he raise or lower the price?
(b) How much was the increase or decrease per pound?

A large sandbox with a base 10 ft. long and 9 ft. wide is built in a park. A dump truck carrying 5 cubic yards of sand is emptied into the box. If the sand is leveled off, what is its depth? Give the answer both in feet and in inches.

A boy has 24 ft. of wire fence to make a rectangular pen for his pet rabbit. He plans to use all the fence in making the pen. Could he make a pen 12 ft. long and 12 ft. wide? Why or why not? Could he make a pen 8 ft. long and 3 ft. wide? How about 8 ft. long and 4 ft. wide? Give five examples of lengths and widths he could use for his pen.

In all the discussions about applied mathematics, no one has ever questioned the value of such problems. We only wish that there were more, and a much greater variety, of them.

The next class of problems in our textbooks, perhaps the most abundant of all, is that which uses words from everyday life outside of mathematics to make the problem "sound good." The key feature of all these problems is that a certain amount of translation from English to mathematics is required before one can start, and the point presumably is to practice such translation along with practicing the subsequent mathematical technique. The statement of such problems rarely questions the honesty or genuineness of the connection of the problem to the real world, but the connection is often false in one or more ways. Some examples:

An electric fan is advertised as moving 3375 cubic feet of air per minute. How long will it take the fan to change the air in a room 27 ft. by 25 ft. by 10 ft.?

The trouble with this problem is that it is based on the assumption that all the old air in a room is removed before any new air enters, while there is, in fact, intermixing of old and new air and a gradual dilution of the former by the new. Are we not aware of how long it takes even a powerful fan to get the smell of a burnt pot of beans out of the kitchen? The answer to the problem is at best a lower bound.

112 tulip bulbs are to be planted in a garden. Describe all possible arrangements of the bulbs if they are to be placed in straight rows with an equal number of bulbs per row.

This is, in fact, quite a realistic problem. People do, of course, consider other kinds of patterns for planting than rectangular arrays, but the problem could easily go on to these. The further problem might be: "What pleasing patterns, regular in some interesting way, can be made from 112 tulip bulbs?"

The next examples are taken from J. M. Hammersley, *Bulletin of the Institute of Mathematics and Its Applications* (*October 1968*). They are examination questions.

Question A16. The mean survival period of daisies after being sprayed with a certain make of weed killer is 24 days. If the probability of survival after 27 days is ¼, estimate the standard deviation of the survival period.

Now, is the candidate expected to apply some cookbook method which assumes that survival times are normally distributed; or is he to try to make his mathematical model realistic? If the latter, then he will have to remember that the distribution is a mixture of two components—the lifetimes of daisies which escape all effects of the spray and of those which do not—and neither of these two distributions is likely to be normal; and he is up against some pretty awkward mathematics. The question hardly suggests that the examiner has extensive experience of constructing mathematical models.

In the S. M. P. Ordinary Level paper we have some multiple choice questions, and the candidate has to encircle the letter or letters corresponding to any correct answer. Question 16 runs as follows:

"Passengers are allowed 40 lb. of luggage free of charge; any amount in excess of 40 lb. is charged at 3d. per lb." If W lb. is the weight of the luggage (W is an integer) and C shillings is the cost, the regulation quoted above is equivalent to

(a) $C = 3(W + 40)$;   (b) $C = 1/4\,(W - 40)$;

(c) $C = 40 + 3W$;   (d) $C = 1/4\,W - 40$.

Since all four choices are false, how does the examiner distinguish between a candidate who answers the question correctly and one who does not attempt it at all? The notable point about this question is that there is no need to scrutinize the individual coefficients in these formulae; all the formulae are linear and therefore obviously false since the situation is non-linear.

The same objection applies to all the pipes of various diameters that empty and fill tanks and swimming pools, to railroad schedules (accurate to the nearest second), to constant-velocity infinite-acceleration trains, to all the factories with linear production costs and known customer response to price, and to many other stereotypes. There will be, in a fair number of cases, a kernel of truth in the situation being used—for example, in a stable economy, sales will probably decrease if prices increase—and it is easy to bound the error due to an assumption of constant velocity. Bounding the error, of course, represents the point of view we need to take in the classroom in order to practice approximation with the students. After all, calculation is often approximate, and this is not just for ease and convenience or for getting one's feelings for the problem in order. Approximate calculation may, in fact, be the only justifiable response to the approximations made in obtaining the mathematical model of reality which the problem represents.

"Word" problems that pretend to come from other scholarly or engineering discipines tend, once again, to be exercises in translation and in the subsequent mathematical techniques, and the reality of the application is often neglected.

To find out how far to tunnel through a hill, a surveyor lays out $AX = 100$ yards, $BY = 80$ yards, $CX = 20$ yards, and $CY = 16$ yards. He finds, by measurement, that $YX = 30$ yards. How long is the tunnel, *AB?*

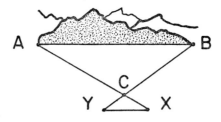

The assumption that A, B, C, X and Y are all in a plane should perhaps be stated; the problem requires it, but perhaps it is reasonable to expect that this assumption will be understood. The only difficulty is that if the land on the near side of the hill is flat, no one would dream of building a tunnel!

A more suspect example is the following alleged application of combinatorial reasoning to linguistics:

It is a rule in Gaelic that no consonant or group of consonants can stand immediately between a strong and a weak vowel; the strong vowels being *a, o, u;* and the weak vowels *e* and *i*. Show that the whole number of Gaelic words of $n + 3$ letters each, which can be formed of n consonants and the vowels *aeo*, is $2(n + 3)!/n + 2$ where no letter is repeated in the same word.

The context of Gaelic orthography here is really questionable. Does it not matter whether the resulting word is pronounceable, and is there really an arbitrary number of consonants? How large is the Gaelic vocabulary of such words?

Another example, which was specifically intended to show the application of mathematics to science, is the following:

The specific weight of water (s) at a temperature $t°c$ is given by the equation:

$$s = 1 + at + bt^2 + ct^3 . \text{ (For } 0° < t < 100° \text{ C)}$$

Where

t = temperature in degrees centigrade

$a = 5.3 \times 10^{-5}$

$b = -6.53 \times 10^{-6}$

$c = 1.4 \times 10^{-8}$

At which temperature will the water have the maximum specific weight? Solution: $ds/dt = a + 2bt + 3ct^2$. When $ds/dt = 0$, $t = 4.09°$C. Since the second derivative, $d^2s/dt^2 = 2b + 6ct$, is negative in the above-mentioned range ($0 < t < 100$—all temperatures at which water is liquid—under pressure conditions), s is a maximum when $t = 4.09$.

Now it is perfectly possible that, for future purposes, one might want a cubic approximation to the experimental curve, plotting the specific weight of water against temperature. It would, of course, be much more exciting if we had some physical intuition leading us to the reasonableness of a cubic and if a, b, and c had an interesting interpretation. However, it is unlikely that the cubic approximation to the real data, or any other analytic fit, would be used to find the maximum specific weight—you would certainly refer to the original data for that. "Eyeballing" the experimental points would give a far better guess for the location of the extremum than would fitting a cubic over a very wide range and then differentiating it.

At the far end of typical textbook problems that are made to look like applications are problems which can best be described as representing pure whimsy. These exercises use words from daily life or from the various disciplines, but it is quite clear to everyone that no real application is intended. The function of such problems, and there are many of them in our textbooks, is not quite clear. Perhaps they serve to bring a tolerant smile from a weary student or to distract him momentarily from an otherwise dreary lesson by diverting his imagination to some more pleasant scene. At any rate, it is difficult to see how they can do much harm. Here are some examples:

Two bees working together can gather nectar from 100 hollyhock blossoms in 30 minutes. Assuming that each bee works the standard eight-hour day, five days a week, how many blossoms do these bees gather nectar from in a summer season of fifteen weeks?

In working on a batch of 100 blossoms, one of the bees stops after 18 minutes (just to smell the flowers), and it takes the other bee 20 minutes to finish the batch. How long would it take the diligent bee to gather nectar from 100 blossoms if she worked all by herself?

Sometimes such problems can have considerable mathematical interest. For example, at his summer school for secondary school students in 1966, A. N. Kolmogorov gave the following problem (the writer does not have his exact phrasing):

A bee and a lump of sugar are located at different points inside a triangle. The bee wishes to reach the lump of sugar, while traveling a minimum distance, under the requirement that it must touch all three sides of the triangle before coming to the sugar. What is the shortest path?

In this series of apiarian problems, no actual relation to the real world is implied. The stories serve to introduce some simple algebra problems on the one hand or a highly ingenious and educational geometry problem on the other.

The applications of mathematics that we have examined thus far—whether genuine or false or whimsical—have all been simple specific problems whose solutions required only the direct translation of the story into mathematical terms and the application of standard mathematical techniques. Actual applications of mathematics, of course, are often not so simple. Rather than beginning with a precisely stated problem, we will probably be given a messy, fuzzy situation which we must try to understand. It may often be more difficult to find the right problem to solve than to solve the problem after it has been found. For example, consider the simple question, "What is the best way to get from here to the airport?" The difficulty begins with trying to understand what is meant by "best." If one has a rented car and is in no particular hurry, then probably minimum distance is meant. Under other conditions, one might well mean the way expected to require minimum time. At certain times of the day, although one might usually prefer a reasonably short drive, the route with the minimum number of intersections at which one does not have the right-of-way may be the "best." There are also other factors that one may wish to take into account such as the danger involved or the police patrol on a particular route. If the person going to the airport is late because of bad weather, is the airplane also likely to be late? After talking to a number of people, the writer has reached the conclusion that persons asking the question mean, by the "best" route to an airport, not the route requiring *minimum expected time* but the one for which there is *minimum variance in time*. People are willing to put up with a longer average time if the spread is smaller.

Supermarkets are a wonderful source of real situations which are subject to useful mathematization. When a product comes in several sizes, which is the cheapest? On one (the immediate) level, this question can be answered by simple arithmetic. There may, however, be other levels. If too large an amount is purchased, is it likely to become spoiled, stale, or moldy before the supply is exhausted? If one gets a free bath towel with one size and a free dish towel with another, which is really cheaper? And the extra-large roll of paper towels is no bargain if it is too fat to fit the purchaser's kitchen rack.

An excellent exercise in applications of mathematics may be achieved by forming a group of students into a firm of junior consultants for an hour. Here is an example of how this exercise might be used: In most supermarkets there is typically one check-out line labeled "express lane," for n packages or less. In using this situation in an experimental teaching procedure, it was learned that students in their experience had found n to vary between 5 and 15. Obviously, if a number varies this much, people do not understand what it should be. The problem, therefore, is to find out how many packages should be allowed to a customer in an express lane. The group of students had a wonderful time with this problem. First of all, what is the express lane for? Obviously, one purpose is to increase the profits of the stockholders, but how is that done? Should the average waiting time be minimized? If so, do we mean average per package or average per customer? Do we want to minimize the expected maximum waiting time? Is it desirable to minimize the probability that the wait exceeds ten minutes (or any other period of time that it appears feasible to choose)? Next, if there is agreement on what is being attempted, how does one construct a mathematical model? What is the relationship between check-out time and the number of packages? Is it good enough to assume a linear relation? Obviously, such a straight line would not go through the origin. However, if the number of packages is sufficiently large, a second sack will be needed. Perhaps a discontinuous, piece-wise linear function should be used! Is it sufficient to assume a deterministic model for check-out time, or is a probabilistic description necessary? How should the model differ between supermarkets that weigh produce at the check-out position and those that weigh and price at the produce counter? Next, what is to be said about the arrival behavior of the customers? How far apart are they likely to be? There are, of course, many other questions that might arise—questions that would provoke lively student debate.

There are innumerable situations in everyday life that can lead to similar mathematical questions. What is the best strategy for raking leaves on a lawn? If a pile of freshly washed socks are hung up on a line in the basement, what are the chances of finding a pair adjacent to each other? What is the best distance for spacing cars in a tunnel? Given the pattern of the traffic lights in New York City, what is the quickest way to walk between two locations? It is quite clear that not every situation of this sort will be formulated successfully into a precise mathematical problem—not to mention into one that the students are ready to solve. Furthermore, there is no certainty at the beginning as to what kind of mathematics will result. Nevertheless, it is very important for students to have practice in seeing situations in which mathematics might be helpful and in trying their hand at formulating useful problems. They will, incidentally, discover that for some situations mathematics is quite irrelevant. This too is very valuable.

Applications of mathematics to other scientific, scholarly, and engineering disciplines follow very much the same pattern. Once again, the understanding of given situations needs to be improved and formulating the right mathematical problem is likely to be half the battle. It is important to realize that situations to be mathematized will arise from many different disciplines. Besides physics (which has long been recognized as a major field of applied mathematics), all branches of engineering, all the other physical sciences, as well as the social and biological sciences, are nowadays leading to interesting mathematics. For example, biologists are making models of the prey-predator cycle and attempting to analyze the spread of epidemics, as well as continuing to develop the more familiar theory of mathematical genetics. Engineers apply topology to printed circuits, probability to random vibrations, and modern optimization techniques to production and inventory control, and they still use lots of differential equations.

Even lawyers sometimes get into serious mathematics. The following is an extract from Section 217 (on the taxability of reimbursed moving expenses) of the current (1969) Internal Revenue Code:

(a) Deduction Allowed—There shall be allowed as a deduction moving expenses paid or incurred during the taxable year in connection with the commencement of work by the taxpayer as an employee at a new principal place of work. . . .
(c) Conditions for Allowance—No deduction shall be allowed under this section unless—(1) the taxpayer's new principal place of work—(A) is at least 20 miles farther from his former residence than was his former principal place of work, or (B) if he had no former principal place of work, is at least 20 miles from his former residence.

Where are all former residences satisfying these conditions? How is the problem made different by the use of air miles as opposed to highway miles?

It is crucial that mathematics problems which claim to be applications of mathematics to other disciplines be *honest* applied mathematics. This means that the relationship between the mathematical model and the situation in the outside world that is being mathematized must be clearly understood. It is rather ridiculous to just use some words from another discipline and then exhibit some equation which is said to be relevant. How was it found? What approximations were made in obtaining this equation? How can it be demonstrated that the mathematical conclusions are meaningful in the original real-world situation?

Here are some examples in which the process of creating the mathematical model for the physical situation is perhaps insufficiently explored:

Consider a tube parallel to the x-axis containing fluid. Suppose that along with the fluid the tube also contains other material. If the concentration of the material increases to the right, there will be a net flow of molecules to the left. The concentration c of the material will be a function of both distance and time and from Fick's law can be shown to satisfy

(1)
$$\frac{\partial c}{\partial t} = D \frac{\partial^2 c}{\partial x^2}$$

where D is a proportionality constant known as the diffusion constant. Show that

$$c = \frac{1}{\sqrt{4\pi Dt}} \, exp \, (- \, x^2/4Dt) \text{ satisfies (1)} .$$

The reaction of the body to a dose of a drug can be represented by the following function:

$$R \, (D) = D^2 \left(\frac{C}{2} - \frac{D}{3} \right)$$

where

    $C =$ a positive constant
    $R =$ the strength of the reaction (for example—if R is the change in blood pressure, it is measured in mm mercury; if R is the change in temperature, it is measured in degrees, and so on.)
    $D =$ the amount of the drug

We will assume that whenever the drug is administered, the concentration of the drug already in the body is insignificant; for if there is already a certain concentration of the drug in the body, the reaction will depend upon this initial concentration (Weber-Fechner Law).

D is defined in the range of O to C. (In other words, C is the maximum amount that may be given.)

Find the range of dose for which the medicine has maximum sensitivity— in other words, where there is the greatest change in R for a small change in D, or equivalently where $R'(D)$ is at a maximum.

In the first of these problems, the introductory paragraph is to be welcomed (and is more than is often given), and the diffusion equation (1) is familiar to many mathematicians. It is, however, probably new to the students, and they are certainly entitled to participate personally in the processes of (*a*) deriving this particular approximation to reality, and of (*b*) analyzing the nature of the errors likely to have been made in the process of mathematization. What is Fick's law, and where does it come from?

The equation in the second problem is much more suspect, if only because it is less familiar. What leads to the belief that this relation is true? How does the functional form arise from first principles? What exactly is measured, and why? How can the units possibly work out right? What kinds of useful understanding can be derived from such a model? A lot needs to be added to make this into a good example of applied mathematics.

It is also possible to think of games and puzzles in mathematics instruction as varieties of applications. They are often totally impractical, but they are good fun and allow the development of both mathematical technique and concepts in a relatively painless context. Many puzzles are simple logical problems:

Three cannibals and three missionaries want to cross a river. They must share a boat which is large enough to carry only two people. At no time may the cannibals outnumber the missionaries, but the missionaries may outnumber the cannibals. How can they all get across the river using only the boat?

Puzzles in which the student has to figure out which of several people are telling the truth and which are lying,[1] questions about polyominoes,[2] attempts at circle and sphere packing, number games, very simple magic squares, nim, tick-tack-toe, bridgit, and many others can be used very successfully.[3] These games and puzzles vary from whimsy to rather serious applications to mathematics itself. Puzzles can be quite helpful in developing the premathematical intuition for new areas of mathematics.

It would be incomplete to leave the subject of the variety and reality of applications of mathematics in the schools without considering the possibility of physical experiments and data collection in connec-

1. School Mathematics Study Group, *Puzzle Problems and Game Projects* (Studies in Mathematics, Vol. XVIII, Stanford University, 1968).

2. Solomon W. Golomb, *Polyominoes* (New York: Charles Scribner's Sons, 1965).

3. Alfred Lehman, "A Solution of the Shannon Switching Game," *Journal of the Society for Industrial and Applied Mathematics* (SIAM), XII, No. 4 (December, 1964).

tion with classroom work. It is possible to use thumb tacks and bags of marbles and spinners in connection with probability. We can construct polyhedra, measure shadows, take all kinds of astronomical data, track the growth of plants, and work with pendula, lenses, springs, and inclined planes. We can record queues in banks and on major highways. We can use balance boards (including loaded ones), and we can find innumerable examples of linear relations in the physical and biological sciences. All of these activities can be excellent for relating mathematics, particularly on the elementary level, to real life. The systematic use of such motivating and illustrative examples becomes more difficult as we proceed through secondary school. The main reason is that any particular sequence of instructional material has to have an internal logic to its own development. While it is very commendable (many would say essential) for an instructor to build up the intuition for each successive topic in mathematics from situations outside of mathematics, here must be a structure to the course—that is, a logical sequence of topics to be undertaken. A difficulty arises when the natural sequence of events in the mathematics does not agree with the natural order of the scientific topics which are being used for motivation. In the elementary school, where we have wisely concentrated on the methodology and the phenomena of science more than on a structured development, this presents less of a problem. The mathematics can perhaps suggest the sequence of events, and conflicts of order will hopefully be gracefully resolved. If a topic is needed for science before it has appeared in the mathematics sequence, this discrepancy is unlikely to be a major problem for either discipline. In the secondary school, however, we attempt to teach systematically biology, chemistry, physics, and perhaps many other subjects which are possible sources of mathematical problems. Furthermore, mathematics has become more complex. If one really tries to integrate science and mathematics teaching, he risks the danger of interfering with the development of at least one of the two partners. Someone will have to be the "boss."

There have been complaints in recent years, some of them quite vociferous, that curriculum reform in mathematics has paid insufficient attention to the applications. This is probably true in many cases and current work is doing much to remedy the situation. Two comments, however, are perhaps in order. First of all, a number of critics have proceeded from the more or less explicit assumption that only applications to physics count as real applications, and that, if these have not been used, nothing has been done. They have thus tended to give less credit than is perhaps justifiable to problems relating mathematics to other disciplines and to the everyday world. Such a monocratic view of fields of applications tends to make the curriculum problems much harder to solve and to distract from the essential goal of having the student experience and share the *process* of model-building. Secondly, we must not underestimate the importance of what recent curriculum reform *has* achieved: an understanding of arrangements, presentations, and priorities of material which are both mathematically sound and pedagogically reasonable. We now have a much firmer base for the next stages of curriculum revision in mathematics, and these certainly include the further development of the interactions with other disciplines. In a sense, it was extremely important for mathematicians to get their own house in order first.

The Process of Applying Mathematics

On the basis of the above glimpse of a taxonomy of applications of mathematics in the classroom, we can now return to the question of what we mean by such applications and see what we have learned. We have seen first of all that almost all major fields of human endeavor, and innumerable situations in everyday life, are likely to lead to significant applications of mathematics. The traditional picture of applications only to physics is very much behind the times. Nowadays, mathematics has significant practical applications in chemistry, biology, economics, and psychology; in all branches of engineering; in geology; in the management sciences; and even in such "far-away" fields as philology and politics. Furthermore, as we have seen, the greatest variety of situations in everyday life can also be the source of interesting mathematical problems. When we therefore consider applications of mathematics in the classroom, we must be sure to have a sufficiently broad view of the fields of human endeavor to which mathematics applies.

The above-mentioned breadth of fields of application necessitates a correspondingly broad understanding of the various branches of mathematics—any of which might prove useful in a consideration of such applications of mathematics in the classroom. Current experience is that all the mathematics ever considered for the elementary and secondary school, all the mathematics taught at the under-graduate level, and much graduate school material are all likely to come up in the course of making practical applications. A typical issue of the *SIAM Journal* (see footnote 3), for example, is likely to contain papers not only on classical applied mathematics and com-puting, but also on functional analysis, probability theory, game theory, graph theory, linear and nonlinear programing, number theory, matrix theory, Boolean algebra and logic, and statistics. Many of these papers are written by industrial mathematicians whose long-range success depends on actual as well as possible applicability of their product.

As we have said above, the list of applicable mathematics includes everything that has recently been considered as additional ingredients of the elementary and secondary school curriculum. Thus, sets and functions, logic, absolute values, inequalities, linear algebra, matrices, probability, statistics, limits, calculus, computing, and modern alge-bra are all eminently important for applications, as well as interesting mathematics in their own right. This points to an important fact, namely, that it is not really possible to choose among alternative new curricula purely on the basis of the potential usefulness of any addi-tional subject matter they might contain. If a particular series of text-books appeals to a selection committee on the basis of the mathe-matics involved, its correctness, and its probable ease of teaching, the Committee should not be swayed from a decision in its favor on the alleged ground that the mathematics itself might not be useful.

We do not mean to imply, of course, that all areas of mathematics are equally important to the principal areas of applications. If we consider the major destinations of students taking mathematics in college—that is, the physical sciences, the biological sciences, the social sciences, engineering, and the teaching and practice of mathematics and computing—then the greatest needs in mathematical subject mat-ter (other than classical analysis) are linear algebra, probability and statistics, and the computer sciences. The current direction of effort in curriculum reform at the secondary level is toward moving more and more of just these areas into high school mathematics. From the point of view of applications, this is exactly what the "doctor or-dered."

In judging the relative claims of these various areas of mathematics to priority of time in the secondary school, there are, of course, many criteria other than a binary choice on applicability. If one argues the number and variety of courses in higher education which depend on the material in an essential way, then calculus would most likely win out. It probably has the largest number of direct descendants in the college curriculum. If one argues usefulness in the everyday lives of the maximum number of high school graduates, then the writer suspects that probability and statistics would be the most important. A large number of judgments in everyday life are likely to involve probabilistic or statistical reasoning. If the argument was in terms of the greatest impact on the human condition during the lifetime of the present school population, the outcome probably would be computer science, for the computer is likely to influence our lives more fundamentally than any other current development.

The next major point which we have learned about applications of mathematics is that applications are about real things and must be connected honestly to the real world. Anyone who thinks that mouthing words from some other discipline and then pulling a formula out of a hat will motivate students is probably misleading himself. Honest applications of mathematics begin with a situation in some other field that is not well understood and that would be worth understanding better. The hope is that a mathematical problem can ultimately be found whose solution will give insight (or even predictive power) in the original situation. Thus, the first stage in actual applications of mathematics is the recognition that something needs exploring.

The next (and frequently the most difficult) step is to formulate a precise mathematical problem that will shed some light on the situation that has been recognized. There are two kinds of difficulties here. First of all, it is necessary to formulate a mathematical problem which is complicated enough to represent the real situation honestly, yet simple enough that there is at least a slight chance of solving it. It is very difficult to obtain these two attributes simultaneously. If one wakes up one morning feeling particularly virtuous and decides that this time he is going to put everything into the problem that might be really important, he is likely to produce a system of relations three pages long which he will never look at again. One therefore may decide that perhaps he has been too virtuous and that some aspects are really not as important as others, and he may begin to

throw things away to simplify the problem. He will probably ultimately reach a problem that can be solved, but quite possibly will
have "thrown the baby away with the bath water": The solution no
longer means anything physically. The process of buffeting between
the Scylla of the real world and the Charybdis of mathematical technique is one of the real difficulties in the formulation of a precise
mathematical problem in an applied situation.

A second difficulty in formulation is often to try to figure out
exactly what one is trying to understand or to build or to optimize.
It is impossible to optimize the design of supermarket check-out
counters or of an anti-aircraft missile system for a task force without facing the question of what one is really trying to achieve. Thus,
the attempt to build a satisfactory mathematical model will force
many important questions about the original situation to come to the
surface. Part of the model-building will be to answer these questions.

After the problem has been successfully formulated, the next step,
of course, will be to solve it. In all honesty, as we have seen, the
process moves back and forth among recognition, formulation, and
solution many times while the work is going on.

Next, there very well may be a stage of computation. If specific
numbers are relevant to the problem, then computing some examples
will give additional insight into the nature of the solution that has
been discovered. Beyond this, however, preparing a problem for
computation frequently forces one to be far more careful and precise than is ever necessary in mathematics. Mathematical work is ofen
very sloppy and uses intuitive check points (that naturally occur in
every branch of the analysis) to determine if everything is proceeding reasonably. The computer does not have this intuition, and the
check points therefore have to be built into the program ahead of
time. This process of thinking through every contingency within the
program forces one to become very much more precise in his thinking, and may, in fact, turn up significant features of the original
situation.

There is finally, in real applications of mathematics, a stage of exposition—of relating the mathematical results and new understanding
to the original situation in the outside world. The job is not finished
until the significance of the results has been explored and until people
in the field of application have a chance to see and understand what
has been done.

An interesting observation about the use of mathematics in the oldest field of application—namely, physics—was made by Hans Freudenthal. He remarked that physicists tend to teach the mathematics in any particular branch of their discipline by using exactly the methods which were used when the work in that discipline was first done. If this is true, it can be rather unfortunate. For example, the use of matrices, differential forms, and operators can simplify a great deal of classical mathematical physics.

Speculation on the possible reasons for such a phenomenon is interesting. It is an unfortunate fact that in much of our physics teaching the relation between the phenomena that we are trying to understand and the corresponding approximate mathematization has been "lost in the shuffle." There is a tendency to start a derivation in physics by writing down the mathematical equation and going on from that point. The student is typically not given the opportunity to participate in making the abstraction from the physical reality to the mathematical model. Why not? It is of course possible to argue (a) that the particular mathematization has been familiar for many years, (b) that it is well known that it works very well, and (c) that it is a waste of time to rederive it. Similarly, it is sometimes argued that it is a waste of time to worry about existence and uniqueness for solutions of the resulting differential equations since they are after all physically obvious. The trouble with these arguments is that they are not good physics but just bad applied mathematics. The student has as much right to participate in deriving the mathematical model and in checking the degree of its validity as he has to repeat any experiment in order to satisfy himself of *its* validity. If the emphasis were, as it should be, on the mathematical modeling of the original physical situation, then everyone would naturally look to the best mathematics for handling the resulting problem. Thus, the use of outdated mathematical models on physical problems is perhaps another piece of evidence that mathematical physics is sometimes taught as bad applied mathematics.

A side remark: Many mathematicians have written down a coriolis term in the differential equations of hydrodynamics. Before the wonderful fluid mechanics films were made at MIT,[4] who had even

4. National Committee for Fluid Mechanics Films, Education and Development Center, Newton, Mass. See, for example, its *Newsletter*, No. 6.

seen the physical phenomenon which this term is supposed to represent?

Another important point about applications of mathematics which we have learned (in the course of our development) is that applications do not have to be deep or remote or recondite. Interesting applications of mathematics can be found in lots of everyday situations. Not every problem that we attack will turn out to be easily solvable, but the potential for interesting situations is all around us.

The Pedagogy of Applications

We shall next examine some effects of applications of mathematics on the teaching process itself. Just how is the pedagogy of applications different from that of the rest of mathematics? In order to answer this, let us restate very briefly what an application of mathematics is. Applications typically begin with an ill-defined situation outside of mathematics—in economics, physics, engineering, biology, or almost any field of human activity. The job is to understand this situation as well as possible. The procedure is to make a mathematical model which hopefully will shed some light on the situation which we are trying to understand. Thus, the heart of applied mathematics is the injunction: "Here is a situation; think about it." The heart of our usual mathematics teaching, on the other hand, is: "Here is a problem; solve it" or "Here is a theorem; prove it." We have very rarely, in mathematics, allowed the student to explore a situation for himself and find out what the right theorem to prove or the right problem to solve might be. Many mathematics educators agree that this absence of individual exploration by the student actually makes for bad mathematics teaching. We very much want our students to experience the creative acitvity of discovering mathematics for themselves. Much recent work in curriculum reform, in fact, has involved the infusing of our textbooks with the possibility of discovery, and much effort at institutions preparing teachers has gone into readying them for discovery teaching.

We are, in fact, giving a dishonest picture of mathematics if we do not allow the student to participate in finding the right problem or theorem. It has often been said that, once a mathematician knows what he is trying to prove, his job is half over. This may be an oversimplification; nevertheless, the normal state of mathematical activity is one that involves (*a*) a situation that is crying out for understanding, and (*b*) a search for the right way to look at it. Unfortunately, we often exclude this intuitive discovery aspect of mathematics from our teaching. A carefully organized course in mathematics is sometimes too much like a hiking trip in the mountains that never leaves the well-worn trails. The tour manages to visit a steady sequence of the "high spots" of the natural scenery. It carefully avoids all false starts, dead-ends, and impossible barriers, and arrives by five o'clock every afternoon at a well-stocked cabin. The order of difficulty is carefully controlled, and it is obviously a most pleasant way to proceed. However, the hiker misses the excitement of risking an enforced camping out, of helping locate a trail, and of making his way cross-country with only intuition and a compass as a guide. "Cross-country" mathematics is a necessary ingredient of a good education.

Let us summarize our conclusion on pedagogy. Applications of mathematics essentially consist of situations to be understood. They have to be taught in this spirit. This is different from much of the usual pedagogy in mathematics but only because the usual pedagogy is not sufficiently inclusive. If we allow students to participate in the mathematical discovery experience and give them this more honest picture of mathematical activity, the pedagogic difference between mathematics and its applications disappears.

An important part of recent curriculum change in mathematics has been a new emphasis on understanding *when* and *how* and *why* the mathematics works. It is interesting to note that this kind of understanding is also essential for applications. The traditional picture of the user of mathematics as a man who looks up a formula in a handbook and turns the crank is very much out of date. The trouble is that when one applies mathematics in practice, the problems which arise are not exactly the problems in the textbook. Something that is new in one respect or other will always be presenting itself. If one has understood his mathematics and the conditions for its success, then he has a chance, because he can examine what is required to make it fit the new situation. If one has not understood his mathematics, then one of two things will happen. Either he will recognize that he has not understood it (an unlikely situation)—in this case, he is just plain "stuck" and can get help—or he will not know that he has not understood the mathematics and will plunge ahead with a method that has nothing to do with the problem at hand. The outcome is guaranteed nonsense. While many people complain about fashions in the teaching of mathematics, it is never fashionable to get the wrong answer. Understanding when and how and why the mathematics works is the best guarantee against mistakes and is therefore essential to applications of mathematics as well as to mathematics itself.

One of the interesting aspects of applications of mathematics, which we have not yet touched upon and which also bears on teaching is that of its evaluation. How does one judge whether a good job has been done? The ultimate proof must always be in terms of the real world. One has done a good job if his understanding of the original "physical" situation has been improved and if he is better able to predict than before. If the model does a poor job of mirroring reality, then, no matter how "pretty" the mathematics, is is not particularly successful as applied mathematics. Consider, for example, the beginnings of the mathematical theory of epidemics. It is clear that at any given time there are three kinds of people: (*a*) those who have not had the disease and are susceptible, (*b*) those who are currently infected and can infect others, and (*c*) those who are cured and can neither receive nor transmit the disease. Furthermore, there are various reasonable ways to describe the time element in relation to each of the three populations. Some model by which the sick infect others, and some model for the duration of an infection are needed. The obvious assumptions lead to simple systems of difference or differential equations whose solutions indeed yield a certain amount of insight. Unfortunately, they do not seem to do very well in predicting the spread of the epidemic in detail. Apparently much more complicated models will be needed to make this application of mathematics really successful.

It might be worthwhile to summarize some of the attributes of a successful mathematical model. A model is always an approximation of reality and should therefore be stable with respect to small changes in the assumptions on which it is based. If a small perturbation causes a major change in the mathematical outcome, then the conclusions must be viewed with considerable suspicion. After all, we can not be completely sure of precision in our assumptions. Secondly, when we have made a mathematical model, we are obliged to consider all of its consequences—those that we like because they agree with our physical intuition about the problem, as well as those whose implications bother us considerably. The latter are very likely to lead to improvements in the mathematical model. It is also true that most mathematizations of outside situations will contain features that are not relevant to the real problem. In a successful model, these must not get in the way. As a very simple example, we regularly apply the real numbers to problems involving measurement or money. Two of the basic properties of the real numbers are that the numbers may be arbitrarily large and also that they may be arbitrarily close together. Money is neither infinite nor infinitely divisible. Nevertheless, in our use of the number system to handle financial problems, we successfully avoid any unreal implications of infinity and infinite divisibility.

An example of the opposite kind, although more advanced, deals with communication signals. There are two basic engineering facts about such functions of time: (*a*) they are limited in *extent*—that is, they vanish outside of some finite time interval—and (*b*) they are limited in *frequency*—that is, their *Fourier Transforms* vanish outside of some finite frequency interval. These two assumptions are known from analytic function theory to be contradictory. It is true that much of signal theory is built on one or another of the two assumptions, but we must be extremely careful to avoid the use of both in one argument.

In the light of the view that we have developed for applications of mathematics and the associated pedagogy, let us now examine what is being done and what has to be done to find a proper expression for applications in mathematics education. On the elementary level, such efforts as the Cambridge Conference on the Correlation of Science and Mathematics in the Schools[5] have pointed out many opportunities for the mutual strengthening of the two fields. Much experimental work remains to be done, however, and we are far from wide availability and acceptance of suitable materials.

The need for the interaction of mathematics and its fields of application continues on the secondary school level. The problem is perhaps easier at this level because the students by this time are likely to know more about both science and everyday life. It may also be

5. *Goals for the Correlation of Elementary Science and Mathematics* (Report of the Cambridge Conference on Teacher Training [Published for Educational Services, Inc. by Houghton Mifflin Co., 1969]).

harder because contradictory natural sequences of events in science and mathematics may get in the way. There is a great need for good applied examples at the secondary level, and there is much effort at collecting them. Current experimental curriculum materials such as the second round of SMSG[6] are likely to contain a great many applications, and very interesting experimental materials which motivate all of secondary mathematics from applications have been developed by Arthur Engel in Stuttgart.[8] Current planning of secondary materials almost invariably includes the early introduction of probability, statistics, linear algebra, computing, and even intuitive calculus. This is, of course, excellent for applications. In addition, the need to connect mathematics education more strongly with the real world comes to the forefront most forcefully when we work seriously on the education of *all* children. Serious proposals have been made to offer parallel mathematics courses—one of which would be more intellectually and structually motivated, and the other of which would motivate and apply every single topic in the real world. Methods of school organization are being sought which would facilitate free transfer between such alternatives.

A principal problem on the college level is that of teacher training. We cannot expect teachers to use, and to be comfortable with, the discovery method unless it has been experienced by them at some time in their own education. The confidence necessary for open-ended teaching may not come naturally. Furthermore, we cannot expect teachers to understand applications and bring their spirit into their own teaching if they have never seen any real, honest applications of mathematics. A recent exploratory step in this direction has been the development of an experimental course on applications of mathematics for prospective secondary teachers. These materials, shortly to be available on an experimental basis from the Committee on the Undergraduate Program in Mathematics of the Mathematical Association of America, attempt to show applications of college mathematics to many different fields of human endeavor in precisely the spirit which we have been discussing. A volume with similar motives, although not primarily intended for teachers, is *Applications*

6. School Mathematics Study Group, *Newsletter,* No. 29, Stanford University, 1969.

7. Arthur Engel, "Systematic Use of Applications in Mathematics Training," *Educational Studies in Mathematics* (Dordrecht), I (May, 1968), 202–21.

of Undergraduate Mathematics in Engineering by Noble.[8] This contains about fifty examples, most of them very recent work, of the
use of calculus and differential equations, probability and statistics,
and linear algebra in a great variety of fields of engineering. Excellent materials on applications of mathematics at the early-college or
late-secondary level may also be found in the series "The Man Made
World," prepared by the Engineering Concepts Curriculum Project.[9]
The work on computing and on stability and feedback in dynamical
systems is particularly interesting. Finally, the Committee on the
Undergraduate Program in Mathematics has strongly urged the development of deeper courses of applied mathematics at the upper-
undergraduate level. Two detailed studies—one for a course of models
in the area of the physical sciences and the other in the social sciences
—have been prepared. Much current effort is directed towards making curriculum materials of this nature available.

It has been assumed throughout this discussion that we had some
particular purpose in mind in bringing honest applications of mathematics into the schools. Why bother? Perhaps the most serious answer is that we believe that this aspect of mathematics is essential for
an honest and full picture of the subject. We have simply not done
our job if we present mathematics purely as an intellectual structure,
or, even worse, as a series of isolated and meaningless tricks to be
memorized. It is an important part of both the value and the heritage
of mathematics to see and to practice its usefulness. Furthermore,
applications of mathematics are important in the motivation of students. It is sometimes difficult to get a mathematician to admit that
some of the students in his class might be there, not for the pure love
of the subject, but in the hope of applying it to something. Nevertheless, this may, in fact, be true of many students. They are not content
to be told to be patient and wait to see, someday, the usefulness of
what they are learning, and there is no reason why they should be. It
is necessary, and it is possible, to organize our presentations of mathematics in such a way that motivations and applications from other
disciplines occur frequently.

There are perhaps other, more mundane or possibly more cynical,

8. Ben Noble, *Applications of Undergraduate Mathematics* (New York: Mac-
millan Co., 1967).

9. Engineering Concepts Curriculum Project, *Man-Made World* (3 parts;
Manchester, Mo.: Webster Division, McGraw Hill Book Co., 1968).

purposes for applications: Maybe they will help to keep students awake, or maybe they will make students forget that they are studying mathematics and fool them into enjoying it. We must, however, be careful that, in the process of fooling the students into liking the work, we do not make fools of ourselves. Fraudulent and obviously stupid examples of alleged applications of mathematics are bound to do more harm than good.

We should perhaps bring to the surface one more fundamental assumption of this brief study of applications of mathematics and their relations to mathematics teaching. We have assumed throughout that it is possible and proper to attack the problem rationally, that is, that a logical and hopefully well-reasoned discussion will contribute to the solution of the problem. It is currently fashionable at times to question the relevance of reason to matters of education. We also are forced to question the relevance of reason, but on grounds totally different from those associated with current educational disturbances. No one seriously questions the importance of applications of mathematics, and yet we have had (and continue to have) enormous difficulties in obtaining a proper place for them in the curriculum. Why? There exists at least a possibility that a fair number of people go into mathematics precisely because they wish to hide from the real world. They conceive of mathematics as a beautiful, orderly structure that has nothing to do with life; amazingly enough, it is possible to make a living at it. If this is the case with sufficient numbers and the real source of difficulty in introducing applications into mathematics teaching, then the writer is afraid there is no hope.

CHAPTER IX

Evaluation and the Classroom Teacher

J. F. WEAVER

Several years ago Maurice L. Hartung presented an approach to the evaluation process in a way that was particularly appropriate for teachers of mathematics (B5: 21–42).[1] At the outset of his discussion Hartung advanced a definition of evaluation that was based upon two other defined terms which, in turn, were based upon two *undefined* terms. It may be both informative and helpful for us to identify briefly the key characterizations in Hartung's approach to the evaluation process.

The undefined terms of the theory are *behavior* and *situation*. The three key defined terms are the following:

(1) *experience* is behavior in specified situations;

(2) *objectives* are desired experiences; and

(3) *evaluation* is the process of finding the extent to which actual experiences conform to objectives (B5: 21–22).

Professor Hartung concludes his discussion of the nature of the evaluation process by asserting that ". . . the purpose of education is to change students from a given state of experience to a desired state by means of a variety of appropriate learning experiences, some of which may be used as a basis for evaluation of achievement. . . . Evaluation is the means we use to discover where we stand on the path between present experience and the objective" (B5: 23).

Our approach to evaluation in this chapter is a less structured one; however, our interpretation of terminology will be in keeping with the undefined terms and definitions just identified. We also shall find it convenient to use the term *outcomes* to refer to actual (and hopefully, observable) experiences. Thus, evaluation may be

1. This notation is intended to signify pages 21–42 of reference no. 5 in section B of the bibliography at the end of this chapter. A similar interpretation should be made of other instances of this notation as used throughout the chapter.

viewed as the process of determining the extent to which outcomes agree with objectives.

Let us recognize from the outset, and keep in mind throughout the chapter, two important things about this process:

1. *Value judgments* are a necessary part of evaluation. They are crucial in determining objectives, in selecting situations in which behavior is to be observed, in deciding when to make particular observations of behavior, and in interpreting outcomes.

2. From the standpoint of the classroom teacher in particular, frequent *informal* observations of student behavior have a vital role to play in the evaluation process. They neither replace nor are replaced by the more formal observations of student behavior that are made on the basis of tests and the like.

Some Delimitations

Somewhat arbitrarily, this chapter will emphasize evaluation involving *cognitive* behaviors—those associated with "thinking." Less explicit attention is given to *affective* behaviors—those associated with "feeling"—despite the fact that they are believed to be important in mathematics instruction. *Psychomotor* behaviors—those associated with "physical action"—are encountered relatively infrequently in any significant way in mathematics instruction[2] and are given no particular emphasis or attention in relation to evaluation in this chapter.

More generally, the material on evaluation in mathematics education presented here is selective rather than exhaustive or definitive. Readers wishing to extend their study beyond the delimitations imposed on this chapter will find numerous helpful references cited in the accompanying bibliography.[3] In this connection it should be

2. Such behaviors rarely play a *crucial* role in mathematical learning. However, a recent approach to geometry through constructions that was intended for children in the primary grades (I and II) did not meet with resounding acceptance and success due, in no small part, to the inability of many six- and seven-year-olds to manipulate compasses properly for the drawing of arcs and circles.

3. Some degree of historical perspective for present-day evaluation in mathematics education can be sensed from references B1-4, 6-8, and C1-6. Sources published within the past five or six years include D-13, E1-31, F1 and appropriate sections of G1. A contemporary approach also is reflected in B5 (1961). General references on measurement and evaluation, without any particular regard for mathematics education, include A1-6.

noted that, as with many other things pertaining to school mathematics, the relevant literature which deals explicitly with the elementary school level is much more extensive than that which deals specifically with the secondary school level. Comparatively little of this literature on evaluation in mathematics education gives broad coverage to all levels, K-XII.

Some Significant Characteristics of Contemporary Evaluation in School Mathematics

What are some of the significant characteristics of contemporary evaluation in school mathematics? In this chapter we consider this question particularly as it relates to the classroom teacher and to his interest in evaluation as associated with ongoing instruction.

INSTRUCTION AND EVALUATION ARE PLANNED WITH APPROPRIATE ATTENTION TO RECURRING, UNIFYING MATHEMATICAL IDEAS

One of the hallmarks of contemporary mathematics is its organization around relatively few central ideas which serve to unify and give coherence to the discipline at all levels. Such ideas are emphasized in current programs of school mathematics and they need to be included in the framework of evaluation.

What are these key ideas? One set of unifying ideas for grades K-XII was suggested in the Twenty-fourth Yearbook of the National Council of Teachers of Mathematics.[4] A similar set of "strands" for grades K-VIII was suggested in the most recent Report of the California Statewide Mathematics Advisory Committee.[5] The particular ideas included within each of these two sets have been identified in Chart 1.

These two sets of key ideas are not identical. The differences, however, are not of as great consequence as might appear to be the case. For instance, "Geometry" is identified as a strand in the California report but not in the NCTM Yearbook. However, even a cursory reading of the latter reference makes it clear that geometric

4. Phillip S. Jones (ed.), *The Growth of Mathematical Ideas, Grades K-12* (the Council, 1959).

5. Statewide Mathematics Advisory Committee, *Mathematics Program, K-8: 1967 Strands Report* (Sacramento: California State Department of Education, 1967, 1968).

content has been subsumed under other unifying ideas. It should not be disturbing, either for instruction or for evaluation, that the content of mathematics can be organized around sets of key ideas that differ from each other to some degree. Evaluation is relative to a particular program of instruction, and the unifying ideas which are reflected in a given instructional program are the ones to be considered in connection with evaluation associated with that program.

CHART 1

COMPARISON OF TWO SETS OF UNIFYING IDEAS FOR SCHOOL MATHEMATICS

NATIONAL COUNCIL OF TEACHERS OF MATHEMATICS (TWENTY-FOURTH YEARBOOK, 1959) Grades K-XII	CALIFORNIA STATE-WIDE MATHEMATICS ADVISORY COMMITTEE REPORT (1967–68) Grades K-VIII
1. Number and Operation	1. Numbers and Operations
2. Relations and Functions	2. Geometry
3. Proof	3. Measurement
4. Measurement and Approximation	4. Applications of Mathematics
5. Probability	5. Statistics and Probability
6. Statistics	6. Sets
7. Language and Symbolism	7. Functions and Graphs
* Mathematical Modes of Thought	8. Logical Thinking
	9. Problem Solving

* "These modes are not quite mathematical concepts themselves, but are rather understandings and procedures which are implicit in the study of all mathematical topics." (Preface, p. v)

INSTRUCTION AND EVALUATION ARE PLANNED WITH APPROPRIATE
ATTENTION TO DIFFERENTIAL LEVELS OF ANY PARTICULAR
MATHEMATICAL IDEA

This characteristic is closely allied to the preceding one. Points of view such as the following, which give a rationale for the spiral development of programs of mathematics instruction, have clear implications for evaluation:

Understanding and meaningfulness are rarely if ever "all or none" insights in either the sense of being achieved instantaneously or in the sense of embracing the whole of a concept and its implications at any one time.[6]

6. Jones, *op. cit.*, p. 1.

Teachers must plan so that pupils continually have recurring but varied contacts with the fundamental ideas and processes of mathematics.[7]

Teachers in all grades should view their tasks in the light of the idea that the understanding of mathematics is a continuum, and understandings grow within children throughout their school career.[8]

Although these points of view were phrased in relation to an understanding of mathematical ideas, they could be restated to apply equally well to other aspects of mathematical ability (e.g., the development of skills).

Let us use place-value numeration systems to illustrate specifically some differential levels of a particular mathematical idea. We might test a student's ability to interpret a decimal numeral such as 5273.94 at quite different symbolic levels, such as:

(1) $5273.94 = 5000 + 200 + 70 + 3 + .9 + .04$

(2) $5273.94 = (5 \times 1000) + (2 \times 100) + (7 \times 10)$
$$+ (3 \times 1) + (9 \times .1) + (4 \times .01)$$

(3) $5273.94 = (5 \times 10^3) + (2 \times 10^2) + (7 \times 10^1)$
$$+ (3 \times 10^0) + (9 \times 10^{-1}) + (4 \times 10^{-2})$$

These certainly do not exhaust the interpretation possibilities, which include this generalized polynomial expression for any decimal numeral written in a place-value system:

$$\ldots + (a_3 \times 10^3) + (a_2 \times 10^2) + (a_1 \times 10^1) + (a_0 \times 10^0)$$
$$+ (a_{-1} \times 10^{-1}) + (a_{-2} \times 10^{-2}) + (a_{-3} \times 10^{-3}) + \ldots$$

In each instance we are concerned with essentially the *same* idea, but the illustrations involve different levels of mathematical sophistication.

Within the domain of place-value numeration systems, we might extend the interpretations to include non-decimal bases (e.g., 304.2_{six}) and the following more generalized polynomial expression:

$$\ldots + a_3b^3 + a_2b^2 + a_1b^1 + a_0b^0 + a_{-1}b^{-1} + a_{-2}b^{-2} + a_{-3}b^{-3} + \ldots$$

Effective instructional planning takes into consideration various differential levels of mathematical ideas and content. So does effective planning for evaluation.

7. *Ibid.*, p. 2.   8. *Ibid.*, p. 3.

Thus far we have identified two significant characteristics of contemporary mathematics programs that have implications for the evaluation of instruction. We may synthesize these characteristics into a view of the domain of school mathematics, as suggested by Figure 1. This view in turn provides a framework for extending our conceptualization of contemporary evaluation.

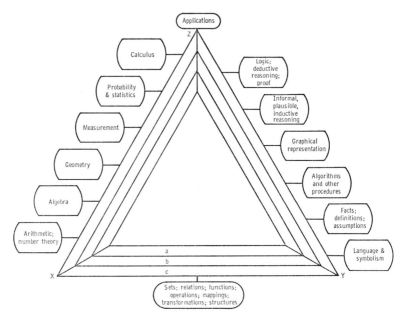

FIG. 1.—A view of the domain of school mathematics

In Figure 1, the domain of school mathematics is represented by the region bounded by $\triangle XYZ$. Associated with $\overline{XY}$ of $\triangle XYZ$ are certain primitive concepts and other key ideas which recur throughout the study of school mathematics: e.g., sets; relations; functions; operations; mappings; transformations; structures; and so on.[9]

Associated with $\overline{ZY}$ of $\triangle XYZ$ are aspects of mathematics that embrace conventions or agreements, techniques, and processes. That which we often refer to as *problem-solving* necessitates the use of some or all of these things.

9. There is some redundancy in these terms, since some may be subsumed under others. But this redundancy may be more helpful than not in making explicit some of the concepts that are to be included in this category.

Associated with $\overline{XZ}$ of $\triangle XYZ$ are familiar categories that at times are helpful in classifying and organizing mathematical content. These are not to be considered as mutually exclusive, nor are they to be considered as the only categories that might be used to advantage in classifying mathematical content.

The subregions of $\triangle XYZ$ which are identified as *a*, *b*, *c* in Figure 1 are intended to suggest that there are different levels—different degrees of depth—at which mathematical content may be considered.

Finally, Figure 1 makes explicit that school programs also are concerned with *applications* of mathematics to other subject matter fields (e.g., science) and within a variety of environmental contexts. The use of mathematics outside the discipline itself must be illustrated as a vital part of a school mathematics program.

The boundary conditions which determine the nature, scope, and organization of an instructional program in mathematics for a particular educational unit (district, school, grade, class, or whatever) are based on decisions made regarding the factors suggested by Figure 1: (*a*) the things associated with $\overline{XY}$, $\overline{YZ}$, and $\overline{XZ}$ of $\triangle XYZ$; (*b*) the differential levels at which mathematical content is to be considered (as suggested by subregions *a*, *b*, *c*,); and (*c*) the attention given to applications of mathematics. These boundary conditions become, in turn, the boundary conditions within which the evaluation of instruction is planned.

Within a given period of time—a day, a week, a year—and with a given group of students, a teacher's instruction embraces a particular subset of the domain of school mathematics. His plans for evaluation must be relevant to each such subdomain.

INSTRUCTION AND EVALUATION ARE PLANNED WITH APPROPRIATE
ATTENTION TO COGNITIVE HIERARCHIES OR LEVELS WITHIN THE
DOMAIN OF SCHOOL MATHEMATICS

For educational objectives that are of a cognitive nature, probably the most familiar and most widely used classification scheme is the so-called Bloom taxonomy (H1). The major categories of this taxonomy usually are arranged in the following hierarchy (from low level to high level): (1) knowledge, (2) comprehension, (3) application, (4) analysis, (5) synthesis, and (6) evaluation.

Adaptations of the Bloom taxonomy to the domain of school

mathematics have been developed by a number of persons. For instance, Avital and Shettleworth (E2) identified three levels of mathematical thinking which correspond, collectively, to five of the six categories of the Bloom taxonomy. Illustrative objectives and test items are given for each of their three levels.

Romberg and Wilson (E27) identified seven levels of cognitive behavior in mathematics that were used by the Research and Test

CHART 2

MAJOR CATEGORIES OF THREE TAXONOMIES OF THE COGNITIVE DOMAIN
FOR SCHOOL MATHEMATICS COMPARED WITH MAJOR
CATEGORIES OF THE BLOOM TAXONOMY

Avital-Shettleworth Taxonomy	Bloom Taxonomy	NLSMA Taxonomy (Romberg-Wilson)	ETS Taxonomy (Epstein)
1. Recognition, recall	1.00-Knowledge	1. Knowing 2. Manipulating	1. Recall factual knowledge 2. Perform mathematical manipulations
2. Algorithmic thinking, generalization	2.00-Comprehension	3. Translating	3. Solve routine problems 4. Demonstrate comprehension of mathematical ideas and concepts
3. Open search	3.00-Application	4. Applying	5. Solve nonroutine problems requiring insight or ingenuity
	4.00-Analysis	5. Analyzing	
	5.00-Synthesis	6. Synthesizing	6. Apply "higher" mental processes to mathematics
	6.00-Evaluation	7. Evaluating	

Development Section of the School Mathematics Study Group (SMSG) in connection with the National Longitudinal Study of Mathematical Abilities (NLSMA). Epstein, e.g., identified six categories of an ability-process dimension that are used in the mathematics department of the Test Development Division at Educational Testing Service (ETS).

An attempt has been made in Chart 2 to compare the major categories of the Avital-Shettleworth, the NLSMA, and the ETS taxonomies with the major categories of the Bloom taxonomy.[10]

10. The relation between the Bloom and Avital-Shettleworth taxonomies is made explicit in reference E2. This author, however, takes full responsibility for

Avital and Shettleworth make this significant point:

In the [Bloom] *Taxonomy* there is a sixth category, Evaluation, which is assumed to be the most complex level of performance, but in mathematical performance we cannot distinguish evaluation as psychologically distinct. Such tasks as judging the correctness of a proof by an internal analysis of the steps, which might by their wording be placed in the category of Evaluation, seem to be an integral part of the process of proof itself and, therefore, belong in the category of Analysis or Synthesis[11] (E2: 7).

Let us use a geometric context to illustrate this idea of different cognitive levels. It is one thing for a student simply to recall as a geometric fact that "an angle inscribed in a semicircle is a right

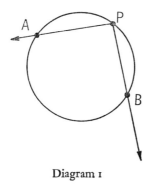

Diagram 1

angle." It is another matter for a student to be able to recognize that for the circle represented in Diagram 1, in which A and B are endpoints of a diameter and P is a point of the circle distinct from A and B, it is true that $\angle APB$ is a right angle. And it is still another matter for a student to be able to prove this as a theorem, or to be able to use (apply) this geometric "fact" in connection with particular geometric constructions.

Let us cite another illustration—but from a different mathematical context. It is one thing for a pupil to be able to compute quickly

the relations suggested between the Bloom and NLSMA taxonomies and between the Bloom and ETS taxonomies. Hopefully, this author's interpretations do no injustice to the taxonomies in question.

11. Lest the naive reader be misled unwittingly, we should call attention to the fact that "Evaluation" as a level of a cognitive taxonomy has a different connotation than does "evaluation" as used in the theme of this yearbook chapter, which is characterized by Hartung's definition given at the outset of the chapter.

and accurately the sum of 27 and 68, for example. It is another thing for him to relate his efficient algorithm to the use of expanded notation, such as "$(20 + 7) + (60 + 8)$." And it is yet another matter for him to sense the association between "$27 + 68$" and "$(2x + 7y) + (6x + 8y)$" when $x = 10$ and $y = 1$.

We will find it helpful to include explicitly in connection with Figure 1 the added dimension of *cognitive level or depth*. This is the intent of Figure 2 which, as an extension of Figure 1, suggests a more

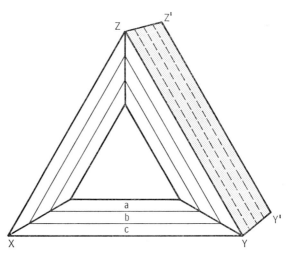

Fig. 2.–An added dimension of *cognitive level or depth* to the domain of school mathematics (Figure 1).

complete view of the domain of school mathematics. This added dimension of cognitive level or depth influences both instruction and evaluation.

It is of interest to illustrate at this point several instances of test models that reflect a multidimensional view of the domain of school mathematics. We shall identify two such models in particular: (*a*) a model suggested by Epstein (E9) for the development of a hypothetical test, and (*b*) a model used in connection with one phase of the National Longitudinal Study of Mathematical Abilities [NLSMA] (E31g).

Chart 3 is adapted from Epstein's Table 1 (E9: 317), and shows how the forty items to be developed for a hypothetical end-of-year test in "fifth-grade arithmetic" might be distributed among the cells of a matrix based on five content categories and three ability-process levels. The components of each of the two dimensions of the matrix must be characterized in a definitive way, of course.

A two-dimensional matrix that has been used in a much broader context is illustrated by Figure 3. This particular matrix served as the basis for classifying a large number of mathematics achievement "scales" (sets of related test items) over a wide range of grades (IV through XII) in one phase of the NLSMA data analysis (E31g). It

CHART 3

A TWO-DIMENSIONAL DISTRIBUTION OF ITEMS IN A HYPOTHETICAL
END-OF-YEAR MATHEMATICS TEST FOR GRADE V
[ADAPTED FROM EPSTEIN (E9: 317)]

CONTENT DIMENSION		ABILITY-PROCESS DIMENSION			Total
		Computation	Routine Problems	Non-routine Problems	
Whole Numbers	Multiplication	2*	3	1	6
	Division	4	4	1	9
Fractions		6	3	2	11
Decimals		4	3	1	8
Measurement		0	4	2	6
Total		16	17	7	40

* The numeral in each cell of the matrix signifies the number of a particular classification to be included in the hypothetical test.

LEVELS OF COGNITIVE BEHAVIOR	CATEGORIES OF MATHEMATICAL CONTENT		
	Number Systems	Geometry	Algebra
Computation	A_1	A_2	A_3
Comprehension	B_1	B_2	B_3
Application	C_1	C_2	C_3
Analysis	D_1	D_2	D_3

FIG. 3.—NLSMA classification model for studying achievement in school mathematics. (Subscripted letters have been used here to facilitate identification of the matrix cells.)

is closely associated with the test development work described by Romberg and Wilson (E27) and by Becker (E3).

In the model illustrated by Figure 3, the components of each dimension are characterized as follows:

1. Categories of Mathematical Content
   Number Systems—Items concerned with the nature and properties of whole numbers, integers, the rational numbers, the real numbers, and the complex numbers; the techniques and properties of the arithmetic operations.
   Geometry—Items concerned with linear and angular measurement, area, and volume; points, lines, planes; polygons and circles; solids; congruence and similarity; construction; graphs and coordinate geometry; formal proofs; and spatial visualization.
   Algebra—Items concerned with open sentences; algebraic expressions; factoring; solution of equations and inequalities; systems of equations; algebraic and transcendental functions; graphing of functions and solution sets; theory of equations; and trigonometry.

2. Levels of Cognitive Behavior
   Computation—Items designed to require straightforward manipulation of problem elements according to rules the students presumably have learned. Emphasis is upon performing operations and not upon deciding which operations are appropriate.
   Comprehension—Items designed to require either recall of concepts and generalizations, or transformation of problem elements from one mode to another. Emphasis is upon demonstrating understanding of concepts and their relationships and not upon using concepts to produce a solution.
   Application—Items designed to require (1) recall of relevant knowledge, (2) selection of appropriate operations, and (3) performance of the operations. Items are of a routine nature. They require the student to use concepts in a specific context and in a way he has presumably practiced.
   Analysis—Items designed to require a non-routine application of concepts.[12]

Other instances in which levels of cognitive behavior are combined with categories of mathematical content to develop a classification scheme include the so-called National Assessment Project (E22) and the International Study of Achievement in Mathematics (E19, 20).

As we shall see, the usefulness of such models is not restricted to the development of tests and test items.

---

12. These characterizations are given in E31g and also will appear in a number of subsequent *NLSMA Reports*.

OBJECTIVES FOR SCHOOL MATHEMATICS ARE FORMULATED AND EXPRESSED
IN SUFFICIENTLY SPECIFIC TERMS SO THAT A TEACHER MAY INFER AP-
PROPRIATE SITUATIONS AND STUDENT BEHAVIORS, BOTH FOR INSTRUC-
TION AND FOR EVALUATION

We have characterized evaluation as the process of determining
the extent to which outcomes agree with objectives—i.e., the extent
to which actual behaviors in specified situations agree with desired
behaviors in the same or comparable specified situations. If objectives are to serve their intended purposes, they must be phrased in
ways that suggest to a teacher (*a*) appropriate instructional activities that may effect desired student behaviors in particular situations, and (*b*) appropriate activities that may be used to observe
actual student behaviors in particular situations.

All too often in the past, objectives have been stated so nebulous-
ly as to be virtually meaningless for instruction and, also, for evaluation. Consider, for instance, "objectives" such as these:

1. To use exponents correctly
2. To understand subtraction
3. To know the distributive property
4. To be familiar with integration techniques

Each of the preceding "objectives" is stated in a manner that
leaves much to the imagination, to say the least. All are lacking in
more than one respect, as we shall illustrate. And in (1), "correctly"
seems to be somewhat redundant. Is it at all likely that "To use
exponents *incorrectly*" would be an "objective" of school mathematics? Putting facetiousness aside, let us look more closely at (3)
as an example of the shortcomings inherent in such a vaguely stated
"objective."

There is not just one distributive property; instead, there are
several distributive properties.[13] Which one(s) is(are) of concern
in connection with this "objective"?

Furthermore, just what does it mean to *know* a distributive
property? What distinguishes knowing a distributive property from
not knowing it? Does a student know a particular distributive prop-

13. For instance: For the operations of union and intersection applied to sets,
it is true that union is distributive over intersection; and it also is true that intersection is distributive over union. For the operations of multiplication and addi-

erty when he can symbolize it? When he can verbalize it? When he can cite specific instances of it?

"To know the distributive property" is, in effect, no objective at all. It is vague to the point of being meaningless—mathematically, and also with respect to cognitive behavior.

Contrast the four preceding "objectives" with these:

1. To estimate the area of an irregular plane region by use of a grid where an approximation to the area is the average of the inner and outer areas

2. To interpret space as the set of all points

3. To determine the factors of a counting number (a whole number other than zero)

4. To use the vertical algorithm in the addition of three addends with one-place numerals

5. To recognize the multiplicative inverse (reciprocal) for every positive rational number except zero and use it in the division of rational numbers[14]

Each of the preceding items illustrates the essential features of an objective pertaining to school mathematics in that it indicates clearly some desired particular behavior (in this case, a cognitive behavior) in some particular mathematical context.

In keeping with these essential features and with representations emphasized earlier in this chapter (particularly in connection with Figures 1 and 2), we may use Figure 4 as a model for formulating any set of instructional objectives within the domain of school

---

tion applied to real numbers, it is true that multiplication is distributive over addition. But it is not true that addition is distributive over multiplication. Furthermore, for every a, b, and c which are non-zero real numbers,

$$(a - b) \div c = (a \div c) - (b \div c)$$

but

$$c \div (a - b) \neq (c \div a) - (c \div b).$$

That is to say, within the set of non-zero real numbers, division is distributive over subtraction in the first of the two forms symbolized above but not in the second form.

14. These five objectives have been selected from among the many which are included in I₂.

mathematics. Such objectives should imply or suggest two things
to a teacher: (*a*) particular appropriate instructional activities that
may lead to attainment of the objectives, and (*b*) particular activities
that are appropriate for observing the outcomes of instruction. Evaluation, then, becomes the process of determining the extent to which
observed outcomes of instruction agree with a particular set of instructional objectives.

Let us see how a classroom teacher may use this model.

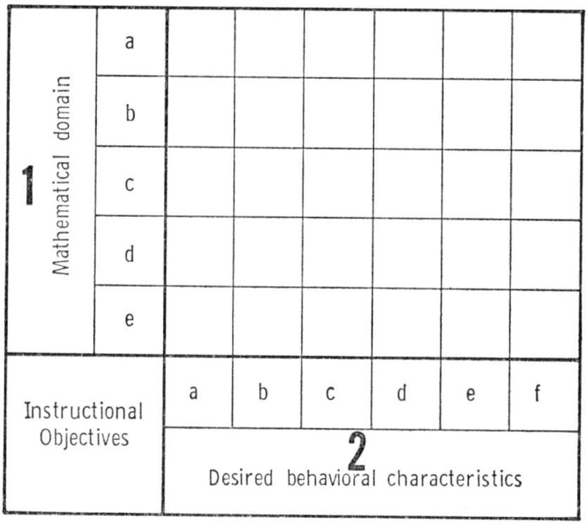

Fig. 4.—A model for formulating a set of instructional objectives within the
domain of school mathematics.

The model of Figure 4 is intended to suggest that the objectives
for a particular instructional unit are formulated from an interaction of (1) specifically identified aspects of the domain of school
mathematics, and (2) specifically identified behavioral characteristics desired of learners. The components of each of these two dimensions may be delimited either narrowly or broadly, depending
upon the scope, nature, and intent of that particular instructional
unit. The matrix for a one-week, third-grade unit dealing with an
informal exploration of primes and composites in relation to rectangular arrays would be quite different in its delimitations from
the matrix for a one-year, tenth-grade unit dealing with geometry
and topology of the complex plane and with linear algebra (as sug-

gested in the Report of the Cambridge Conference on School Mathematics).[15]

Let us use the following situation to illustrate how the model of Figure 4 might function in the formulation of instructional objectives. Consider a secondary school unit in which some consideration is given to integers and fractional numbers (non-negative rational numbers) when each kind of number is interpreted in terms of ordered pairs of counting numbers or whole numbers. Chart 4 indi-

CHART 4

NOTATION AND DEFINITIONS FOR ILLUSTRATIVE
UNIT IN SCHOOL MATHEMATICS

	Integers	Fractional Numbers*
Notation†	(a,b) where $a \in C, b \in C$	(a,b) where $a \in W, b \in C$
Equality (=)	$(a,b)=(c,d)$ iff $a+d=b+c$	$(a,b)=(c,d)$ iff $ad=bc$
Order $\quad$ (>) $\quad$ or $\quad$ (<)	$(a,b)>(c,d)$ iff $a+d>b+c$ $(a,b)<(c,d)$ iff $a+d<b+c$	$(a,b)>(c,d)$ iff $ad>bc$ $(a,b)<(c,d)$ iff $ad<bc$
Sum (+)	$(a,b)+(c,d)=(a+c,b+d)$	$(a,b)+(c,d)=(ad+bc,bd)$
Product (×)	$(a,b)\times(c,d)=(ac+bd, ad+bc)$	$(a,b)\times(c,d)=(ac,bd)$

* Non-negative rational numbers.
† $C = \{1, 2, 3, 4, 5, 6, \ldots\}$ and $W = \{0, 1, 2, 3, 4, 5, \ldots\}$

cates the nature of certain aspects of this content. (In relation to Figure 1 of this chapter, the content is at the level of one of the inner regions of $\triangle XYZ$ and represents a more sophisticated interpretation of number than students experienced earlier in their program of school mathematics.)

Chart 5 illustrates a matrix that might be used to formulate a set of instructional objectives for such a unit. The matrix reflects decisions that were made concerning (1) aspects of the mathematical domain to be considered in the unit, (2) student behaviors to be considered in connection with the unit, and (3) specific associations desired between (1) and (2), as indicated by check marks ($\sqrt{}$).

15. *Goals for School Mathematics* (Report of the Cambridge Conference on School Mathematics [Boston: Houghton Mifflin Co. for Educational Services, Inc., 1963]), p. 44.

The check marks of the matrix imply objectives such as these: A student is able to:

1. State symbolically the definition for the equality relation within the set of integers and within the set of fractional numbers.
2. Associate particular integers and particular fractional numbers with points of a line.

CHART 5

ILLUSTRATIVE MATRIX FOR FORMULATING A SET OF OBJECTIVES
FOR AN INSTRUCTIONAL UNIT IN SCHOOL MATHEMATICS

		State definitions symbolically	Apply definitions to numerical examples	Associate numbers and points of a line	Demonstrate whether or not hypothesized properties are valid ones	Illustrate hypothesized properties with examples or counterexamples
Integers and Fractional numbers	Equality relation (=)	√	√			
	Equivalence classes		√			
	Order relations (>,<)	√	√			
	Graphical representation			√		
	Addition operation (+)	√	√		√	√
	Multiplication operation (×)	√	√		√	√

3. Apply to particular numerical examples the definition for the sum of two integers and for the sum of two fractional numbers.
4. Demonstrate whether or not a particular hypothesized property of multiplication is valid for integers and for fractional numbers.[16]
5. Use the definitions of equality to specify particular equivalence classes of integers and of fractional numbers.

16. For instance, is the student able to demonstrate for integers and for fractional numbers whether or not it is true that (n,n) is a right-hand identity for multiplication; i.e., $(a,b) \times (n,n) = (a,b)$? (It is true for fractional numbers but not for integers.)

The preceding objectives are simply illustrative. They in no way exhaust the objectives implied by the matrix of Chart 5. Regardless, they should make it clear that specifically stated objectives may serve to guide a teacher in planning his instruction and in planning his evaluation of that instruction.

Notice that the evaluation of which we speak is not a matter of assessing the "merit(s)" of the objectives. By definition, the objectives already have "merit" in the sense that they represent *desired* experiences. Rather, we are concerned with evaluation as a process of finding the extent to which outcomes (actual, observed experiences) agree with objectives (desired experiences).

THE PROCESS OF INSTRUCTIONAL EVALUATION IN SCHOOL MATHEMATICS UTILIZES A VARIETY OF APPROPRIATE INSTRUMENTS, PROCEDURES, AND TECHNIQUES FOR OBSERVING INSTRUCTIONAL OUTCOMES.

This significant characteristic of contemporary evaluation in school mathematics may be suggested by extending Figure 4 to develop a model of the form illustrated by Figure 5.

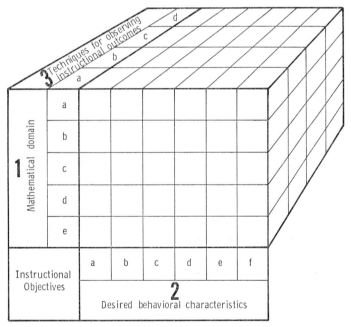

FIG. 5.—A model for planning instructional evaluation within the domain of school mathematics.

It should be quite clear that in terms of the point of view developed in this chapter, "evaluation" and "testing" are not synonymous. One step of the evaluation process involves the collection of samples of student behaviors (instructional outcomes). Tests are but one means of collecting such data, and they are not always the most appropriate means for doing so.

Grossnickle, Brueckner, and Reckzeh list the following "most valuable methods" for gathering data pertaining to outcomes of instruction:

1. Standard tests and objective test procedures
   a. Standard tests
      (1) Achievement tests
      (2) Readiness tests
      (3) Diagnostic tests, dealing with specific phases
   b. Unstandardized short-answer objective tests
      (1) Simple recall or free response
      (2) Alternate response
      (3) Multiple choice
      (4) Completion
      (5) Matching
2. Evaluation by less formal procedures
   a. Analysis of behavior in some problematic situation
   b. Use of behavior records
      (1) Controlled conditions involving check lists, rating scales, time studies, recordings
      (2) Uncontrolled conditions involving anecdotal records, diaries, reports by self and others, observation of behavior in the classroom and elsewhere, records of social agencies
   c. Inventories and questionnaires about attitudes, interests, activities, methods of study
   d. Interviews, conferences, personal reports
   e. Analysis of the qualities and merits of some product, such as a graph
   f. Sociometric procedures to study social relations [D5: 386, 388]

These authors also illustrate the appropriateness of certain techniques for selected broad instructional outcomes (not all of which are stated in behavioral terms) in Table 1 [D5: 387]:

TABLE 1—OUTCOMES OF LEARNING AND TECHNIQUES TO EVALUATE THEM

Outcomes	Evaluative Techniques

The learner is:
1. Developing a clear understanding of the structure of numbers and of the decimal system of numeration
  a. Understands the significance of place value in numbers
  b. Understands grouping and regrouping of numbers in operations
  c. Understands the number line
  d. Understands number properties
	Objective tests of understanding
	Observation of daily work
	Interview with learner
	Anecdotal records about contributions
	Demonstration by learner

2. Becoming skillful in fundamental operations and the ability to apply them
  a. Has control of knowledge of basic number facts
  b. Understands the meaning of the four number operations and their interrelationships
  c. Has skill in performing computations
  d. Can solve real and vicarious problems
	Standard tests
	Informal tests, from textbooks or teacher-prepared
	Observation of behavior
	Analysis of daily written work
	Interviews to test understanding
	Anecdotal records
	Problem-situation tests

3. Developing competence in utilizing systems and instruments of measurement and quantitative procedures in dealing with problems of daily living
  a. Can read and use the ruler
  b. Has skill in using measurements to describe and define quantitative aspects of objects, events, and ideas
  c. Constructs and interprets methods for communicating by graphic and tabular means
	Objective tests
	Behavior records and ratings
	Rating of product of student's work
	Interview with learner
	Reports of responses in other curriculum areas

4. Developing meaningful concepts in algebra and geometry
  a. Uses manipulative and visual aids effectively
  b. Uses mathematical sentences intelligently in solving problems
  c. Knows how to solve equations
	Observation of daily work
	Interview with learner
	Questionnaires
	Analysis of reports of methods of study

5. Developing desirable interest in and attitudes toward mathematics
  a. Makes voluntary contributions of significance to class discussions
  b. Reads widely about mathematics and its uses
  c. Is resourceful and inventive in dealing with quantitative aspects of problems and situations
	Interest inventory
	Ratings of interest in activities and toward curriculum content
	Observation of behavior
	Self-rating devices
	Interview with learner
	Questionnaires
	Anecdotal records

6. Developing desirable behavior patterns and good citizen traits as a result of group activities
  a. Reveals qualities of leadership
  b. Participates effectively in group work, committee assignments
  c. Is able to attack real problems systematically and effectively
	Observation of behavior
	Problem-situation tests
	"Guess who" tests
	Rating scales
	Interview with learner
	"What would you do" tests
	Tape recordings

It is significant to note that *tests* of one form or another are by no means the only evaluative technique suggested by Grossnickle, Brueckner, and Reckzeh. Various other means of observation are suggested, some of which are quite informal. Objective tests (standardized and others) are but one aspect of dimension 3 of Figure 5.

Some Emerging Distinctions

It is not unlikely that the terms *summative evaluation* and *formative evaluation* will be used with increasing frequency in the near future. Each of these terms has implications for the classroom teacher within the context of instruction and evaluation in school mathematics, although formative evaluation commonly is also associated with program development.

Bloom makes explicit ". . . a distinction between the teaching-learning process and the evaluation process. At some point in time, the results of teaching and learning can be reflected in the evaluation of students. But these are *separate* processes."[17]

The term *summative evaluation* is being used increasingly to refer to the "evaluation process" which Bloom distinguishes from the "teaching-learning process." Associated with the instructional process, however, is the term *formative evaluation*. Tests have a role to play in both summative evaluation and formative evaluation, and the testing context may be helpful in clarifying the distinction between these things.

The familiar standardized mathematics achievement test is a good illustration of a *summative* evaluation instrument. Among other things, such a test generally samples a relatively large block of content (e.g., that of a semester or a year). As a "standardized" test, it is "norm referenced" in that it rates or ranks each student's achievement in relation to the achievement of students in a particular norming group (reference group). These and other characteristics associate its use with the "evaluation process" as distinguished by Bloom from the "teaching-learning process."

17. Benjamin S. Bloom, "Learning for Mastery." *Evaluation Comment*, 1, no. 2 (May, 1968), not paged. (Bloom's paper will be published as a chapter in *Formative and Summative Evaluation of Student Learning* by Bloom, Hastings, Maddaus, and others [McGraw-Hill]).

By contrast, consider a mathematics test which samples a much smaller block of content (e.g., a week or two of instruction). Add to this a diagnostic feature which facilitates subsequent instructional prescription on the basis of a student's test performance. And make the instrument "criterion referenced" in the sense that achievement is interpreted in terms of an absolute criterion score rather than on a relative basis in terms of the achievement of other students. Such an instrument illustrates a *formative* evaluation test and the use of a test of this nature ". . . should be regarded as part of the learning process and should in no way be confused with the judg-

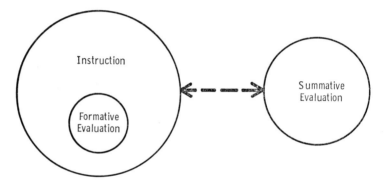

Fig. 6.—Instruction, formative evaluation, and summative evaluation

ment of the capabilities of the student or used as part of the grading process."[18]

The preceding illustrations have oversimplified the distinction between summative and formative evaluation in their broader contexts. The essential point to be made here is that there are different purposes and kinds of "evaluation."

We may view the relationship between instruction, formative evaluation, and summative evaluation as shown in Figure 6.

Formative evaluation is an integral part of instruction. Such evaluation uses a variety of means for gathering samples of student mathematical behavior in order to facilitate instruction and make it more effective from day to day. Non-normed criterion reference tests (CRTs) have a role to play in formative evaluation. But this kind

18. *Ibid.*

of evaluation also uses to advantage a variety of less formal observational techniques.

Summative evaluation, on the other hand, is not directly a part of
the instructional process. It, too, may use a variety of instruments
(including normed tests) for gathering samples of student mathematical behavior. But its intent is to "evaluate" in a different sense
and for a different purpose.[19] It may influence indirectly one aspect
or another of instruction, but it is a separate process.

It should be noted that the same mathematical situation might be
used in connection with either summative or formative evaluation
and it might be used either formally or informally. Consider the
following instance (Diagram 2):

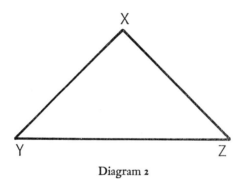

Diagram 2

$\triangle XYZ$ is an isosceles triangle in which $\overline{YX} \perp \overline{ZX}$ and $m\overline{YX} = 6$
(units). What is the area of the region bounded by $\triangle XYZ$?

This situation might appear as an item on a standardized achievement test, or it might appear as an item on a CRT. Furthermore, the
situation might be used in connection with one variety or another
of informal observation of student mathematical behavior. Such less
formal procedures often are of value when we are interested in

19. For instance, summative evaluation often is associated with *groups* of students rather than with individual students. A summative evaluation instrument
then may be built on the basis of "item sampling," in which not every student
in the group is measured on every mathematical behavior sampled by the instrument as a whole. Formative evaluation, on the other hand, is often associated with
individual students. Each student is measured on each mathematical behavior
sampled by the instrument as a whole, although different equivalent items may
be used to sample a particular behavior.

knowing how a student interprets and attacks a particular mathematical situation. Consider these three solutions for the given problems:

Illustrative Solution I (See Diagram 3)

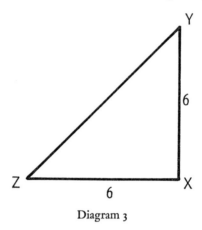

Diagram 3

$\triangle XYZ$ is a right triangle. If we think of turning or rotating $\triangle XYZ$
so that it is in the position shown above, it is immediately evident
that both the base and the altitude of the triangle are known, since
$\triangle XYZ$ is isosceles. Thus, the area of the region bounded by $\triangle XYZ$
is $\frac{1}{2}(6)(6) = 18$ (sq. units).

Illustrative Solution II (See Diagram 4)

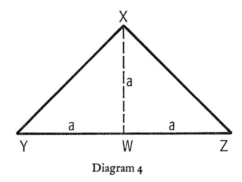

Diagram 4

The altitude XW of $\triangle XYZ$ is perpendicular to the base YZ and bi-
sects it, from which it can be established that $\overline{YW} \cong \overline{WZ} \cong \overline{XW}$.

$$a^2 + a^2 = 6^2 ; \qquad a = \sqrt{18}.$$

The area of the region bounded by $\triangle XYZ$ is

$$2[\tfrac{1}{2}(\sqrt{18})(\sqrt{18})] = (18 \text{ sq. units}) \,.$$

Illustrative Solution III (See Diagram 5)

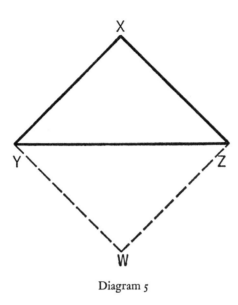

Diagram 5

$\overline{YZ}$ is a diagonal of square $XYWZ$, and the area of the region bounded by $\triangle XYZ$ is one-half the area of the region bounded by square $XYWZ$ (since $\triangle XYZ \cong \triangle WYZ$). The area of the region bounded by $\triangle XYZ$ is

$$\tfrac{1}{2}(6^2) = 18(\text{sq. units}) \,.$$

These three illustrative solutions represent quite different perceptions of and approaches to the same mathematical situation. Informal observational procedures are significantly useful in gathering information about *how students think* in particular mathematical situations. Such *patterns of thinking* are highly relevant in contemporary programs of mathematics instruction.

Gray (E16), for one, has emphasized the use of an informal interview as a valuable technique in gathering information about students' thinking patterns in mathematical contexts—a technique pioneered by Brownell several decades ago.[20] This procedure also is applicable to formative evaluations associated with classroom instruction, as suggested by Weaver.[21] Although the technique has been used more extensively with elementary school students, it can be used to advantage equally well with secondary school students.[22]

A Concluding Observation

Advances in media and technology already have influenced some of our evaluation instruments, methods, etc.,—and further influences can be expected.[23] But these advances cannot eliminate the need for value judgments at certain stages of evaluation, whether it be summative or formative.

The school administrator is concerned more directly with summative evaluation in mathematics than with formative evaluation. His need is not for "evaluation" as an integral part of the ongoing process of instruction.

The teacher of mathematics, on the other hand, is concerned very directly with formative evaluation and its role in facilitating effective instruction. He also has a concern for aspects of summative evaluation and its indirect relationship to the separate instructional process.

Both school administrators and teachers of mathematics must accept responsibility for making professional value judgments as a necessary part of their evaluations and for the courses of action which result from those evaluations. This is a responsibility which neither the school administrator nor the mathematics teacher can disregard.

20. William A. Brownell, *The Development of Children's Number Ideas in the Primary Grades* (Supplementary Educational Monographs, No. 35 [Chicago: University of Chicago Press, 1928]); more recently, see: William A. Brownell, *Arithmetical Abstractions: The Movement Toward Conceptual Maturity under Differing Systems of Instruction* (U.S. Department of Health, Education, and Welfare, Office of Education, Cooperative Research Project No. 1676 [University of California at Berkeley, 1964]).

21. J. Fred Weaver, "Big Dividends from Little Interviews." *Arithmetic Teacher* II (April, 1955), 40–47.

22. See, for instance: Jeremy Kilpatrick, "Analyzing the Solution of Word Problems in Mathematics: An Exploratory Study" (unpublished Ph.D. dissertation, Stanford University, 1967).

23. For instance, see: Thomas A. Kriewall, "A Prototypic Instructional Management System Designed for Individualized Mathematics Curricula" (unpublished Ph.D. thesis, University of Wisconsin, 1969).

Bibliography

A. GENERAL REFERENCES ON MEASUREMENT AND EVALUATION

1. DAVIS, FREDERICK B. *Educational Measurements and Their Interpretation.* Belmont, Calif.: Wadsworth Publishing Co., 1964.
2. EBEL, ROBERT L. *Measuring Educational Achievement.* Englewood Cliffs, N.J.: Prentice-Hall, 1965.
3.. FINDLEY, WARREN G., ed. *The Impact and Improvement of School Testing Programs.* Sixty-second Yearbook of the National Society for the Study of Education, Part II. Chicago: University of Chicago Press, 1963.
4. NOLL, VICTOR H. *Introduction to Educational Measurement.* 2d ed. Boston: Houghton Mifflin Co., 1965.
5. REMMERS, H. H.; GAGE, N. L.; and RUMMEL, J. FRANCIS. *A Practical Introduction to Measurement and Evaluation.* 2d ed. New York: Harper & Row, 1965.
6. STANLEY, JULIAN C. *Measurement in Today's Schools.* 4th ed. Englewood Cliffs, N.J.: Prentice-Hall, 1964.

B. YEARBOOK REFERENCES ON EVALUATION IN MATHEMATICS EDUCATION

1. BROWNELL, WILLIAM A. "The Evaluation of Learning in Arithmetic." *Arithmetic in General Education.* Sixteenth Yearbook, National Council of Teachers of Mathematics (Final Report of the National Council Committee on Arithmetic), pp. 225–67. New York: Bureau of Publications, Teachers College, Columbia University, 1941.
2. CLARK, JOHN R., ed. "The Evaluation of Mathematical Learning." *Emerging Practices in Mathematics Education.* Twenty-second Yearbook, National Council of Teachers of Mathematics, pp. 339–409. Washington: the Council, 1954.
3. GREENE, CHARLES E., and BUSWELL, G. T. "Testing, Diagnosis, and Remedial Work in Arithmetic." *Report of the Society's Committee on Arithmetic.* Twenty-ninth Yearbook of the National Society for the Study of Education, pp. 268–316. Bloomington, Ill.: Public School Publishing Co., 1930.
4. HARTUNG, MAURICE L., and FAWCETT, HAROLD P. "The Measurement of Understanding in Secondary-School Mathematics." *The Measurement of Understanding.* Forty-fifth Yearbook of the National Society for the Study of Education, Part I, pp. 157–74. Chicago: University of Chicago Press, 1946.
5. JOHNSON, DONOVAN A., ed. *Evaluation in Mathematics.* Twenty-sixth Yearbook, National Council of Teachers of Mathematics. Washington: the Council, 1961.
6. REEVE, W. D., ed. "Evaluation of the Progress of Pupils." *The Place of Mathematics in Secondary Education.* Fifteenth Yearbook, National Council of Teachers of Mathematics (Final Report of the Joint Com-

mission of the Mathematical Association of America and the National Council of Teachers of Mathematics), pp. 162–86. New York: Bureau of Publications, Teachers College, Columbia University, 1940.

7. SPITZER, HERBERT F. "Testing Instruments and Practices in Relation to Present Concepts of Teaching Arithmetic." *The Teaching of Arithmetic*. Fiftieth Yearbook of the National Society for the Study of Education, Part II, pp. 186–202. Chicago: University of Chicago Press, 1951.

8. SUELTZ, BEN A.; BOYNTON, HOLMES; and SAUBLE, IRENE. "The Measurement of Understanding in Elementary-School Mathematics." *The Measurement of Understanding*. Forty-fifth Yearbook of the National Society for the Study of Education, Part I, pp. 138–56. Chicago: University of Chicago Press, 1946.

C. SELECTED MONOGRAPH REFERENCES ON EVALUATION IN
MATHEMATICS EDUCATION

1. BUSWELL, G. T. "Methods of Studying Pupils' Thinking in Arithmetic." *Arithmetic 1949*. Supplementary Educational Monographs, no. 70, pp. 55–63. Chicago: University of Chicago Press, 1949.

2. GLENNON, VINCENT J. "Testing Meanings in Arithmetic." *Arithmetic 1949*. Supplementary Educational Monographs, no. 70, pp. 64–74. Chicago: University of Chicago Press, 1949.

3. ROSSKOPF, MYRON F., chm. "Mathematics and Evaluation," in *New Developments in Secondary School Mathematics. Bulletin of the National Association of Secondary School Principals*, vol. 43, no. 247 (May 1959): 150–68.

4. SPITZER, HERBERT F. "Procedures and Techniques for Evaluating the Outcomes of Instruction in Arithmetic." *Arithmetic 1948*. Supplementary Educational Monographs, no. 66, pp. 15–25. Chicago: University of Chicago Press, 1948.

5. STORM, W. B. "Arithmetical Meanings That Should Be Tested." *Arithmetic 1948*. Supplementary Educational Monographs, no. 66, pp. 26–31. Chicago: University of Chicago Press, 1948.

6. SUELTZ, BEN A. "Measuring the Newer Aspects of Functional Arithmetic." *Improving the Program in Arithmetic*, pp. 27–34. Chicago: University of Chicago Press, 1946, 1947.

D. REFERENCES ON EVALUATION IN CONTEMPORARY PROFESSIONAL BOOKS IN
MATHEMATICS EDUCATION

1. BUFFIE, EDWARD G.; WELCH, RONALD C.; and PAIGE, DONALD D. "Evaluation, Diagnosis, and Marking-Grading." *Mathematics: Strategies of Teaching*, pp. 151–81. Englewood Cliffs, N.J.: Prentice-Hall, 1968.

2 BUTLER, CHARLES H., and WREN, F. LYNWOOD. "Evaluation of Instruction." *The Teaching of Secondary Mathematics*. 4th ed., pp. 185–201. New York: McGraw-Hill Book Co., 1965.

3. DUTTON, WILBUR H. *Evaluating Pupils' Understanding of Arithmetic.* Englewood Cliffs, N.J.: Prentice-Hall, 1964.

4. FLOURNOY, FRANCES. "Evaluating Pupil Progress." *Elementary School Mathematics*, pp. 93–101. New York: Center for Applied Research in Education, 1964.

5. GROSSNICKLE, FOSTER E.; BRUECKNER, LEO J.; and RECKZEH, JOHN. "Appraising Outcomes of Elementary Mathematics" and "The Diagnosis and Treatment of Learning Difficulties in Mathematics." *Discovering Meanings in Elementary School Mathematics.* 5th ed., pp. 383–98, 399–416. New York: Holt, Rinehart & Winston, 1968.

6. JOHNSON, DONOVAN A., and RISING, GERALD R. "Evaluation of Achievement." *Guidelines for Teaching Mathematics*, pp. 323–46. Belmont, Calif.: Wadsworth Publishing Co., 1967.

7. KRAMER, KLAAS. "Evaluation." *The Teaching of Elementary School Mathematics*, pp. 373–91. Rockleigh, N.J.: Allyn & Bacon, 1966.

8. MARKS, JOHN L.; PURDY, C. RICHARD; and KINNEY, LUCIEN B. "Evaluating Pupil Progress." *Teaching Elementary School Mathematics for Understanding.* 2d ed., pp. 429–67. New York: McGraw-Hill Book Co., 1965.

9. RAPPAPORT, DAVID. "Evaluation." *Understanding and Teaching Elementary School Mathematics*, pp. 216–24. New York: John Wiley & Sons, 1966.

10. RIEDESEL, C. ALAN. "Evaluation of Learning in Elementary School Mathematics." *Guiding Discovery in Elementary School Mathematics*, pp. 402–32. New York: Appleton-Century-Crofts, Meredith Publishing Co., 1967.

11. SCOTT, LLOYD. "Evaluation." *Trends in Elementary School Mathematics*, pp. 165–83. Chicago: Rand McNally & Co., 1966.

12. SPITZER, HERBERT F. "The Evaluation of Mathematics Learning." *Teaching Elementary School Mathematics*, 4th ed., pp. 314–29. Boston: Houghton Mifflin Co., 1967.

13. WESTCOTT, ALVIN M., and SMITH, JAMES A. "Evaluation and Creative Mathematics." *Creative Teaching of Mathematics in the Elementary School*, pp. 181–92. Rockleigh, N.J.: Allyn & Bacon, 1967.

E. RECENT JOURNAL ARTICLES AND MONOGRAPHS PERTAINING TO EVALUATION IN MATHEMATICS EDUCATION

1. ASHLOCK, ROBERT B., and WELCH, RONALD C. *A Test of Understandings of Selected Properties of a Number System: Primary Form.* Bulletin of the School of Education, Indiana University. Vol. 42, no. 2, March 1966.

2. AVITAL, SHMUEL M., and SHETTLEWORTH, SARA J. *Objectives for Mathematics Learning: Some Ideas for the Teacher.* Ontario Institute for Studies in Education, Bulletin no. 3. Toronto: the Institute, 1968.

3. BECKER, J. P. "Geometry Achievement Tests in NLSMA." *American Mathematical Monthly* 75 (1968): 532–38.

4. BERNABEL, RAYMOND. "A Logical Analysis of Selected Achievement Tests in Mathematics." *Dissertation Abstracts* 27 (1967): 4121–22A.

5. BISHOP, ALAN J. "The Other Modern Mathematics." *Mathematics Teaching*. No. 42 (Spring 1968), 52–55.

6. CALDWELL, EDWARD. "Group Diagnosis and Standardized Achievement Tests." *Arithmetic Teacher* 12 (1965): 123–25.

7. CRAWFORD, DOUGLAS HOUSTON. "An Inventory of Age-Grade Trends in Understanding the Field Axioms." *Dissertation Abstracts* 25 (1965): 5728–29.

8. EDWARDS, ANDREW SOULE. "A Statistical Analysis of the Internal Properties of Three Elementary School Mathematics Tests." *Dissertation Abstracts* 26 (1966): 6546.

9. EPSTEIN, MARION G. "Testing in Mathematics: Why? What? How?" *Arithmetic Teacher* 15 (1968): 311–19.

10. EVANS, EDWARD WILLIAM. "Measuring the Ability of Students To Respond in Creative Mathematical Situations at the Late Elementary and Early Junior High School Level." *Dissertation Abstracts* 25 (1965): 7107–108.

11. FLOURNOY, FRANCES. "Applying Basic Mathematical Ideas in Arithmetic." *Arithmetic Teacher* 11 (1964): 104–8.

12. ——. "A Study of Pupils' Understanding of Arithmetic in the Intermediate Grades." *School Science and Mathematics* 67 (1967): 325–33.

13. ——. "A Study of Pupils' Understanding of Arithmetic in the Primary Grades." *Arithmetic Teacher* 14 (1967): 481–85.

14. GARNER, JEWELL LORAIN. "The Construction and Administration of Two Objective Tests Designed to Assess Basic Arithmetical Understandings of Elementary School Pupils." *Dissertation Abstracts* 26 (1965): 1992–93.

15. GRAHAM, GLENN THOMAS. "Sequentially Scaled Mathematics Achievement Tests: Construction Methodology and Evaluation Procedures." *Dissertation Abstracts* 27 (1967): 3308A.

16. GRAY, ROLAND F. "An Approach To Evaluating Arithmetic Understandings." *Arithmetic Teacher* 13 (1966): 187–91.

17. HALL, DONALD EUGENE. "The Ability of Intermediate Grade Children to Deal with Aspects of Quantitative Judgment." *Dissertation Abstracts* 27 (1967): 2730A.

18. HARTLEIN, MARION L. "Use of Items with Coded Numbers for Measuring Understanding of Elementary Mathematical Concepts." *Arithmetic Teacher* 13 (1966): 540–45.

19. HUSÉN, TORSTEN, ed. *International Study of Achievement in Mathematics*, vol. I. New York: John Wiley & Sons, 1967.

20. ——. *International Study of Achievement in Mathematics*, vol. II. New York: John Wiley & Sons, 1967.

21. MADDEN, RICHARD. "New Directions in the Measurement of Mathematical Ability." *Arithmetic Teacher* 13 (1966): 375–79.

22. Merwin, Jack C., and Higgins, Martin J. "Assessing the Progress of Education in Mathematics." *Mathematics Teacher* 61 (1968): 130–35.

23. Myers, Sheldon S. "Questions Illustrating the Kinds of Thinking Required in Current Mathematics Tests." Unpublished monograph. Mathematics Department, Test Development Division, Educational Testing Service, 1967.

24. Pace, Angela. "Understanding of Basic Concepts of Arithmetic: A Comparative Study." *Journal of Educational Research* 60 (1966):107–20.

25. Pritchett, Edward Milo. "An Instrument of Measurement to Appraise the Arithmetic Abilities of Educable Mentally Retarded Children Ages Six Through Nine." *Dissertation Abstracts* 26 (1966): 7120.

26. Rickard, Esther E. Sidwell. "An Inventory of the Number Knowledge of Beginning First Grade School Children, Based on the Performance of Selected Number Tasks." *Dissertation Abstracts* 28 (1967): 406A.

27. Romberg, Thomas A., and Wilson, James W. "The Development of Mathematics Achievement Tests for the National Longitudinal Study of Mathematical Abilities." *Mathematics Teacher* 61 (1968): 489–95. (See also E31g.)

28. Von Brock, Robert. "Measuring Arithmetic Objectives." *Arithmetic Teacher* 12 (1965): 537–42.

29. Weaver, J. Fred. "Levels of Geometric Understanding: An Exploratory Investigation of Limited Scope" and "Levels of Geometric Understanding among Pupils in Grades 4, 5, and 6." *Arithmetic Teacher* 13 (1966): 322–32, 686–90.

30. Welch, Ronald C., and Edwards, Charles W., Jr. *A Test of Arithmetic Principles, Elementary Form.* Bulletin of the School of Education, Indiana University, vol. 41, no. 5, September 1965.

31. Wilson, James W.; Cahen, Leonard S.; and Begle, Edward G., eds. *NLSMA Reports.* School Mathematics Study Group, Stanford University, 1968, 1969. (Distributed by A. C. Vroman, Inc., Pasadena, Calif.)

    a. *No. 1* (Parts A and B). *X-Population Test Batteries.* Pp. 524.

    b. *No. 2* (Parts A and B). *Y-Population Test Batteries.* Pp. 588.

    c. *No. 3. Z-Population Test Batteries.* Pp. 358.

    d. *No. 4. Description and Statistical Properties of X-Population Scales.* Pp. 260.

    e. *No. 5. Description and Statistical Properties of Y-Population Scales.* Pp. 326.

    f. *No. 6. Description and Statistical Properties of Z-Population Scales.* Pp. 194.

    g. No. 7. *The Development of Tests by Thomas A. Romberg and James W. Wilson.*

32. Wood, R. "Objectives in the Teaching of Mathematics," *Educational Research* 10 (1968): 83–98.

F. A HELPFUL BIBLIOGRAPHY

1. MYERS, SHELDON S., and DELON, FLOYD G. *Mathematics Tests Available in the United States*, rev. ed. Washington: National Council of Teachers of Mathematics, 1968.

G. AN INVALUABLE REFERENCE

1. BUROS, OSCAR KRISEN, ed. *The Sixth Mental Measurements Yearbook.* Highland Park, N.J.: Gryphon Press, 1965. See also earlier editions.

H. SOME REFERENCES PERTAINING TO OBJECTIVES

1. BLOOM, BENJAMIN S., ed. *Taxonomy of Educational Objectives: The Classification of Educational Goals. Handbook I: Cognitive Domain.* New York: David McKay Co., 1956.
2. KRATHWOHL, DAVID R.; BLOOM, BENJAMIN S.; and MASIA, BERTRAM B. *Taxonomy of Educational Objectives: The Classification of Educational Goals. Handbook II: Affective Domain.* New York: David McKay Co., 1964.

I. MISCELLANEOUS

1. LOS ANGELES CITY SCHOOLS. *The Art of Questioning in Mathematics.* Division of Instructional Services, Curriculum Branch, Instructional Bulletin no. EC-123. 1967. (For Workshop Use)
2. WISCONSIN DEPARTMENT OF PUBLIC INSTRUCTION. *Guidelines to Mathematics, K-6.* Madison, 1967.

CHAPTER X

Evaluation of Mathematics Programs

EDWARD G. BEGLE

AND

JAMES W. WILSON

Introduction

Evaluation of mathematics programs is considerably more important today than was the case a decade ago. Radical changes in the curriculum at all grade levels, coupled with a variety of new pedagogical techniques, have resulted in a much greater variety of textbooks and textbook sequences than we have ever had before in this country. School officials responsible for decisions on the choice of textbooks and educational procedures are asking for more and better information and for more powerful ways of evaluating alternatives among which they must choose.

This chapter begins with a general discussion of evaluation, including the important problem of stating the objectives of mathematics education in an organized fashion. This discussion is followed by brief reviews of a number of projects which have been concerned in one way or another with the evaluation of mathematics programs. The final portion is a detailed discussion of the variety of evaluation procedures used by the School Mathematics Study Group (SMSG), the largest of the mathematics curriculum projects in this country.

The authors, through their work with the National Longitudinal Study of Mathematical Abilities (NLSMA), a study conducted by SMSG, have been actively engaged in many phases of the evaluation of mathematics programs. A substantial proportion of this chapter draws upon this NLSMA experience.

Kinds of Evaluation

There are many different kinds of activities that have been called "evaluation." There is no quarrel with the "evaluation" of a mathematics program that is based on the expert opinion of mathematicians and mathematics educators about the quality of mathematics presented and the organization of the material. Book reviews are of this nature. They serve a useful purpose. But as evaluations of mathematics programs, they are inadequate. Insightful analysis of the content and organization of a mathematics program may, in fact, be a commonsense first step in program evaluation. The NCTM guidelines for textbook selection provide one framework for doing this type of evaluation.[1] The criteria for evaluation within this framework pertain to organization of the material, quality of the mathematics, proper use of illustrations, color and typography, cover of the book, or degree of change from the last edition. The point should not be belabored, but evaluation in this sense is too limited and may not be relevant to how well the materials can be adapted to a classroom context in order for students to use them in learning mathematics.

The criteria for evaluation which are stressed in this chapter are *pupil outcomes*. What identifiable changes in students can be observed during or after exposure to the mathematics program? By using the general term, pupil outcomes, a wide variety of criteria are possible. And this is a key point in this chapter: *mathematics programs should be evaluated over a range of criteria*. These criteria may include achievement measures, retention measures, attitude measures, self-concept measures; they may (should) be measures over as many different types of achievement as can be identified in the objectives of the mathematics program.

The mathematics program operates within the total context of the school. Any legitimate evaluation of the mathematics program must take into account this context, describe it, consider its influence, and account for it in the analysis of information. Obviously, the evaluation of a mathematics program can become confounded with other factors in the school context. For example, if the evaluation involves the comparison of two mathematics programs, a suitable experimental design needs to be followed to insure that it is the alternative programs that are being compared rather than other factors. It is a fact of school operation that experimental materials will tend to be used

---

1. Committee on Aids for Evaluators of Textbooks, National Council of Teachers of Mathematics, "Aids for Evaluators of Mathematics Textbooks," *The Mathematics Teacher*, LVIII (1965), 467–73.

by the better teachers with better students unless an explicit evaluation design is accepted by the school and followed.

FORMATIVE EVALUATION

The evaluation of a mathematics program that occurs in the process of the development of the program has come to be called *formative evaluation*. Formative evaluation has as its purpose the production of information, perhaps diagnostic in nature, which can be used to improve the product. It includes, but is not limited to, the preliminary tryout of units of material in classes, the gathering of comments from teachers, or the more large-scale achievement testing to find how well students handle the material in a preliminary version. The purpose of formative evaluation is to obtain information for decision making in the development of a program.

Every curriculum developer, every textbook writer, every program planner, or even every teacher uses some form of formative evaluation in his work. For the most part, these procedures are informal and unsystematic. As such, they may lose some of the potential inherent in having an effective plan for gathering information on which to base decisions. Further, the production of curriculum materials tends to move more rapidly than do most schemes for evaluation. Or, as some critics charge, a systematic scheme of formative evaluation can inhibit the development of a mathematics program or dampen creative writing. For example, the stating of objectives for a unit of material is a highly relevant part of unit writing, instruction, and evaluation. But if writing of objectives in behavioral terms becomes an end, the program itself may never get written. A balance is needed.

Attention to procedures of formative evaluation may well be the most important development in the evaluation of mathematics programs during the next decade. The possible payoff in effective decision making during the development of mathematics programs is very great. There is a need for continued theorizing about and application of formative-evaluation techniques. It is truly an interdisciplinary problem—the mathematician, the psychometrician, the curriculum specialist, the psychologist, the statistician, and the teacher all have something to contribute to the theory and practice of formative evaluation.

SUMMATIVE EVALUATION

Contrasted with the formative evaluation is that evaluation which is done to determine the worth or quality of a finished product—a mathematics program. This has been called *summative evaluation*. It represents the more traditional use of the term "evaluation" as it applies to collecting information upon which to make decisions about the use of a program. There is no clear dividing line between formative and summative evaluation—nor is one needed. In fact, an evaluation activity can be summative in the sense that information is used to make decisions about the use of the program, and at the same time formative in that information is used to lead to the improvement of the program.

An evaluation is inherently comparative in nature. That is, the program that is being evaluated is being compared with something—an alternative program, criteria determined by a norm group, or criteria in some absolute sense. Ideally, mathematics educators should be able to take any task which students are to learn and to develop criteria by which teachers can determine when the student has learned it. There are not very many nontrivial examples of such criteria in the mathematics education literature. Usually, the criteria are what some norm group has done on a measure, or more typically, coverage of mathematical material in class without assessment of student proficiency.

There is no reason to be apologetic for an evaluation that compares alternative programs. Decisions must be made about the selection and operation of a mathematics program, and information on the comparative effectiveness of programs is useful. There are some guidelines which will help to maximize the usefulness of these comparisons, and setting forth these guidelines is the primary concern of this chapter.

Comparison of alternative programs does have limitations, however, and those who utilize evaluation results as well as those who engage in evaluation should be careful to utilize the strengths of comparative evaluation rather than be trapped by its limitations. First, it is rarely possible to establish experimental conditions for a "pure" experiment. Therefore, sources of invalidity will need to be recognized and treated by appropriate means. For example, new programs tend to be used first with the best students in the best schools with the best teachers. There are statistical and experimental means to deal with these problems and they should be used. Second, comparison may be extremely costly and time consuming. A full-blown curriculum comparison experiment may be outside the fiscal and professional resources of an individual school system.

At the current stage of the development of the art and theory of mathematics-program evaluation, comparisons among alternative programs may be the most operational strategy. This procedure may involve compromise with experimental rigor. The typical comparison is a status study which is at best correlational in nature. But progress can be made in improving mathematics programs, instruction, *and* evaluation techniques by bringing resources to bear on doing quality evaluation studies.

Any person who attempts an evaluation of mathematics programs should, as basic homework, make himself familiar with some of the recent position papers which have sharpened some of the concepts of program evaluation. Cronbach[2] has clearly stated some of the purposes and methods of program evaluation. Scriven,[3] partially as a reaction to Cronbach's position, has elaborated and expanded the purposes and means of curriculum evaluation and presented some alternative views. Finally, a reference which has been widely used—perhaps not always in an appropriate way—is the *Taxonomy of Educational Objectives*.[4] A taxonomy exists for both the cognitive domain and the affective domain, but the former is the one commonly called "the taxonomy."

A Model for Mathematics Achievement

The evaluation of mathematics programs must, in part, be based on measures of student proficiency in mathematics. There should be a whole range of pupil-performance criteria. The task of describing or specifying these criteria can be made easier if a schema to organize

2. Lee J. Cronbach, "Evaluation for Course Improvement," *Teachers College Record*, LXIV (1963), 672–83.

3. Michael Scriven, "The Methodology of Evaluation," in Robert Stake (ed.), *Perspectives of Curriculum Evaluation* (AERA Monograph Series on Curriculum Evaluation, no. 1 [Chicago: Rand McNally, 1967]).

4. Benjamin S. Bloom (ed.), *Taxonomy of Educational Objectives: Cognitive Domain* (New York: David McKay Co., 1964); David R. Krathwohl, Benjamin S. Bloom, and Bertram B. Masia, *Taxonomy of Educational Objectives: Affective Domain* (New York: David McKay Co., 1964).

the task is available. For this reason, a model of mathematics achievement is presented in this section.[5]

The model may serve a number of purposes and uses. It may provide a unifying theme for considering problems of mathematics curriculum, instruction, and evaluation. The mathematics achievement of students is at the heart of these concerns.

The model described below assumes that mathematics achievement is a many-component phenomenon. That is, mathematics achievement is not a unitary trait, and therefore a strategy needs to be available to insure sampling of a whole range of measures of mathematics achievement. One strategy is to classify mathematics achievement outcomes in two ways—first by categories of content, and second by levels of cognitive behavior assumed to be associated with the outcome or its measure.

The task of describing the content dimension is not difficult. All that has to be done is to draw on the expertise of the mathematical community. Any group or person who is competent in mathematics can easily describe this dimension and can modify the categories to serve any particular purpose. For instance, early in the operation of NLSMA, a very detailed categorization of mathematics content was used because the task of test development required it.[6] Later, a simpler classification of content was used for organizing the discussion of results.

The primary value of describing cognitive levels is to insure a more balanced coverage of objectives within a content area. It is important that the cognitive levels are defined in terms comprehensible to the mathematics education community, are logically developed and internally consistent, and are potentially related to psychological, or behavioral, phenomena. Without considering such a dimension, mathematics educators, teachers, and test constructors have tended to emphasize some objectives and to ignore others.

The particular model described here was developed during NLSMA and is the one used in organizing the discussion of results.

5. The word "model" is used in the sense of providing an organizational framework; it represents a categorization system with some stated rules and relationships for using the system.

6. Thomas A. Romberg and James W. Wilson, "The Development of Tests for the National Longitudinal Study of Mathematical Abilities," *The Mathematics Teacher*, LXI (1968), 489–95.

Romberg and Wilson[7] have provided a thorough description of the evolution of this model. The explicit statement of the model must acknowledge the contribution of all the NLSMA report writers.[8] The specification of the cognitive-levels dimension is similar to that given by Bloom,[9] but modified for categories appropriate to mathematics achievement.

As mentioned previously, the essential idea of the model is that measures of mathematics achievement, or test items, or objectives of mathematics instruction, can be classified in two ways: (*a*) by categories of mathematical content, and (b) by levels of behavior. The levels of behavior reflect the cognitive complexity of a task (*not* simply the difficulty of a task). In the model presented in Figure 1,

	Number Systems	Geometry	Algebra
Computation			
Comprehension			
Application			
Analysis			

FIG. 1.—A model for mathematics achievement

the categories of mathematical content are number systems, geometry, algebra. The levels of behavior are computation, comprehension, application, and analysis.

The model, as it is presented, requires explicit specification of the terms along each dimension. These specifications are as follows:

CATEGORIES OF MATHEMATICS CONTENT

Number Systems—Items concerned with the nature and properties of whole numbers, integers, the rational numbers, the real numbers, and the complex numbers; the techniques and properties of the arithmetic operations.

7. Thomas A. Romberg and James W. Wilson, *The Development of Tests, NLSMA Reports*, no. 7. See list of *Reports* at end of the chapter.

8. The NLSMA report writers are Edward G. Begle, Stanford University; L. Ray Carry, University of Texas; Jeremy Kilpatrick, Teachers College, Columbia University; Gordon K. McLeod, Stanford University; Thomas A. Romberg, University of Wisconsin; J. Fred Weaver, University of Wisconsin; and James W. Wilson, University of Georgia.

9. Bloom, *op. cit.*

Geometry—Items concerned with linear and angular measurement, area, and volume; points, lines, planes; polygons and circles; solids; congruence and similarity; construction; graphs and coordinate geometry; formal proofs; and spatial visualization.

Algebra—Items concerned with open sentences; algebraic expressions; factoring; solution of equations and inequalities; systems of equations; algebraic and transcendental functions; graphing of functions and solution sets; theory of equations; and trigonometry.

LEVELS OF BEHAVIOR

Computation—Items designed to require straightforward manipulation of problem elements according to rules the students presumably have learned. Emphasis is upon performing operations and not upon deciding which operations are appropriate.

Comprehension—Items designed to require either recall of concepts and generalizations, or transformation of problem elements from one mode to another. Emphasis is upon demonstrating understanding of concepts and their relationships, and not upon using concepts to produce a solution.

Application—Items designed to require (*a*) recall of relevant knowledge, (*b*) selection of appropriate operations, and (*c*) performance of the operations. Items are of a routine nature. They require the student to use concepts in a specific context and in a way he has presumably practiced.

Analysis—Items designed to require a nonroutine application of concepts. The items may require the detection of relationships, the finding of patterns, and the organization and use of concepts and operations in a nonpracticed context.

The second dimension, levels of behavior, is both hierarchical and ordered. It is *ordered* in the sense that analysis is more cognitively complex than application, which is in turn more cognitively complex than comprehension, and the computation level includes those items which are the least cognitively complex. It is *hierarchical* in that an item at the application level may require both comprehension-level skills (selection of appropriate operations) and computation-level skills (performance of an operation).

The use of the model usually requires some rules of thumb. For instance, outcomes are classified at the highest cognitive level even though lower level behaviors are required. Generally, time and practice have to be expended in orientation with the model and in adapting it to a specific problem.

The model is by no means unique. In the following section, various other models which have been used by mathematics projects are discussed to illustrate some similarities to and differences from the model given above.

In emphasizing measures of mathematics achievement, all cognitive outcomes, there is no intent to disregard affective outcomes such as attitude, appreciation, interest, and anxiety. A model could be developed for such outcomes in a mathematics program also—or the present model could be expanded. The first concern of mathematics program evaluation, however, has been, and will continue to be, with cognitive outcomes, or achievement. The affective outcomes are supportive and important but secondary to, or at most of equal importance to, achievement.

Similar Models Used in Other Mathematics Projects

The models which are described here are all alike in that they use some form of content by cognitive processes matrix to describe the different outcomes of mathematics achievement. They each differ from the model presented above, usually being constructed to reflect the purposes of the particular project. In some cases a different point of view is inherent in one or the other of the dimensions. In most cases, only the cognitive processes dimension is discussed.

The Statewide Mathematics Advisory Committee (SMAC) in California has taken the model given above and adapted it to the task of preparing items for a proposed statewide mathematics assessment. The committee kept the definitions of levels of cognitive behavior almost as defined in the model, but replaced the columns by the content categories contained in its 1967–68 "Strands Report."[10] These content categories were whole numbers, rational numbers, real numbers, number line and number plane mathematical sentences, geomtry, measurement, probability and statistics, functions and graphs, and logical thinking. This content breakdown is more appropriate to the purposes of the assessment and reflects the policy statement of the committee as given in the "Strands Report." Teams of writers have produced sets of items to measure mathematics achievement at each level of behavior for each content category. This huge set of

10. Statewide Mathematics Advisory Committee, "The Strands Report, Part 1," *Bulletin of the California Mathematics Council*, 1967, 25(1); and "Reprint of the Strands Report, Part 2," *Bulletin of the California Mathematics Council*, 1968.

items is comprehensive in that it covers the whole range of objectives as defined by the committee. The assessment uses item-sampling procedures so that some measure of the attainment of each objective is obtained for the state.

If a behavioral category dimension is used by a project, in most cases, somewhere in the background, the work of Bloom[11] and his associates will have contributed to its development. The broad cognitive behavior categories used by Bloom are (*a*) Knowledge, (*b*) Comprehension, (*c*) Application, (*d*) Analysis, (*e*) Synthesis, and (*f*) Evaluation. These broad categories were divided into subcategories, and examples were given from several subjects. Mathematics, however, does not fit gracefully into the scheme. For example, where would one put a computation item like $653+281$? It does not seem to be either a knowledge-level item or a comprehension-level item. On the other hand, to call it an application-level item implies a higher cognitive level than comprehension (understanding, translation). This seems unreasonable. Although Bloom's taxonomy has been used in its given form, it seems appropriate to redefine the cognitive levels to better correspond with the study of mathematics when evaluating a mathematics program.

Wood[12] reported the use of a slightly different cognitive behavior hierarchy for the Item Banking Project. His categories were the following:

1. Knowledge and information: recall of definitions, notations, concepts
2. Techniques and skill: computation, manipulation of symbols
3. Comprehension: capacity to understand problems, to translate symbolic forms, to follow and extend reasoning
4. Application: of appropriate concepts in unfamiliar mathematical situations
5. Inventiveness: reasoning creatively in mathematics

This differs from the model in the last section primarily in holding to a separate knowledge level and in the emphasis on creativity in the highest category.

The International Study of Achievement in Mathematics[13] evolved

11. Bloom, *op. cit.*

12. R. Wood, "Objectives in the Teaching of Mathematics," *Educational Research*, X (1968), 83–98.

13. T. Husen, ed., *International Study of Achievement in Mathematics* (New York: John Wiley & Sons, 1967), chapter 4.

a model with a cognitive-behavior dimension. An analysis of mathematics objectives in the United States used the following categories:

1. Ability to remember or recall definitions, notations, operations, and concepts
2. Ability to manipulate and compute rapidly and accurately
3. Ability to interpret symbolic data
4. Ability to put data into symbols
5. Ability to follow proofs
6. Ability to construct proofs
7. Ability to apply concepts to mathematical problems
8. Ability to apply concepts to nonmathematical problems
9. Ability to analyze [problems] and determine the operations which may be applied
10. Ability to invent mathematical generalizations[14]

Eventually, the study developed items for a very detailed list of mathematics content at each of the following levels:

1. Knowledge and information: definitions, notation, concepts
2. Techniques and skills: solutions
3. Translation of data into symbols or schema or vice versa
4. Comprehension: capacity to analyze problems, to follow reasoning
5. Inventiveness: reasoning creatively in mathematics[15]

The similarity of the Item Banking Project categories and the preceding categories is not accidental. Wood[16] acknowledges that the Item Banking categories were made up after a consideration of these categories in conjunction with the Bloom taxonomy. The translation category received considerable emphasis in the *International Study*, (13).

The Committee on Assessing the Progress in Education, the National Assessment Project, uses the following categories of behavior for its mathematics objectives:[17]

1. Recall and/or recognize definitions, facts, and symbols
2. Perform mathematical manipulations
3. Understand mathematical concepts and processes
4. Solve mathematical problems—social, technical, and academic
5. Use mathematics and mathematical reasoning to analyze problem situations, define problems, formulate hypotheses, make decisions, and verify results
6. Appreciate and use mathematics

14. *Ibid.*, p. 93.   15. *Ibid.*, p. 94.   16. Wood, *op. cit.*, p. 89.

17. Committee on Assessing the Progress in Education, "Objectives for National Assessment," *CAPE Newsletter*, II, no. 4 (1969), 6.

This scheme is particularly suited to the purposes of national assessment. The similarity to the previous schemes is obvious, but there are important differences too. In particular, the last item is, in part, noncognitive.

A scheme which has been used to discuss the objectives of mathematics instruction in higher education is that used by the University Grants Commission in India.[18] The objectives were organized as follows:

1. The student will acquire knowledge of definitions, concepts, and theories in mathematics.
2. The student will develop the ability to solve problems on the basis of the theories and methods learned.
3. The student will develop the ability to think in terms of postulations and logical structure.
4. The student will acquire the ability to solve problems by combining different branches of mathematics.
5. The student will become aware of the interrelations between mathematics and other branches of knowledge.
6. The student will develop skill in applying mathematical methods to the solution of problems in other fields of knowledge.
7. The student will develop ability to impart mathematical knowledge to others.[19]

These categories are somewhat different from those reviewed previously. It is doubtful that strong assumptions on the hierarchical nature of the categories can be made.

These various schemes indicate a common point: a model with a content dimension and a levels-of-behavior dimension can be adapted to the purposes of an evaluation project so that a range of criteria are delineated.

Evaluations of Mathematics Programs

No comprehensive review of evaluation studies will be attempted. Rather, a few studies will be discussed to illustrate some of the problems in evaluation.

Hungerman[20] contrasted ten classes who had used SMSG texts in

18. University Grants Commission, *Evaluation in Higher Education* (New Delhi: U. G. C., 1961).

19. *Ibid.*, p. 247.

20. Ann D. Hungerman, "Achievement and Attitude of Sixth-Grade Pupils in Conventional and Contemporary Mathematics Programs," *Arithmetic Teacher,* LX (1960), 30–39.

Grades IV, V, and VI with ten classes who had used a conventional text in Grades IV, V, and VI. A strong point of this study was an attempt to obtain several measures of conventional mathematics achievement, several measures of contemporary mathematics achievement, and a measure of attitude. *The California Achievement Test: Arithmetic* and the *Contemporary Mathematics Test* (Experimental form from the California Test Bureau) were used. Subscores were calculated on each test as determined by items of similar content. No attempt was made to discuss the items in terms of levels of behavior. Most items on either test probably would be at the computation level.

On the conventional test, significant differences were found for two of the seven subscores, both in favor of the conventional group. On the contemporary tests, the SMSG group performed significantly higher on four of seven content subscales and on both terminology subscales. No differences were found on the attitude measures.

The relationships of socioeconomic level, IQ, and sex with achievement were explored in the study. Secondary analyses on the items were performed to aid in interpreting the results.

The study by Hungerman was done with intact groups. Analysis of covariance was used to adjust for IQ and socioeconomic level. The unit of analysis was the student whereas the class would have been the most appropriate unit.[21] The significant differences may not translate to any practical differences due to the increased power of the statistical tests resulting from the large number of data cases.

Williams and Shuff[22] reported studies conducted during 1960–61 in the Roseville (Minnesota) Schools in Grades VII, VIII, IX, and X. The SMSG text materials were used in the experimental classes, and traditional text materials were used in the control classes. The experiment was carefully designed, students randomly assigned to classes, and care taken to control for teacher effects. The dependent variables were the measures obtained on the *Sequential Tests of Educational Progress (STEP): Mathematics* and the appropriate grade and course test from the *Cooperative Tests* (COOP). Both of these sets of tests were based on conventional mathematics programs.

21. The "appropriate" data unit is the smallest group that could be independently assigned to and administered one of the experimental treatments in a study. In this study, classrooms were selected rather than students.

22. Emmet D. Williams and Robert V. Shuff, "Comparative Study of SMSG and Traditional Text Material," *The Mathematics Teacher*, LVI (1963), 495–504.

Williams and Shuff found no advantage, as far as measured by these tests, for the SMSG group. They recognized that the tests were not measuring important objectives in the SMSG program, but abdicated the responsibility as evaluators to obtain, or develop, appropriate measures as dependent variables. Here again, the appropriate unit of analysis appears to have been the class, but student data was used instead.

The Minnesota National Laboratory conducted an extended program of evaluation which was summarized by Rosenbloom.[23] The studies of Williams and Shuff were related to the work of the Minnesota National Laboratory. Rosenbloom described several experiments which for the most part supported the results of an evaluation by the Educational Testing Service, discussed below. For most of these studies, the results obtained on the STEP tests were used as the dependent variable. There is no discussion of how well these tests match the goals of mathematics instruction. One suspects that the choice of the STEP tests was one of expediency and availability. In some of the studies, the "comparison" was between the performance of the SMSG classes and the norms on these tests.

An evaluation conducted by the Educational Testing Service for SMSG during 1960–61 was reported by Payette.[24] The study was designed for replication over five grade levels—Grades VII, IX, X, XI, and XII—and had as its fundamental purpose the comparison of student achievement in SMSG courses with student achievement in non-SMSG mathematics courses.

Evidence pertinent to the three following questions was secured:

1. Does the SMSG curriculum detract from student achievement with respect to traditional mathematical skills?
2. Does the SMSG curriculum result in a measurable extension of developed mathematical ability beyond that of conventional mathematics instruction?
3. How effectively is the SMSG curriculum communicated to students at various levels of scholastic ability?

The design of these studies called for the analysis of data from classrooms of teachers selected randomly from those willing to par-

23. Paul Rosenbloom, "Minnesota National Laboratory Evaluation of SMSG, Grades 7–12," *SMSG Newsletter*, no. 10 (November, 1961), 12–26.

24. Roland F. Payette, "Educational Testing Service Summary Report of the School Mathematics Study Group Curriculum Evaluation," *SMSG Newsletter*, no. 10 (November, 1961), 5–11.

ticipate. There were approximately thirty teachers in each group at each grade level, and the unit of data for the analysis was the class (i.e., the mean for all students in a class). The dependent variables were scores on standard traditional mathematics tests on the one hand and those on tests prepared by SMSG on the other.

The results, taken collectively, led to the conclusions that (a) students exposed to conventional mathematics have neither a profound nor a consistent advantage over students exposed to SMSG mathematics with respect to learning of traditional mathematical skills; (b) students exposed to SMSG instruction acquire pronounced and consistent extensions of developed mathematical ability beyond that developed by students exposed to conventional mathematics instruction, and (c) scholastic aptitude (as measured by SCAT) is not sufficient for predicting achievement; students at all SCAT levels can learn considerable segments of SMSG materials.

Maier[25] reported specific results of the ninth-grade replication of this evaluation and presented results consistent with the conclusions stated above. Bock[26] used this data as an illustrative example and did not arrive at the same conclusion when the data was subjected to a multivariate analysis.

The evaluation produced very little information useful for further curriculum revision or for decision making in the schools. Obviously, there were many questions left unanswered. It underscored the need for a more comprehensive study of mathematics achievement. Although not realized by the curriculum builders or evaluators at that time, it underscored the need for a conceptual framework, such as the model, for analyzing and specifying mathematics achievement outcomes.

Weaver[27] analyzed the performance of fourth- and fifth-grade students, using experimental SMSG textbooks during 1961–62. A random sample of approximately 200 students at each grade level from the eight tryout centers was selected. Scores were obtained in the fall

25. Milton Maier, "Evaluation of a New Mathematics Curriculum," *American Psychologist*, XVII (1962), 336 (Abstract).

26. R. Darrell Bock, "Contributions of Multivariate Experimental Design to Educational Research," chap. 28 in *Handbook of Multivariate Experimental Psychology*, ed. Raymond B. Cattell (Chicago: Rand McNally, 1966).

27. J. Fred Weaver, "Student Achievement in SMSG Classes, Grades 4 and 5," *SMSG Newsletter*, no. 15 (April, 1963), 3–8.

on *SRA Primary Mental Abilities*, in fall and spring on the *SRA Arithmetic Achievement Test*, in spring on specially constructed SMSG mathematics tests, and in fall and spring on a measure of attitude constructed by an SMSG-sponsored project.

Weaver found the sample to be above average in IQ and arithmetic aptitude. This placed some restriction on the generality of the results. Either the tryout centers were in schools with above-average-aptitude students, or tryout classes within the centers tended to be above average.

The analysis of the *SRA Arithmetic Achievement Test* scores found the difference in approximate grade-equivalent scores from fall to spring to be between .8 and 1.4. The "reasoning" and "computation" scores were analyzed; the "concepts" scores were dismissed by Weaver as invalid measures since the items tended to measure only reading of numerals and vocabulary.[28] Weaver concluded that the use of SMSG textbooks did not inhibit the achievement of students in Grades IV and V as measured by the test administered and its norms.

The data on the SMSG mathematics tests were examined, but they were strictly normative since this was the first time the tests had been administered.

The attitude data were subjected to a factor analysis in order to identify subscales. As a whole, very little change in attitude was found, but again, the data were only normative.

In an important sense, this study should be considered an exercise in formative evaluation, since an important objective was to obtain information useful for the revision of the experimental materials during the summer of 1962. The study is noteworthy for its attempts to measure attitudes toward mathematics as one of the outcomes.

SMSG originally prepared textbooks for Grades VII, VIII, and IX for the college-capable student. Later, revisions of the textbooks were prepared for the average student, and the mathematics in the original textbooks was maintained, but presented in a different style. Fleming[29] demonstrated that the change in style did not result in the loss of any of the mathematics when both were used with high-ability

28. *Ibid.*, p. 4.

29. Walter Fleming, "Comparison Experiment of SMSG 7M and 9M Texts with SMSG 7th and 9th Grade Texts," *SMSG Newsletter*, no. 15 (April, 1963), 11–16.

students. Classroom tryouts and subsequent use of these textbooks confirmed their appropriateness for average students. It was further proposed that the textbooks in the "M" series would be suitable for lower ability students (i.e., in the 25th to 50th percentile range on arithmetic aptitude) if a slower pace was used—perhaps taking two years to cover the material rather than one year.

Herriot[30] reported a rather large-scale study of the mathematics achievement of several hundred junior high school students believed by their counselors and teachers to be "slow-learners" in mathematics. The slow-learner classes in seventh grade and ninth grade, fall of 1963, studied seventh-grade mathematics or ninth-grade algebra for two years, using the SMSG "M" series textbooks. Comparison groups using the same SMSG textbooks were selected from the same schools in the fall of 1964 to cover the course in one year. Standardized aptitude and achievement tests were used; SMSG achievement tests and measures of attitude toward mathematics were also used. The aptitude tests included *SCAT-Q, SCAT-V, Davis-Comprehension,* and *Davis-Speed.* In the analysis, a random one-half of the data was used for "data snooping" or hypothesis generation. The second half was used for hypothesis-testing to follow up the hypotheses generated in the first part of the analysis.

Regression analysis, correlational analysis, and analysis of covariance were used to explore the data in the two-phase procedure. Initial measures of quantitative ability and of mathematics achievement were strongly related to criterion measures; the relationships of all aptitude variables to the criterion measures were essentially the same for both groups. These were the main results.

An analysis of covariance found the adjusted scores of the slow-learner, two-year groups significantly higher than the adjusted scores for the above-average, one-year groups. The differences in initial aptitudes make the analysis of covariance procedure extremely tenuous as a statistical technique. It is quite possible that the criterion scores for both groups were adjusted into a range where the errors of estimate were large.

The study is a provocative and fruitful exploratory evaluation. Below-average students studying mathematics over a two-year period

30. Sarah T. Herriot. *The Slow Learner Project: The Secondary School Slow Learner in Mathematics* (*SMSG Reports*, no. 5 [Stanford: School Mathematics Study Group, 1967]).

can perform at a level similar to that of above-average students studying the same material for only one year.

Biggs[31] has reported a rather large-scale status study in the third year of the English junior schools in 1959. In part, the study was an evaluation of three kinds of teaching methods:

1. *Traditional*—teaching children to calculate with speed and accuracy; formal method
2. *Structural*—developing understanding; use of rods, blocks, and concrete materials
3. *Motivational*—informal; emphasis on real-life problem situations

The information on schools, in order to classify them by teaching method, was obtained by questionnaires. Test batteries were given to obtain measures of verbal reasoning, computational skill, problem-solving, and understanding of concepts. An attitude scale and a student questionnaire were included.

The results were as a whole inconclusive. There seemed to be no support for unimodel structure materials such as Cuisenaire or Stern materials. Multimodel structural materials such as Dienes materials were associated with higher mechanical and concepts scores and especially favored the slow learner in mathematics. There were a very few classes using multimodel structural materials, however, and this result is very tentative.

A strong point of this study is the thoroughness and care with which its results are stated. It suffers, however, from a limited range of measures from which to do an evaluation.

The *International Study of Achievement in Mathematics*[32] is usually not considered an evaluation of mathematics programs. A few results from the study do have an evaluation flavor to them, though. For example, learning-centered or "discovery" approaches, as contrasted to drill or rote methods, were found to be correlated with mathematics performance and interest in mathematics.[33] There is the curious statement that "students who had had courses in 'new mathematics' achieved higher scores than other students on items in traditional mathematics".[34] In fact, the data on courses in new mathematics was lost and new mathematics exposure was "determined" by

---

31. J. B. Biggs. *Mathematics and the Conditions of Learning* (Slough: National Foundation for Educational Research in England and Wales, 1967).

32. Husen, *op. cit.*   33. *Ibid.*, p. 298.   34. *Ibid.*, p. 196.

response to a set of items. Nevertheless, there are a number of conclusions in the report that are "evaluation" in nature. It is a pacesetting study and one which needs to be better understood by the mathematics education community.

This brief review of a few evaluation studies indicates that a concern for evaluation has existed along with the rapid changes in school mathematics during the past decade. Yet few systematic assessments of the outcomes of these programs—particularly the long-range effects that a good many innovators think are of prime importance—have been attempted.

The absence of long-term studies is no surprise. A tremendous amount of resources must be brought to bear to organize a study over a period of time longer than one school year.

The studies reviewed lack an explicit framework within which to discuss the outcomes. Where a model has been used, often items across several cognitive levels, or across content levels, have been combined. The inclusion of items spanning cognitive or content levels can mask differences. This point will be illustrated in the "NLSMA Results" section which follows. Suppose a group using textbook A scores 55 on a computation measure and 35 on a comprehension measure, and suppose a group using textbook B scores in the opposite way—35 on computation and 55 on the comprehension. If separate variables measure these two levels, then the contrast of the textbooks can be meaningful and the decision as to which textbook is better depends on a judgment (e.g., the school district policy) as to which outcome is more important. If, on the other hand, a single criterion is obtained by ignoring levels, both textbook groups obtain the same score, 90, and one could be led to the erroneous decision that the textbooks are equally good.

This rather involved discussion does have a point in the review. Many standardized tests are of a type which includes items from several cognitive or several content levels. The reliance on relatively long standardized tests in the evaluation of mathematics programs may represent a serious weakness. None of the studies reviewed used a multivariate analysis of the data. But mathematics achievement is a multivariate phenomenon. A model is useful for identifying, selecting, or developing the several measures for an evaluation; it is appropriate that multivariate methods be used in the analysis.

The NLSMA effort has confronted a number of these evaluation issues. It is instructive, therefore, to examine this project in considerable detail.

National Longitudinal Study of Mathematical Abilities

The School Mathematics Study Group, beginning in 1958, undertook a large curriculum development project and the preparation of sample mathematics textbooks. This development started with textbooks at the high school level and proceeded down through the grade levels until sample textbooks had been prepared for kindergarten through twelfth grade. These textbooks were subjected to two kinds of evaluation.

The first evaluation involved those procedures and information used in the development and revision of the material. On the one hand, each text was prepared by a writing team of mathematicians and mathematics teachers. As the material was prepared for tryout in classrooms, there was considerable comment, judgment, and selection exercised by the various members of the team. Classroom tryouts were then arranged to find out whether the text could be used comfortably by reasonably well-trained teachers. For most of the writing teams, one or more of the team members conducted a tryout classroom for extended use of the material. During these classroom tryouts, considerable information was obtained from the teachers which could be used by the writing teams in revising the text. The procedures for this formative evaluation varied from one writing team to the next. The procedures were informal, and the amount and quality of information gained from the classroom tryouts varied considerably. Yet this evaluation was extremely valuable[35] to the writing teams and contributed much to the quality of the textbooks. These procedures have also been described by Wooten.[36]

Once the classroom tryouts and the revisions of the text had been completed, and the presentation deemed feasible from the experience, there was further evaluation to find out whether the textbooks were actually doing anything; to see whether the students were actually learning mathematics while using them.

35. School Mathematics Study Group, *Philosophies and Procedures of the SMSG Writing Teams* (Stanford: SMSG, 1965).

36. William Wooton, *SMSG, The Making of A Curriculum* (New Haven: Yale University Press, 1965).

The wave of mathematics curriculum reform, represented by SMSG and by several other projects, had resulted in two diametrically opposed points of view in the scientific community. There were some who felt that the new curriculum materials were an unfortunate departure from the tried and true curriculum of the past and that their use would result in drastically inferior student achievement of skills and knowledge. Many others felt that the new curriculum materials were a vast improvement over what had been available in the past and that their use would result in great improvements in student achievement.

Such feelings, in the mathematical community at least, were so strong that an early evaluation of the new materials and a comparison of them with conventional curricula seemed necessary. Accordingly, achievement over one academic year by students using the secondary school texts produced by the School Mathematics Study Group was compared with achievement by students using a conventional text. This study was carried out in the academic year 1960–61.[37]

The results showed that both the fears and the hopes had been exaggerated. While there were some differences in achievement in the two groups of students, the differences were not spectacularly large.

Unfortunately, this reduction of fears and hopes was the only outcome of this evaluation. The instruments used in the evaluation were so broad and covered such a wide variety of topics and problem types that no conclusions could be drawn as to which aspects of the curricula were responsible for such differences as did appear. Consequently, no guidance was provided for further curriculum development.

Furthermore, while the evaluation did demonstrate that students using the SMSG texts did learn certain topics not included in the conventional curriculum, no evidence was provided about the value of these topics either for problem solving or for further learning of mathematics. Consequently, no guidance was provided to those school administrators responsible for selection of textbooks.

Realizing the shortcomings of this evaluation and the continuing need for curriculum revision, the SMSG Advisory Board asked that a large-scale effort be undertaken to obtain quantitative information

37. Payette, *op. cit.*

which would be useful in further curriculum development and also would be useful to school administrators in making decisions about curriculum problems. It was also noted at this time that the field of mathematics education needed a great deal of information on how students learn mathematics and on the variables that are related to mathematics achievement. With these considerations, and the interest in evaluation of the new mathematics curricula voiced by the National Science Foundation, school personnel, and the public, the National Longitudinal Study of Mathematical Abilities (NLSMA) was organized. The SMSG Panel on Tests[38] was appointed in the fall of 1961 and assigned the responsibility of organizing and directing the study. This panel of mathematicians, psychologists, and psychometricians adopted three objectives of the study, corresponding to the above types of needed information. These were: (*a*) to obtain information which could be used in future curriculum development, (*b*) to obtain information which could be used in the schools for decision making on curriculum problems, and (*c*) to obtain, as far as possible, information useful for basic research in mathematics education.

At its first few meetings, the Panel on Tests made a number of basic decisions about the first steps to be taken. The most important of these were:

1. Information gathering rather than hypothesis testing should be stressed. It was felt that not all important hypotheses could be stated in advance. Therefore, a large pool of measured subjects should be established from which samples could be drawn to test various hypotheses as they were developed. (On the other hand, many of the tests developed during the study were obviously based on hypotheses, even though they may not have been completely formulated.)
2. Student achievement, both cognitive and affective, should be measured for students in a wide variety of curricula.
3. Long-term effects were of major interest, so students should be tested periodically over several years.
4. A large number of variables could be identified which might influence mathematics achievement. As many of these as possible should be measured.

---

38. The members of this Panel were Richard Alpert, Harvard; Max Beberman, University of Illinois; E. G. Begle, Stanford; Robert Dilworth, California Institute of Technology; Jerome Kagan, Harvard; M. Albert Linton, Jr., William Penn Charter School; William Lister, SUNY-Stony Brook; Samuel Messick, Educational Testing Service; J. Fred Weaver, Boston University and University of Wisconsin; Arthur P. Coladarci, Stanford: and Lee J. Cronbach, Stanford.

5. Since it was unlikely that all relevant variables could be identified in advance and measured, the population to be studied should be large so that the effects of unmeasured variables could hopefully be randomized out.
6. The type of mathematics tests then available would not provide the detailed information desired, so new tests, restricted to fairly narrow specified topics, should be developed.
7. Since modern curricula for the primary grades had, at the time, only a restricted use, the study should begin with Grade IV.

Design of NLSMA

Figure 2 illustrates the design of NLSMA. A large population of students at each of the three grade levels was tested in the fall and spring of each year, beginning with the fourth, seventh, and tenth

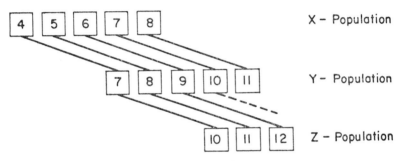

FIG. 2.–Design of NLSMA

grades in the fall, 1962. The X-Population and Y-Population were tested for five years. The Z-Population was tested for three years and then followed by means of a questionnaire after graduating from high school. The design stressed three features: (1) the long-term study of groups of students—up to five years, (2) study of the same grade level at different times—for instance, the seventh and eighth grades in 1962–64 for the Y-Population and again in 1965–66 for the X-Population, and (3) extensive data on mathematics achievement for the fourth through the twelfth grades.

In the fall of 1962, there were over 110,000 students from 1500 schools in forty states participating in the study. There were about 35,000 students who were starting fourth grade, about 45,000 students who were starting seventh grade, and 30,000 students who were starting tenth grade. Schools were asked to participate with the understanding that they would not be required to make any adjustments in their curricula or in their procedures because of this study. The study was to be conducted in actual everyday situations. Care was taken to obtain schools using a variety of mathematics curricula.

In any long-term study following the same set of students, attrition will be a problem. Approximately 15 percent of the remaining population each year was lost in this study. This was due to a number of causes: families moved and the students were no longer in the schools participating in the study; a *few* schools decided that the time commitment of three hours for testing each fall and of three hours for testing each spring was too much; and some students were lost from the study in moving from an elementary school to a junior high school, or from a junior high school to a senior high school.

A tremendous mass of information was collected over the five years. Mathematics achievement was measured in each of the spring test sessions and in three of the fall sessions. A large number of psychological variables believed to be potentially relevant to the learning of mathematics were measured. Measuring instruments included cognitive tests such as those of IQ, spatial visualization, numerical reasoning, logical thinking, etc., and also a number of affective tests which provided measures of attitude toward mathematics, attitude toward schools, self-concept, and anxiety.

A good deal of information was obtained about the teachers—how much experience they had had, what their training had been like, and how they felt about teaching and about mathematics, Questionnaire data were obtained to describe the schools and the communities in which they were located.

A full description of each of the variables is given in the *NLSMA Reports*,[39] numbers 1–7 and 9.

Mathematics Tests in NLSMA

The mathematics tests used in NLSMA require a little more discussion. The NLSMA staff and its consultants, from the very beginning of the study, had a firm conviction that mathematics achievements is not a single thing. It is a very multivariate quantity; there are many aspects of mathematics achievement. The framework which was finally used for specifying mathematics achievement meaures is

39. The *NLSMA Reports* are detailed background and reference documents. A full list of them is given at the end of this chapter.

the model presented earlier in this chapter. The mathematics content was divided into a large number of compartments; but in general there were three major ones—number systems, geometry, and algebra. There are a few topics toward the end of the high school, such as analysis, functions, logarithms, and exponentials, for which measures do not fit well under these major headings, but the bulk of the mathematics achievement measures do. Under any particular major heading there are many smaller ones. For instance, within the number systems category there is "whole numbers" and within that there are the four major operations, the structure of the whole number system, and special topics such as systems of numeration.

More important than to make the finer content distinction, it was desired to test the mathematical abilities of students at different cognitive levels. For example, it was certainly desirable to know about the ability of the student to carry out routine computation. It may be a little hard to think of what computation would be in geometry, but within the definition of the computation level given with the model, there are a few things such as the routine construction involved in bisecting an angle. Carrying on the example with whole numbers for other cognitive levels, it was important to know how well students understood a given mathematical topic, or how well the students understood what the addition of whole numbers really means. And beyond that, it was desirable to assess how well students could solve both routine and nonroutine problems.

During the five years, a large number of mathematics achievement tests were developed. It was not possible to have an entry in every cell of the matrix, but a sample from year to year and from each of the three populations was attempted. For each student who participated in all five years of the study, there were approximately 100 different mathematical scales, sampling all of the cells of the matrix appropriate for the student's mathematics program. At the end of five years, there were data for a very substantial number of students and for each student a very long *vector* of measures, including mathematics achievement scores, psychological variable scores, a socioeconomic index, demographic data, teachers' scores, and school-community description variables.

From this immense bank of data many different kinds of information can be extracted. Some very substantial analyses have been undertaken by the SMSG Research and Analysis Section. The data bank will eventually be made available for mathematics educators who have questions of their own which can be answered from the NLSMA data.

Textbook Comparison Analyses in NLSMA

The first set of analyses completed by the SMSG Research and Analysis Section is a series of textbook comparison analyses. That is, it is a comparison of groups determined by the textbook which the students used in their mathematics classes. These analyses investigate the effects on student achievement that seem ascribable to the textbooks which they are using.

The design for these analyses involved an elaborate sequence of statistical procedures. The details of the procedures and the results are provided in *NLSMA Reports*, numbers 10–18. A brief description and summarization will be attempted here.

For each student, in each year of the study, the major textbook used in his mathematics instruction was identified. This information was examined and textbook groups were determined for the analyses on the basis of the textbook used in a particular grade, or a sequence of textbooks used over two or three grades. For the X-Population two analyses were possible. Data from students using specified textbook series in Grades IV, V, and VI were used for the first analysis, and the second analysis was of data from those students using specified textbook series in Grades VII and VIII. Four analyses were made for the Y-Population. The first was a comparison of groups using specified textbook series in Grades VII and VIII. The second was a comparison of groups using specified algebra textbooks in Grade IX. The third was a comparison of groups using specified geometry textbooks in Grade X, and the fourth was a comparison of groups using specified algebra 2 or intermediate mathematics textbooks in Grade XI. For the Z-Population, three analyses were done, one for each of the three years: Grade X, Grade XI, and Grade XII. The Grade X and Grade XI analyses parallel those done for the Y-Population in Grades X and Grade XI except that they were at an earlier year of the study. The Grade XII analysis is a comparison of groups determined by the type of mathematics course taken rather than of groups determined by a specific textbook. These analyses are reported in *NLSMA Reports*, numbers 10–18.

The unit of data for these analyses was the school. Actually, an elaborate design, fully described in *NLSMA Reports* noted above, was used to examine the data for boys and for girls separately and jointly in each school. Almost no interaction of sex and textbook effects was found[40] and therefore the analyses are based on the mean for each school.

The textbook groups were not formed just for this study. Rather, they were existing groups of schools, and it was known that the groups differed prior to the study. Analysis of covariance was judged most appropriate for analyzing the possible textbook-related effects when measures such as *Lorge-Thorndike Intelligence Tests* scores and previous mathematics-achievement test scores were used as the covariates. The use of analysis of covariance does not make an evaluation study such as this into an experiment. It remains correlational and differences between the groups are at most textbook related. That is, the differences that can be found between textbook groups may in fact not be caused by the textbook, but by other factors which also determine textbook selection. The results of such analysis are *hypotheses* about textbook-related phenomena, rather than conclusions.

An Illustrative Analysis from NLSMA

The analysis of mathematics achievement in Grades IV, V, and VI is the topic of *NLSMA Report* number 10.[41] It is a comparison of six textbook groups over a period of three years' use. The achievement data were obtained from test batteries administered in the spring of 1963, 1964, and 1965, and from the fall of 1965 as the students began Grade VII. Six textbook series were identified as being used in enough NLSMA schools to be included in the analysis. Data for those students who used the same textbook series in the same school over the three grades were selected from the NLSMA files. School data on each variable were obtained by taking the mean for all boys and the mean for all girls in the school. The school-sex means were then combined to form the school units.

40. This does not mean that differences between boys' and girls' performance were not found, but rather that the effect of textbook was the same both for boys and for girls. Differences between boys' performance and girls' performance were of minor interest in these analyses.

41. L. Ray Carry and J. Fred Weaver, *Patterns of Mathematics Achievement in Grades 4, 5, and 6: X-Population, NLSMA Reports,* no. 10. See list of *Reports* at the end of the chapter.

The six textbook groups were contrasted on 38 variables. The analysis was completed in four parts—one part for each of the test sessions. Significant (p < .001) multivariate F-statistics were found for each part, indicating variation across the vectors of mean scores in the groups after adjustment for scores on verbal IQ, nonverbal IQ, and mathematics achievement variables from the beginning of Grade IV. These multivariate analyses were followed by univariate analysis of variance on the adjusted scores to locate the source of variation in each of the vectors. Significant (p < .05) variation was found on 37 of the 38 variables. There were approximately 300 schools in the analysis.

The variables on which significant variation occurred included eleven measures of number systems-computation, sixteen measures of number systems-comprehension, two measures of geometry comprehension, one measure of algebra comprehension, three measures of number systems-applications, two measures of number systems-analyses, and two measures of geometry analysis.[42]

One of the textbook groups, T1, was determined by the use of the SMSG textbooks in Grades IV, V, and VI. For each of the variables with significant variation, contrasts of the SMSG textbook group mean with each of the other textbook group means were examined and a t-statistic computed. These contrasts were discussed to analyze the *patterns* of mathematics achievement associated with each of the textbook groups.

Before discussing the additional means of examining and describing patterns of achievement, it should be noted that three of the six textbook groups were determined by their use of textbooks judged to be modern, and three groups were determined by their use of textbooks judged to be conventional in point of view and presentation of material. This identification of texts as modern or conventional was of course associated with a number of expectations—even though hypothesis testing was not a goal of the analysis. Rather, the goal was hypothesis *formation*.

Patterns of mathematics achievement were analyzed and displayed in three other ways. First, multiple discriminant analyses[43] were

42. These labels of groups of variables correspond to the cells of the model in Figure 1.

43. Multiple discriminant analysis is a statistical procedure in which the linear combination of variables is determined which maximally spreads the groups. The

performed on the vector of adjusted scores. While no claim can be made that the discriminant functions were the *same* for each of the parts of the analysis, there was some consistency. In most cases, two clusters of textbook groups did appear—the three modern textbook groups in one cluster and the three conventional ones in the other. The first dimension (the first, most important, discriminant function) usually was some contrast of comprehension-level scales on one end and computation-level scales on the other; the modern cluster tended to be toward the comprehension side and the conventional cluster toward the computation side. Also, in most cases, the second dimension was determined by an unusual spread of the textbook groups on one scale. Where distinct clusters were not formed, there seemed to be an unusual spread af the textbook means on one scale in the vector of scores.

Second, the adjusted scores were normalized to a mean of 50 and a standard deviation of 10. Then, for each scale, the means for the textbook groups were plotted and a 90 percent confidence interval displayed around each mean.

Third, a profile of achievement scores was plotted for each textbook. On these profiles, the means for all textbook groups were plotted in order to show the spread of groups on each variable and the position of a particular textbook on each variable indicated within the plot. For instance, the SMSG textbook group profile is given in Figure 3. The darkened marks are the SMSG group means. Scale codes for the 37 scales with significant variation are given across the bottom of the figure. These scales are grouped by cognitive level and then by content as indicated at the top of the figure.

These profiles use standardized scores; they communicate the position of a textbook group *relative to* the other groups in the analysis. They are useful for identifying areas of strength and weakness among

---

weights in the linear combination, the discriminant function coefficients, can then be examined to hypothesize or characterize the function of dependent variables. In a sense, this "describes" how the groups differ on the set of variables. The first discriminant function is then followed by a second which maximally spreads the groups in a way orthogonal to (uncorrelated with) the first. When scores from these two dimensions are plotted on a coordinate system, visual inspection can sometimes identify groups which cluster.
See R. Darrel Bock, "Contributions of Multivariate Experimental Designs to Educational Research," chap. 28 in *Handbook of Multivariate Experimental Psychology,* ed. Raymond B. Cattell (Chicago: Rand McNally, 1966), for a discussion of the use of discriminant analysis in this context.

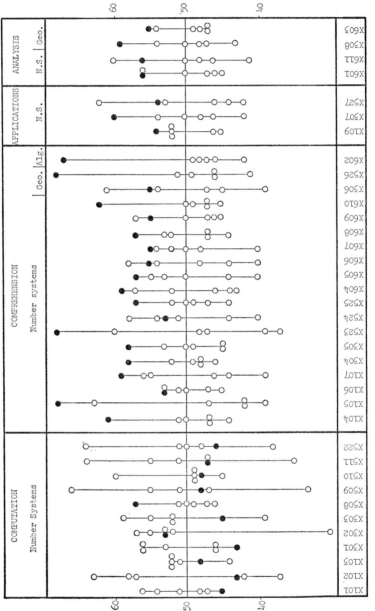

Fig. 3.—Profile for Textbook Group T1 (X-Population; Grades 4, 5, 6; Years 1, 2, 3)

the scales for each textbook.[44] It can be seen from Figure 3 that the SMSG textbook group exhibited relative weakness for computation scales. It was lowest, however, on only two of the eleven computation scales. The group was low on computation, but not extremely low. On the comprehension scales, the SMSG group is quite high relative to the other text groups, and similarly for the few applications and analysis scales. On the 37 scales, T^1 had the highest mean on 19. The weakness in computation scales is not severe; no mean is more than a standard deviation away from the grand mean of 50. On comprehension scales, several are more than a standard deviation above the grand mean.

One of the conventional textbook groups in the analysis was T_2.[45] The achievement profile for textbook T_2 is given in Figure 4. To some degree, this profile is almost a mirror image of that for the SMSG group, although for the entire set of variables this group is probably best characterized as average. Where the SMSG textbook group tended to be below the grand mean on computation, the T2 textbook group mean is above it, but not far above. And whereas the SMSG textbook group was above the grand mean on all comprehension, application, and analysis scales, textbook group T2 tends to be below or near the grand mean.

Unfortunately, these patterns do not generalize. That is, the modern textbook groups do not all have an achievement profile like that in Figure 3, and the conventional textbook groups do not all have an achievement profile like that in Figure 4. On the contrary, there appears to be as much variation among the modern textbook groups as there is between the modern and the conventional. Also there is considerable variation among the conventional.

One additional profile from this analysis will suffice, for this example of a NLSMA analysis, to show a rather different pattern for a conventional textbook group, T6. This profile is given in Figure 5. The group is very strong on computation measures, shows great variability across comprehension measures, generally improving from

44. The profiles, however, are subject to misinterpretation. The reader should not infer that the SMSG textbook group does better on scale X_{105} than on scale X_{104} (see Figure 3) for the between group variation on X_{104} is less than the between group variation on X_{105}. To infer that the SMSG group does better on X_{105} than on X_{104} does not take into account the characteristics of the measures.

45. See Carry and Weaver, *loc. cit.*, for a full identification and comparison of the textbook groups.

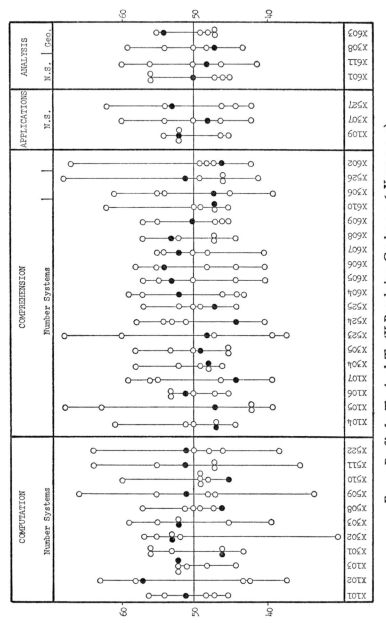

FIG. 4.—Profile for Textbook T2 (X-Population; Grades 4, 5, 6; Years 1, 2, 3)

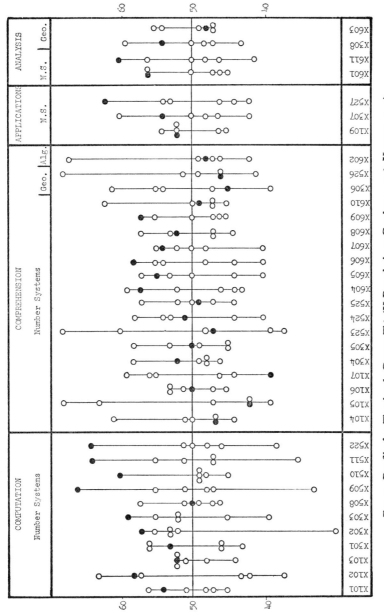

FIG. 5.—Profile for Textbook Group T6 (X-Population; Grades 4, 5, 6; Years 1, 2, 3)

fourth grade to sixth grade, and is fairly strong in application and analysis.

General Observations on the NLSMA Results

The preceding section gave an example of one of the NLSMA textbook comparison analyses. General trends in the results of these analyses, insofar as they have been identified, are noted in this section.

First, in general, the higher the grade level, the less seems to be the effect associated with the textbook. The greatest variation among textbook group means, and the greatest number of variables on which significant variation is found, occur in the lower grades. As one examines the analyses up to eleventh and twelfth grades, it is observed that the differences between textbook groups are quite small. It is clear that the trend is in the data; it is also clear that there is no simple explanation of it. The trend is probably the result of several factors—among which *may* be included the more adequate background of teachers, narrower range of aptitude in the students, increased capacity of students for individual study, and difficulty in building satisfactory measures of achievement at the upper grades. The NLSMA data does not provide much evidence for or against any of these possibilities (or others); the NLSMA data does indicate quite clearly that the trend is there.

The difference between the SMSG textbook group and most conventional textbook groups at any grade level is largely a contrast of computation-level scales on the one hand and understanding of mathematical ideas as indicated by comprehension-, application-, and analysis-level scales on the other. There are exceptions to this of course. In the example analysis in the last section, textbook group T6 did as well or better than the SMSG textbook group on most of the application- and analysis-level scales.

The sequence in which mathematical topics are taught, and the emphasis given them, varies from one textbook sequence to the next. This sequence must be kept in mind carefully in interpreting the NLSMA textbook comparison analysis results. For example, it was found at the end of Grade IV that one of the modern textbook groups was doing quite poorly on a measure of division of whole numbers—more than a standard deviation below the grand mean. One of the conventional textbook groups was just the opposite; it appeared to be doing very well. Another measure of division of whole numbers was given at the end of Grade V and both of these textbook groups were right at the grand mean. Examination of the textbooks showed that the conventional one put a lot of emphasis on division in Grade IV and then very little more in Grade V. The modern text barely introduced division in Grade IV and put a lot of time on it in Grade V. The sequence of mathematical topics must be considered in interpretation of the data.

The example above can be extended a bit to underscore the importance of examining the long-term development of mathematics achievement. At the end of Grade IV the conventional text was clearly superior to the modern text on division. At the end of Grade V they were equally good. But on a similar measure at the end of Grade VI for division of decimals, the modern textbook group was far above the average and the conventional textbook group was average. The long-term cumulative effects for development of a division algorithm seemed to support the sequence and emphasis in the modern text. Unfortunately, these NLSMA textbook comparison analyses do not deal with long-term, cumulative effects. Textbook sequences are not identifiable in the upper grades. Hence, the Grade IX algebra textbook comparison does not build on the cumulative effects of a sequence through Grades VII, VIII, and IX. Instead, these effects are adjusted out of the Grade IX analysis by using end of Grade VIII achievement measures as covariates.

In general, the results for the SMSG textbooks were favorable. But not all modern textbooks produced the kind of results that were expected for them. Some of them in fact did rather poorly on *all* levels —from computation to analysis. Those textbooks which did not do very well were for the most part considerably more formal and more rigorous than the SMSG textbooks. In the upper grades, more attention was paid to axiomatics and strict deduction than is paid by SMSG, and less, apparently, to understanding the basic concepts. This remark on the greater formalism is conjectural; it is an opinion as to a possible general explanation of the poor showing of some modern textbooks. It is an interesting lead into what could be helpful for further research. Parenthetically, no similar seemingly consistent observation has been made across conventional textbooks showing poor results.

The results of the NLSMA textbook comparison are exceedingly complex. There are not very many clear generalizations that can be made. There is variability among modern textbook groups and variability among conventional textbook groups, as well as the variability between modern and conventional textbook groups. The NLSMA results demonstrate that the simplistic question of "Which textbook is better?" is not appropriate and they emphasize the multivariate nature of mathematics achievement.

The NLSMA results have demonstrated well the importance of a range of criteria. There are clear examples in most every analysis of the reversal in the rank order of the means of two textbook groups in going from measures at one level to measures at another. The use of a single criterion, such as most standardized tests provide, will force one of two situations: Either (a) the criterion will come entirely from one level, and hence other levels will be ignored, or (b) the criteria will be summed across levels, and differences such as many of those found in the NLSMA analysis will be hidden.

Concluding Remarks

The revolution in school mathematics of the past decade or so has consisted mainly of the proposal, development, and dissemination of alternative curriculum programs. The same forces that spawned this revolution have brought about a modest amount of work in assessing the outcomes of these programs. But progress in mathematics program evaluation has been slow. This is partly because the object of an evaluation—a mathematics program—is a very complex phenomenon. Progress in mathematics program evaluation has also been delayed because of a lack of powerful evaluation techniques and a theoretical framework for organizing such evaluation, and because of the necessity to develop adequate instruments for the assessment of mathematics incomes.

This chapter has emphasized some of the general guidelines for mathematics program evaluation rather than attempting to provide specific advice on how to do an evaluation. Such specific advice just does not exist in any satisfactory form—again because the outcomes of mathematics instruction are very complex and because a wide variety of evaluation activities is needed. Grobman[46] has reviewed some

46. Hulda Grobman, *Evaluation Activities of Curriculum Projects: A Starting Point* (AERA Monograph Series on Curriculum Evaluation, no. 2 [Chicago: Rand McNally, 1968]).

evaluation activities of curriculum projects and offers some advice on how to do an evaluation. But, as her title suggests, what has been done and what is available represents only a starting point.

It is to be hoped that the development of practical and effective evaluation procedures will be carried out without delay so that school administrators and other interested parties can obtain the information needed for better curriculum decision making.

NLSMA has demonstrated the varying patterns of results that can occur when an organized multiple-outcome view of mathematical learning is taken. The evaluation of a mathematics program that is based on a single criterion will at best produce limited information; at worst it can be misleading by failing to show important characteristics.

A model of mathematics achievement can be extremely useful for an evaluation project. Within the basic framework of the model, the dimensions can be stated in greater detail for finer distinctions to suit the purposes of a particular evaluation. If there is a "how to do it" aspect of this chapter, it is an admonishment to use a model to analyze the outcomes of the mathematics program to be evaluated, to guide selection and preparation of measuring instruments, and to analyze the results.

Formative evaluation has received very little emphasis. This does not relegate it to a place of less importance. On the contrary, the potential for systematic formative evaluations is extremely good. Yet, there is only a limited body of literature on formative evaluation of mathematics programs. The absence of a thorough discussion and review of formative evaluation is in part a subtle protest that the topic deserves the literature for a full chapter of its own.

Another topic, hardly discussed in this chapter, is the noncognitive outcomes of mathematics programs such as attitudes, motivation, and appreciation. Future mathematics program evaluations should give more consideration to these outcomes in addition to mathematics achievement measures. Very little is understood about these outcomes and their interaction with cognitive outcomes. Much work is needed in theory building, experimentation, and the development of satisfactory instrumentation for assessing noncognitive outcomes.

NLSMA Reports

Edited by: James W. Wilson, Leonard S. Cahen, and Edward G. Begle

Published by: School Mathematics Study Group, Stanford University

Number

1. *X-Population Test Batteries.* Parts A and B. 1968.
2. *Y-Population Test Batteries.* Parts A and B. 1968.
3. *Z-Population Test Batteries.* 1968.
4. *Description and Statistical Properties of X-Population Scales.* 1968.
5. *Description and Statistical Properties of Y-Population Scales.* 1968.
6. *Description and Statistical Properties of Z-Population Scales.* 1968.
7. *The Development of Tests.* By Thomas A. Romberg and James W. Wilson. 1969.
8. *Statistical Procedures and Computer Programs.* By James W. Wilson and L. Ray Carry. (In preparation)
9. *Non-Test Data.* 1968.
10. *Patterns of Mathematics Achievement in Grades 4, 5, and 6: X-Population.* By L. Ray Carry and J. Fred Weaver. 1969.
11. *Patterns of Mathematics Achievement in Grades 7 and 8: X-Population.* By L. Ray Carry. 1969.
12. *Patterns of Mathematics Achievement in Grades 7 and 8: Y-Population.* By Gordon K. McLeod and Jeremy Kilpatrick. 1969.
13. *Patterns of Mathematics Achievement in Grade 9: Y-Population.* By Jeremy Kilpatrick and Gordon K. McLeod. 1969.
14. *Patterns of Mathematics Achievement in Grade 10: Y-Population.* By Gordon K. McLeod and Jeremy Kilpatrick. 1969.
15. *Patterns of Mathematics Achievement in Grade 11: Y-Population.* By Jeremy Kilpatrick and Gordon K. McLeod. 1969.
16. *Patterns of Mathematics Achievement in Grade 10: Z-Population.* By James W. Wilson. 1969.
17. *Patterns of Mathematics Achievement in Grade 11: Z-Population.* By James W. Wilson. 1969.
18. *Patterns of Mathematics Achievement in Grade 12: Z-Population.* By Thomas A. Romberg and James W. Wilson. 1969.

SECTION IV

SCHOOL ORGANIZATION FOR MATHEMATICS INSTRUCTION

CHAPTER XI

Differentiation of Mathematics Instruction

M. VERE DEVAULT AND THOMAS E. KRIEWALL

Introduction

This chapter is designed to assist educational workers in achieving better utilization of available instructional resources in order to more effectively meet the learning needs of individual pupils. Developing adequate systems for differentiating or individualizing instruction is a difficult task, and progress has been somewhat slower than some authoritative predictions had anticipated. However, there are signs that indicate a growing capability in many schools to cope with the economic, managerial, and instructional problems that differentiation of instruction necessarily incurs. The following remarks summarize the trends in this area and point to new directions which appear to be most promising at this time.

Differentiation of instruction is a concept which is interpreted in many ways by teachers, curriculum workers, mathematicians, and researchers. For the last two or three decades, attention has focused on problems of grouping pupils according to one or more learning parameters. Segregation into grades is the most common example of this practice. Here the parameter on which grouping is based is largely chronological age. In spite of the obvious administrative merits this scheme enjoys, the lock-step grade framework generates many pedagogical problems that have resisted attempts at solution.

The natural response to these problems has been to seek other, more effective, attributes on which to base grouping practices. The term "non-graded" comes to mind immediately as the notion opposite to grading. By itself, however, it is a negative concept and mainly suggests what not to do. In order to operate a non-graded system, one actually must seek other parameters on which to base the organization of learners into units for instruction. The uniqueness of the individual learner is, of course, the ultimate attribute on which to base differentiated instruction. Experience has shown, however, that one-to-one tutoring is not an economically viable approach to instruction, even where many of the management, sequencing, and record-keeping problems can be resolved.

Aptitude and achievement tests provide easily obtained measures which have been used to form instructional subgroups. One of the properties from which this technique suffers is the relative stability of these measures, an ironic property perhaps, but one that tends to keep individuals locked into a given group. This effect tends to demoralize further those students in the lower ability groups who probably are most in need of motivation and encouragement.

Another of the more obvious differential characteristics, detectable in any classroom, is the learning rate of the individual. This characteristic of learners is relatively easy to identify, witness the common use of such terms as the "slow," "average," or "fast" learner. In spite of some difficulties, rate of learning has been widely used as a basis for forming "rate homogeneous" learning groups.

These various techniques for organizing pupils into classes share one common objective. The purpose of grouping is to gather together learners having common attributes which presumably define a single set of learning needs. Therefore, in theory, the same instruction should be as effective for the group as it is for any one member. Partly because we can never successfully form a homogeneous group with respect to one parameter, let alone the several that significantly influence learning, the groups formed are sufficiently heterogeneous that group instruction invariably fails to meet important learning needs of some individuals in the group. For this and other reasons, instruction given to groups segregated according to one parameter usually seems to result in no significant difference when compared to the effects of instruction given to groups formed on the basis of another parameter.

In spite of the fact that measurable learning benefits are hard to identify, grouping practices continue for a variety of reasons. How we group children for common learning experiences depends on our educational purposes. In some areas of the curriculum, group dynamics are the *sine qua non* of the learning experience. In the elementary school especially, the socializing process as well as the democratization process depends vitally on having groups possessing the maximum possible variation in attributes. In certain kinds of special education, such as teaching the emotionally disturbed or the physically handicapped, one may have to go to some lengths to minimize the all-too-obvious individuality of the exceptional child. In such cases, the instructional strategies may be primarily directed toward integrating individuals into a natural framework of group interaction.

However, to teach mathematics effectively demands that one be concerned with the individual, for mathematics learning is a highly individual matter. Mathematical ideas, skills, and structures surely are learned on an individual basis even though we can, as individuals, benefit from assistance given by others or by witnessing their behavior in performing mathematical processes as an example for our own behavior.

Suppes has been one of the most assiduous investigators of the inherent differences which exist between individuals in their capacity to learn mathematics. From his observations, he has formed one definition of individualization of instruction that places emphasis on the need to provide a unique experience for each learner. Individualization, he writes, is the "adaptation of an educational curriculum in a unique fashion to individual learners—each of whom has his own characteristic initial ability, rate, and even 'style' of learning, to provide him a successful learning experience."[1]

More modest conceptions of individualized instruction are entertained by those who face the insurmountable obstacles which put such an ideal well beyond the pale of present practice. Gage and Unruh, for example, suggest that much individualization of instruction goes on in the conventional classroom. This form of individualization is due primarily to the selectivity of the learner rather than as a result of any special plan by the instructor. In this view, there is a "kind of 'spraying' of stimuli, ideas, questions, and answers that goes on in a relatively unplanned (unprogrammed) way in the conventional classroom [which] does succeed nonetheless, by virtue of its near randomness, in hitting most pupils where they are."[2]

These two concepts of individualized instruction, diverse as they

1. Patrick Suppes, "The Uses of Computers in Education," *Scientific American*, CCXV (September, 1966), 207–20.

2. N. L. Gage and W. R. Unruh, "Theoretical Formulations for Research in Teaching," *Review of Educational Research*, XXXVII (June, 1967), 358–70.

appear to be, do share at least one common feature. That is the sensed need to do a better job of meeting the unique needs of the individual in a system of mass education—of "hitting the learners where they are."

Much of the innovative effort of the 1960's has focused on problems associated with the differentiation of instruction. Encompassing not only mathematics but the entire curriculum as well, the National Society for the Study of Education and the Association for Supervision and Curriculum Development published in 1962 and 1964, respectively, yearbooks entitled *Individualizing Instruction*.[3] In the field of mathematics education, Weaver has presented a comprehensive review of the literature concerned with differentiation of instruction in which individualization was seen as only a part of the total effort to meet the individual needs of learners.[4]

Just as the perceptions of what constitutes individualized instruction vary with observers, the purpose of seeking to perform this educational service varies greatly from one situation to another. The first significant attempts to build programs especially designed to meet individual needs were probably the programed texts that grew out of the work of Skinner,[5] Crowder,[6] and many others. The pragmatic concern of these materials, which appeared in many classrooms nearly a decade ago, was to feed material to the learner at a rate consistent with his unique intellectual metabolism. After a brief flurry, stirred up by the belief that a solution had been found, hopes waned considerably while criticism of the process grew. Not only was it hard to find convincing evidence that the quality of the learning experience had been enhanced by the use of these materials, but also

3. *Individualizing Instruction* (Sixty-first Yearbook of the National Society for the Study of Education, Part I [Chicago: Distributed by the University of Chicago Press, 1962]); *Individualizing Instruction* (1964 Yearbook of the Association for Supervision and Curriculum Development [Washington, D.C.: The Association, 1964]).

4. J. Fred Weaver, "Differentiated Instruction and School-Class Organization for Mathematical Learning within the Elementary Grades," *The Arithmetic Teacher*, XIII (October, 1966), 495–506.

5. B. F. Skinner, "Teaching Machines" in *Teaching Machines and Programmed Learning: A Source Book*, eds. A. A. Lumsdaine and R. Glaser (Washington, D.C.: Department of Audiovisual Instruction, National Education Association, 1960).

6. Norman A. Crowder, "Automatic Tutoring by Means of Intrinsic Programming" in *Teaching Machines and Programmed Learning: A Source Book*, eds. A. A. Lumsdaine and R. Glaser (Washington, D.C.: Department of Audiovisual Instruction, National Education Association, 1960).

there was a growing conviction that indeed the experience provided by such materials was the very opposite of individualization, at least insofar as the purpose was concerned. Every learner traveled the same path to the same end, varying only the time at which he arrived at the prescribed objective. Although the use of programed materials in the schools declined perceptibly, researchers continued to explore the potential of the medium. An important path was opened by Crutchfield and others who worked toward extending programed instruction to embrace teaching creativity.[7] Others in recent years such as Lindvall and Bolvin have attempted to implement means of varying the *paths* as well as the *rate* in their individually prescribed instructional programs.[8]

Many are looking carefully today at the possibilities of utilizing the technology of time-sharing computer facilities to monitor the learner's performance and to diagnose and prescribe automatically the next step to take in the pupil's learning experience. For the most part, these efforts appear to share a common goal—the purpose being to let the gifted students achieve to the maximum of their potential without undue stress, tension, and pressure while permitting the less talented to proceed to the best of their abilities, free of frustration and humiliation. Johnson has summed up this approach by saying that individualized instruction should challenge " . . . each child, at all times during his continuous development, to reach his maximum intellectual, social, and emotional growth."[9]

Notwithstanding the heavy preponderance of generalized statements about what individualization of instruction involves, there seems to be a growing consensus that if individual learning needs are to be met in our classrooms, patterns of differentiated instruction must move increasingly from grouping to individualized modes. Summarizing his review of fourteen experimental studies of arithmetic grouping, Brewer concludes that ". . . more favorable achievement results can be expected from arithmetic teaching as grouping prac-

7. Richard S. Crutchfield and Martin V. Covington, "Programmed Instruction and Creativity," *Theory into Practice*, V (October, 1966), 179–83.

8. C. M. Lindvall and John O. Bolvin, "Programed Instruction in the Schools: An Application of Programing Principles in 'Individually Prescribed Instruction,' " *Programed Instruction* (Sixty-sixth Yearbook of the National Society for the Study of Education, Part II [Chicago: University of Chicago Press, 1967]), pp. 217–54.

9. Charles E. Johnson, "Grouping Children for Arithmetic Instruction," *The Arithmetic Teacher*, I (February, 1954), 16–20.

tices move toward the individualized end of the continuum."[10] On the assumption that educators and their curricula have placed ceilings on children's learning rates, the Rasmussens say that "The basic and most difficult job ahead of teachers is to analyze their classroom role and to modify it if needed in order not to stand in the way of children's learning."[11] Suppes expressed the belief that the more individualized classroom teaching becomes, the more it will facilitate a speed of learning and a depth of understanding that now seems impossible to achieve.[12]

Although there seems to be minor disagreement about what differentiation of instruction really involves and about what procedures have the greatest promise for solving problems in this area, there does seem to be general consensus on a number of related basic assumptions. The first of these is that individual differences among learners in our classrooms do exist and that they exist along a number of dimensions which may include learning rate, learning style, interest, motivation, and background. There seems to be consensus that children are capable of learning more and also more effectively than they now do in our schools. That the search for an easy answer to this complex problem is doomed to disappointing results also appears as a general view in the mathematics education community. Finally, there seems to be consensus that the world of technology must be thoroughly explored as to its potential in providing solutions to some of these problems. True, there is little agreement concerning the extent to which this source of assistance is likely to produce significant improvements in our educational efforts, but most educators agree that we should make full exploration of the possibilities of technology. Much of the innovative effort at the time of this writing seems to be moving in this direction.

Consensus is conspicuously lacking at the point of our commitment to differentiation or individualization of instruction in mathematics. Full individualization of instruction implies that the content, the sequence, the processes, and the very goals of the curriculum will differ from one learner to the next. The historical role of the school

10. Emery Brewer, "A Survey of Arithmetic Intraclass Grouping Practices," *The Arithmetic Teacher*, XIII (April, 1966), 310–14.

11. Don Rasmussen and Lore Rasmussen, "The Miquon Mathematics Program," *The Arithmetic Teacher*, IX (April, 1962), 180–87.

12. Patrick Suppes, "Plug-in Instruction," *Saturday Review* (July 23, 1966), 25–30.

in this country has been one of providing a common education for all. Until quite recently, the great need in mathematics education as well as in other aspects of the total educational enterprise was to provide a means of melding one society out of the peoples coming from many cultural backgrounds. The recognition of need for the continued development of this common educational background seems to be well entrenched and runs counter to the idea of building programs which will extend the diversity of products coming from our schools. In fact, part of the confusion here might well be related to the fact that the task of providing the common educational experience for all youth has not been satisfactorily achieved, and now we have been directed to answer questions about problems designed to counter the direction of an unfinished task in American education.

A Systems Approach to Differentiation of Instruction

One way of looking at a complex problem which is useful for identifying and isolating important sub-components is the *systems approach*. Romberg and DeVault have recently developed a systems model of mathematics curriculum which seems especially well suited for the analysis of differential mathematics instruction.[13] In this view of the mathematics curriculum, we consider four major inputs, as shown in Figure 1. The content, the instruction, the teacher, and the learner all possess certain variable characteristics or parameters which are essential to consider when designing the operational stage of the system, i.e., the individual learning experience. The parameters which either singly or in some combination have been the basis of design for both theoretical and applied projects of individualized mathematics instruction are shown in the input boxes. Currently, various new programs, development projects, research activities, and school practices frequently reflect innovation at the point of input for one or more of these four components. However, the state of the art at the present time is such that the focus of any given innovation can be described in terms of a single component.

Variability is the key to successful individualization of instruction. If we are to understand the nature of optimal individualization, we must understand the potential for variability at every input point of

13. Thomas Romberg and M. Vere DeVault, "Mathematics Curriculum: Needed Research," *Journal of Research and Development in Education,* I (Fall, 1967), 95–112.

the instructional system. At each input we need to search for those parameters which when altered result in improved mathematics learning for the individual student.

THE CONTENT COMPONENT

Within the content input as presented in Figure 1, one has a number of options to exercise, either singly or jointly, in order to tailor

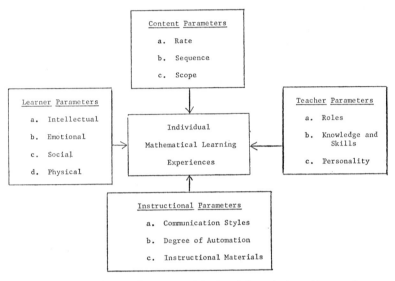

FIG. 1.—Mathematics curriculum model: the differentiation of instruction

the learning experience to individual needs. Perhaps the most common technique of individualizing the content input has been the provision for the learner to proceed at his own rate through some body of material with fixed scope. The early Skinnerian teaching machines were especially concerned with this particular form of individualization.

However, rate seems not to be the only important parameter to adjust to the learner's special needs. If variable rate is provided for, two kinds of problems frequently occur. One is that the learner still may proceed at an inappropriate rate—one not well adapted to his own learning needs. This maladaptive behavior has many causes and seems to require closer control of the learning process than simple forms of programed learning appear to be able to provide. This problem has been partially responsible for increased attention being given to computer-assisted instruction.

The second kind of important problem which arises in programs which focus entirely on the adjustment of rate is a variety of effects which can be lumped under the general heading of stimulus deprivation. Most such programs may broaden the stimuli to include listening to tape recordings. But almost all are deficient in verbal interaction between pupil and peer or pupil and teacher.

Ironically, rate-dedicated programs can provide significantly less individualization of instruction than other techniques, simply because all pupils follow the same path to the same end with the only difference lying in the time it takes to get there. Such programs may prove in actuality to be little more than effective drill programs of limited scope and utility.

One of the early variants of simple programing, often referred to as Crowder or branched programing, attempted to make use of the student's errors to decide which of several alternate branches or *sequences* he should undertake to learn next. This option is indicated in the content input of Figure 1 as the second adjustable parameter for individualizing instruction. In the simplest form that such a program might take, the scope of the content remains fixed but alternate paths to the fixed goals are provided. This technique not only has the same deficiency as the linear program mentioned before in that all learners ultimately are expected to reach the same goal, but it also introduces a difficult new problem related to the technique for deciding at a branch point *which* of the several available alternative branches a given learner should take. Decision systems of various kinds have been and are being worked on. However, the complexity of the problem is such that no early solution seems to be in sight.

Recently, a number of efforts have been made to provide more effective individualization by varying the *scope* of the curriculum, the third parameter indicated in the systems diagram of Figure 1. One might include under the heading of "variable scope" such a practice as *enrichment*.

Enrichment, in the usual sense, envisions a basic curriculum menu with a little dessert. However, some thought has been given to the possibility of opening up the curriculum from the fixed forms characteristic of past practice to include a wide variety of topics in which learners might conceivably be interested. Efforts are underway to ex-

tend mathematics learning experiences far beyond the four fundamental operations on whole numbers and fractions to include serious
forays into areas of mathematics regarded only a decade ago to be of
sole interest to mathematicians and far too advanced for elementary
school pupils.

One simple way of attempting to provide variable scope is through
the use of a textbook series which provides a great variety of topics
for study. The particular choice can be made either by the teacher or
by the learner. In view of the increased emphasis being given to the
need for the learner to learn how to take increasing responsibility
for his own educational goals, as urged by the American Institute for
Research (AIR) in the conclusions drawn from Project TALENT,[14]
two kinds of variable scope programs are currently under study.
One, typified by a number of computer-assisted tutorial programs,
attempts to employ modern high-speed computers to monitor student responses, decides what learning experience to provide as the
next step, and presents and controls the step decided upon. In this
way, each learner conceivably could be routed through different
material toward different goals within the same broad subject matter
areas. A second approach is to turn responsibility for the selection decision over to the learner, using members of a teaching team to assist
and guide him as the need arises. The project known as IMCP (Individualized Mathematics Curriculum Project) under the direction of
DeVault at the University of Wisconsin is an example of this second
approach to the problem of individualized scope.[15]

THE LEARNER COMPONENT

The complexity of the task of individualization is rooted in the
nature of differences which exist among learners. Problems centered
around the nature of these differences may be seen at two levels. One
level is the point of contact between the individual learner and the
experiences he derives from the environment in which he finds himself. Notwithstanding the extensive progress which has been made in

14. John C. Flanagan, "Developing a Functional Model on an Educational
System for the '70's" (paper delivered to the American Institute for Research,
Westinghouse Learning Corporation, February 19, 1967).

15. K. A. Neufeld, *Differences in Personality Characteristics between Groups
Having High and Low Mathematical Achievement Gain under Individualized
Instruction* (unpublished doctoral dissertation, University of Wisconsin, 1967),
pp. 49–53.

some areas through psychological investigation and research, very little is known about the nature of the individual learner which can be useful to the teacher who seeks information about matching learner characteristics with learning opportunities in a classroom. In the absence of such knowledge, programs which emphasize self-selection and self-pacing by the individual learner would seem to be preferred over those which prescribe specific learning environments for specific learners on the basis of scant evidence—research or otherwise.

The success of a self-selection, self-pacing environment is dependent on both the quality and the variety of learning opportunities in content, in instructional mode, and in person-to-person contact. Such self-pacing environments obviously do not now exist. Their development and establishment in schools is essential if we are to provide a context within which problems centered around the nature of learner differences and their impact on classroom learning are to be better understood.

Because the learner variables which seem to be of importance are both elusive and numerous, the interaction of the various input components as shown in Figure 1 can be investigated most thoroughly, if not always with the greatest precision, in the complex environment of the classroom designed to optimize self-selection and self-pacing.

Intellectual factors.—Differentiation of instruction has often been provided for through some kind of homogeneous grouping. Tyler, several years ago, reported on the intraindividual variability among pupils in a given junior high school and concluded that the "... data unmistakably show the existence of extensive intraindividual differences ... that groups or grades or classes, homogeneous with respect to scores on some specific test, are far less homogeneous, and likely quite heterogeneous, as far as their scores on other tests are concerned."[16] Such evidence, which is corroborated by many studies, explains the lack of consistently effective results of homogeneous grouping practices as procedures in organizing for differentiation of instruction.[17]

Undoubtedly there is a great array of intellectual factors upon

16. Fred T. Tyler, "Intraindividual Variability," *Individualizing Instruction*, (Sixty-first Yearbook of the National Society for the Study of Education, Part I [Chicago: Distributed by the University of Chicago Press, 1962]), pp. 164–74.

17. Ruth B. Eckstrom, *Experimental Studies of Homogeneous Grouping: A Review of the Literature* (Princeton, N.J.: Educational Testing Service, 1959).

which learners in a given classroom differ. Each of these in its own way and in interaction with other factors contributes to the appropriateness of a given experience at a particular time in the academic life of the learner. Ability and past achievement are the most obvious ones and those which have received the greatest emphasis in the testing and measurement field. They are, therefore, the ones to which we turn most readily for bases on which to make choices for individual learners. It is likely, however, that learning styles[18] and learning sets[19] are both intellectual factors which contribute to the success or lack of success of a given mathematical learning experience.

Emotional factors.—Individualization of instruction which emphasizes the importance of self-selection and self-pacing places a heavy reliance on the independence with which a learner is able to deal with the decision-making situations he faces. The dependence-independence factor in youth is one which has been the subject of much study. Independence apparently varies greatly among learners in our classes. The extent of independence which boys and girls develop has been reported by various researchers to be related to factors associated with home background and relations with parents.[20] These results add another dimension to the complexity of any attempt to individualize instruction. It becomes evident that for some children self-selection becomes an act requiring a degree of independence which they do not possess. Therefore, the extent of self-direction expected of a learner must also be treated as an important parameter.

Social factors.—As stated earlier, mathematics would seem to be one subject area of study which could be undertaken without major concern for the role of one's peer group. As opposed to social studies where the objectives of instruction can hardly be met without participation in discussion and other activities with classmates, certain mathematics goals can be achieved independently. This is not to say

18. Zoltan P. Dienes, "Some Basic Processes Involved in Mathematics Learning," in *Research in Mathematics Education*, ed. J. M. Scandura (National Council of Teachers of Mathematics, 1967), pp. 21–34; John W. French, "The Relationship of Problem-Solving Styles to the Factor Composition of Tests," *Educational and Psychological Measurement*, XXV (Spring, 1965), 9–28.

19. Harry F. Harlow, "The Formation of Learning Sets," *Psychological Review*, LVI (January, 1949), 51–65; Robert M. Gagne, "The Acquisition of Knowledge," in *Research in Mathematics Education*, ed. J. M. Scandura (National Council of Teachers of Mathematics, 1967), pp. 6–20.

20. Harold E. Jones and Mary C. Jones, *Growth and Behavior in Adolescence* (Berkeley: University Extension, University of California, 1960).

that they can best be achieved independently by all learners. Some children working in individualized programs seem to require the motivation which is engendered through a close working relationship with peers with whom they make choices and plan their learning activities. The degree of participation in this kind of group-structuring activity would seem to be an important adjustable parameter of the fully individualized learning environment.

Another social factor involved in the environment is the relationship between teacher and learner. This relationship may involve the one-to-one tutor role, or it may be in the form of the small seminar in which learners with similar interests and backgrounds work together in the development of particular mathematical understandings. There seems to be some evidence, however, that for many children—perhaps particularly for those alienated youth whose motives prompt a rejection of authority figures in the classroom—the "adult-free learning environment" might have a high priority among their choices of factors designed to enhance mathematics learning activity. This suggests something of the variation in the teacher's role one might consider when designing an individualized curriculum.

Physical factors.—Particularly among young children, physical readiness is an important input factor to consider in any plans for building mathematics learning experiences. Such factors play an especially important role among students who are in various special-education categories.

Within the instruction component, the primary variable that must be considered is the *communication style* of the teacher. The communication modes also interact strongly (*a*) with the degree of automation made possible through the use of computer-assisted instruction and (*b*) with the use of various instructional materials. All three parameters—method of communicating, automation, and materials—must be carefully considered when designing the instructional input to the system. Present educational research and development efforts are directed toward finding more effective modes of instruction and toward increasing understanding of their role in the improvement of learning. Little has been done to investigate the advantages of specific modes for learners of particular characteristics as they study given mathematical content. Until a wide variety of instructional modes—each appropriate at a given moment—become available to learners, optimal individualization cannot be claimed. Although little has been done to make a wide variety of modes available to a given learner, much work is under way to improve our understanding of specific communication styles, the role of computer-assisted instruction, and the value of instructional materials.

Communication styles.—At the outset it should be said that in the elementary school all teachers individualize instruction. This is a fact which should be strongly emphasized even though it has often been overlooked. Many of the new programs which emphasize individualization have little acceptance among teachers because they begin within a context which is foreign to elementary school classroom practices. The task the teacher faces in adopting these new programs appears to be overwhelming, and teachers too often choose not to become involved in such extensive reorientation. A more modest approach to the improvement of instructional strategies (and yet perhaps more fruitful in producing desired results in the long run) may be to emphasize the ways in which teachers are currently individualizing and to extend their ideas in what seem to be productive directions.

The lecture is one form of instruction in which no individualization takes place. A lecture may be given to a group of pupils about whom the lecturer knows very little; it may be put on audio or video tape and replayed to classes without losing its initial impact. The lecture is a method of providing information in a manner not unlike that of a book or a film. We recognize that the book is not a teacher but too often we fail to recognize that the lecturer is also not a teacher. Teachers in the elementary school seldom lecture; however, a predominate form of teaching in the elementary school classroom is the lecture-discussion. It is through *discussion* that individualization may proceed. If individual differences are met in these kinds of conventional classroom settings, it happens to the extent that the teacher is perceptive of the needs, the interests, the abilities, and the achievements of his pupils on a day-to-day, moment-to-moment basis. There has been little research related to the role of *teacher perception* in the meeting of individual differences. It may be assumed, however, that teachers vary considerably in their perceptiveness of differences among their pupils. We know almost nothing of the ways in which this perception affects communication or of the ways in which teacher perception can be enhanced.

It is through listening to the pupil that the teacher learns of the pupil's understanding. The lecture-discussion may be seen as a sequence through which the teacher provides information about the content of the lesson and the pupil provides information about himself. Whether the learner is asking or answering questions, the teacher has an opportunity to evaluate that learner as an individual each time he speaks. Olver discusses this matter in the context of the expansion-reduction communication theory in teaching.[21] The teacher makes a statement about a particular phenomenon and either through a question or other verbal means invites response from the class. A child's response reflects his understanding of the topic. He has reduced the statement made by the teacher to one which meets his understanding. Taking the cue from this reduction response, the teacher responds by expanding a bit on the pupil's comment. The same pupil or another picks up the communication and responds again with an indication of reduction in comparison to the teacher's comment. This reduction-expansion sequence continues as the teacher expands the pupils' understanding of the concept.

The teacher individualizes throughout a discussion in still other ways. In the direction of questioning, the teacher attempts to "tailor" the question to the pupil. Being asked to answer a question which is either too easy or too difficult is embarrassing to a student. It contributes nothing to his understanding. It is likely to decrease his self-confidence and increase his antipathy toward mathematics. Therefore, the teacher selectively directs his questioning. As the sequence progresses, he is aware of the nature of the challenge represented in the question and of the students for whom that particular question might extend understanding and those for whom it will not. The skillful teacher also carefully evaluates the kinds of questions he is asking and the kinds of understandings which are required by the appropriate responses.[22] Individual differences are respected, encouraged, and nourished through the kind of acceptance the teacher gives

21. Rose Olver, "Tutor and Learner," *Learning about Learning: A Conference Report,* ed. J. S. Bruner (Cooperative Research Monograph No. 15, Office of Education, U.S. Department of Health, Education, and Welfare, Washington, D.C., 1966), pp. 93–97.
22. Norris Sanders, *Classroom Questions: What Kinds?* (New York: Harper & Row, 1966).

pupil responses. The master teacher recognizes that his questions should be varied in the extent to which they require different kinds of answers. Some questions require factual or knowledge responses, whereas others require more of an application or synthesis-type response.[23] The competent teacher uses questions from among these various types. Responses from some higher types, beyond the simple fact kind of question, may provoke a wide variety of secondary responses and, here again, the effective teacher is able to draw heavily upon this variety to support the individual differences of his students. He is also aware that a kind of response which represents a particularly thoughtful reaction on the part of one student will not represent the same thoughtfulness on the part of another, and the reward embodied in his reaction is adjusted by this awareness.

Another aspect of communication relates to the importance of pupil-pupil interaction. By far the greatest amount of communication in the classroom is of the teacher-pupil variety. Nonetheless, we have long known that much learning takes place when peers communicate among themselves. In many classrooms this is encouraged through open discussion. Experienced teachers report times when their own efforts to explain something to a pupil have been eclipsed by another pupil who interjected briefly with an effectiveness to be envied by any master teacher. Recent recognition of this phenomenon is represented in some of the efforts in the inner-city programs to have much of the assistance and leadership come from among those to be helped. A kind of empathy and understanding exists in such a situation which is difficult for an outsider to emulate. And the teacher is, for the most part, an outsider.

Computer-assisted instruction (CAI).—Progress in the application of CAI can be measured by looking at the kinds of problems that have in some sense been solved and those which are still under study. For this purpose, it is convenient to classify programs (after Suppes) as drill-and-practice systems, tutorial systems, and dialogue systems.[24] The first kind, drill-and-practice, closely resembles earlier forms of programed instruction in which the material was tightly sequenced and presented in small bits to the learner; a response was accepted and

23. Benjamin A. Bloom *et al.*, *Taxonomy of Educational Objectives Handbook I: Cognitive Domain* (New York: David McKay Co., 1956).

24. Suppes, "Plug-in Instruction," *loc. cit.*

checked for speed and accuracy; and a decision was made by the computer as to what the next question or problem would be. Two advantages of special importance come through use of the computer. First, one can use either *error rate* or *response latency* (the time between presentation of the stimulus and the learner's response) as the basis for branching. Latency, as measured by an internal clock in the computer, has appeared to be a more important and useful guide for branching decisions than the error rate. Without the computer, there would be no convenient way of measuring latencies on each trial.

The second important advantage that accrues from using a computer lies in *data collection* and *manipulation*. Considerable amounts of data concerning the individual student and his performance can be collected, stored, referenced, and analyzed quickly and accurately. The main effect of this capacity lies in the reduction of the feedback time between student response and reinforcement, and in improved techniques for prescribing the next step.

The second kind of CAI program is much more sophisticated than simple drill-and-practice work. In the tutorial mode, the computer stores portions or possibly all of a course of study in memory, on film loops, or on audio tapes. In this mode, the individual pupil sits before a TV-like scope terminal which has something resembling a typewriter keyboard attached and perhaps a rear-view projection device under computer control situated next to the scope face. The learner may wear a headset to listen to audio messages which are in a state of rapid development; the most common mode by which the pupil may respond to the computer at the present time is through the teletype keyboard or by pointing a "light-pen" at some portion of the light-sensitive scope face. The computer accepts either the typed response or the coordinates at which the light appears on the scope face and determines the appropriateness of the response. Present systems are capable of handling simultaneously numbers of pupils approximating a small class, and they provide individual sequences of study, careful control of step-by-step performance, and a fair variety of visual and auditory stimuli. The capacity to use a central computer facility to handle larger numbers of remote terminals in the schools is currently under study and development. Tutorial modes are of such recent development that few have progressed to the "model school" stage of development. Serious problems of hardware reliability and cost as well as problems of software or program development remain to be solved before the model-school and wide-dissemination stages are likely to be reached.

There is less to report concerning the third kind of CAI system, the dialogue system. Some hope exists that means of interaction between pupil and computer can be simplified and extended to include direct voice communication at some time in the future. Regardless of the mode of man-machine communication, dialogue systems will attempt to accept the kind of variable conversations that arise in ordinary human interaction, evaluate the response, and proceed accordingly—much as two humans might do. Perhaps the closest approach to developing dialogue capacities is typified by the work of Starkweather at the University of California, Berkeley.[25] He has developed a kind of language called an "author language" which can be used to accept and respond to a wide variety of ordinary language communications which the learner might type in at the terminal. The PILOT system (Programed Instruction, Learning, or Teaching) had its genesis in an earlier problem which Starkweather attacked: that of interviewing subjects by means of computer terminals. In the last few years he has experimented with applications of the language in elementary school education with encouraging results.

TEACHER COMPONENT

There is ample evidence to indicate that teachers vary considerably in their knowledge of mathematics and in their attitudes toward mathematics. Although there is every reason to expect that these differences affect the achievement and attitudes of their students, the results of research on the matter are not clear. This is due, we suspect, to the many other uncontrolled variables which contribute to the behavior of every teacher as he meets students in the mathematics class. Personality, teaching style, and sensitivity to learners as individuals are all factors which influence the teacher's effectiveness with a given learner.

Thelen has hypothesized that particular teachers are more effective with some learners than with others and has tested the theory of teachable groups.[26] In his early reports he discussed ways in which

25. J. A. Starkweather, "A Chatty Computer in Room B-3," *Educom*, III (March, 1966), 3–6.

26. Herbert A. Thelen, *Education and the Human Quest* (New York: Harper & Row, 1960).

teachers might select those pupils with whom they believed they could be most effective. More recently it has seemed that with the flexibility of team teaching and non-graded forms of elementary school organization, it may become increasingly possible for learners to make choices from among those teachers who are available.

If it is possible to organize schools so that learners make choices among available teachers, then it would seem reasonable to expect that teachers should be made available to learners in greater variety than we typically find today. Teacher education programs may well turn their attention to the matter of individualizing their programs so that a variety of teacher characteristics rather than stereotypes emerge as products of our teacher education institutions.

In keeping with these ideas of providing the right teacher for the right child, Sears has suggested that research should be undertaken to determine the effect of the similarity between child and teacher on learning and the effects of one teacher versus multiple teachers on children's performance.[27] These suggested efforts are indicative of the attention which can be focused on parts of the total problem of determining the importance of adjusting specific teacher characteristics to the specific learner.

Technology and Individualization

In the last decade, great efforts have been made to harness the forces of technology to break the stubborn logjam of problems which have beset virtually all attempts to individualize instruction. Teaching machines in a number of forms made their appearance in the late fifties, and in the early sixties one began hearing about the marvelous things that soon would be done with the help of computers. New techniques of decision making based on something called *systems management* rumbled out of engineering schools around the country in the years following World War II. By the late fifties, the terminology and a little of the systems method were being applied to the problems of education. Man and machine slowly came to be viewed as an interacting unit called a *cybernetic system*. Reports circulated that rather astounding breakthroughs were being made that would

27. Robert Sears, "Product Pleasure," *Learning about Learning: A Conference Report*, ed. J. S. Bruner (Cooperative Research Monograph No. 15, Office of Education, U.S. Department of Health, Education, and Welfare, Washington, D.C., 1966), pp. 47–50.

soon show the way toward the brave new world. These somehow seemed slower in coming than expected. With several millions of dollars now having been spent on these efforts, it is appropriate to ask where we stand and what we can reasonably expect in the way of help to differentiate instruction and learning through partial automation.

It is easy to describe the present position of the schools with regard to automation of instruction. Aside from a very few exceptional schools, computer-assisted instruction is presently of little practical consequence in American elementary and secondary education. This means that there is no teaching of conventional mathematics subject matter being done with the assistance of computers that cannot be done just as effectively and at lower cost by means that do not involve computers. That is where we stand now.

These facts do not mean, however, that technology has no future in elementary and secondary mathematics education. In view of the many problems that remain essentially unsolved in spite of lengthy and strenuous efforts to find effective means of individualizing mathematics instruction without the assistance of computers, it is easy to agree with Suppes when he says that computers offer the only real hope for providing learning experiences that are individually tailored to the unique needs of each pupil. The question seems to be mainly one of time. How long will it be before the development of computer hardware, of communications terminals, and of computer-based learning programs can support individualized mathematics instruction in elementary and secondary school classrooms?

Informed opinion in regard to this question varies greatly. A debate on the topic "CAI: Bane or Boon" at the 1968 annual meeting of the American Educational Research Association[28] was instructive, not so much because the question was decided one way or the other, but rather because it revealed the dimensions of the gulf that separates the thinking of the several representatives of important institutions which are vitally concerned with the implementation and dissemination of computer-based systems of instructional management. Suppes spoke hopefully of the future for CAI. His optimism was based in part on the modest but significant accomplishments that have

---

28. "CAI: Bane or Boon?" Harry F. Silberman, moderator; Patrick Suppes, Anthony Oettinger, Ross Tullian, Robert Taylor, participants; Daniel Alpert, Louis Bright, discussants (AERA Annual Meeting, Chicago, February 8, 1968).

been achieved at Stanford in the last four or five years in the development of arithmetic drill and mathematical logic programs. Oettinger, taking an opposite position based in part on the harsh realities of cost considerations, estimated that the hopeful future was perhaps thirty years away and that this fairly remote time schedule would be met only if quantities of money exceeding that of our annual national defense budget were expended in the development of computer capabilities for instruction. He took sharp issue with those who have for some time gone on record in favor of encouraging schools to include the provision and use of computer hardware in their planning. While Bright defended the U. S. Office of Education for giving such encouragement—partly on the basis of the total assistance that computers can offer schools both in the instructional and administrative areas—he conceded that present computing equipment is not being especially designed to meet educational needs. Oettinger remained firm in his conviction, however, that with respect to CAI the USOE was engaged in an "artificial dissemination of nonexistent information."

Where do such strongly held and widely divergent opinions of the experts leave the school administrator who must plan realistically for the immediate as well as the long-range future and who must take into account the very real need to individualize not only mathematics instruction but other subject areas as well? Where does it put the researcher who has modest facilities but a deep commitment to finding better methods of mathematics instruction through the more effective use of the existing tools that technology provides? Should one simply set the matter of CAI aside to await whatever the dozen or so institutions around the country which have the most sophisticated machinery and expertise can provide? Or are there levels at which one can make contributions in a large and growing field—contributions that will return immediate benefits in today's classrooms?

The answers to such questions must be made individually, of course, but there is some information currently available that may assist those concerned to reach a satisfactory conclusion and to chart a reasonable course of action. One may readily concur with the discussant who said in regard to Oettinger's realistic but harsh judgments that he agreed with the substance but not the tone of the remarks made—that although the present situation is not especially encouraging in terms of an immediate breakthrough, one certainly must proceed with a spirit of optimism and hope to isolate parts of the total problem, seek solutions to those parts that are tractable within the present state of the teaching and computing art, and in this way build systematically toward the time when our larger aspirations and expectations may more fully be met.

At what level, then, ought one to begin to search for ways in which to feed in new ideas for tests and trial? A description of just where we are in the present state of the art may help provide the orientation needed to make such a decision. Two descriptions of the present and projected situation have been given recently which help to summarize present accomplishments and to indicate trends. Suppes has spoken of three stages of development through which a program may go.[29] The first is one in which the concern is basic research and limited trial with a few pupils under laboratory conditions. The second stage is a demonstration stage at which perhaps one school is set up to model the system's operation. The final stage is widespread dissemination—a real penetration into the classrooms in a wide geographic area.

As to the kinds of CAI programs presently in different stages, Suppes has cited his "Drill-and-Practice" program in fundamentals of arithmetic as one approaching the third stage of wide dissemination. This program assumes that the fundamental learning of concepts and skills has taken place through presumably conventional means and that the skills can be maintained and sharpened through brief but regular practice at a teletype keyboard which serves as the communication link between a pupil and the central computer which controls the program. Recently certain schools in New York, for instance, joined the "Drill-and-Practice" network originating in Palo Alto, California—at least until the local computer system in New York becomes operable.[30]

The drill-and-practice type of program is not primarily instructional in the sense of initiating learning. To initiate learning requires a higher level of sophistication in program development. Thus the next step toward the automation of instruction, as Suppes sees it, is the development of a tutorial program. At present, the work at Stan-

29. Patrick Suppes, "Tomorrow's Education? Computer-Based Instruction in the Elementary School," *Education Age*, III (January–February, 1966), vol. II.

30. *The New York Times*, March 19, 1968.

ford at the tutorial level of operation is somewhere between the first stage of limited laboratory trial and the second stage of single-school demonstration.[31] Interestingly, the cost of operating one terminal jumps by a factor of ten (comparing present experimental terminal cost for the tutorial program to the cost of a simple teletype used in drill). In terms of dollars, a system which operates a few teletype terminals may cost in order of magnitude about $1000 per month at present while the much more elaborate system consisting of a TV-like scope, light pen, audio headset, keyboard, and film-projector system may rent for upwards of $10,000 per month. The cost, of course, is representative of the kind of investment required to do the basic research and development needed to create the programs. It is anticipated that the cost will be considerably reduced when the system gets to the point at which widespread dissemination takes place. Obviously, cost reduction is a necessary precondition to widespread dissemination, and it is on this point that the controversy centers. How far in the future widespread dissemination of tutorial systems may be is anyone's guess.

Watching a tutorial system in operation leaves one with the impression that the computer-substitute for the teacher resembles a new teaching situation in which the automatic teacher is not terribly perceptive nor very imaginative and sometimes rather slack in supplying a response to the youngster's reaction. Part of the problem here is hardware limitation—primarily in the capacity of the input/output devices to communicate with the learner. For those who dream far into the future, it is possible to think of the computer as understanding ordinary voice communication as a human teacher does. The achievement of this capability would help make possible the third level of program sophistication, which Suppes calls the *Dialog Mode*.[32] This mode seems an unlikely achievement in this generation, given the present rate of progress in the field. It is barely at the first stage of basic research and limited experimentation.

There are others who see the development of computer-oriented instruction somewhat differently. Becker, at Research for Better Schools, Inc., describes four levels of programing in place of Suppes'

31. Patrick Suppes, "Computer Technology and the Future of Education," *Phi Delta Kappan*, XLIX (April, 1968), 420–23.

32. Suppes, "Plug-in Instruction," *loc. cit.*

three.[33] The first mode is called *Individually Prescribed Instruction* (IPI) and operates in the pencil-and-paper or manual mode. At present, IPI is developed to a point between stages two and three; some 27 schools across the country are field-testing the system.

The second level of program, in Becker's scheme, is called the *Automated Learning Management System* (ALMS). The idea of instructional management has received considerable attention in recent years. At the heart of this approach is the problem of determining how to imitate the teacher's ability to diagnose learning difficulties and then prescribe learning experiences which are appropriate for the individual. So far, the diagnosis-prescription-decision problem has presented formidable obstacles to progress in the area of learning management through the use of computers. The fundamental techniques for dealing with it usually employ either some form of linear regression equation to predict pupil performance or alternatively the computation of optimum learning path on the basis of probability distributions and individually determined parameters which define a Markov learning model for a given learner. These statistical or probabilistic approaches lack real power for this type of problem. The first approach makes good sense when applied to the prediction of group behavior where randomization effects can act to stabilize the reliability of the prediction. However, it is the kind of approach which can very well be wrong in its diagnosis of every individual case and be right only with regard to the average. The second approach is so complex from a computational point of view as to render it practically worthless. As we are fond of incanting in such situations, more work needs to be done in this area. And of course more work is being done, mostly at the stage-one level of limited experimentation with group, not individual, learning management.[34]

The third mode that Becker identifies is the *CAI Mode*. This re-

33. James W. Becker, "Toward Automated Learning" (paper delivered at American Educational Research Association Annual Meeting, Chicago, February 8, 1968).

34. Harry Silberman, "Design Objectives of the Instructional Management System (IMS)" (paper delivered at American Educational Research Association Annual Meeting, Chicago, February 8, 1968). Beverly Y. Kooy, "Definition of Course Objectives and Preparation of Design Tests for IMS" (paper delivered at American Educational Research Association Annual Meeting, Chicago, February 8, 1968).

sembles Suppes' tutorial system in structure and is also at the first stage of development.

The fourth mode, which Becker calls the *Interactive Mode*, is similar in concept to Suppes' *Dialog System*. The purpose behind the development of the interactive mode is to make the computer "so reactive to the child that it becomes unique to him."[35] Oettinger's cost and time estimates seem especially conservative when thinking of this level of programing service.

Thus, it seems that, for the schools, the level at which one might expect the most immediate profit from exploring and inventing new approaches to individualized mathematics instruction is at the non-automated level or, at most, at the level of a relatively simple drill-and-practice program on a teletype. In the non-automated field, there is much yet to be learned about grouping techniques, all of which ultimately should contribute to our understanding of individualized instruction. What definable learning parameters can be used in the formation of homogeneous groups (i.e., homogeneous with respect to the selected parameter) that will enable one to develop learning experiences which will yield perceptible gains in learning for the children? Is it possible to form groups that are homogeneous with respect to more than one significant learning parameter?

Another form of non-automated instruction which needs further exploration is that by teams of teachers. Should the team members be roughly equivalent in their teaching competence or should the members represent different areas of special strength—in effect, should each member be a specialist to some degree? The specialist concept makes some sense from the standpoint of division of labor, a practice which has yielded dividends in other areas of endeavor heretofore. If evidence were accumulated which favored the use of specialists, it certainly could have a radical effect on our elementary-school teacher-education programs which are currently adjusted to the anachronistic goal of producing generalists capable of teaching all subjects in Grades K-VIII.

Finally, programed learning falls within the province of non-automated instruction, as we are using the term here. The role and value of programed materials are not yet fully known, and further experimentation in the use and development of these materials is warranted.

35. Becker, *op. cit.*

As for computer-facilitated instruction, one is somewhat at the mercy of events. Some schools may be able to afford (or may have access to) computers for instructional experimentation. Certainly the merits of regular drill and practice in the fundamentals of arithmetic deserves to be given a thorough tryout. There is yet another development here that deserves mention. That is the use of specially simplified languages, called author languages, which can be used by children and teachers to actually create certain kinds of learning and teaching programs for a computer. Starkweather's PILOT (Programed Instruction, Learning, or Teaching) is an illustrative effort in this direction.[36] The author-language field seems one of the most promising from the standpoint of economy and simplicity and, from all appearances, seems to be one which is receiving relatively little attention at the present time.

Summary

Through the use of a systems model of individualized mathematics instruction, we have attempted to describe how four kinds of parameters—content, learner, teacher, and instruction—may affect the design of a given program. The virtue of the systems model is that it avoids narrow, single-minded approaches to a complex problem and thereby reduces the tendency to search for easy "breakthroughs" and panaceas. It also should help to reduce the tendency toward fadism that is an ever present danger in educational program development. We look to technology, especially to computers, to provide important assistance in building better programs of differentiated mathematics instruction in the years to come, but we realize that much can and should be done to strengthen non-automated techniques of individualization in the meantime.

36. J. A. Starkweather, "Computest: A Computer Language for Individualized Testing, Instruction, and Interviewing," *Psychological Reports*, XVII (August, 1965), 227–37.

CHAPTER XII

Administration and Supervision

MILDRED KEIFFER

New Emphases in Curriculum Reform

For many years before World War II, administrators were accustomed to a gradual process of curriculum development which reflected the relatively gradual evolution processes occurring at the same time in society. After World War II, the situation changed. Unprecedented advances occurred in technology and in scientific and mathematical research. The general community indicated a growing interest in educational matters and pressed for action.

Repeated layers of minor revisions of the curriculum had been applied, year after year, and the time was overdue for a complete rethinking. As scientists and mathematicians became aware of the situation, many indicated interest in accepting responsibility and assisting with the problem. Their resulting involvement in precollege curriculum improvement assisted both in producing change and in influencing the character of the change.

One of the characteristics of this movement was that it was discipline centered rather than child centered. The emphasis was upon updating and reorganizing the academic disciplines which constitute preparation for college. Thus it attended to the special needs of middle-class and upper middle-class, college-bound students.

In effect, the effort for curriculum change received its momentum from forces and interests mostly outside the local system which is legally responsible for the schools and the content of their instruction. Subject matter specialists proposed the content, but care was usually taken to see that classroom teachers participated in the writing. Temporarily, at least, decisions concerning what is to be taught in the schools, who is to determine what is to be taught, and who is to conduct and control the ongoing curriculum revision waited upon

433

the recommendations of content specialists. Local administration, however, remained aware of the possibility that students tomorrow may be served better by subject combinations different from those in effect today and that piecemeal planning by separate content areas does not provide for across-the-board study of the total experience of the school child. Administrators could see science, mathematics, social studies, and language arts all making separate efforts at internal improvement and became concerned about how to bring them all together in terms of the life of the individual learner.

Current Curriculum Situation

The current curriculum situation is a matter of concern to administrators and to supervisors, who are aware that the schools are responsible for educating all children. Impatient observers find improvements too slow and often more talked about than accomplished, but many school administrators feel that they are moving quite fast enough—if not too rapidly. They face problems relative to teacher selection, in-service training, staff utilization, school organization, curriculum construction, pupil counseling, pupil programing, community relations, parent concern, and budget considerations. Admittedly, persons with administrative and supervisory responsibilities face such problems whether they have a new program in mathematics or not, but some of the problems appear to be intensified because of the developments in mathematics.

TEACHER SELECTION

It is increasingly necessary for administrators to study carefully the qualifications and the mathematics backgrounds of teacher applicants. School employment officers must be far more selective than once was acceptable. This is a major problem at a time when there is a general shortage of mathematically trained personnel and competition for their services is brisk in business and industry. Occasionally announcements are made that the shortage no longer exists. This may be true in prosperous "Suburbia Gardens," but inner-city schools continue to be aware of the scarcity of competent applicants.

Schools report that recruiting well-prepared teachers is a grave problem at all levels of mathematics instruction, but the shortage seems to be especially acute for the elementary and junior high school grades. Teachers at the junior high school level should have completed a solid major in college mathematics including calculus, abstract algebra, modern geometry, probability, statistics, and applied mathematics. The problem is that such preparation also equips them for attractive posts in industry. It also indicates an interest in the content of mathematics and in the teaching of pupils of more than junior high school maturity. The matter of prestige enters the picture and able junior high school teachers after a few years often apply to teach at the senior high school level. Preparing young adolescents for an updated college-preparatory sequence in mathematics requires a teacher who appreciates the elementary program and knows the modern high school content as well. Teaching early teen-agers also requires a teacher who understands the restless energy of these pupils and knows how to harness it for educational purposes. Retaining such teachers is another problem for junior high school administrators.

At the elementary level, teachers in an improved program teach much more than how to compute. They must know enough about number theory and elementary geometry to give their young charges a proper start on the long spiral course ahead in their mathematics future. It is difficult for some teachers to accept the spiral plan of teaching. Instead, they work for mastery at a pupil's first contact with an idea. Both teachers and pupils need encouragement and reassurance. Administrators find it necessary to learn enough about changes in content and methods of presentation to be able to understand what is going on in the classroom. They must be able to recognize whether pupils are thinking mathematics or merely repeating words that sound modern. No program, however new and expertly prepared, can be successful in the face of poor instructional methods and insufficient knowledge of mathematics on the part of the teacher.

Difficulties increase as schools seek teachers for slower learners and for inner-city classes of disadvantaged boys and girls. Exciting new materials adjusted to the reading and interest levels of pupils who do not qualify for the college-capable group have been slow in appearing so that school systems often have tried to prepare their own. Teachers and administrators are familiar with classes in which a different third of the pupils are absent each day. The problem of securing the needed zestful, imaginative, gifted teacher is acute. So is the problem of providing such a teacher with the time and resources required to develop materials adjusted to the specific needs of his less favored classes. Encouraging news at the time of this writing is that efforts to produce materials for low achievers in mathematics are proving successful in many different localities and that these materials will soon be available for general study and use.

IN-SERVICE EDUCATION

If well-prepared teachers cannot be found in sufficient numbers among new applicants, in-service problems are thereby increased for the schools which must employ inadequately prepared personnel in order to supply the classrooms. The administrator is called upon to make immediate plans to help the new teacher secure the necessary training. He also may find on his staff experienced teachers whose many years spent in teaching traditional materials give them little confidence as they face new topics presented in unfamiliar ways. These teachers need help too. Teachers who have long regarded themselves as successful in a traditional program require recognition of this success and special orientation to an updated program.

Sometimes administrators have available the services of specialists in mathematics to whom they can delegate the responsibility for in-service training of teachers. The specialist, coordinator, or supervisor—whatever his title—may conduct classes and workshops himself. He may have sufficient funds to secure occasional consultant help on special problems of content or method. In schools which have worked on their improved programs for several years, the initial pressures for immediate training in content background and in methods of teaching the new materials have usually subsided. A dedicated and competent staff can assist the administrator by planning its own on-going, in-service growth program, for such teachers realize that changes will continue to occur. As updated programs are developed further, additional improvements will emerge. Teachers must also be informed of changes occurring in the years preceding and following the grades for which they are responsible. Administrators face the task of keeping themselves informed of the total mathematics program as it continues to develop and of observing how mathematics functions in the entire educational experience of the pupil.

If no one else is available to plan and conduct an in-service program for the teachers of mathematics in his school, the administrator must rely upon himself. In systems which assign this responsibility to the supervisor, the latter must see to it that his own store of knowledge is properly updated. Self-study and additional graduate course work are in order for him, and if he is employed on a year-round basis, he has a problem. He must find time to learn new subject matter and also methods of preparing teachers to teach it effectively.

Teachers have reported that often they cannot find in their colleges the kinds of courses they need. Too often the only graduate courses available are tailored for further graduate study and research. In-service institutes supported by the National Science Foundation have helped this situation by offering after-school and Saturday courses of value to teachers who wished to update their algebra, geometry, or calculus. Sometimes courses in updated teaching methods have also been offered.

Even undergraduates preparing to become teachers report that the courses planned for them continue to follow the traditional path. The first experience of many beginning teachers with an updated school mathematics program occurs after they see the textbooks they will use in their new teaching assignments. School systems face serious problems in making available to teachers the time and the funds they need to attend institutes, conferences, and workshops in which they can learn how to increase their skills in an updated mathematics program. It is encouraging that many college mathematics departments are making known their sincere interest in assisting schools and in co-operating with administrators in planning and providing appropriate contemporary training programs, both the content and the presentation techniques.

Responsibilities of Administrators and Supervisors

RESPONDING TO PRESSURES

In order to maintain their position of respected leadership, administrators have had to learn to accept change and to become conversant with what improved mathematics programs require of teachers. Popular zeal for keeping abreast has required the administration in some communities to resist adopting a new program and to insist upon time in which to help the staff prepare. Sometimes the pressures exerted by parents and interested citizens in the community are increased because a neighboring school system has adopted a new mathematics program. Pressure from publishers, professional organizations, and colleges and universities to make changes and thus be identified as progressive educational leaders has added to the problems of school administrators and supervisors. Successful implementation of an improved mathematics program requires teachers prepared in content, in appropriate teaching techniques, and in an updated philosophy of mathematics education. Staff preparation requires *time* for planning and *more time* for carrying out the plans. Teachers who are already occupied with many responsibilities are not always able to respond to the call to in-service training programs.

In a different situation, a qualified staff, ready to move ahead in a new mathematics program, may find its action questioned by the community. Misinformed criticism and publicity must be offset by supplying appropriate individuals and organizations with correct information. Administration and staff must be prepared to answer questions about the goals of the new program and to explain why and how it constitutes an improvement over the traditional one which they had supported previously.

Monthly newsletters from the schools to parents have been useful and so have open meetings and personal conferences. Parents who are disturbed by the unfamiliarity of the materials their sons and daughters are using can be invited to attend special evening classes conducted by teachers and supervisors. Although many books written for the information of parents are now available (some even on the shelves of the local supermarkets), a very helpful resource has been the pupil textbook used in the school program. The seventh-grade textbook has been found most useful for a class of parents interested in learning about the elementary-school program, since this book ties together all the elementary ideas and shows how they are used at the next level.

On the whole, general publicity about new mathematics programs during the early developmental periods was favorable and supportive. There were some expressions of reservation, but the public mood seemed to be one of approval. Now the public attitude appears to have settled into an expectant stage, waiting for the schools to produce evidence that the new mathematics programs are right and sound for children. School staff members must be sure of their own thinking and prepared to answer more searching inquiries than ever before.

ADOPTING AND IMPLEMENTING NEW PROGRAMS

New local supervisors are being employed to coordinate the various levels as schools adopt updated mathematics programs. Someone who knows the field is needed to advise on the decisions to be made and to make certain that the new spirit actually permeates the classroom. There is need for increased observation and supervision of instructional processes to guard against a mere trading of new vocabulary for old and new expedients for old tricks. It becomes necessary for the school administrator to delegate responsibility for the mathematics program to some qualified persons or to become sufficiently familiar with it himself to serve as an in-school consultant in both content and teaching methods. Maintaining an up-to-date reference library for teachers is one way an administrator can encourage them to pursue a continuous personal re-education program.

PROVIDING RESOURCES

Schools find that they must devote increased time and resources to helping teachers locate and make effective use of appropriate equipment and supplementary materials. Searching for material to fit the unique needs of a particular school or class places added demands upon a staff which is already fully occupied. An updated program requires materials for children to handle, count, compare, and measure as they formulate ideas. The market is filled with teaching aids which their manufacturers are eager to sell, and the school administrator's outer office is filled with salesmen ready to oblige. There is no lack in the quantity of material—programed, filmed, taped, prepared on transparencies, or ready for instant duplication. The problem lies in the quality and instructional effectiveness of these products of current technology. When useful and appropriate teaching aids are secured, space in which to store them and space in which pupils may use them must be found. No less important, money must be obtained to pay for them.

COORDINATING THE MATHEMATICS CURRICULUM

Securing articulation between elementary- and secondary-school mathematics offerings requires meetings and committee work on the part of the teachers involved. Where elementary, junior high school, and senior high school buildings are separated geographically, they may also be separated in educational philosophy. It is important to bring the teachers together so that each level recognizes and understands the goals of the others. All levels must be aware of the unifying general concepts which underlie the total program. The spiral treatment of content and the planned extension of depth of understanding in successive units over the years require communication up and down the entire sequence. This notion of repeated attention as the pupil advances is a new one to some established teachers. They need help in revising their philosophy and methods. "Cover the book" and "Master this topic before you start a new one" are inconsistent with modern objectives.

In large junior and senior high schools, teachers of mathematics usually teach only mathematics. In the elementary school, a teacher is often responsible for the total educational program of a class. Thus the elementary teacher must be an expert in teaching reading, language arts, science, social studies, music, art, health, and physical education—as well as a person thoroughly informed about new ideas in mathematics. The question of specialization in the grades is a thorny one and will not become less so as more new programs become available in other subject areas. The teacher in a self-contained classroom may have grown up disliking mathematics and may, indeed, be uncertain in her own computation. In some schools, administrators attempt to attack the problem by moving to a departmentalized situation in mathematics and simply assigning to one teacher who likes mathematics all the mathematics classes in Grades IV, V, and VI. In others, administrators may count upon at least one teacher to have some additional training and interest in mathematics. This teacher is then relied upon to answer the questions of the other teachers. Some school principals hope to find a solution in developing team teaching or in establishing ungraded schools. Some anticipate that perhaps a change in the way time is scheduled during the day may help to solve the specialization problem in the elementary school. All these factors add to the problems of the administrator as he works on organizing the school for effective instruction and optimum staff and space utilization.

Programing for all students.—Initially, the improved programs in mathematics were designed for college-bound and college-capable pupils. As schools use the new materials, they learn that they must give careful attention to appropriate grouping of pupils. A class which follows a new program must be a carefully selected group. Moreover, it has to be retained as a unit, sometimes for several years. Pupils from a traditional program are not easily scheduled into a class with pupils from an updated program. Transfers are not conveniently made into or from classes following a new program. The general mobility of pupils means that, as families move from one community to another, a child can enter a school and find no mathematics class suitable for him. Administrators continue to be concerned about how to provide a transitional period for transfer pupils.

Both vertical and horizontal coordination are affected. Special sequences are in order for different subsets of the ablest group of pupils. Some accelerate in order to participate in the Advanced Placement Program. Some prepare to start with calculus in college. Others anticipate college majors not requiring more than two years of high school mathematics.

Pupils in the middle or average group include a subset with college plans also. A less demanding modern mathematics program seems appropriate for them, with a worthy four-year sequence available for those who wish it. Such pupils will need further preparation in college if they find it necessary to study calculus, but as a rule they will be interested in majors which do not require additional mathematical background. As more special groups of pupils are defined, counseling and scheduling problems increase geometrically.

The matter of offering algebra in the eighth grade instead of the ninth raises questions about the validity of early selection of pupils. It also increases the number of courses offered at each grade level and introduces the need for a fifth year of high school mathematics different from the Advanced Placement Program. The Advanced Placement Program is designed for a highly gifted and specialized group of high school students in the top four or five per cent of the school population. It is a college calculus course and requires a high degree of motivation and industry as well as mathematical insight. Able pupils who are not eligible for such rigorous treatment should have available a worthy course appropriate to their level of mathematical maturity. The content of this fifth-year course must be decided upon and suitable text materials must be found. Also, it is important to maintain channels of communication with college admissions offices so that colleges have complete information about the full extent of the mathematics preparation of high school graduates. In some schools, eighth-grade algebra may bring about changes in graduation requirements, since high school credit may not be granted for eighth-grade work. Accelerated and advanced programs raise questions concerning marking practices and provision for appropriate adjustments in assigning class rank. Rank in class is important to pupils because of its influence upon college admission.

After the college-capable classes are sectioned off, it seems reasonable to inquire about what should constitute minimum essentials in an improved program for less favored groups. Worthy programs for low-average and slower groups of pupils need study. Teachers have been obliged to rely upon their own resources and the office duplicating machine. Interest has been growing in providing mathematics laboratories or resource centers with a variety of updated textbooks, supplementary reading materials, manipulative devices, computers, production equipment, display items, and similar aids to teaching and learning. At the same time, budget considerations require caution and discrimination in order to be sure that the purchased materials add to the effectiveness of the instruction and learning processes. Large sums of money obtained by schools under various acts of Congress are more thoughtfully spent on useful materials when supervisors and administrators know what will support the mathematics program and what will merely gather dust. Questions about the place of team teaching, individualized-instruction materials, non-graded organization, and modular scheduling remain to be resolved for the high school as well as for the elementary school.

The principal disadvantage of books in the eyes of the very limited pupil is that books are supposed to be read and he cannot read. He does not remember the addition or multiplication facts either, and, by the time he reaches the seventh grade, he has lost any zeal he ever had for learning mathematics. The schools are gravely concerned. They need to know what kind of improved mathematics program is appropriate for these pupils and what constitutes reasonable success for them. They are concerned about the best way to provide for slower pupils in a school organization and ponder the arguments for and against assigning fast-moving and slow-moving pupils to different classes. Sociological considerations support heterogeneous groups, but teaching convenience suggests ability groups.

More selective grouping of pupils means more classes, and more classes require more teaching stations. The administrator's task of scheduling space grows in complexity. Also, teachers need work space and time to develop plans and materials for the various ability levels. They need time to help in the adjustment of pupils who received their previous instruction in a traditional program or in a contemporary program in which a different sequence of topics was followed.

Choosing suitable materials.—There was a time when textbooks in mathematics continued to be used for decades, since the subject matter remained constant and only the prices in the practical applications increased. Now, change in the mathematics curriculum is an accepted fact, and schools are prepared to expect this situation to persist. Textbooks will not continue to be appropriate for long periods of time but will be revised at frequent intervals. Schools will find it necessary to anticipate frequent new adoptions to keep pace. They must not be misled by a bright new cover on a book or a few modern appearing illustrations and think the book represents a worthy contemporary product. A chapter on sets and much emphasis on words like "commutative" do not guarantee that a book is suitable. The way the topics are presented, as well as the topics themselves, must be studied by the selection committee. The rigor and abstraction must be appropriate to the maturity of the pupils who will use the book. Administrators and supervisors must be prepared to evaluate textbooks and allied materials and to support their evaluations from the point of view of correct mathematics as well as of appropriate pedagogy. They may wish to seek the assistance of the mathematics department of a nearby college as they and the teachers involved examine textbooks for correct content, emphasis, and terminology. It is important, if the school contemplates the adoption of a series of books for a succession of grades, to study the development of concepts and the extension of understanding provided for in the sequential treatment. The number of attractive and well-written books available on the current market offers a wide range of choice. Each local school system needs only to decide upon its own goals and then to select appropriate textbooks which provide the best fit.

From the beginning, the new experimental materials in mathematics were prepared with the interests and needs of the teacher in mind. Each pupil text was accompanied by a carefully prepared commentary or manual for teachers in which the writers included background mathematics information for the teacher and specific teaching techniques recommended for the topic at hand. As commercial books were produced, the publishers tended to follow the example of the experimental materials, and they provided complete commentaries also. Administrators and supervisors must be sure that teachers have these commentaries and make effective use of them.

Critical Problems

Secondary schools may look forward to fused courses in algebra and geometry and to an end of the compartmented sequence. In each school, decisions must be made about where in the program various topics are taught most effectively and efficiently. Even now, schools seem to be more carefully selective than formerly in their choices of textbooks and supplementary materials, establishing local criteria and fitting their choices to their own situations. Each level of difficulty has its unique need for which text material must be found. The chances are good that suitable material will continue to be available for accelerated, gifted, able, and high-average classes. Textbooks for low-average pupils often promise more than they produce, and teachers must supplement them with their own ideas. The slower classes present the most serious problem. Their needs have not been met and possibly are not even known or understood.

ISSUE OF PRACTICAL APPLICATIONS

Practical applications were mentioned above as one aspect in which former textbooks became outdated. A criticism of modern textbooks is that practical applications have been slighted, if not frankly omitted. It is further stated that new mathematics programs tend to separate mathematics from other school subject areas even more firmly than traditional treatments did. Pupils seem to be no more able than before to use their mathematical competence in science, shop courses, home economics, or other fields of study. There is no provision for developing competence in dealing with ordinary problems in computation as encountered by the consumer, the wage-earner, or the taxpayer in day-to-day experience. Teachers must find time to supplement once more, and supervisors must be prepared to help locate examples and arrange for the production and distribution of the needed materials.

As more advanced topics are presented earlier in a pupil's school experience and as increased emphasis is placed upon understanding and appreciation of pattern and structure, less class time remains available for providing drill on the facts and skills of computation. Statements are made from time to time that there is a noticeable decrease in proficiency in computation among school children and that this is particularly evident among slower learners. Administrators and supervisors are concerned as they observe children who do not know their addition and multiplication facts. These pupils seem not to recall the facts at all, much less as rapidly as they need them. They are able to supply reasons but cannot complete a process. They work so slowly that they forget what they are doing and where they are in the process. There appears to be a stigma attached to the word "drill' and teachers are reluctant to emphasize practice. They feel obliged to emphasize *principles and structure* at the expense of *practice* and to be creative at all costs.

Slower pupils tend to become confused when several different methods or procedures are presented to them. Perhaps a single good way rather than several ways to approach a problem would be more profitable for them. Able pupils can generalize and recognize pattern, but slower pupils are only confused. For example, a slower pupil learns that he may add by starting at the top or at the bottom of a column, and he proceeds in the same way in subtraction. Thus, when 62 is the minuend and 38 is the subtrahend, he subtracts 2 from 8 and then 3 from 6 and offers 36 as his answer. More information is needed as to how content and teaching methods should be adapted for slower classes.

Search for Realistic Goals

Schools are searching for realistic goals and for means of determining what constitutes reasonable success for teachers and for pupils. They need help in developing different sets of competencies and in identifying the pupils who are to achieve these sets of competencies. Administrators are uncertain about how to evaluate the progress of pupils in the new programs. They know that the old, familiar testing instruments are not satisfactory. They are aware of the concern of the community and its interest in assessing the soundness of the new programs. They await the development of suitable instruments and techniques which will provide answers acceptable to the community and to the school.

Schools in many communities are trying to follow the advice of college mathematicians and are making earnest attempts to update their mathematics programs in the manner proposed. Administrators in such schools encounter problems in securing teachers trained in the new approach, both in content and in teaching methods. They are beset by pressures exerted by parents, teachers, influential community leaders, and other interested persons or agencies to keep up to date on the one hand and to hold the line on the other. They face problems of providing suitable instructional materials for pupils and for teachers, arranging schedules for pupils and teachers which take into account individual talents and interests, and answering to the board of education and the taxpayers for the satisfactory progress of pupils in mathematics. Finally, they have to be sure that Johnny can add.

A BRIEF LOOK AHEAD

CHAPTER XIII

A Changing Mathematics Program

TRUMAN BOTTS

The Mathematical Sciences Today

In earlier chapters, and especially in chapters i and viii, we have indicated something of the growing role that mathematics and its applications are playing in our society today.

This role has deep roots in the past. The basic idea of abstracting a useful mathematical structure from man's physical experience was implicit in the earliest developments of the counting numbers. To make this idea explicit was the crowning achievement of the axiomatic geometry of the ancient Greeks. Another great landmark was the invention of the calculus in the seventeenth century. This was decisive for the enormously fruitful developments in the physical sciences and engineering that followed in the succeeding centuries and, indeed, have continued to the present day. Already by the end of the nineteenth century these developments, together with further developments within mathematics itself, had had a revolutionary effect on man's intellectual attitude toward his environment and on his practical control of this environment.

It is, however, the twentieth century that has witnessed not only a remarkable flowering of mathematical discovery but also an unprecedented penetration of mathematical methods into other fields of human activity. In addition to the physical sciences and engineering, these fields now include the biological and medical sciences, the social and behavioral sciences, various domains within the humanities, and the general field of business operations and management. During the past twenty years, this virtual "mathematization of culture" has been greatly accelerated and intensified by the evolution of the high-speed electronic computer.

Today the areas of mathematical activity are so broad and diverse that it no longer seems adequate to speak simply of mathematics, and in consequence a new term has arisen: *the mathematical sciences*. The mathematical sciences comprise not only the various subfields of mathematics and the classical applied mathematics of the physical sciences and engineering, but also statistics, computer science, and what is usually called operations research or management science. We also find more and more subfields of other disciplines with designations such as mathematical biology, mathematical psychology, mathematical linguistics, mathematical economics, and the like.

The Increasing Need for Mathematically Trained People

The current growth in all forms of mathematical activity has produced a need for mathematically trained people at every level and in unprecedented numbers.

At the broadest level, there is the mathematical training appropriate for our citizens generally. Today this includes more than just basic mathematical skills. Increasingly important is an informed mathematical literacy as well—a genuine grasp of the nature of the various mathematical sciences and of the many ways in which they are contributing to the solution of real-world problems. The number of people who need mathematical training at this level is quite large. It may be estimated that already about one-fourth of the adult population of the United States has at least two years of high school mathematics; and perhaps eight to ten million have a fundamental mathematical education extending through two years of college. These are the basic numbers involved, and they can only be expected to grow in the future.

At a less broad but deeper level, there are the varied needs for mathematical education on the part of professionals in other fields—physicists, astronomers, chemists, engineers, biologists, pychologists, economists, administrators, and others—who regularly use methods from the mathematical sciences in their own areas of work. Statistics and computer science, especially, have a rich and continuous interplay with such other domains. The pervasive and valuable way in which the mathematical sciences figure in other fields is through *mathematical models*—not always explicitly formulated or realized—for situations arising in these fields. It is the function of such models to abstract from diverse real situations the essential feature at issue, so that powerful mathematical knowledge and techniques can be brought to bear in solving problems. The number of people in the United States who need this deeper level of training in the mathematical sciences is now perhaps one or two million.

At the deepest level, there is the training required by professionals in the mathematical sciences themselves. The number of such professionals now approaches 400,000. The largest groups are high school mathematics teachers, perhaps 120,000 in number, and computer programers, now estimated to number over 200,000. In addition, there are somewhat over 50,000 people who are engaged in research or in college and university teaching in mathematics, statistics, computer science, and operations research—management sciences. This now includes nearly 10,000 Ph.D.'s in the mathematical sciences, over 1,500 of whom are consistently active in discovery and innovation. It has been estimated that the number of full-time teachers of the mathematical sciences in universities and four-year colleges alone, who numbered around 11,000 in 1966, will need to be expanded to about 20,000 by 1971, if we are to approach fulfillment of national needs.

Recent Progress in Mathematics

In spite of widespread discussion of the "new math," there are still people who think of mathematics as a "dead" subject, one whose development was essentially completed in the remote past. Such people are very much surprised to learn that the twentieth century, especially the past twenty-five years, has proved to be a "golden age" for new discoveries in mathematics.

At the turn of the century, it was still possible to subdivide mathematics into three broad domains: algebra, geometry, and analysis—the last of these being the mathematics of infinite limiting processes growing out of the calculus. New developments were, however, already brewing, among them topology and mathematical logic.

The evolution of topology illustrates one of the most characteristic trends of contemporary mathematics—the confluence or flowing-together of various subfields. Stimulated initially by unresolved questions in analysis, topology developed in the early decades of the twentieth century as a kind of generalized geometry in which one studied qualitative features of geometric figures that survive under transformations, like crumpling and knotting, which drastically change sizes and shapes. It was then found that a powerful and fruitful approach to this generalized geometry was, via the methods of modern abstract algebra, giving rise to what is now called algebraic topology. Concurrently, though, there was a continuing cross-fertilization between topology and analysis, witnessed in the development of analytic topology, topological analysis, topological dynamics, and most recently, differential topology. In addition to bringing new insights and techniques to other branches of mathematics. topology is now seeing significant application outside mathematics altogether.

Although the study of logic and formal mathematics goes back to the ancient Greeks, mathematical logic really dates its systematic development from the late nineteenth century, stimulated partly by Cantor's theory of infinite sets, with its logical paradoxes. In the early decades of the twentieth century, mathematicians hoped to formalize all mathematical reasoning in a single logical system. A crucial discovery by Gödel in 1931, however, led to the realization that in any formal logical system adequate for ordinary arithmetic there will always be *unprovable* true statements about the whole numbers. Cantor had conjectured that there is no set "intermediate in size" between the set of all natural numbers and the set of all points on the real line. In 1939 Gödel established that this conjecture can never be *disproved* in the logical system commonly used in mathematics; and in 1963 P. Cohen showed that it can never be *proved* in this system, either. The formal manipulation of symbols envisioned in mathematical logic is actually realized in the algorithmic procedures of electronic computers; and, in fact, two distinguished mathematical logicians, von Neumann and Turing, played important roles in developing the theory and design of the modern computer.

There have been many other developments in contemporary mathematics—more than we can possibly mention here. Algebra in the twentieth century has evolved into a theory of abstract structures so general and powerful that its results and techniques are now used in every other branch of mathematics. Linear algebra, nowadays viewed as the theory of finite dimensional vector spaces, is central in statistics and numerical analysis and, partly through these, has found very important applications in fields ranging from engineering to the social sciences and business.

Analysis, too, has recently witnessed many interconnected advances in its various branches. Complex function theory, formerly rather self-contained, now has a flourishing interplay with other parts of mathematics and promises to have profound applications in elementary particle physics. Harmonic (or Fourier) analysis, stemming from problems of vibration and heat-flow considered 150 or 200 years ago, has since found applications throughout mathematical physics and has helped to stimulate such important twentieth-century mathematical advances as the Lebesgue integral and Schwartz distributions. In turn, Lebesgue's theory of measure and integration has furnished a solid foundation for the theory of probability, which underlies much of statistics, while Schwartz distributions have afforded a new and fruitful viewpoint in the field of differential equations. This last field has had a development in the past twenty-five years which is nothing short of explosive, with applications—aided crucially by the new electronic computers—in areas as diverse as control theory (e.g., for satellites) and numerical weather prediction.

Statistics

Against this background of growth in mathematics and in the mathematization of more and more aspects of our lives, we now examine a bit more closely two fields in which demands for educated manpower are especially pressing today, namely, statistics and computer science. These fields have sometimes been called *"partly* mathematical sciences" in recognition of the strong extra-mathematical components motivating and shaping their development. Statistics, the older of the two, is discussed first.

Statistics is concerned with observational data—with analyzing such data and drawing inferences from them. Statistics is mathematical in that it invents or adapts mathematical theories and techniques for use in the analysis of data and the drawing of inferences. Mathematical knowledge and techniques may also figure in the design of the experiments yielding the data. Above all, statistics draws on, and indeed merges into, the theory of probability, a branch of mathematics.

Probability theory arose initially out of statistical questions regarding games of chance. Although it is usually dated from the seventeenth-century work of the French mathematicians Pascal and Fermat, probability theory was definitely foreshadowed in the sixteenth-century investigations of the Italian Cardano.[1] At first, the theory applied only to probability situations with "discrete" outcomes (like tossing coins or dice), but by the early nineteenth century the analysis of "continuous" situations, requiring calculus methods, was well established in probability theory, most brilliantly in the work of Laplace. There were other notable advances in probability during the eighteenth and nineteenth centuries, but the definitive logical foundation of the whole theory awaited the development of the Lebesgue integral in the early years of the twentieth century.

It would, however, be misleading to speak only of the mathematical roots of statistics, for many other threads have contributed vitally to its development and character. Over the past century and a half, these have included: the study of errors of observation in astronomy and surveying, the systematic analysis of census data, the development of methods of actuarial and insurance practice, the correlation of anthropological traits, the design and analysis of experiments in agriculture and biology, the control of quality in industrial production, the development of sampling techniques generally, the drawing of conclusions from psychological and educational testing, and the evaluation of surgical techniques and the effectiveness of drugs, to name only some of them. Often it was the challenges of needs in other fields that called forth statistical inventions of the highest order and originality; and often it was mathematically gifted experts in these other fields, rather than professional mathematicians, who met these challenges and produced these inventions.

Today, statistics is a well-developed field in its own right, and statisticians are needed in a variety of roles. Some are required for research and teaching in the field of mathematical statistics itself in order to continue the discovery and evaluation of new statistical approaches and techniques. Others are needed for consultation or collaboration in solving the statistical problems of workers in other fields—in other sciences, in industry, in government, and in insurance

1. Oystein Ore, *Cardano, The Gambling Scholar* (Princeton, N.J.: Princeton University Press, 1953).

and business. The latter types of statisticians generally require both research-level training in mathematical statistics and an appreciation and understanding of the objectives of statistical applications. Statisticians with such training may be called upon to formulate more clearly the needs of an application, to tailor or adapt existing mathematical techniques to such needs, or perhaps to devise new ways for bringing modern computing systems to bear on statistical problems.

While computers may have blunted the need for routine statistical workers, there is still a need for statisticians expert in conducting surveys and data-gathering operations. There is also a need for people, trained in both statistics and computing, to provide improved computer programs for statistical tasks and sometimes to modify statistical procedures in order to take maximal advantage of modern computers. Finally, there will be a growing need for teachers with up-to-date training who can communicate these various new techniques and skills to others.

Computers and Computer Science

Physically, a modern computer is a complex of electronic and mechanical components. Functionally, these are organized into interconnected memory units, processing units, and input-output devices. The memory units, serving the purpose of storing suitably coded information, may consist of electronic circuits, wired arrays of tiny circular magnets, magnetic tapes or drums or discs, plastic strips, punched paper tape or cards, etc., or combinations of these. The processing units execute programs of instructions, themselves stored in the memory. Each instruction causes segments of stored information to interact, producing both new information, which is again stored in the memory, and also an indication of where in the memory the next instruction is to be found. The power of a computer is measured roughly by the rate at which it executes instructions.

The first such computers were constructed hardly more than twenty years ago. Since that time, sweeping advances in sophistication have been made, both in the design and componentry of the machines and in the art of programing. This evolution is still in full swing today and has, most experts believe, tremendously much further to go than it has gone already. Yet the computer's profound effects on the capabilities of our technological era are already everywhere in evidence, and the potentialities of even present-day computers have only begun to be exploited. Twenty-five years ago, computer-programing was a non-existent employment, but today the United States has over half again as many computer programers as it has high school mathematics teachers. By 1967 there were already over 40,000 electronic computers in the United States, and during that year the federal government alone spent over $2 billion for acquisition and use of computers.

Everyone knows that one of the most phenomenal aspects of the electronic computer is *speed*. Great gains in this respect have been made over the past twenty years, and comparable factors of further gain are definitely foreseeable for the near future. The computers of the late 1940's could execute a sequence of several thousand instructions per second. Nowadays computers can carry out several *million* instructions per second, a factor of gain of roughly one thousand. Rates of tens and hundreds of millions of instructions per second are virtually within our grasp now, and rates of thousands of millions of instructions per second are clearly in prospect within the next few years.

Quite as important as speed is the computer's *versatility*. The heart of this versatility lies in the fact that any desired program of instructions can be "read into" the computer's memory, where the computer can then itself modify these instructions in a prearranged fashion as it executes the given program. This crucial idea—that a computer should store its own instructions along with the data on which it operates—is generally credited to the distinguished mathematician John von Neumann (early 1940's).

Speed, versatility, and the capacity to store great masses of data in accessible form permit the computer to cope directly with complexity that would otherwise be hopelessly unmanageable. In this respect computers go beyond mathematics, for mathematics can deal with a complex situation only by seeking to abstract from it the simple features of central importance.

Very impressive gains can result when the abstractions of mathematics and the speed and capacity of computers are employed together. A striking example of this is numerical weather prediction. Here the atmosphere and its changes are first represented by a simplified abstract mathematical model, in the form of certain differential equations of hydro- and thermodynamics. Computers are then employed in the rapid approximate solution of these equations, making running use of great masses of atmospheric data gathered on a continuous round-the-clock and round-the-world basis.

Computer science, the systematic study of computers and their uses, is today centered around three interrelated kinds of activities: first, the designing of computer "hardware"—the systems of electronic and mechanical components that make up computers; second, the devising of computer "software"—the basic languages and programs, compilers, control schemes for time-sharing, and so forth that make the electronic machines into effective computing systems; and third, the invention and study of techniques and methods for using computers to solve problems. All these kinds of activities point up the fact that computer science, like statistics, is only partly mathematical in character. The design of actual computer hardware is, of course, primarily an engineering activity. Apart from computer-oriented numerical analysis, the most highly mathematical part of computer science today is perhaps the theory of programing languages, which also involves mathematical linguistics.

Like statistics, however, computer science has also been strongly influenced in its development by its wealth of applications and the interests it shares with other fields. We have already mentioned that computer science has in common with engineering an interest in design, and shares with linguistics an interest in problems of language and communication. It shares with psychology an interest in the characteristics of intelligent behavior. Along with library science, it is concerned with the storage and retrieval of masses of information. In fact, most of the applications of computers rest more or less directly on their capacity for speedy and flexible processing of large amounts of information—whether this be crystallographic or nuclear-reactor data, telemetered information from satellites, or the multi-form records of businesses or governments. It is this capacity that gives computers their great power in simulation and in the automation of commercial and industrial processes that affect the lives of all.

Implications for the Schools

The picture we have been painting—the growth of the mathematical sciences, their increasing penetration into other fields, and especially the strong interaction of these other fields with statistics and computer science—has implications for mathematical education at every level.

At the elementary school level, curriculum reform in mathematics education is of course not a new thing; the present vigorous movement goes back at least into the 1950's. From the outset the rallying-cry was "Not rote learning but understanding!" There are few who would deny that this movement has been in a healthy direction, though regrettably there are still many school systems in which it has scarcely made an impression on traditional practices; and, ironically, even where it has caught on, the reform itself has all too easily ossified into new rote patterns. Thus, there is still much to be done along trails already broken.

There are also new currents in these reforms today, currents toward a closer integration of mathematics-teaching with the teaching of the experimental sciences, and, in particular, toward a more effective presentation of mathematical models as powerful tools in gaining an understanding of the world around us.[2] Ideas of probability and statistics may be expected to appear naturally in this setting through manipulations of observational data, especially in simple situations with built-in uncertainty, such as coin-tossing. As long ago as 1961, the Committee on the Undergraduate Program in Mathematics (CUPM) recommended that the college training of at least 20 per cent of the teachers of elementary mathematics in a school should contain several of the "Level II" courses, including a basic course in probability.[3] The new trends underline the need for such training, perhaps now on the part of an even broader group.

For the near future, computer use in mathematical education at the elementary school level appears to be somewhat problematical. At present, the principal area of experimentation is computer-aided instruction, paced to the individual student. In general, this may be described as a more sophisticated and promising outgrowth of the

2. This was, in fact, one of the principal themes at the 1967 Cambridge Conference on School Mathematics.

3. See recommendations for the training of teachers in *Course Guide for the Training of Teachers of Junior High and High School Mathematics,* Committee on the Undergraduate Program in Mathematics, Mathematical Association of America, 1961.

programed-learning movement and earlier attempts at "teaching machines." The progression from simple graduated-drill activities to effective "dialogue" between student and computer, however, still offers many problems as yet largely unsolved.[4]

At the secondary level, the stronger schools have been responding increasingly to mathematical curriculum-reform movements begun over ten years ago. Many feel that this response has already played a significant part in the improvement now apparent in the mathematical preparation of students entering four-year colleges and universities.[5] Again, however, there is much yet to be done in bringing improved mathematical curricula to more of our schools. We should emphasize, too, that further change in the mathematical curricula of all secondary schools is likely to be the order of the day for the foreseeable future.

Much of the training that secondary schools offer in the mathematical sciences is college preparatory, and therefore trends in college level work in these fields may be expected to induce trends at the secondary school level. For one thing, there is a strong trend in four-year colleges and universities toward making analytic geometry, calculus, and courses of equivalent or higher level the initial mathematics courses for entering Freshmen. This implies that these colleges and universities will be relying increasingly on the secondary schools to do a good job of teaching "college" algebra, trigonometry, and courses of equivalent or lower level.

Though the absolute numbers involved are sometimes small, the sharpest *percentage* increases over the period 1960–65 in college-level mathematical science enrolments are in the fields of finite mathematics (700 per cent), linear and matrix algebra (475 per cent), probability and statistics (187 per cent), computer-programing and re-

4. See the essays, Patrick Suppes, "On Using Computers To Individualize Instruction," pp. 11–24; Judson T. Shaplin, "Computer-Based Instruction and Curriculum Reform," pp. 36–44; and others in *The Computer in American Education*, eds. Donald D. Bushnell and Dwight W. Allen, Commissioned by the Association for Educational Data Systems (New York: John Wiley & Sons, 1967).

5. For impressive documentation of this improvement, see John Jewett and Clarence B. Lindquist, *Aspects of Undergraduate Training in the Mathematical Sciences* (Report of the Survey Committee, Vol. I, Conference Board on Mathematical Sciences, 1967), especially p. 16.

lated mathematics (500 per cent), topology (300 per cent), and real analysis (300 per cent).[6] Some of these especially sharp increases have only general implications for the importance of mathematical training in the secondary schools; but at least in several of these fields —linear and matrix algebra, probability and statistics, and computer-programing and related mathematics—high school level work seems quite feasible, and introductory texts for such work have already appeared, some of them excellent. For education in the mathematical sciences, however, the truly pressing problem of the day—not just at the secondary level, but at every level from kindergarten to post-Ph.D.—is to produce qualified teachers in sufficient numbers.

6. *Loc. cit.*, p. 19.

Index

461

INFORMATION CONCERNING THE NATIONAL SOCIETY
FOR THE STUDY OF EDUCATION

1. PURPOSE. The purpose of the National Society is to promote the investigation and discussion of educational questions. To this end it holds an annual meeting and publishes a series of yearbooks.

2. ELIGIBILITY TO MEMBERSHIP. Any person who is interested in receiving its publications may become a member by sending to the Secretary-Treasurer information concerning name, title, and address, and a check for $8.00 (see Item 5), except that graduate students, on the recommendation of a faculty member, may become members by paying $6.00 for the first year of their membership. Dues for all subsequent years are the same as for other members (see Item 4).

Membership is not transferable; it is limited to individuals, and may not be held by libraries, schools, or other institutions, either directly or indirectly.

3. PERIOD OF MEMBERSHIP. Applicants for membership may not date their entrance back of the current calendar year, and all memberships terminate automatically on December 31, unless the dues for the ensuing year are paid as indicated in Item 6.

4. DUTIES AND PRIVILEGES OF MEMBERS. Members pay dues of $7.00 annually, receive a cloth-bound copy of each publication, are entitled to vote, to participate in discussion, and (under certain conditions) to hold office. The names of members are printed in the yearbooks.

Persons who are sixty years of age or above may become life members on payment of fee based on average life-expectancy of their age group. For information, apply to the Secretary-Treasurer.

5. ENTRANCE FEE. New members are required the first year to pay, in addition to the dues, an entrance fee of one dollar.

6. PAYMENT OF DUES. Statements of dues are rendered in October for the following calendar year. Any member so notified whose dues remain unpaid on January 1 thereby loses his membership and can be reinstated only by paying a reinstatement fee of fifty cents.

School warrants and vouchers from institutions must be accompanied by definite information concerning the name and address of the person for whom membership fee is being paid. Statements of dues are rendered on our own form only. The Secretary's office cannot undertake to fill out special invoice forms of any sort or to affix notary's affidavit to statements or receipts.

Cancelled checks serve as receipts. Members desiring an additional receipt must enclose a stamped and addressed envelope therefor.

7. DISTRIBUTION OF YEARBOOKS TO MEMBERS. The yearbooks, ready prior to each February meeting, will be mailed from the office of the distributor only to members whose dues for that year have been paid. Members who desire yearbooks prior to the current year must purchase them directly from the distributors (see Item 8).

8. COMMERCIAL SALES. The distribution of all yearbooks prior to the current year, and also of those of the current year not regularly mailed to members in exchange for their dues, is in the hands of the distributor, not of the Secretary. For such commercial sales, communicate directly with the University of Chicago Press, Chicago, Illinois 60637, which will gladly send a price list covering all the publications of this Society. This list is also printed in the yearbook.

9. YEARBOOKS. The yearbooks are issued about one month before the February meeting. They comprise from 600 to 800 pages annually. Unusual effort has been made to make them, on the one hand, of immediate practical value, and, on the other hand, representative of sound scholarship and scientific investigation.

10. MEETINGS. The annual meeting, at which the yearbooks are discussed, is held in February at the same time and place as the meeting of the American Association of School Administrators. Members will be notified of other meetings.

Applications for membership will be handled promptly at any time on receipt of name and address, together with check for $8.00 (or $7.50 for reinstatement). Applications entitle the new members to the yearbook slated for discussion during the calendar year the application is made.

5835 Kimbark Avenue   HERMAN G. RICHEY, *Secretary-Treasurer*
Chicago, Illinois 60637

i

PUBLICATIONS OF THE NATIONAL SOCIETY FOR THE STUDY OF EDUCATION

NOTICE: Many of the early yearbooks of this series are now out of print. In the following list, those titles to which an asterisk is prefixed are not available for purchase.

POSTPAID
PRICE

*First Yearbook, 1902, Part I—*Some Principles in the Teaching of History*. Lucy M. Salmon...
*First Yearbook, 1902, Part II—*The Progress of Geography in the Schools*. W. M. Davis and H. M. Wilson...
*Second Yearbook, 1903, Part I—*The Course of Study in History in the Common School*. Isabel Lawrence, C. A. McMurry, Frank McMurry, E. C. Page, and E. J. Rice.............
*Second Yearbook, 1903, Part II—*The Relation of Theory to Practice in Education*. M. J. Holmes, J. A. Keith, and Levi Seeley..
*Third Yearbook, 1904, Part I—*The Relation of Theory to Practice in the Education of Teachers*. John Dewey, Sarah C. Brooks, F. M. McMurry, *et al*..........................
*Third Yearbook, 1904, Part II—*Nature Study*. W. S. Jackman....................
*Fourth Yearbook, 1905, Part I—*The Education and Training of Secondary Teachers*. E. C. Elliott, E. G. Dexter, M. J. Holmes, *et al*...............................
*Fourth Yearbook, 1905, Part II—*The Place of Vocational Subjects in the High-School Curriculum*. J. S. Brown, G. B. Morrison, and Ellen Richards............................
*Fifth Yearbook, 1906, Part I—*On the Teaching of English in Elementary and High Schools*. G. P. Brown and Emerson Davis..
*Fifth Yearbook, 1906, Part II—*The Certification of Teachers*. E. P. Cubberley............
*Sixth Yearbook, 1907, Part I—*Vocational Studies for College Entrance*. C. A. Herrick, H. W. Holmes, T. deLaguna, V. Prettyman, and W. J. S. Bryan...................
*Sixth Yearbook, 1907, Part II—*The Kindergarten and Its Relation to Elementary Education*.Ada Van Stone Harris, E. A. Kirkpatrick, Marie Kraus-Boelté, Patty S. Hill, Harriette M. Mills, and Nina Vandewalker..
*Seventh Yearbook, 1908, Part I—*The Relation of Superintendents and Principals to the Training and Professional Improvement of Their Teachers*. Charles D. Lowry................
*Seventh Yearbook, 1908, Part II—*The Co-ordination of the Kindergarten and the Elementary School*. B. J. Gregory, Jennie B. Merrill, Bertha Payne, and Margaret Giddings.........
*Eighth Yearbook, 1909, Part I—*Education with Reference to Sex: Pathological, Economic, and Social Aspects*. C. R. Henderson...
*Eighth Yearbook, 1909, Part II—*Education with Reference to Sex: Agencies and Methods*. C. R. Henderson and Helen C. Putnam......................................
*Ninth Yearbook, 1910, Part I—*Health and Education*. T. D. Wood..................
*Ninth Yearbook, 1910, Part II—*The Nurses in Education*. T. D. Wood *et al*..............
*Tenth Yearbook, 1911, Part I—*The City School as a Community Center*. H. C. Leipziger, Sarah E. Hyre, R. D. Warden, C. Ward Crampton, E. W. Stitt, E. J. Ward, Mrs. E. C. Grice, and C. A. Perry..
*Tenth Yearbook, 1911, Part II—*The Rural School as a Community Center*. B. H. Crocheron, Jessie Field, F. W. Howe, E. C. Bishop, A. B. Graham, O. J. Kern, M. T. Scudder, and B. M. Davis...
*Eleventh Yearbook, 1912, Part I—*Industrial Education: Typical Experiments Described and Interpreted*. J. F. Barker, M. Bloomfield, B. W. Johnson, P. Johnson, L. M. Leavitt, G. A. Mirick, M. W. Murray, C. F. Perry, A. L. Stafford, and H. B. Wilson................
*Eleventh Yearbook, 1912, Part II—*Agricultural Education in Secondary Schools*. A. C. Monahan, R. W. Stimson, D. J. Crosby, W. H. French, H. F. Button, F. R. Crane, W. R. Hart, and G. F. Warren...
*Twelfth Yearbook, 1913, Part I—*The Supervision of City Schools*. Franklin Bobbitt, J. W. Hall, and J. D. Wolcott...
*Twelfth Yearbook, 1913, Part II—*The Supervision of Rural Schools*. A. C. Monahan, L. J. Hanifan, J. E. Warren, Wallace Lund, U. J. Hoffman, A. S. Cook, E. M. Rapp, Jackson Davis, and J. D. Wolcott...
*Thirteenth Yearbook, 1914, Part I—*Some Aspects of High-School Instruction and Administration*. H. C. Morrison, E. R. Breslich, W. A. Jessup, and L. D. Coffman....................
*Thirteenth Yearbook, 1914, Part II—*Plans for Organizing School Surveys, with a Summary of Typical School Surveys*. Charles H. Judd and Henry L. Smith...................
*Fourteenth Yearbook, 1915, Part I—*Minimum Essentials in Elementary School Subjects—Standards and Current Practices*. H. B. Wilson, H. W. Holmes, F. E. Thompson, R. G. Jones, S. A. Courtis, W. S. Gray, F. N. Freeman, H. C. Pryor, J. F. Hosic, W. A. Jessup, and W. C. Bagley..
*Fourteenth Yearbook, 1915, Part II—*Methods for Measuring Teachers' Efficiency*. Arthur C. Boyce...
*Fifteenth Yearbook, 1916, Part I—*Standards and Tests for the Measurement of the Efficiency of Schools and School Systems*. G. D. Strayer, Bird T. Baldwin, B. R. Buckingham, F. W. Ballou, D. C. Bliss, H. G. Childs, S. A. Courtis, E. P. Cubberley, C. H. Judd, George Melcher, E. E. Oberholtzer, J. B. Sears, Daniel Starch, M. R. Trabue, and G. M. Whipple..
*Fifteenth Yearbook, 1961, Part II—*The Relationship between Persistence in School and Home Conditions*. Charles E. Hollye..
*Fifteenth Yearbook, 1916, Part III—*The Junior High School*. Aubrey A. Douglas...........
*Sixteenth Yearbook, 1917, Part I—*Second Report of the Committee on Minimum Essentials in Elementary-School Subjects*. W. C. Bagley, W. W. Charters, F. N. Freeman, W. S. Gray, Ernest Horn, J. H. Hoskinson, W. S. Monroe, C. F. Munson, H. C. Pryor, L. W. Rapeer, G. M. Wilson, and H. B. Wilson..
*Sixteenth Yearbook, 1917, Part II—*The Efficiency of College Students as Conditioned by Age at Entrance and Size of High School*. B. F. Pittenger..............................

vi   PUBLICATIONS

POSTPAID
PRICE

Fifty-third Yearbook, 1954, Part II—*Mass Media and Education.* Prepared by the Society's
Committee. Edgar Dale, Chairman. Cloth $4.50
    Paper.. 3.75
Fifty-fourth Yearbook, 1955, Part I—*Modern Philosophies and Education.* Prepared by the
Society's Committee. John S. Brubacher, Chairman. Cloth............................ 4.50
    Paper.. 3.75
Fifty-fourth Yearbook, 1955, Part II—*Mental Health in Modern Education.* Prepared by the
Society's Committee. Paul A. Witty, Chairman. Cloth.............................. 4.50
    Paper.. 3.75
*Fifty-fifth Yearbook, 1956, Part I—*The Public Junior College.* Prepared by the Society's Com-
mittee. B. Lamar Johnson, Chairman. Cloth...
    Paper..
Fifty-fifth Yearbook, 1956, Part II—*Adult Reading.* Prepared by the Society's Committee.
David H. Clift, Chairman. Cloth.. 4.50
    Paper.. 3.75
Fifty-sixth Yearbook, 1957, Part I—*In-service Education of Teachers, Supervisors, and Adminis-
trators.* Prepared by the Society's Committee. Stephen M. Corey, Chairman. Cloth 4.50
    Paper.. 3.75
Fifty-sixth Yearbook, 1957, Part II—*Social Studies in the Elementary School.* Prepared by the
Society's Committee. Ralph C. Preston, Chairman. Cloth........................... 4 50
    Paper.. 3.75
Fifty-seventh Yearbook, 1958, Part I—*Basic Concepts in Music Education.* Prepared by the So-
ciety's Committee. Thurber H. Madison, Chairman. Cloth......................... 4.50
Fifty-seventh Yearbook, 1958, Part II—*Education for the Gifted.* Prepared by the Society's Com-
mittee. Robert J. Havighurst, Chairman. Cloth...................................... 4.50
    Paper.. 3.75
Fifty-seventh Yearbook, 1958, Part III—*The Integration of Educational Experiences.* Prepared
by the Society's Committee. Paul L. Dressel, Chairman. Cloth....................... 4.50
Fifty-eighth Yearbook, 1959, Part I—*Community Education: Principles and Practices from
World-wide Experience.* Prepared by the Society's Committee. C. O. Arndt, Chairman. Cloth 4.50
    Paper.. 3.75
Fifty-eighth Yearbook, 1959, Part II—*Personnel Services in Education.* Prepared by the Soci-
ety's Committee. Melvene D. Hardee, Chairman. Cloth............................ 4.50
    Paper.. 3.75
Fifty-ninth Yearbook, 1960, Part I—*Rethinking Science Education.* Prepared by the Society's
Committee. J. Darrell Barnard, Chairman. Cloth.................................... 4.50
Fifty-ninth Yearbook, 1960, Part II—*The Dynamics of Instructional Groups.* Prepared by the
Society's Committee. Gale E. Jensen, Chairman. Cloth 4.50
    Paper.. 3.75
Sixtieth Yearbook, 1961, Part I—*Development in and through Reading.* Prepared by the Society's
Committee. Paul A. Witty, Chairman. Cloth.. 5.00
    Paper.. 4.25
Sixtieth Yearbook, 1961, Part II—*Social Forces Influencing American Education.* Prepared by
the Society's Committee. Ralph W. Tyler, Chairman. Cloth.......................... 4.50
Sixty-first Yearbook, 1962, Part I—*Individualizing Instruction.* Prepared by the Society's Com-
mittee. Fred. T. Tyler, Chairman. Cloth.. 4.50
Sixty-first Yearbook, 1962, Part II—*Education for the Professions.* Prepared by the Society's
Committee. G. Lester Anderson, Chairman. Cloth.................................. 4.50
Sixty-second Yearbook, 1963, Part I—*Child Psychology.* Prepared by the Society's Committee.
Harold W. Stevenson, Editor. Cloth.. 6.50
Sixty-second Yearbook, 1963, Part II—*The Impact and Improvement of School Testing Programs.*
Prepared by the Society's Committee. Warren G. Findley, Editor. Cloth.............. 4.50
Sixty-third Yearbook, 1964, Part I—*Theories of Learning and Instruction.* Prepared by the
Society's Committee. Ernest R. Hilgard, Editor. Cloth.............................. 5.50
Sixty-third Yearbook, 1964, Part II—*Behavioral Science and Educational Administration.* Pre-
pared by the Society's Committee. Daniel E. Griffiths, Editor. Cloth................. 4.50
Sixty-fourth Yearbook, 1965, Part I—*Vocational Education.* Prepared by the Society's Com-
mittee. Melvin L. Barlow, Editor. Cloth.. 5.00
Sixty-fourth Yearbook, 1965, Part II—*Art Education.* Prepared by the Society's Committee.
W. Reid Hastie, Editor. Cloth.. 5.00
Sixty-fifth Yearbook, 1966, Part I—*Social Deviancy among Youth.* Prepared by the Society's
Committee. William W. Wattenberg, Editor. Cloth.................................. 5.50
Sixty-fifth Yearbook, 1966, Part II—*The Changing American School.* Prepared by the Society's
Committee. John I. Goodlad, Editor. Cloth... 5.00
Sixty-sixth Yearbook, 1967, Part I—*The Educationally Retarded and Disadvantaged.* Prepared
by the Society's Committee. Paul A. Witty, Editor. Cloth........................... 5.50
Sixty-sixth Yearbook, 1967, Part II—*Programed Instruction.* Prepared by the Society's Com-
mittee. Phil C. Lange, Editor. Cloth... 5.00
Sixty-seventh Yearbook, 1968, Part I—*Metropolitanism: Its Challenge to Education.* Prepared
by the Society's Committee. Robert J. Havighurst, Editor. Cloth.................... 5.50
Sixty-seventh Yearbook, 1968, Part II—*Innovation and Change in Reading Instruction.* Pre-
pared by the Society's Committee. Helen M. Robinson, Editor. Cloth................. 5.50
Sixty-eighth Yearbook, 1969, Part I—*The United States and International Education.* Prepared
by the Society's Committee. Harold G. Shane, Editor. Cloth........................ 5.50
Sixty-eighth Yearbook, 1969, Part II—*Educational Evaluation: New Roles, New Means.* Prepared by the Society's Committee. Ralph W. Tyler, Editor. Cloth.................... 5.50
Sixty-ninth Yearbook, 1970, Part I—*Mathematics Education.* Prepared by the Society's Committee. Edward G. Begle, Editor. Cloth.. 7.00
Sixty-ninth Yearbook, 1970, Part II—*Linguistics in School Programs.* Prepared by the Society's Committee. Albert H. Marckwardt, Editor. Cloth 5.50

Distributed by

THE UNIVERSITY OF CHICAGO PRESS, CHICAGO, ILLINOIS 60637

1969